AUSTRALIAN CITIES

RESHAPING AUSTRALIAN INSTITUTIONS

Series editors: John Braithwaite and Geoffrey Brennan, Research School of Social Sciences, Australian National University

Published in association with the Research School of Social Sciences, Australian National University

This program of publications arises from the School's initiative in sponsoring a fundamental rethinking of Australia's key institutions before the centenary of Federation in 2001

Published in this program will be the work of scholars from the Australian National University and elsewhere who are researching and writing on the institutions of the nation. The scope of the program includes the institutions of public governance, intergovernmental relations, Aboriginal Australia, gender, population, the environment, the economy, business, the labour market, the welfare state, the city, education, the media, criminal justice and the Constitution.

Brian Galligan   *A Federal Republic*
Ian Marsh   *Beyond the Two Party System*

AUSTRALIAN CITIES

Issues, Strategies and Policies
for Urban Australia
in the 1990s

Edited by
PATRICK TROY

Research School of Social Sciences
Australian National University

Published by the Press Syndicate of the University of Cambridge
The Pitt Building, Trumpington Street, Cambridge CB2 IRP, UK
40 West 20th Street, New York, NY 10011–4211, USA
10 Stamford Road, Oakleigh, Melbourne 3166, Australia

Printed in Hong Kong by Colorcraft

National Library of Australia cataloguing-in-publication data

Australian cities : issues, strategies and policies for urban
Australia in the 1990s.
Bibliography.
Includes index.
1. City planning – Australia. 2. Urban policy – Australia.
3. Cities and towns – Australia – Growth. 4. City and
town life – Australia. I. Troy, Patrick N. (Patrick
Nicol). (Series : Reshaping Australian institutions).
307.760994

Library of Congress cataloguing-in-publication data

Australian cities : issues, strategies, and policies for urban
Australia in the 1990s / editor, Patrick Troy.
p.   cm.
Includes bibliographical references and index.
1. Cities and towns – Australia. 2. Urban policy – Australia.
3. City planning – Australia. I. Troy, Patrick.
HT149.A8A78 1995
307.76'0994–dc20   94–46810

A catalogue record for this book is available from the British Library.

ISBN 0 521 48197 X Hardback

Contents

Figures

Tables

viii

Preface

Because cities are the places where most people live, where most goods and services are produced and traded, and because they are the primary sources of advanced technology and business innovation, what happens in them and to them is of central importance to a society.

The better they are planned and developed, the more effective they can be in aiding wealth creation. Their structure, nature and functioning also affect the quality of life, social justice and equity and the natural environment. They provide the setting for and are an expression of a nation's cultural development.

Growing concern over the environment, increasing globalisation of the economy, the rapid uptake of information technology, and the persistence and deepening of divisions between groups within the city are leading to new and unstable patterns of working and living. The future of cities as we know them is uncertain. They need to and are replacing their infrastructure, but what kind of government and administration should be making decisions about the new structure is problematical.

The challenge is to find a way of accommodating diverse and changing urban activities. How do we provide and finance 'urban' services, and how do we democratise governance of the emerging urban space? How do we manage the transition from the inherited form and structure to the new urban space and accommodate new patterns of urban development within it? These questions do not imply either physical or technological determination but a recognition of the impact of dynamic economic forces and changing social attitudes on physical development, which is itself long-lived and shapes subsequent development. The relationships between activities within cities may both reflect and shape the distribution of well-being among the population. They may also affect the meaning of citizenship by shaping the effective rights

ix

of citizens and their access to facilities, services and cultural and employment opportunities.

This book is a response to the challenge of whether our cities have a future. It is the first contribution to a debate in which all contributors feel we must engage.

Patrick Troy
Research School of Social Sciences
Australian National University

Acknowledgements

All books are the product of a collective enterprise. This is the product of an exceptionally large enterprise. My authors and I are indebted to Hugh Stretton and an anonymous reviewer, to Phillipa McGuinness and John Braithwaite and to colleagues in our respective institutions who have been generous with their comments and criticisms on earlier drafts of these chapters. The greatest debt however is to Barbara Norman and Rita Coles.

Note on Contributors

BLAIR BADCOCK is Reader in Geography at Adelaide University

TIM BONYHADY is a Senior Research Fellow at the Urban Research Program, Research School of Social Sciences, Australian National University

RAYMOND BUNKER is Associate Professor in Town Planning, University of South Australia

TONY DINGLE is Associate Professor in Economics, Monash University

LIONEL FROST is Lecturer in the School of Economics, Faculty of Social Science, La Trobe University

RENATE HOWE is Associate Professor in History, Deakin University

ALEC MCGILLIVRAY is a PhD student in the Department of Urban and Regional Planning, University of Sydney

PATRICK MULLINS is Senior Lecturer in Sociology, University of Queensland

MAX NEUTZE, AO, is Professor of Urban Research, Urban Research Program, Research School of Social Sciences, Australian National University

LIONEL ORCHARD is Director of Studies, Politics, Flinders University

MARK PEEL is a Research Fellow at the Urban Research Program, Research School of Social Sciences, Australian National University

PETER SELF is Emeritus Professor and Visiting Fellow, Urban Research Program, Research School of Social Sciences, Australian National University

PATRICK TROY, AO, is Professor of Urban Research, Research School of Social Sciences, Australian National University

SOPHIE WATSON is Professor of Urban and Regional Planning, Sydney University

Abbreviations

ABS	Australian Bureau of Statistics
AFR	*Australian Financial Review*
AIHW	Australian Institute of Health and Welfare
ALP	Australian Labor Party
ALGA	Australian Local Government Association
AMCORD	Australian Model Code for Residential Development
AMCORD URBAN	Guidelines for Urban Housing
ARRB	Australian Road Research Board
AURDR	Australian Urban and Regional Development Review
AWRC	Australian Water Resources Commission
BA	Balmain Association
BBC	Building Better Cities
CBD	Central Business District
CFC	chlorofluorocarbon
CHC	Commonwealth Housing Commission
CSPC	Central Sydney Planning Committee
DEET	Department of Employment, Education and Training
DHHCS	Department of Health, Housing and Community Services
DHHLGCS	Department of Health, Housing, Local Government and Community Services
DPUD	Department of Planning and Urban Development
DURD	Department of Urban and Regional Development
EAC	Ethnic Affairs Commission
EH	*Eastern Herald*
EPAA	Environmental Planning and Assessment Act
EPAC	Economic Planning Advisory Council
ESB	English Speaking Background
FA	*Fairfield Advance* (local newspaper)

GDP	Gross Domestic Product
HACC	Home and Community Care
HR	House of Representatives
HRSC–LTS	House of Representatives Standing Committee for Long-Term Strategies
ICI	Imperial Chemicals Industry
ILAP	Integrated Local Area Planning
IPA	Institute of Public Affairs
IPC	Indicative Planning Council
LA	Los Angeles
LARP	Local Areas Review Program
LC	Leichhardt Council
MAV	Municipal Association of Victoria
MFP	Multi Function Polis
NESB	Non-English Speaking Background
NHPR	National Housing Policy Review
NHS	National Housing Strategy
NIMBY	Not in My Back Yard
NOROC	Northern Regional Organisation of Councils
NSWPD	New South Wales Parliamentary Debates
NUDP	National Urban Development Program
OECD	Organization of Economic Cooperation and Development
OEMA	Outer Eastern Municipalities Association
OLG	Office of Local Government
PCB	polychlorinated biphenyls
PMC	Prime Minister and Cabinet
RAPI	Royal Australian Planning Institute
REDO	Regional Economic Development Organisation
RRR	Review of the Residential Regulations
SAHT	South Australian Housing Trust
SAPR	South Australian Planning Review
SEQ	South-East Queensland
SH	*Sun Herald*
SMH	*Sydney Morning Herald*
TCF	Textile, clothing and footwear
TFRD	Task Force on Regional Development
TFUD	Task Force on Urban Design
TM	*Telegraph Mirror*
URP	Urban Research Program
VFT	Very Fast Train
WESROC	Western Sydney Regional Organisation of Councils
WSC	*Western Suburbs Courier*

Introduction

Patrick Troy

In recent years urban issues which have attracted little attention or sense
of urgency since the Whitlam era have risen up the political agenda
again. One immediate reason is official concern about the public costs
of urban growth, accompanied by the goal of making Australian cities
more economically efficient and competitive in terms of the global
economy. A second reason has been rising concern over environmental
issues which are essentially urban in origin (air, water and noise
pollution which are problems of big cities and the environmental
impacts and worsening congestion caused by motor traffic). A third,
more muted but very real cause of social concern is the impact of
unemployment, increasing poverty, inequality of housing provision and
living conditions upon associated levels of crime and conflict.

The time is thus ripe for a fresh exploration of the issues and
problems bound up with the current growth and functioning of
Australian cities. All the major concerns – economic, environmental and
social – are examined here in a fresh and original manner. It is not to be
expected that a simple or single solution can be found for this diverse
range of problems; indeed, one of the conclusions which emerges from
several chapters is that the currently fashionable doctrine of creating
more compact cities ('urban consolidation') as the best cure for urban
problems is inadequate for this purpose. Instead, the various authors
shed light upon the underlying character of current urban changes and
point to some new directions which could reduce the adverse features of
big city life. Their different perspectives also bring out the importance of
a balanced set of goals aimed at making Australian cities more equitable
as well as more productive, and offering a better quality of life as well as
enhanced economic efficiency.

1

The first part of this introduction provides a contextual description of changes in Australian cities and urban policy since World War II. The impacts of these factors are reflected in the following chapters which deal with particular aspects of urban growth.

It is commonplace that the Australian population has continued to grow over the post-war period and that most of the growth has been in the urban areas. The greater part of the urban growth has occurred in the State and national capitals although more recently the urban growth in coastal south-east Queensland and north-east New South Wales has resulted in a major concentration of development in that region. Within the capitals the residential population growth occurred mostly in new outer suburbs and the population in the older inner areas has fallen relatively and, in recent years, absolutely. Table (i) shows that within the broad areas covered by Sydney, Melbourne, Adelaide and Perth in 1921, the populations continued to increase until 1971 and subsequently declined. The majority of the growth in all the cities (all of it after 1971) occurred by geographic expansion rather than by increased population density in the established areas. Since the 1921 boundaries are not defined in a consistent way the table cannot be used to make comparisons between cities. One feature is clear, however: the percentage of urban populations in the older inner areas has fallen consistently and substantially over time. That is, most of the population growth has been in the suburbs of the capitals.

The continuing urban growth is the subject of this book. The following chapters explore the historical background of the growth of Australian cities, the policies which have been adopted to manage it and how its future course might be shaped.

This suburban expansion was a continuation of the form and structure of Australian cities which had been established over the previous century and was both the spatial expression of social aspirations and the result of economic and social processes (see Frost and Dingle, chapter 1).

In the early post-war period the relatively high standard of living and the willingness of Australians to invest a good deal of their resources in acquiring housing enabled an increasing proportion of the population to realise its aspiration for a better quality, larger dwelling set in its own garden. By 1961 home ownership had been attained by seven out of ten households – the majority of the dwellings were in the form of single family houses. Suburban development was also accompanied by more equitable provision of public facilities such as schools – the catchment area of primary schools became the building block for most of the urban planning of that era. More equitable access to public open space and recreation facilities was among the objectives which the post-war town planning system was also designed to deliver.

Table (i) *Population change in selected capital cities, 1921–1991*

		1 Metropolitan/ urban population (000's)	2 Population in 1921, metro boundary (000's)	3 % of total living in 1921 boundary
Sydney	1921	899	899	100
	1947	1484	1279	86
	1961	2183	1362	62
	1971	2725	1513	56
	1981	2865	1356	47
	1991	3098	1351	44
Melbourne	1921	718	718	100
	1947	1226	1085	88
	1961	1911	1161	61
	1971	2408	1199	50
	1981	2579	1023	40
	1991	2762	977	35
Adelaide	1921	255	249	98
	1947	383	348	91
	1961	588	504	86
	1971	809	575	71
	1981	883	544	62
	1991	957	544	57
Perth	1921	155	127	82
	1947	273	202	74
	1961	420	218	52
	1971	731	228	31
	1981	809	197	24
	1991	1019	205	20

Notes: The 1921 metropolitan area boundary was used for column 2 except where it could not be traced in later years because of boundary changes. In the case of Perth some additional areas were omitted because the 1921 boundary was very wide. In all cases the area used for column 3 is constant.
For 1921 and 1961 the metropolitan boundaries were not consistently defined for different cities. In later years, consistent criteria were used to define the 'urban centre' boundaries (*Australian Year Book 1968*: 123).
Source: Australian Census of Population and Housing 1921, 1947, 1961, 1971, 1981, 1991.

The population growth which has occurred since 1945 was not some chance event but the outcome of a sustained attempt by the Commonwealth to populate and 'develop' the country. In the early post-war period urban planning was predicated on the assumption of a continuation of pre-war social mores and behaviour. In particular, it was built on

AUSTRALIAN CITIES

the assumption that the future would be demographically stable. In the event, people have married later and family sizes have fallen as living standards have increased. Without a high level of immigration, urban growth in Australia would have been significantly lower. One immediate consequence of the demographic change is that the efficacy of using the older 'average' household size – in particular the numbers of school-age children per household – to establish the relationship between the number of dwellings per primary school has now been brought into question. The idea that the efficient size of schools for education purposes happily coincided with notions of the maximum distance a primary-school child could be expected to walk to school was one of those felicitous relationships which was bound into planning rules. The 'quarter-mile' radius which this calculus produced also happily buttressed prevailing notions of the size of the catchment, needed to sustain convenience shopping and a variety of local services, including open space and recreation, and was supported by the contemporary attraction for romantic notions of 'community'. It also provided an arbitrary but seemingly appropriate development unit for planning and providing roads when rising car-ownership levels led to increased demands for more and better private transport.

By the mid-1980s the breakdown in these relationships was manifest. Increasing pressure on the public sector forced governments to review their policies on school provision. The 1000 to 1200 dwellings which in the 1950s were thought to be sufficient to support a primary school, by the 1980s yielded hardly enough children to maintain a full range of classes. In some areas which had been developed rapidly, the subsequent ageing of the population had led to enrolments falling to a fraction of the school's capacity. Education policies adopted in the 1960s, 1970s and 1980s of subsidising private schools accentuated these processes, leading in the late 1980s to widespread 'rationalisation' of the public school systems which resulted in many schools being closed. The rigidities resulting from the development of the road system now meant that primary-school-age children were required to make longer journeys than were earlier considered acceptable and they were more likely to be expected to cross busy roads.

The neighbourhood (the primary-school catchment area) also came under attack as a basic planning unit because of changes in retailing and the increase in car ownership which increased mobility and led to greater accessibility. This dissolving of verities resulting from social processes over which they had little influence left town planners with feelings of impotence – often exaggerated because frequently they were blamed for outcomes or developments which they had warned of or advised against. To some extent the feelings of impotence grew out of a recognition by town planners that the preoccupation with physical determinism in their training and embodied in planning laws and regulations had proved inadequate in coping with the growth and management problems they faced.

The effort during the 1950s, 1960s and 1970s to enhance and defend ordinary living standards, secured by such means as the shorter working week and rising real wages, had important consequences for the uses and the populace's expectations of urban goods like recreational and cultural facilities, parks and playgrounds, all of which required more space. Technological innovations in transportation, energy production and distribution and in communications and information processing facilitated changes in retailing, the organisation of production and financial services. These changes enabled firms to relocate from the centre to other areas within the cities, and allowed government services to be decentralised. This was reflected in an increasing proportion of jobs being 'displaced' to the suburbs as production, distribution and exchange functions were reorganised to take advantage of the economies offered by the new technologies and the simultaneous growth of labour supplies in the suburbs.

Innovations in marine transport technology have wrought major changes to the structure of all Australian port cities as the focus of shipping has shifted from the centre to suburban and even outer suburban locations. The development of aviation has similarly shifted the focus of passenger travel from centrally focused rail services to suburban locations which in turn has led to major structural changes in the cities. The increased preference for and access to the private car gave residents greater choice of job locations. This was reflected in diffused origins and destinations in the long distance trips throughout the urban areas. These changes in transport wrought major structural changes.

The use and development of other technological innovations indirectly led to forces which also have tended to restructure the city. Many of the jobs in the increasingly important service sector are close to where the population growth occurred – in the suburbs.

The reduction in the working week, increased workforce participation of women and increased availability of private transport which gave greater mobility to household members enabling them to pursue a wider range of interests was reflected in changes in the trip patterns of households. The journey to work became relatively less important with non-work trips now accounting for over 60 per cent of all trips. Although the cities have become extensive, the average trip length has not increased. Fewer than one in five of all work trips are to the city centre and these are the only work trips whose average length has increased.

Transport investments continue to be made, however, to meet the demand for city-centre-oriented work travel.

Over the same period expectations of the level of urban services grew. People expected water supply, sewerage and drainage, sealed roads, open space, schools and other community facilities to be provided as new areas were developed. For most of the period, these expectations were met by governments (State and local) either from their own resources or by making their provision a condition of development permission. The massive expansion of the cities has required large public investment in social and urban infrastructure. As Max Neutze shows in chapter 10, many of the services have been financed and priced according to strategies and philosophies which are no longer regarded as appropriate. In some cases, the financing and pricing policies have resulted in inefficiencies in the provision of the service, environmental stresses which are difficult to resolve and outcomes which are inequitable. In the light of their experience in the 'long boom' people's expectations about their standard of housing also increased. They sought larger houses with better facilities than their parents had enjoyed but they typically had much smaller blocks of land.

Toward the end of the period the situation had changed. By 1983 Australian governments had departed from their uneven but important commitment to notions of more egalitarian social and economic outcomes which had characterised Australian public policy since 1945. The income and wealth distributions had become markedly less equal with increasing numbers living in poverty. The economy was faced with a situation where every round of inflation was met with demands by the unions for an increase in wages to retain their relative position. The new Commonwealth government developed an Accord with the unions so that their share in the increasing wealth of the nation would be received partly through increases in wages and partly by giving their members better access to what was called the social wage. This social wage was intended to encompass those elements of collective consumption such as better public services, more equitable access to education and health services and housing, as well as more generous cash transfers for the less fortunate. That is, it was meant to encompass services regarded as 'urban services'.

In the event, successive renegotiations of the Accord watered down these commitments, reducing them to valuable but limited increases in family income support schemes. This was accompanied by the replacement of universalist notions of social welfare provision by a targeted approach. In spite of this, the incidence of after-housing poverty increased by over 20 per cent during the 1980s (Australian Institute of Health and Welfare (AIHW) 1993). Over the last decade unemployment has risen and the number experiencing long periods of unemployment has increased. Regional inequalities in unemployment have increased. There has been a simultaneous loss of the middle – what Gregory calls the 'disappearance of the middle' (1992) – which may well be due to the restructuring of firms and government agencies which have been able to take advantage of new information technologies and new approaches to management. But this has also led to the decline in the middle class and therefore in the demand for the kinds of housing and urban services it enjoyed.

Manufactured housing and the numbers living permanently in caravan parks have increased. Commencing with the fundamental changes to the Commonwealth Housing Agreement forced on the States by the Commonwealth in 1978, public housing programs have been inexorably reduced to residual welfare or social housing programs. Some of the effects of these policies are discussed by Mark Peel and Blair Badcock in chapters 2 and 9. Since then, the proportion of housing in public ownership has fallen. Waiting lists for welfare housing increased over the 1980s. Home ownership rates, as measured by the level of owner occupation, fell among the younger age group households in both the 1986 and 1991 censuses suggesting that purchase of their own home was becoming less affordable for increasing proportions of the population. Although housing appeared to be more affordable since 1989, the decline in owner occupation may be due as much to the uncertainties people feel about their employment prospects as to their relative decline in income or wealth.

For some time governments and the public have been assailed by market advocates and business interests with arguments about the desirability of reducing taxes. A 'conventional wisdom' has evolved that the community will not pay higher taxes and the impression has been created that Australia is a highly taxed society (notwithstanding evidence to the contrary from other OECD countries). Few politicians have explained the purpose of and need for public expenditure but have competed over proposals to lower taxes. In the face of the apparent decline in community readiness to pursue collective solutions to urban issues and a desire to reduce what is perceived by them to be an onerous tax burden, governments have recently sought different ways of coping with the problems of urban growth and management. In many instances they have sought to withdraw from fields of concern by privatising the services or to 'distance' themselves from the financing of services by corporatising them wherever possible. These responses have had limited success and problems posed by the growth and management of urban areas remain a subject of political concern. The responses have been complex because of the tension between the ideologically driven desire to withdraw from the public provision and/or management of urban services on the one hand and the political pressures and imperatives to be engaged in the solution to problems on the other.

The Commonwealth government has undertaken a series of initiatives ranging from reviews of housing (National Housing Policy Review 1988–1989; National Housing Strategy 1990–1992) to a review of urban and regional development (Australian Urban and Regional Development Review (AURDR) 1993) and two task forces (Task Force on Urban Design (TFUD) 1993; Task Force on Regional Development (TFRD) 1993) to explore the problems arising from continued urban growth. In addition, it has commissioned reports from the Industry Commission on Urban Transport; Public Housing; Impediments to Regional Industry Adjustment; and Taxation and Financial Policy Impacts on Urban Settlement – all issues which are central to the debate on urban policy. Furthermore, the parliament itself has taken up the issue through the House of Representatives' Standing Committee on Long-Term Strategies which reported in 1992 in the publication *Patterns of Settlement: Consolidating the Future*? The Federal Opposition has implicitly recognised the significance of urban issues by designating a shadow minister with responsibility for the development of urban and regional strategy.

The Commonwealth has also committed resources to projects (the Multi Function Polis (MFP)) and programs (Building Better Cities (BBC)) which it believes will materially improve the functioning of the cities largely by their demonstration effects. The history of such demonstration programs suggests that we should not be sanguine about realising the aims of current initiatives. The present review of the MFP will substantially revise downwards the prospects for that project.

In the 1970s the Whitlam government had an administrative structure which had clear responsibilities for analysis, policy development and program management in urban and regional development (see Lionel Orchard's discussion of the Department of Urban and Regional Development in chapter 3). Although it initially eschewed this approach, the present Commonwealth government has nonetheless stumbled toward the development of a capacity to address urban issues through the Department of Health, Housing, Local Government and Community Services (DHHLGCS).

The uncertain commitment by the Commonwealth to the area and failure to identify clearly urban issues can be seen in the mix and piecemeal accretion of functions in that department. It is also reflected in the failure to develop a professional capacity within the administration to deal with them. The fact that the Housing Division of the department had nine internal reorganisations and no less than six new division heads (only one of whom had previous policy experience in housing or urban development) in the period 1987 tó 1993 can be seen as evidence of failure to develop a professional capacity within the administration to deal with them. A similar pattern is revealed in the staffing of the Housing Division where only a handful of the almost one hundred officers transferred to the department in 1987 worked continuously in it through to late 1993. This turnover of staff significantly reduced the ability of the department to develop a sophisticated understanding of housing and urban issues and meant that there was little development either of institutional memory or historical understanding of the issues.

Over the last decade most of the State governments have also taken initiatives to address urban 'problems' (see chapter 6). These have included adoption of policies to 'contain' urban expansion and the introduction of user charges for a variety of urban services. They have also led to major reviews and reorganisations of the housing and planning activities in most States. In New South Wales housing was first reorganised following the retirement of the post-war generation of administrators. It was reorganised again following a change in government to introduce a more managerialist approach to the delivery of housing services and subjected to a review which proposed even greater regionalisation and privatisation. More recently it was fused with the urban planning activities which were themselves undergoing massive changes in function and powers.

The housing services in Victoria, South Australia and Queensland have undergone similar reorganisations and amalgamations with the urban planning functions.

In part these reorganisations and amalgamations have flowed from the change in housing programs from public to welfare or 'social' programs forced on the States by the Commonwealth in the 1978 changes to the Commonwealth-State Housing Agreement. They have also flowed from the adoption of managerialist approaches in the public sector more generally and the concurrent decline in public sector investment. The reorganisation of planning and the diminution of its range of activities has followed from the general climate of deregulation and the concomitant retreat from large-scale and interventionist public projects, towards the more localised emphasis associated with post-modern experiments in urban design and planning.

In most cases, the reorganisations have been accompanied by significant shedding of staff and replacement by recruits who have not necessarily had experience in the field. This has necessarily led to a significant loss of 'corporate knowledge' in the fields. One feature of this recent phase in administration of housing and planning services is that the senior positions in the States have often been held by people who have had little or no reputation for expertise or competence in housing or urban planning. That is, at State and Commonwealth levels, housing and urban policy formulation and program management has been increasingly in the hands of officers who have little experience or training in the fields but are seen as 'generalists' or have some special understanding of the philosophical position adopted by the government.

There can be little doubt that the growth of urban areas has resulted in major stresses. These are stresses on the environment and on the economic and social system. The decline in professionalism in this field of policy, the lack of an appropriate information and research base and the reluctance of political leaders to focus on urban issues has created a situation where simple solutions to complex issues are grasped. Unfortunately these 'solutions' are almost always inappropriate.

We need to develop a debate about the size, nature, form and structure of Australian cities. Are our cities too large in terms of population or area covered (see chapter 11)? How do/can we know? Are there more efficient ways of distributing the population over the national system of cities? Would they result in greater equity? Is the structure of the cities – heavily influenced by their history – now appropriate? What strategies should we follow to restructure them? Is the form of our cities appropriate? Does it offer opportunities consistent with our present life styles and concern for the environment? Is the present system of governance capable of dealing with the economic and social forces which now act on our cities? Are there alternative ways of providing, financing and pricing the delivery of desired urban services which produce less environmental stress?

Governments at State and Commonwealth level have prejudged many of the answers to these questions. Policies have been adopted which are forcing changes on the cities with no guarantee that they will have desirable economic effects, will reduce environmental stress, will not reduce standards of amenity and will not lead to considerable increases in inequity in the city. Local authorities and communities have had their power to object to development proposals curtailed. This loss of autonomy has occurred simultaneously with claims that administrative changes have been introduced to increase local engagement in planning and environmental control.

Some may argue that most of the problems in Australian society should be seen as problems *in* cities, not those *of* cities, but there can be little doubt that the way cities grow and are administered, their form and their structure, can exacerbate or ameliorate them. The moment we acknowledge that people pursue their activities in real time occupying real space and that the opportunities open to them are significantly influenced by their location relative to one another and to the range of facilities available in the city, we begin to accept that 'the urban' is a useful way of thinking about social policy. The problems created by urban growth then become important issues in the way we discuss the future of Australian society.

This book has two purposes. The first is to contribute to the debate on urban growth and to open for discussion issues which have so far been ignored. The second is to begin the exploration of the issues raised by growth and by governments' current responses to it. It will become clear to the reader that the book canvasses different positions. This catholicity of attitude is recognition that there is ground for differences of opinion. The book identifies some areas where we simply do not know enough to understand with any clarity how to specify the problem or reach finality on appropriate policy responses. But in other areas the book arrives at conclusions or indicates, with confidence, directions in which they will be found.

The book is the result of a discussion and exchange which took place between the authors during 1993. Their views were then exposed to critical review at a national workshop late in that year and revised early in 1994 in the light of that review.

It is difficult to conduct a debate on urban growth as though that growth took place outside the general economic and political context or processes occurring in society. More importantly, it is undesirable to do so. This book attempts to discuss urban growth and the issues which arise from it in Australian cities in the current of intellectual debate. It also attempts to ground its comment on policy in the context of the contemporary economic and political situation.

The book is in three parts: Part I provides a perspective on the state of Australian cities, including an historical analysis of their development; Part II discusses current policies and their origins; and Part III explores possible avenues for policy development.

Part I   The Development and State of Australian Cities

In chapter 1 Lionel Frost and Tony Dingle explore the issues arising from the past growth and suburbanisation of the major Australian cities. They remind us that the past conditions and influences present options. Many structures have physical lives which exceed the lives of those who built them and their economic usefulness. Urban services frequently have 'design lives' of a century or more. Land subdivisions and road reservations are useful conventions for dividing up and representing private rights in real property to ensure that access to it is preserved. The sanctity of continuity of use and preservation of access rights, once designated, make subdivision boundaries difficult to change. Although some pieces of land can and have been used for only one purpose since their designation, many allotments and structures have been used for a variety of purposes. Dwellings can be used as commercial premises, warehouses, offices and factories often can be converted to dwellings and, of course, many structures which have been built to house a set of activities continue to be used for those activities even when the activities themselves change radically.

The path dependency to which Frost and Dingle draw attention stems partly from the essentially incremental growth of the city. Once development has occurred those who own it seek to maximise their advantage. Subsequent development is aimed at enhancing the initial investment. As cities grow and economic and political powers are centralised and entrenched it becomes easier for established interests to shape the conditions under which incremental growth can occur. Optimising urban development is difficult because the private interests of established property owners and residents, although short term, usually outweigh the longer term collective benefits of optimisation.

Frost and Dingle point out that the suburban form and highly centralised structure of our cities are the product of a long historical process in which different economic and social forces acted at different times but at all times were influenced by what each generation inherited. Their argument confirms the point, made in response to those who would take an ahistorical approach to urban policy, that the essentially suburban nature and relatively low density of Australian cities predates recent developments in transport technology by attributing it to the increasing popularity of the motor car.

Mark Peel in chapter 2 takes us on a different but no less significant journey of consideration of urban issues. His history reminds us that one of the central tenets of the early town planning reformers was concern for the injustices which the poor experienced. Their determination to ameliorate the injustices as efficiently as possible simply presented policy choices in the correct order: the mitigation of the problems resulting from a market-oriented society and the improvement of health and housing conditions were the goals – efficient use of resources and the relationship of activities to one another was simply the means.

In his critique Peel shows how the loss of vision of what constitutes 'the good society', the confusion over ends and means and re-emerging physical determinism in the management of urban growth, have served to obscure the important issue of disadvantage by focusing on economic efficiency. Peel acknowledges that where people live in the city affects disadvantage and he points out that some policies in housing and urban management have located them in places which have increased their disadvantage. He examines the way that the policy debate specifies, and effectively understates, the 'urban problem'. The processes of defining the problem help carry the planning agenda away from intervention in inequality towards a kind of 'servicing' for an unequal society. In asking whether we want to do anything about reducing polarisation and inequality he invites us to consider how we might best shape urban growth to that end but cautions that the answer goes to the heart of the nature of Australian society and its values.

In traversing the history of national urban policy over the last twenty-five years Lionel Orchard (chapter 3) sees three main phases: social democratic, libertarian and corporatist. His description of the Whitlam government's essay into urban policy as interventionist and regionalist and that of the Fraser government as libertarian and indicating a withdrawal by the Commonwealth to a position of minimal engagement in urban policy, accurately summarises those eras. There are few fuller explorations of the pros and cons of the policy of urban consolidation so vigorously adopted by the Commonwealth late in the 1980s. Orchard's discussion, although focused on the national scene, resonates with the more historical exploration by Frost and Dingle of the form of the Australian city and with the sociological review by Mullins in chapter 4 of the importance of consumerism and notions of community to the achievement of national policy objectives. Orchard cautions that present policy might fail in its objectives.

The household is a central unit of the discussion if not the analysis of urban planning and management. Patrick Mullins argues that, in spite of its importance in the discourse, we know little about the role played by households in urban development. He explores the link between households, consumerism, residential development and urban policy. Mullins begins by discussing what is meant by 'the household' and how it relates to residential organisation, offering us a useful account of the limitations to the notion of 'community' which tends to impart energy to debates over urban policy without throwing light on the subject. His review of the impact of consumerism on Australian cities opens new ways of thinking about the forces which are restructuring them. Mullins confirms from a different perspective the conclusions reached by Frost and Dingle, that the suburban nature of Australian cities is the result of the high living standards which Australians have enjoyed for the last 130 years. In his discussion of households and consumerism Mullins then goes on to question whether contemporary urban policy initiatives, such as the preoccupation with consolidation, are based on a full understanding of the nature and strength of the obsession with consumerism.

In different but complementary ways all four chapters in Part I raise important questions about the efficacy of the present dimensions and directions of urban policy. They all query the reversion to physical determinism and implicitly suggest that we need more information about the aspirations and behaviour of the population as well as a clearer articulation of the social and distributive consequences of urban policy options before we travel further in the direction current initiatives are taking.

Part II   Current Policies and Options

The story of Balmain by Tim Bonyhady, as described in chapter 5, is not simply 'a rattling good yarn'. We have all too few studies of urban decision-making which explore the role of different participants – State government, developers, property owners, planners, councillors, courts, residents, consultants – their values and their actions. Bonyhady lets us see how State and local governments may contest an issue and how the rights and expressed preferences of citizens may be given little weight in disagreements with either level of government or major private economic interests. This study shows that, although the law in theory enables citizens, individually or collectively, to exercise their rights and to obtain redress, the cost of the process may make it impossible. This effectively means that the legal process is open only to the rich and powerful.

Bonyhady's analysis shows how policies which are not rooted in the expectations and desires of citizens or do not take full cognisance of them may fail to achieve their objectives. The analysis also shows how failure to observe due process can be fatal to government initiatives. Although Balmain residents may have won the battle and have yet to win the war, they have shown how guerilla-like resistance to unpopular State and local government initiatives may, at the least, significantly delay them. Bonyhady shows the environmental and social limits to urban consolidation in places like Balmain.

Raymond Bunker gives us a more traditional account of recent State planning activities. His chapter 6 accepts the general 'failure' of physically determinist planning in the post-war period. His account of the recent Planning Review in South Australia acknowledged the potential value of employing people on such an exercise who were 'largely unfamiliar with metropolitan planning' but set against it the problems raised by the innocence of understanding by those same people and their failure to address important planning issues.

One of the paradoxes which emerges from Bunker's account is that although the limitations of physical determinism are recognised, the South Australian Planning Review (SAPR) was unable to interest the government in the relationship between economic issues and urban development. As a consequence, its recommendations were couched in older physical determinist terms and the action taken by the government endorsed them when it reorganised the Department of Housing and Urban Development to embrace a number of agencies including housing and land development agencies.

In their report on planning in Sydney in chapter 7, Sophie Watson and Alec McGillivray explore problems and opportunities raised by the fact that Australian society is increasingly ethnically diverse. The authors point out that although the migration program has been in place for nearly fifty years the planning system has been slow to recognise the resulting cultural diversity of the population and to adjust its policies and practices accordingly. They discuss the tensions which arise as established members of the community find the religious and cultural activities of new citizens threatening.

At the heart of this exploration is the notion that the planning system has hitherto been predicated on notions derived from Anglo-Saxon conventions and norms. The authors suggest that this approach is no longer valid. They imply that there is a need for greater recognition by planners that the old verities have dissolved and by both the community and its planners that the situation is much more dynamic and uncertain than it was and that we need a new kind of planning in a multicultural environment.

Local government has traditionally been seen as the weakest of the three levels of government in Australia. Its weakness flows from the fact that it has no independent existence but is the creature of State governments. Renate Howe in chapter 8 argues that changing economic circumstances are leading to changes in the power and significance of local government. She points out that hitherto State governments have ignored local government in their development of metropolitan plans. Federal concerns that their initiatives aimed at improving local government have to some extent been frustrated by State governments has led to attempts by the Commonwealth to deal directly with local government.

Howe identifies some of the ambiguities which exist in relation to local government in most Australian cities and which affect the way they respond to growth issues: central city local governments may have interests which are in conflict with those of fringe councils, State governments are loath to strengthen and are more likely to weaken local government's capacity to deal with growth issues because that might reduce the authority of the State government, local governments which are the focus of major development may not be competent to cope with the growth and consequently make planning mistakes which are costly even in the relatively short run. Nonetheless, Howe is optimistic about the future of local government and the need for it to be given stronger powers.

The issue of equity is picked up by Blair Badcock in chapter 9 who argues that the prospect of achieving greater equity in Australian cities is receding. He finds that the restructuring policies which opened Australia to global economic forces simultaneously lead to greater inequality in labour and housing markets. Badcock also argues that urban policies contribute to these inequalities and lead to concentrations of disadvantage in the cities. In discussing current urban policies Badcock concludes that neither the Building Better Cities (BBC) program nor the focus on consolidation is likely to reduce disadvantage. In the case of the BBC this is because the demonstration effects of the projects chosen, focus on efficiency and the extent to which the projects are successful is likely to accentuate the differences between poorer and richer areas. Regardless of the stated objective of a better mix of more affordable housing enabling a choice of life styles, the actuality of consolidation practices is producing a distribution of housing choices which will accentuate difference and reduce the choice of the lower income households.

Badcock's discussion of increasing inequality and its spatial expression reminds us that while the underlying causes may not be found in urban policies they have been exacerbated by them. And he suggests that urban policy can do no more than ameliorate some of the problems of inequality.

The discussion in Part II focuses on the current situation and how cities and State governments are dealing with urban growth. The first four chapters recommend, explicitly or implicitly, how urban growth could or should be better managed. They concentrate on the process of decision-making and the distribution of powers between the institutions and agencies which together comprise the system of urban management. At the heart of all four chapters is a concern by the authors of the need for greater measures to protect and even enhance the rights of citizens and for a strengthening of local democracy. In the fifth chapter Badcock's exploration of inequality and how government policies exacerbate it, serves to remind us that we cannot be sanguine about the outcome of urban policy.

Part III   Avenues for Development

In discussing the financing of urban services in chapter 10 Max Neutze takes the exploration of policy options into new territory. The provision and financing of urban services is a central element in deliberations over policies to cope with urban growth, but so far the agenda for debate has been set by existing conventions – a classic case of the path dependency referred to by Frost and Dingle. Neutze reconsiders the issues from first principles. He identifies the objectives pursued in financing services, then discusses the different ways services might be financed and their economic consequences. His refreshing exploration of the determinants of cost leads him into a discussion of more rational ways urban services might be funded. The institutional effects of the charging options are then explored.

There has recently been an increased adoption of user charges for a variety of urban services. Neutze argues that wider use of such charges would produce significant economies in the operation of the services and lead to reduction in environmental stress. He recognises that the adoption of user charges raises equity issues which would need further exploration – in some cases, user charges might increase equity while in others action would be needed to ensure that the poor could still have access to the service. He acknowledges that, to realise the benefits which could flow from changes in the way services are financed, people would have to change their behaviour. This might involve changes in the location as well as the way they use urban space. Neutze's argument is a salutory reminder that economic mechanisms are available and can be used to complement physical planning and control measures.

Problems of urban growth have frequently been seen as the problems of the big cities. In chapter 11 Peter Self makes the point that we cannot confine the consideration of urban growth to the big cities, that the development of regional Australia offers the possibility of reducing pressures on them and of leading to a more balanced and satisfactory settlement pattern for Australia as a whole. He draws lessons from earlier regional policies, discusses the growth dilemmas of the big cities and reviews regional development prospects. Self argues that developments in information technology and the diseconomies of scale in the big cities provide the opportunity for a gradual switch of employment to smaller regional cities.

There are many areas of Commonwealth government responsibility where its policies have a major effect upon patterns of urban growth. Self explores the ways in which immigration, transport policy, rational pricing of urban services and Federal assistance to local government affect regional development. He argues that there is a need for a Commonwealth regional development policy but that it should be selective and developed in collaboration with State and local government.

In chapter 12 Patrick Troy discusses the history of cooperation between the States and Commonwealth, suggesting that the reasons for failure to develop more productive cooperative relations over urban growth issues lie in the institutional history of the States and the distribution of powers between them and the Commonwealth. He argues that the scale and changing nature of urban problems has led to a situation where the various levels of government can no longer attempt to deny their responsibility. Regardless of constitutional niceties, the political realities require governments to cooperate in resolving issues over which there is public concern. This is leading to a de facto redefinition of constitutional responsibilities – one which might need to be formally recognised.

Part III of the book is essentially optimistic. Neutze, Self and Troy all argue that we do not have to accept the present specification of the urban growth problem nor the currently limited policy prescriptions. They hold that a return to a discussion of the objectives of policy coupled with a reaffirmation of the rights and obligations of citizens wedded to a vision of what kind of urban system we desire, can lead to better policies more appropriate to our current needs.

The overall conclusion of the book is that there is a strong need for public intervention in the resolution of urban growth problems and that such intervention can produce better outcomes than will otherwise occur from the present policy.

PART ONE

The Development and State
of Australian Cities

CHAPTER 1

Sustaining Suburbia: An Historical Perspective on Australia's Urban Growth

Lionel Frost and Tony Dingle

Few people who each day battle traffic jams, suffer from pollution, or face shortages of services in far-flung suburbs appreciate how much the modern urban landscape is a creation of the past. At the start of the twentieth century Australia's major cities had either already developed a low-density townscape with significant decentralisation of housing and jobs, or were beginning to sprawl at the edge of their old, compact core. This low-density physical form was built in an attempt to avoid the sort of urban problems which can develop in a high-density setting. As city populations grew, heavy investment in public transport and infra-structure was needed if this land-extensive housing stock was to be replicated and improved. During the twentieth century, improvements in public transport encouraged commuting and the creation of new suburbs, but the system eventually became congested. Jobs came to be increasingly located away from the old downtown and commuters began to switch to private transport. Road building enabled cities to sprawl further and eventually outrun their public transport systems. The costs mounted up over time as the provision of infrastructure lagged behind population growth and the dependence of new, distant suburbs on cars saw an increase in the volume of traffic and associated disamenities. What were once seen as solutions to urban problems – the opening up of new low-density suburbs and the building of roads and freeways to improve the flow of cars – have now become urban problems in themselves.

There is a substantial element of what economic historians call 'path dependency' here, as the consequences of one historical era have been carried over to the next. Concerns about the ability of Australian cities to cope with population growth, to provide affordable and functional housing, to cost-effectively maintain and extend infrastructure, and to avoid externalities such as pollution, are the result of the implications of past decisions being played out. Australian cities began to sprawl in the nineteenth century because a large proportion of the population was able to afford to live in a suburban setting, and because this ideal was generally supported and encouraged by governments. Suburbanisation was sustained in the twentieth century by the persistence of these factors, and by new developments which encouraged dispersal, such as large-scale manufacturing, assisted immigration, government subsidisation of home ownership, and the internal combustion engine. While the current push for planned areas of consolidated urban land use, with more space-intensive housing located close to workplaces, public transport, shops and community services, is to be applauded, it is working against a big load of history, as past city-building has caused jobs and housing to be scattered far and wide.

The Spacious Suburb: A Realisable Goal

To live in quiet, clean and spacious suburbs, away from the noise, dirt and crowds of town centres, is something that most people have desired from a very early stage in Australian history. Governor Phillip's first town plan for Sydney stipulated that main streets would be 200 feet wide and that town lots would have a minimum frontage of 60 feet (Fletcher 1989:53-5). This plan was ignored by subsequent governors, but the objective of creating healthy and spacious living conditions underlay much of the physical development of Australian cities. All the capitals developed suburbs before their centres were fully built up. Town lots tended to be purchased by speculators and thus many people lived and worked at cheaper sites further out (Statham 1989:22-6).

The spread of suburbs during the nineteenth century was most pronounced in Melbourne, Adelaide and Perth. These were part of a 'New Urban Frontier' – a region of cities in North America and Australasia which coped with population growth by spreading outwards through the replication of suburbs. Compared to the concentrated cities of Europe and eastern North America, cities like Los Angeles, Denver, Vancouver, Auckland and Christchurch were of arrestingly low density and covered immense areas of ground. The New Frontier cities generally averaged a population density of around 5 persons per acre at the end of the nineteenth century, compared to between 8 and 93 per acre in cities in Britain and eastern North America. Melbourne's most densely populated district in 1891, Fitzroy, had an average of 37 persons per acre, well below the peak density of, say, London (365 per acre), Chicago (273) or Boston (184). At the turn of the century Perth sprawled as far from south-west to north-east as did London from north to south (Frost 1991b:24–8).

Three factors have been commonly suggested to explain the sprawling, low-density character of Australian cities. First, it may be argued that an abundance of cheap land provided ample space for low-density suburbs. Second, because Australian cities grew large during an era of improvement in public transport technology, they could suburbanise more easily than older cities which had built up a high-density housing stock during earlier periods when public transport was expensive or nonexistent. This is similar to the case made by those who suggest that the sprawl of Los Angeles began in the twentieth century with the automobile. Third, Australian cities were built this way because of preferences which are embedded in Australian culture.

None of these explanations is convincing. While it is easy to cite examples of cities being hemmed in geographically, by hills (such as Sheffield), waterways (Boston) or large areas of permanent parkland (Stuttgart), one can also find examples of high-density cities surrounded by large areas of cheap, flat land, such as Chicago, Cleveland and Toronto. A number of cities in North America, central and eastern Europe grew large during the same period as did Australian cities, yet took on a markedly different physical and spatial form (Frost 1991b:31–3).

The cultural preference for suburbia is quite widespread, having originated in England. From the mid-eighteenth century, London's merchant elite began to sell their town-houses and move to new villas located in the open countryside around villages such as Clapham and Hampstead. These areas were sufficiently distant to shield a family from urban problems, yet close enough for a breadwinner to commute to a town workplace each day. The 'classic suburb' was thus a 'marriage of town and country' (Fishman 1987), with suburbia forming the 'borderland' where the city ended and the countryside started (Stilgoe 1988). While city-dwellers in most of continental Europe, Scotland and Ireland followed the Paris fashion of living as close as possible to city centres in apartments or other high-density residential buildings, what was valued in English towns was the ability to live in an individual house, with maximum privacy, sunlight and fresh air (Olsen 1986). English emigrants took this preference with them to Australia, and to the United States, Canada and New Zealand. In the New Frontier cities the preference for living in a suburban setting was no more widespread than in other Anglo-Saxon cities, but was a more realisable goal.

The clue as to why this was the case lies in the fact that suburbs are expensive to build. The costs of building, equipping and servicing the urban environment and getting people to work are inflated in low-density suburbs: a family living in a detached house would require more land and building materials than would have been the case if they had lived in multi-storey or terraced housing, the breadwinner would usually have to pay train or tram fares each day, and the infrastructure needed by the family would have to be spread over great distances. The costs of living in a 'classic suburb' in England and most of North America were generally beyond the lower-middle and working classes, and the inaccessibility of suburbs was something the middle classes valued. Thus, most of the population lived in compact housing, generally on flat, badly drained areas close to factories and railway yards, where the number of dwellings ranged from about 10 to 60 per acre (Frost 1991b:14).

That so many Australians could bear the high costs of suburbanisation can be attributed to the high average incomes which were generated by a prosperous economic base. The function of towns was largely administrative during the convict era, and this stimulated urban growth. As the economy developed further, towns played a crucial role as providers of commercial services for the export sector. A large part of the urban workforce was employed in providing goods and services for other urban inhabitants. Throughout the nineteenth century the Australian urban population accounted for a larger share of total population than was the case in other new societies colonised by white settlers (Frost 1990:17). Australian cities were largely commercial-tertiary, rather than industrial, centres. Because of high labour costs, a limited domestic market and high transport costs, manufacturing was confined to a limited range of activities associated with the needs of the urban population, such as building materials and food and drink, and accounted for a smaller share of the labour force than was the case in most North American cities (Frost 1991b:68–9).

Much urban work involved labour-intensive, often unskilled activity such as building, digging, delivering, loading and so on. Productivity growth in the export sector created a continuing demand for urban work. Furthermore, because the costs of emigrating to Australia were sufficiently high to discourage low-income groups, most migrants were literate, skilled workers, such as tradespeople, merchants or pro-fessionals. Their spending on housing and other goods and services further increased economic activity and the demand for labour.

These labour market conditions created a general level of affluence. For instance, by the early twentieth century an unskilled labourer in an Australian city could expect in a full week of work to earn around twice as much as his British counterpart. This relative advantage is effectively widened if low Australian food costs are taken into account. Provided that they stayed able-bodied, Australian workers could earn, and reasonably expect to continue to earn, wages which gave them large disposable incomes.

High disposable incomes allowed most people to spend heavily on housing. During the gold rushes, the number of permanent dwellings had roughly kept pace with population growth, but by 1861 the housing stock waš of poorer quality, size and durability than had been the case a decade earlier. N. G. Butlin calculates that in 1861 one-fifth of the total population lived in substandard, impermanent housing, such as tents and shanties. In Victoria, where there was a large goldfield population, the proportion was almost one-third (Butlin 1964:215–17). During the subsequent 'long boom' from around 1860 to 1890, when Australians enjoyed rates of economic growth and living standards which were equalled by few, if any, contemporary nations, the standard of the housing stock improved markedly. Expansion of the housing stock more than kept pace with population growth, even during periods such as the Adelaide boom, when the city grew at a rate of almost 9 per cent per annum from 1876 to 1881, or during the 1860s, 1880s and 1890s, when Sydney grew at an average rate of 5 per cent per annum, as did Melbourne during the 1880s.

Houses became larger and better appointed on average, but improvements in building technology kept construction costs down (Pikusa 1986). In Adelaide during the mid-1870s, the rent of an average sized four-room cottage cost 20 per cent of a skilled builder's weekly wage; thirty years later the typical suburban house had five rooms, yet the rent cost only 17 per cent of a skilled builder's weekly wage (Frost 1991a:36). Unskilled workers in Melbourne spent up to 30 per cent of their weekly income to rent four-room cottages which were simple but far superior to those in which most of their parents would have lived (Lack 1991). In contemporary British cities, only slum dwellers whose incomes were low spent such a high proportion of income on rent. Skilled workers normally spent around 10 per cent of income on rent.

Home buyers needed to find cash for a deposit and make mortgage payments which were usually higher than rents. In Adelaide in the early 1880s, home buyers had to pay a deposit of £40–50, when unskilled wages averaged around £2 per week. Mortgage payments absorbed around 31 per cent of average unskilled wages (*Adelaide Advertiser* 1881). However, home buyers could partially offset these costs by buying a smaller house, say, of three rooms rather than the average four or five, and then extending later. Most urban dwellers seem to have strongly desired to become home owners, and studies of Melbourne have shown that as new suburbs were opened up the majority of houses were occupied by owners rather than tenants (Dingle & Merrett 1972).

High incomes are a necessary, but not sufficient condition for extensive suburban development. An institutional framework must exist or be developed which allows suburban developers to be subsidised by public provision of infrastructure, especially public transport. Australian suburbanisation has been boosted by the provision of infrastructure by colonial and State governments, rather than local governments or private developers (Davison 1993:8–9). In virtually all North American cities, street railroads (tramways) were built into open countryside to lure people to suburban home sites, but the cost of this was normally absorbed by land owners and developers, who either owned streetcar companies or paid subsidies to them. In Australia, many of the costs of suburban development were financed by government borrowing and general taxation revenue. This was to the considerable advantage of new suburbs, with the costs of providing the required new schools, sanitation and suburban railways being shared by the general community (trams, however, were the exception, being built and operated by private companies or municipal councils).

Although the promotion of population growth in rural areas was given a high priority by colonial governments, as evidenced by such policies as the sale of Crown land on credit to selectors, rural railway building, irrigation and closer settlement (Frost 1992), high rates of urban population growth encouraged public investment which facilitated suburban expansion. This was especially so in Victoria and South Australia, where most members of parliament represented or lived in the capital city (Hirst 1973). An important factor in the Melbourne building boom of the 1880s was a bold program of government railway extension to a number of areas which had suburban potential but were only lightly populated (Davison 1978).

The siting and planning of Melbourne, Adelaide and Perth encouraged railway building and suburbanisation: railways were needed to Williamstown, Port Melbourne, Port Adelaide and Fremantle because these ports were located some distance from their respective town centres, and this encouraged decentralisation of jobs and housing. The railway to Fremantle became Perth's main suburban corridor. Each of these cities had a grid of wide streets which was well-suited to the building and operation of trams.

Sydney and Brisbane were not so favoured. These were also high-income cities, but because of planning and political constraints their suburbs were slow to develop. Their sites were more confined, with the docks adjacent to the town centre. Brisbane's suburban developers were hampered by a shortage of bridges to take commuters across the Brisbane River. In Sydney, a lack of available space when the first railway was built made it difficult for a terminus to be built close to the major workplaces. Narrow, and in places crooked, streets became quickly clogged with trams and other traffic. The New South Wales parliament, dominated by country interests, was hostile to Sydney and under-invested in the city's infrastructure. This encouraged most people to live in compact housing, within walking distance of workplaces or the city's limited public transport facilities. While governments in Melbourne and Adelaide built effective water supply and sewerage systems (Dingle & Rasmussen 1991; Frost 1991a:37–8), Sydney's sanitation was built cheaply and its ineffectiveness made living conditions dismal in the crowded areas close to the city centre (Fitzgerald 1987, 1992).

Suburbia: Sustaining Factors

By the early 1970s, 86 per cent of all Australians lived in towns or cities. The populations of the capital cities expanded sixfold on average during the twentieth century. So too did their housing stock, so that the overwhelming bulk of our urban built environment is a twentieth-century creation. This development has been overwhelmingly suburban, having taken the nineteenth-century model of the suburb and extended it with larger subdivisions, fewer people per house and higher levels of owner occupation. For the first three-quarters of the twentieth century, governments took a larger and a more direct role in expanding and sustaining suburbia than they had during the nineteenth century. They did this by protecting industry from foreign competition, thereby creating more work in urban areas, by assisting immigrants, most of whom settled in urban areas, by subsidising the provision of suburban services, by assisting low-income earners to purchase their own home and by establishing minimum housing standards appropriate to suburbia. Although Australia slipped gradually down the international league table of average incomes throughout the twentieth century, this did not erode the capacity of Australians to pay for a suburban lifestyle.

In the nineteenth century, urbanisation had stimulated manufacturing but as the twentieth century progressed it was the growth of manufacturing which generated city growth. Manufacturing provided the major single source of employment in all the capital cities by 1911, with one in four jobs in Hobart and Perth, the smallest capitals, rising to 32 per cent in Sydney and 37 per cent in Melbourne. These percentages do not appear to have risen substantially before the outbreak of World War II (the 1933 census was taken at the wrong time to assess long-term trends); nevertheless, the aggregate additions to the manufacturing workforce were impressive. Between 1911 and 1921, Sydney acquired an extra 38 000 factory jobs and Melbourne 29 000, then between 1921 and 1947 there were net additions of 110 000 and 81 000 respectively (Commonwealth censuses 1911–1947).

It was the clusters of industries that grew rapidly around the new technologies of electricity and the internal combustion engine which gave manufacturing a new direction and impetus in the 1920s and 1930s. Increasingly, the products of the new industries – items such as cars, electric power, electric irons, toasters, fridges and vacuum cleaners – were aimed at suburban consumers (Forster 1964; Sinclair 1970). The protective Greene Tariff of 1921 and subsequent tariff increases allowed these local industries to increase their share of the local market somewhat during the 1920s. Devaluation and further tariff increases during the Depression then gave them greatly increased shares in the 1930s, amounting to three-quarters of the total in metals and machinery and two-thirds in chemicals (Schedvin 1970:55, 304). The redistributional effects of protective tariffs were a major political issue during the inter-war years. They boosted the incomes of those in protected manufacturing industries and reduced the incomes of exporters (Brigden 1929), thus redistributing income from rural to urban areas, from small State to large States and from small towns to large cities. It has been calculated that the tariff between 1929 and 1932 alone may have boosted city incomes by as much as 3 per cent (Ward 1983:104). Foreign firms established branches in Australia as a way of ducking under the tariff barriers. General Motors, ICI and many others were consequently creating jobs in Sydney or Melbourne rather than Detroit or Northwich.

Government activity stimulated a flow of resources into the cities in other ways. Until the Depression of the 1930s State governments were primarily concerned with the promotion of rural development and, like their colonial predecessors, invested heavily in rural development projects. But instead of following the lead of governments, private investors turned increasingly to more promising prospects that were opening up in urban areas through the emergence of new technologies. As a result, urban growth continued to demand a larger slice of public investment. Public capital formation accounted for roughly half of all capital formation in the first three decades of the twentieth century. It had been dominated by railway construction before 1900 but thereafter roads and bridges, water and sewerage and telegraph took increasing shares. Investment by local government rose from 20 per cent of public capital formation in 1900 to 40 per cent in the 1930s, and much of this was for road improvements and services (Butlin 1962). Governments which sought to promote closer rural settlement ended up financing the infrastructure for the growing suburbs (Sinclair 1970).

The programs of assisted immigration after World War I were an integral part of the plan to settle more Britons on the land. They never reached their targets and many of those who came ended up in the cities rather than the bush, so this was another way in which urban growth was subsidised. Overseas immigrants, most of whom had been assisted in some way, made varying contributions to the growth in population of the capital cities between 1911 and 1947; they accounted for 15 per cent of Perth's growth, 7 per cent of Sydney's, but only 4 per cent of Brisbane's and 3 per cent of Melbourne's. They contributed nothing to the growth of either Adelaide or Hobart (Merrett 1978:191).

Between 1911 and 1947 Australia's urban population more than doubled; capital city populations alone rose from a total of 1.7 to 3.8 million. The stock of housing also more than doubled to accommodate them. This urban growth was heavily concentrated in the outlying suburbs of Sydney and Melbourne, which accounted for 72 per cent of capital city population growth from 1911 to 1947 (New South Wales, Victorian censuses 1911–1947). Pent up wartime demand resulted in a rush for housing from 1919 and the price of materials and buildings increased considerably. However there was no shortage of land. Subdividers worked so enthusiastically that many suburban lots had not been built on before the Depression brought expansion to a halt. The inter-war suburb was invariably dominated by the Californian bungalow, set well back on its sizeable block. A minority of people in Sydney and to a lesser extent in Melbourne went to the opposite extreme and lived in flats, but there was no inter-war equivalent to the higher density row-housing built in some inner suburbs in the second half of the nineteenth century. The experiences of Melbourne and Sydney were replicated on a smaller scale elsewhere.

Improvements and extensions to public transport opened up enough new land to allow low-density suburban expansion to continue. In Melbourne electrification of the suburban rail network immediately after World War I speeded travel and increased carrying capacity. On congested lines the track was duplicated and the grade altered to eliminate level crossings. These improvements allowed people to live much further out and still spend the same 30 minutes commuting, a length of time which most people appear to have regarded as tolerable (Ward 1983:222–35). Electrification of the railways did not start until 1926 in Sydney but then had a similar impact. The opening of an underground rail loop in 1926 and the Harbour Bridge in 1932 also improved access to new suburbs. Tramway links opened up many areas including the eastern suburbs and were the major public carrier (Kelly 1980; Gibbons 1983). Melbourne's various systems of private and municipal horse and cable tramways were brought under the control of the Melbourne and Metropolitan Tramways Board in 1919, which then electrified and extended the network.

This new investment in public transport contrasted sharply with the situation in American cities. American transport companies suffered severe financial difficulties after World War I, mainly because municipal governments refused to alter franchise agreements which required that a flat fare, usually 5 cents, be charged on all journeys. These low fares were popular with voters but did not provide adequate revenue for companies to maintain or update capital equipment. Few city governments subsidised public transport, and as systems became congested and run-down commuters began to use their own automobiles, driving them on roads paid for by the general taxpayer (Jackson 1985:168–77; Bottles 1987). In the United States the number of people per automobile fell from 13 in 1920 to 5 in 1930; in Australia the corresponding figures were 62 in 1921 and 10 in 1930 (Jackson 1985:163; Vamplew 1987:171).

One reason why Australia's inter-war suburbanisation was somewhat more sluggish than that of the United States was that in Australia, public transport remained the main link between suburbia and the workaday world. America's cars and roads could open up new residential areas away from public transport routes, and so for developers 'every multi-lane ribbon of concrete was like the touch of Midas, transforming old pastures into precious property' (Jackson 1985:176). This type of development was relatively unimportant in Australia until after World War II.

House prices varied according to area. In affluent Woollahra in 1919 the average cost of a new dwelling was £1200 and in working-class Bankstown slightly less than half that amount. Home sites cost at least £100 and often much more at a time when the basic wage was less than £190. Thereafter both prices and wages rose, but the cheapest housing continued to cost a little more than three times the annual basic wage. Lower income earners were unable to bridge the deposit gap and borrow from building societies and trading banks. Even the State Savings Bank in New South Wales, which financed about 17 per cent of new buildings in New South Wales during the 1920s, would not lend more than three-quarters of the value of the property, leaving a deposit gap of £150 on a cheap house costing £600 (Spearritt 1978:30–1).

From the early years of the century there was a growing desire at both State and Commonwealth level to facilitate higher levels of home ownership amongst people on lower incomes. Labor parties at State and Commonwealth level never spoke with one voice on this issue, but many Labor people saw this as a way of getting workers out of the grasp of landlords and giving them the independence and security that they needed to fight strongly for their industrial interests. The mass evictions of the 1890s Depression, especially in Melbourne, were a reminder of how swiftly families could be deprived of shelter. Conservatives also supported home ownership because it would make those with a stake in the country less revolutionary, less likely to tear down capitalism (Williams 1984:172–81). There was bipartisan support for home ownership, reflecting its widespread acceptance as a desirable goal for all in a property-owning democracy.

There were various ways in which lower income earners could be given access to housing. The deposit gap could be narrowed by lending more against valuation. The repayment period could be extended and the interest rate reduced, especially if governments guaranteed the loans and used their borrowing power to raise the finance necessary for such schemes. All these approaches were tried in varying degrees by legislation introduced in all the States (Hill 1959:ch.5).

In Victoria the *Housing and Reclamation Act* of 1920 gave municipalities the power to build houses costing not more than £800 to sell to people earning less than £400 a year. The municipalities took no action and so the State Bank of Victoria became the main agent implementing the legislation. It built up a book of approved plans which were carefully designed so that they could be built within the cost limits of the Act on 10 per cent deposit. These modest Californian bungalows went up in their tens of thousands in Melbourne's outer suburbs during the 1920s. Repayments were at the rate of 14/2d. per month for every £100 borrowed, or nearly 24 shillings per week on the maximum loan of £720. The level of repayment acceptable to the State Bank was 20 per cent of income – this was also the amount spent on rent by the average family during the 1920s according to official cost-of-living surveys – so someone seeking the maximum loan would have needed an income of £6 a week or just over £300 a year, which was well above the basic wage (Garlick 1983; Ward 1983). The State Bank of Victoria lent in a similar way through the War Service Homes scheme, a Commonwealth initiative, as well as through its Credit Foncier and Savings Bank schemes so that it appears to have provided nearly a third of Melbourne's housing finance during the 1920s (Ward 1983:378). It is unclear how many home buyers benefited from the subsidies incorporated in these schemes to help low-income earners, but in 1922–1923, 16.5 per cent of the new houses financed by the bank were under the Housing and Reclamation Act and 27.5 per cent under the War Service Homes Act (Murray & White 1992:210). This suggests that home ownership had been brought within reach of a wider section of the population.

The new suburbs were overwhelmingly peopled by home owners or home purchasers. Rates of home ownership in both middle- and working-class outer suburbs were typically above 60 per cent and often above 70 per cent (Commonwealth Census 1921). Overall, more than 40 per cent of all private capital formation in the 1920s went into residential construction and over half of this was for owner occupation (Butlin 1962:21). It is difficult to gauge the impact of the 1920s building boom on overall levels of owner occupation. On the face of it, levels rose only modestly in Melbourne but hardly at all anywhere else between the censuses of 1921 and 1933 (see table 1.1). Unfortunately the census returns from 1911, 1921 and 1933 were not taken at the most appropriate time for our purposes. The biggest gains, of 9 percentage points or more in each of the capital cities, came between 1911 and 1921 but it is unclear how much of this had occurred before or after the war. Likewise the 1933 census was measuring the situation in the depths of the Depression which may have impacted differently on the housing market in the various capital cities.

Various influences combined to lessen the population density of suburban expansion. Legislation in most States in the first quarter of the century gave local authorities power to establish minimum sizes for subdivisions, setbacks, house and room sizes and heights (Sandercock 1975:62). These powers could be used to protect property values in a locality by preventing the construction of small, crowded, 'slum' housing, indeed such regulations posed problems for those trying to design small, low-cost workers' housing.

Brick houses were more expensive than timber houses during the inter-war years so declaring an area brick only kept out lower income earners. Style also played a part. The popular Californian bungalow was long and low and had to sit across its block rather than running down it as earlier styles had done. Even the State Bank of Victoria's modest designs were 38 feet wide, necessitating a 50-foot frontage if there was to

Table 1.1 *Owner/purchaser occupation in the capital cities, 1911–1986*
(as per cent of all households)

	Sydney	Melbourne	Brisbane	Adelaide	Perth	Hobart
1911	31	37	46	42	41	33
1921	40	45	59	52	55	43
1933	41	49	60	54	56	44
1947	40	46	60	55	56	49
1954	56	63	71	66	68	63
1961	68	73	75	73	73	70
1966	70	74	74	74	73	71
1971	67	71	72	70	67	68
1976	67	71	71	71	69	70
1981	66	69	69	70	68	67
1986	67	73	72	71	71	71

Source: Williams 1984:171–6; Troy 1991:2.

be access around the side of the house. As the car became more common and a side driveway was incorporated, frontages had to be widened to 55 or 60 feet (Freeland 1972:229).

Building activity almost ceased as the Depression bit deep from late 1929. Many proud home purchasers found themselves out of work and unable to meet their mortgage commitments. By mid-1932 two-thirds of the mortgagees with the State Bank of South Australia were in arrears. Some eventually lost their homes, but others managed to hang on. Banks realised that they could not sell property reverting to them until the economy and the housing market recovered. Meanwhile, it was better to have houses occupied rather than empty so many suburbanites remained where they were (Spenceley 1990:61–2). Building activity picked up slowly from the mid-1930s but not at a level sufficient to eat into the accommodation backlog which had begun to build up during the Depression years. During the 1920s those who could not afford to buy a house had been forced into renting older, and increasingly dilapidated, properties in the inner suburbs. They could not afford to rent the new outer suburban properties where rents were comparable to the level of repayments on a mortgage (Garlick 1983:71). Those dispossessed by the Depression were also forced back onto the inner-suburban rental market. It was these deteriorating areas which worried housing reformers such as Oswald Barnett in the 1930s and became the focus of detailed enquiries. These led to the establishment of Housing Commissions in Victoria and New South Wales and the Housing Trust in South Australia, each concerned to provide decent housing for low-income earners.

After 1941 private construction virtually halted. It was clear that there would be a massive housing shortage once the war ended. The Commonwealth Housing Commission (CHC) estimated that by January 1945 the shortfall was 300 000 houses. It proposed a national effort, which would be centrally directed, to eliminate the shortage within a decade. Its guiding principle was that 'the housing of the people of the Commonwealth adequately, soundly, hygienically and effectively, each according to his social and economic life is a national need', therefore housing 'should cease to be a field of investment yielding high profits'. It also absorbed the environmentalism of the inter-war reformers. The essence of the slum was overcrowding, therefore better housing meant lower-density suburban housing. The commission recommended that any government-sponsored house should meet minimum standards for room size, floor area, and be built on an allotment of not less than 4500 square feet with a frontage of at least 50 feet (CHC Final Report 1944:10, 18). It turned what had become the suburban norm during the inter-war years into a minimum housing standard.

Post-1945: More of the Same

Continued urban growth after 1945 was stimulated by much the same forces as in the 1920s, but they did so for far longer and with greater intensity. This 'long boom' was carried along on rates of economic growth which, although not spectacular by international standards, had not been matched in Australia since the nineteenth century. Levels of unemployment, which hovered around 1 per cent for nearly thirty years, were unprecedented and gave a sense of security to wage earners which contrasted with the instability of the previous decades of war and depression. This was well-founded, for real household incomes per head rose by over 1 per cent per year during the 1950s and over 4 per cent per year during the 1960s and early 1970s. Furthermore, the distribution of incomes appeared to be less unequal than it had been (Boehm 1979:280; Jones 1975). It was this sustained growth in incomes which transformed Australia into 'a modern consumer society' (Whitwell 1989:3). The chemical, electrical, automotive and iron and steel industries had been greatly stimulated during the war and they spearheaded manufacturing growth during the 1950s and 1960s. Economies of scale brought productivity increases as manufacturers increasingly bunched in the major urban centres. Melbourne and Sydney had the advantage here because of their size; in Sydney more than 37 per cent of the workforce was employed in manufacturing during the 1950s, while in Melbourne in 1954, 40 per cent of all jobs were in manufacturing. This helped these two largest cities to increase their share of Australia's population from 36 per cent in 1947 to 43 per cent by 1971. All the States bid against each other to attract large firms to their capital city (Head 1986). Adelaide sustained a level of manufacturing employment not far behind that of Sydney, but in Brisbane, Perth and Hobart only a little over a quarter of all jobs were in manufacturing (Commonwealth censuses 1911–1971).

As in the 1920s government policies stimulated urbanisation. After the war it was accepted by governments that if population was to be boosted by a massive immigration program most of the jobs must be created in manufacturing. Import controls until the end of the 1950s, and then 'made to measure' tariffs, offered local industry rising levels of protection against imports (Boehm 1979:ch.6). Overseas companies and foreign capital entered the country to a far greater extent than previously. This prompted concerns about the level of foreign ownership of manufacturing, but the manufacturers were creating more urban jobs. The sustained program of assisted immigration underpinned the expansion of manufacturing, providing both workers and consumers. Between 1947 and 1961, 73 per cent of the increase in the labour force was provided by immigration, falling to just under 50 per cent in the 1960s and early 1970s (Boehm 1979:ch.3). The impact of immigration was greatest in Sydney, Melbourne and Adelaide contributing 38, 47 and 47 per cent respectively to the total population growth of each city between 1947 and 1961, whereas in the other capitals it played a lesser role than natural increase (Merrett 1978:191). The migrants made their biggest contribution where most manufacturing employment was located.

Manufacturing also stimulated a profound spatial reorganisation of cities after the war. The old inner-city industrial areas became increasingly congested with the buildup of road traffic. There was little room for expansion and land prices were high. Car makers and their industries wanting large areas of land to set up large, single-storey buildings to house continuous flows of production moved to cheap 'greenfield' sites on the suburban fringe. The increasing use of truck transport had freed them from reliance on the railways. People followed the factories to the outer suburbs (Dingle 1984:226–30; Spearritt 1978:121–7). As a growing proportion of jobs was located in the outer suburbs the fixed-track, largely radial network of tram and train transport, which had worked so well when people moved towards the city for their work, proved increasingly irrelevant. The bus was more flexible but population densities in the outer suburbs were so low and job locations so dispersed that it was uneconomic for buses to provide the frequency of service which inner-suburban locations had enjoyed from trams or trains. It was the private motor car which triumphantly fulfilled the transport needs of suburbanised, decentralised employment.

In 1945 there was one motor vehicle for every 8.7 people but by 1968 there was one for every 2.8 people. The fivefold increase in the number of cars which this represented was made possible because they became more affordable. In the early 1950s a new Holden cost 77 weeks of work at average weekly earnings. By 1970 only 30 weeks of wages were required (Whitwell 1989:3). Most families had one car, many had two. The post-war suburbs were shaped to the requirements of the car. The spatial form of all suburbs reflects the dominant form of transport when they were constructed; those of the nineteenth and early twentieth century clustered around railway stations and spread along tram routes. The car has had a more pervasive impact than any of its predecessors, largely because it is such a land-hungry form of transport. It has required wider frontages to accommodate driveway and garage, as well as wider suburban streets and regional shopping centres surrounded by large car parks.

The hegemony of the car has been hastened by the imperialistic tendencies of its owners. Competition for road space saw bus and car users urge the elimination of trams: Sydney began tearing up its tramlines in 1939 and the last one ran in 1961 (Gibbons 1983). Resources devoted to speeding up traffic flow encouraged more people to use cars. As in other Australian cities, with increasing sprawl came a clear trend away from public transport which strengthened with every road widening and extension project. By 1974 two-thirds of Melbourne's workforce journeyed to work by car.

Most post-war suburbanites soon owned the house they lived in as well as the car, although this was not what the planners in Canberra had anticipated in the mid-1940s. The Commonwealth Housing Commission assumed that government funds would flow into the provision of rental housing for low income earners and this would play a major role in eliminating the post-war housing shortage, especially in the first few years (CHC Final Report 1944). The shortage was overcome by the mid-1950s as almost 700 000 dwellings went up, increasing Australia's housing stock by a quarter. But only about one in seven of these were built by public authorities. Private enterprise built the rest and well over a third of all houses were built by their owners (*Commonwealth Year Book* 1957). This often involved working weekends and nights, scavenging scarce materials and living in the garage in an epic of hard work and determination (Rehak 1988:119–27).

In the seven years between the censuses of 1947 and 1954 there were unprecedented increases in levels of owner occupation (see table 1.1). Adelaide experienced the smallest rise, but even here it was 11 percentage points. There were further large increases in the next seven years to 1961 to bring the levels of owner occupation almost to their peak. There has been much discussion on the causes of this increase (e.g. Kemeny 1986; Berry 1988; Allport 1980; Kass 1987; Bethune 1978). No consensus has emerged but there is at least wide agreement on the major forces at work. As already noted, these were years of low unemployment, rising disposable incomes and a vigorously growing economy. While housing costs rose, the admittedly scattered evidence from the 1950s and 1960s suggests that only 10–12 per cent of personal expenditure was going on housing, little more than half pre-war levels (Whitwell 1989:30; Podder 1971). This was partly a consequence of rising incomes, but governments were also subsidising the costs of home ownership in various ways. Initially direct subsidies came mainly through the favourable terms offered through the War Service Homes scheme; nearly 18 per cent of all housing advances made between 1945 and 1956 came from this source (Hill 1959:128). After 1956 a new Commonwealth and State Housing Agreement encouraged State housing authorities to sell public housing to sitting tenants at favourable rates as part of the Menzies government's policy of boosting levels of owner occupation.

Large numbers of government-financed properties were subsequently sold off and this must have had a significant impact on the increase in levels of owner occupation during the late 1950s (Berry 1988). While it was reducing the cost of ownership, government was also reducing the supply of private rental properties. After the war, rent controls fixed rents at pre-war levels. Landlords forced to accept subnormal profits sold their properties to their tenants or whoever would buy them and invested their assets where they could yield a better return. Between 1947 and 1961 the number of private rental properties in Sydney declined by 44 000 and in Melbourne by 39 000. If all these converted to owner occupation this alone would have increased ownership levels by 8 percentage points in both cities (Bethune 1978:165–7).

Public rental housing was in short supply and young couples who missed out on it were forced to live with their parents or try to raise the finance to buy their own home. They took the latter route because the suburban ideal remained a cherished goal for the majority. For nearly two decades depression then high unemployment and war had deprived many young married couples of the suburban lifestyle their parents had often enjoyed. Once the opportunity did become available they seized it with enthusiasm, even though it did not always live up to expectations (Rehak 1988). The pioneers often had to go without roads, sewers and other basic facilities because developers subdivided with scant regard to the provision of infrastructure. Metropolitan planners sought to coordinate expansion and curb the excesses of the developers but they too remained committed to the detached suburban home on its own sizeable block (Dingle & Rasmussen 1991:ch.9). Stiffer and more uniform minimum building and site regulations also reduced the number of houses which could be built on each acre of land.

Kenneth Jackson has identified five characteristics of urban development in the United States between 1945 and 1973. First, it was located on the periphery of the cities. Second, it was low-density detached housing with more land allotted to streets and open space than previously. Third, the suburbs were architecturally similar with a limited range of styles and house sizes. A fourth characteristic was the easy availability of suburban housing: 'it was quite simply cheaper to buy new housing in the suburbs than it was to reinvest in central city properties or to rent at the market price'. Fifth, the post-war suburb was distinguished by economic, age and racial homogeneity. He might have stressed also that the new suburbs were car-dependent. Jackson assumed that these features were uniquely American: 'the creation of good, inexpensive suburban housing on an unprecedented scale was a unique achievement' (Jackson 1985:238–45). In fact, the features apply equally well to Australia, with the important qualification that there has been nothing here to compare with the exclusion of blacks from suburbia; Australian suburbs have been far less exclusionist than American suburbs and its cities are relatively free of large ethnic ghettos and the effects of urban blight.

Conclusion

The periods after the gold rushes and the two world wars were marked by initial housing shortages, and then bursts of suburban development as economic growth allowed Australians to devote a large slice of their resources to the form of housing to which they aspired. Government support was a further prerequisite for suburbanisation, and over time the level of subsidy increased. By the early 1970s the overwhelming majority of Australians lived in this way. Perhaps all who wished to live the suburban life were doing so.

Since the early 1970s some of the forces sustaining suburbia have weakened. Urbanisation halted, then so too did the increase in levels of home ownership (see table 1.1). The world economy was shocked into recession, while at the local level the 25 per cent across-the-board tariff reductions in 1973 marked the end of the policy of high protection for local industry. The manufacturing workforce in the cities had begun to decline as a proportion of total employment in all the capitals from the end of the 1950s, but by the 1970s there was an absolute decline in the number of jobs in manufacturing. By 1986 only one in five jobs in Melbourne, one in seven in Sydney and one in ten in Hobart remained in manufacturing. Wholesale and retail occupations were more numerous, so too were jobs in community services, mainly health and education. Levels of unemployment rose to 6 per cent by the late 1970s and 10 per cent by the early 1980s while economic growth slowed to a crawl along with the rise in incomes. In the past decade rates of population growth in the capital cities have been generally slow, with the exception of Perth and the Brisbane–Gold Coast conurbation, and certain regions such as Melbourne's south-eastern corridor (Population Issues Committee 1992:7–9). By the 1980s there was increasing evidence that the distribution of income was becoming less equal. Governments have gradually wound back the subsidies to suburbia, mainly by withdrawing assistance for home finance. Probably a smaller percentage of the population can afford home ownership today than could do so twenty years ago.

The social costs of car-dependence have also become clearer during the last quarter century. OPEC price rises and strikes by petrol tanker drivers highlighted some of the drawbacks of car-dependence, although petrol prices have remained lower than most people expected in the

1970s. Traffic jams have grown longer and become more frequent. Ambitious plans to build networks of freeways to relieve the congestion were challenged and often defeated by resident action groups, but the freeways which were built destroyed homes, parks and neighbourhoods. The car disappointed in other ways as it pumped lead, greenhouse gases and other pollutants into the suburban air. The people's vehicle was polluting suburbia.

The current debate over the condition of Australian cities is therefore taking place against a background of slower economic growth and mounting concern over the environmental and economic costs of spread out, car-dependent cities. As State governments a decade ago gloomily contemplated the massive costs of more dams, roads or sewage treatment works to service suburbia, and the reduced likelihood of generous help from the Commonwealth government, they saw in urban consolidation a way out of their dilemma. The savings from urban consolidation may turn out to be smaller than hoped, but governments are now promoting high-density living and row-housing that their predecessors would have shied away from as slums in the making. Australian cities are perhaps striking out in new directions but they remain saddled with a massive suburban legacy.

CHAPTER 2

The Urban Debate: From 'Los Angeles' to the Urban Village

Mark Peel[1]

Not before time, more Australian critics are confronting 'economic rationalism', or what David Harvey (1992:597) calls 'market triumphalism': the idea that the organisation of our economic and social life through public policy should mirror the disciplines and principles of the market. While it is a loose coalition of different viewpoints, economic rationalism rests on two fairly basic convictions: that governments tend to be inherently inefficient in their attempts to produce or to distribute wealth and resources, while markets, through which 'sovereign consumers' satisfy their individual preferences, are ultimately the more efficient and equitable means of rewarding effort and generating productive growth. Left to itself, the market will provide. In a sense, the idea seems to be that the skills involved in running the country are not unlike those needed to run a business.

Against these suppositions – and they are, as Frank Stilwell (1993a:31–3) points out, based on highly restrictive and questionable assumptions – critics argue that government activities, from direct investment and regulation through to tax-based redistributions of income, are vital to the efficient functioning of the economy and society and, by extension, the Australian city. Academic and professional debates over the urban future, in league with State government and Federal government reviews of urban policy, have played an important role in challenging the doctrines of market rule. Economic rationalism is waning as an intellectual force, its underlying rationales and arguments revealed as

1 My thanks to Steven Bourassa, Peter Grabosky, Alastair Greig, Penny Hanley, Hugh Stretton, Patrick Troy and the participants in the Urban Growth Debate Workshop for their comments and corrections on earlier drafts.

statements of ideological belief rather than accurate prediction. Yet the principles of smaller government, and a fixation on cost efficiency it helped cement in public policy, still hold sway among those shaping Australian government in the 1990s.

The urban debate of the 1990s has a real sense of moment, even of urgency. As ever, urban planning – and urban policy more generally – rises and falls on its ability to depict the city in crisis and to claim it can produce a better future. Urban reform needs its 'bad city' as the counterpoint to its 'good city' alternative. True to form, we have tended to locate that urban dystopia in someone else's slums and fears that the 'old world' present might become our future. Fifty years ago that was likely to mean some version of London's East End. The image at the centre of contemporary concern is a 'Los Angeles' of uncontrolled urban sprawl, dispossession and despair. Drawing on the work of Mike Davis (1990), Sophie Watson (1993:11–12) gives a stark picture of 'a mad society' and warns that 'Australian cities are on a similar trajectory and . . . the Los Angeles scenario may not be so far away'. Even the normally sober pronouncements of government departments warn that our cities 'are beginning to move closer to Los Angeles' (DHHCS 1992) and that we are 'at the crossroads . . . where decisions need to be taken now about the sort of place in which Australians want their children to live and work' (NHS 1992:15). And what confirms the point are words and pictures of urban inequality, LA-style: gates, walled enclaves, video surveillance.

This emerging disquiet has yet to produce a compelling version of the 'good city'. Certainly, debates about the future of the city range far beyond the simple juxtaposition of 'sprawl' against 'consolidation'. There are complex questions about whether it is feasible to change the basic pattern of urban development – by increasing the population density of established suburbs, providing more housing in central business districts, or building a wider variety of housing types in new suburbs, for instance – and halt the spread of low-density suburbs, or whether this may be a worse medicine than the purported disease. As John Minnery (1992) shows, debates about the basic form of the Australian city have yet to settle on any ideal solution, nor even on the best way of defining and describing the essential 'urban problem'.

Critical assessments of what Australian cities are like and what they might become are emerging all over the place. Every State government is busy on urban strategies and visions; where the timid aim for the year 2000, the more daring press on to 2010 or 2020. Urban policy statements are full of 'prospects' and 'options' and the need for 'making a difference' at a 'vital stage of economic, social and environmental development' (Victorian Department of Planning and Housing 1990:7). The

Federal Minister, Brian Howe (1990:9), has argued for 'strategic investments' which 'lead Australia in directions appropriate to the future, rather than investments which simply add to and perpetuate the patterns of development of the past'. And the renewed excitement of strategic planning at the grand scale does carry with it a disruptive potential. These will be projects to change the basic pattern of urban growth, a reinventing of the city and with it, perhaps, the nation.

My major focus in this chapter is on the relationship between this wide-ranging critique and the urban projects of government, including Building Better Cities, revised metropolitan planning strategies and housing reform. The particular problem I address is why, given the vigour of the critique, the proposals for a better Australian city mount so lacklustre a response to the inequities and injustices they purport to address. Policy documents (and much of the academic work which worries around their edges) routinely open with visions of a 'Los Angeles future'. But translating critique into achievable policy objectives often runs up against the basic commitments to market principles described above as 'market triumphalism'. These commitments so constrain the interventionist scope of public policy that goals like 'increased equity' or 'social justice' are effectively marginalised, and maintain a mostly rhetorical presence.

Essentially, where the first principle of good government is the pursuit of economic efficiency, and not 'getting in the way' of more efficient private interests, goals like equity or social justice become at best a secondary consideration, and at worst a kind of drag on the 'productive efficiency' of the nation. As Stilwell (1993a:36) notes, 'a dualism is established between economic and social issues. The economic is the hard-headed: the social is the soft-hearted . . . and social justice is achievable only at an economic cost which we typically cannot afford.' Little heed is paid to a fairly common-sense dictum: pay now for education and health, or pay later, when the consequences of doing nothing – illiteracy, poor health, social dislocation – come home to roost.

Of course, public policy must always focus on what is politically possible, on means as well as ends. To get their urban projects through the rigours of expenditure review, or past the hard hearts of finance departments, the framers of urban policy must use the required rhetoric of 'market realities' and show how any new policy contributes first of all to productive efficiency. In State and local government too, planners must show their faith in market mechanisms and the benefits of smaller government. Summoned to save the city, they find themselves immobilised by the funding constraints and the distorted order of priorities those principles imply.

All this sets strong limits on how far urban policy can generate a 'better city' for everybody, rather than just those who can afford its entry price. Dominant definitions of 'efficiency' are perhaps the strongest constraint. Here, 'efficiency' means immediate cost-effectiveness, short-term savings and politically-safe cuts in vulnerable areas of welfare provision like public housing. Efficiency means slashing costs in the here and now; rationalising assets and trimming 'waste' become ends in themselves, often with little thought to long-term consequences or the uneven impact of reduced government spending on different areas or groups of people.

Myopic fixations on short-term cost savings are no real answer to the range of problems implied by a 'Los Angeles future'. Nor does a narrow focus on matters of urban form – increasing densities, more diverse housing options, restraining car use, or building 'urban villages' – offer a comprehensive enough response. After all, what makes Los Angeles the 'bad edge of post-modernity' (Davis 1990)? Urban sprawl? Too many cars. An homogenous housing stock? Perhaps, to a degree. Too much government intervention? High taxes? In California, hardly. Surely, as Sophie Watson (1993) points out, the most fundamental problems in the recent history of Los Angeles stem from the savage class inequalities and racial polarisations which are turning the city into walled pockets of uneasy privilege surrounded by the barrios of the poor and the dispossessed.

The origins of those inequalities, in Los Angeles or in Australia, lie in the increasing maldistribution of wealth, in the job losses which have come with restructured industries, in the particular impact of expenditure cuts and de-industrialisation on already disadvantaged individuals, families and communities. Cities do not produce poverty, even if badly designed and inefficient ones increase the penalties people suffer for being poor, and even if bad policy decisions – like restricting the physically segregated public housing stock to the 'truly needy' – intensify the spatial concentration of poor people. Just as important, inequality is not a simple matter of unequal income distribution: as Iris Young (1990:5) argues, 'while distributive issues are crucial . . . it is a mistake to reduce social justice to distribution'. Inequality also measures people's rights and capacities to be self-determining, to exercise freedom and seek opportunity, or to have an effective voice in the making of decisions.

For these reasons, any critical assessment of urban policy must refer more generally to public policy. The particular problem, I think, is how to assert inequality as the central focus of policy and insist that governments are responsible for tackling the consequences and the causes of social division. Debates about cities have always been a vehicle for launching broader reformist ideas into public debate. In a highly urbanised country like Australia, talking about the urban future makes sense as a strategy for talking about a future nation.

The political skills and courage which have pushed better cities and urban planning reforms into the policy limelight should be applauded. Discussions of urban density, consolidation, neighbourhood planning and 'urban villages' have also raised important issues. But there are other trajectories that might be explored. In this paper, I briefly evaluate the urban critique and criticise the notions of 'efficiency' which are deflecting urban policies away from a focus on social polarisation. I also try to suggest ways of highlighting the transformative and disruptive capacity of the urban debate and mobilising concerns about cities around the concepts of public value and justice. The task is not so much to bemoan the fate of good intentions, nor to blame those who are battling to defend even minor gains. The point must be more general: to imagine our urban policies as part of a broader assault on the forces which are consigning more and more Australians to an uncertain future.

The Urban Critique

Arguments about the urban future, before and during their translation into policy discussion, rely first of all on their ability to picture a 'better city'. That also means producing effective critiques of cities as they are, in order to show how and why they should be changed. Such critiques commonly focus mostly on the physical legacy of previous development practices: poorly planned subdivisions, or public spaces which fail as human environments, for instance. Yet representing 'urban problems' always means reflecting on broader social and political issues as well, so our debates on cities always occur within a more general context.

From a variety of starting points, participants in the recent urban critique also anchor their accounts of urban problems in more wide-ranging examinations of Australian political and social life. For those stressing the benefits of market disciplines, for instance, unwieldy planning codes, expensive infrastructure and 'price distortions' mark an 'over-regulated' and 'inefficient' society. From a quite different point of view, our sprawling, car-dependent suburbs reveal an extravagance which may yet lead to environmental suicide. And if the social divisions of the city can be used to portray the basic economic injustices of capitalism, then distinguishing isolated, under-serviced suburbs (for women) from skyscraper-style city centres (for men) is a way of illustrating how patriarchy is etched into the very landscape of the city.

Despite these different viewpoints, contemporary writings about the city share a conviction that the basic physical and social patterns of urban life, along with the relationships between governments, private institutions and citizens, established during the 'long-boom' economy of the 1950s and 1960s, are undergoing profound disruption. For the purposes of this argument, I will focus on three particularly important themes in this critical re-evaluation: the redefinition of urban disadvantage, the shift towards public participation, and the attempt to imagine a changed physical form for Australian cities.

On the first theme, attempts to define the nature and incidence of disadvantage in urban areas have moved beyond simple 'snapshots' of household income to confront such issues as inadequate access to educational, training and job opportunities, the role of long-term income and housing insecurity in perpetuating poverty, and the way that disempowerment extends beyond a lack of money to a lack of the information, knowledge and confidence which people need to participate in decisions about their future (Cass 1989). Also at issue are the ways in which structures of disadvantage based on gender, age, disability, race and family structure interact with and reinforce each other, so that people's encounters with the structural barriers to opportunity are very complex and hard to solve by any simple focus on one parameter of disadvantage (Watson 1988; Cass 1991).

There is also more attention being paid to 'compounding inequality' or 'locational disadvantage' (DHHCS 1991; Maher et al. 1992). These concepts are an attempt to describe the experience of disadvantage as a compounding process, exacerbated by where people live, not as a static or simple condition. People without secure housing, for instance, also find it hard to get and hold jobs, and vice versa. Many sole parents cannot afford full-time child care, but without it they can't look for or take the kinds of jobs which might lead them and their children out of poverty. The same people whose low educational qualifications restrict them to low-paid work are also unable to afford educational resources for themselves or their children, such as time and space for homework and books and computers. In disadvantaged communities where education is the single most important means of getting ahead, people's collective inability to provide money and resources to their local schools compounds the problem of shrinking government expenditure on public education.

These notions of compounding and locational disadvantage far more accurately capture the way people experience disadvantage as a vicious circle of insufficient resources and diminishing life chances. They also generate better strategies for dealing with the complexities of inequality, like the attempt to coordinate the activities of all the public and private agencies which deliver assistance in the same area, or the gathering together of the users of these agencies to involve them in defining specific local needs. As I have argued (Peel 1993b), the community consultation, service coordination and local advocacy initiatives of South Australia's Elizabeth–Munno Para Project (1992) were models in both respects.

The second theme, the emphasis on public participation in urban and social planning, signals a recognition among professional planners that those most affected by change have a right to be involved in making the decisions. The relationships between metropolitan planning and housing authorities and their 'clients' have clearly shifted, with 'increasingly adept' local constituencies (Hedgecock, Hiller & Wood 1991:221) demanding a real say in small- and large-scale development proposals. Moreover, talking about 'participation' has helped push forward other concerns about citizen involvement, so that strategies to increase local involvement in a planning project also create oppor- tunities for 'community development', where local people build on their experience of participation to foster their own projects and discussion groups or manage their own institutions, like neighbourhood houses and community centres.

The rhetoric of community consultation remains rather too innocent about power relationships within communities, especially about who gets to speak and be heard (Peel 1993c). On the one hand, people who are already organised, who have access to the language and styles of bureaucratic decision-making or are adept at lobbying can easily capture consultation and make it serve their own interests, often, it must be said, in the sincere belief that they do represent 'community opinion'. On the other hand, if those organising the consultation process see it primarily as a means of 'selling' an already final product or decision to affected people, it can easily become what Michael Dear (1989:456) calls a 'mechanics of persuasion', especially if the really important decisions or projects are removed from public view or taken before the public is consulted. However, as long as community participation and consultation remain at least technically open to all, they can provide a forum for unexpected voices and demands.

The third theme concerns urban form and whether it is possible and preferable to change the shape of Australian cities. Should our cities continue to grow at the fringe, or should there be positive steps taken to increase the density of housing in established areas, perhaps through dual occupancy, creative medium-density designs, or converting larger houses into units? In newly developed areas, should houses be smaller, with less private garden space but more public open space? Should there also be more apartments, semi-detached housing or other medium- density developments in new areas? Arguments that Australian cities should be 'consolidated' to prevent or at least slow fringe development also propose to revitalise central cities and inner suburbs with new residents and to stage new developments around public transport 'nodes' to encourage commuting by train or bus rather than car (Newman & Kenworthy 1992b).

Critics of the consolidation approach question some of its basic claims, especially that denser development or 're-using' inner suburbs will automatically lead to cheaper infrastructure or housing costs, that 'automobile-dependence' can be easily overcome by using town planning to harness the car, or that central cities are somehow superior to suburbs in 'communal feel' or 'public space'. They also warn that restricting the present lower-density form of development might simply mean that newcomers to the housing market will have to put up with lower-quality smaller housing, narrow roads and less recreational space, while those who currently enjoy low-density suburbs maintain and indeed increase their relative advantages (Troy 1989, 1992b). As Christine Charles (1990) points out, it is difficult to see how consolidation can fulfil its objectives of greatly reducing public expenditure on roads, sewerage or schools without decreasing the standard of those facilities or shifting to a potentially regressive user-pays system.

The idea that many Australians are somehow being forced to inhabit poorly serviced, alienating suburbs is also countered by carefully compiled evidence which shows that outer-suburban residents in Melbourne were largely satisfied with their living standards because their aim was to find a good place to bring up children. They did not regard distance from the central city as a problem, and basically saw their fringe location as a trade-off: good, new housing, plus adequate playing space for children and quiet streets in return for dependence on cars and occasional long trips to work (Australian Institute of Family Studies 1993:456–63).

This research also suggests that using higher prices and taxes to limit fringe expansion would adversely impact the very people consolidation claims to be helping. As Richard Kirwan (1991c) implies, recovering the full cost of fringe development will have to mean that people buy lower-standard houses or spend more for the same standard. Another concern is the impact of rapid medium-density development on areas which already suffer a backlog in many important services, especially if it coincides with a redirection of public spending towards consolidation areas in central cities (Stretton 1989:lxiii–iv). This is already emerging as an issue in western Sydney, where consolidation will have to mean increased spending on infrastructure. (Gooding 1990). Raymond Bunker (1989) provides a useful middle ground on these issues. Recognising the possible benefits of urban infill and more medium-density development in terms of increasing housing choice, he also argues that consolidation programs are ambiguous and 'could be harmful . . . unless there are forceful measures by governments to determine otherwise' (Bunker 1989:42).

Of course, the issues outlined above do not exhaust the current urban debate. Other papers in this volume explore questions about pricing infrastructure, coordinating the actions of historically antagonistic political institutions and reshaping the relationship between urban and regional policy. Elsewhere, there are ongoing debates about the future of public housing – particularly the implications of shifting resources into 'community housing' managed by local governments or housing cooperatives (Paris 1992; Randolph 1993) – or the best ways to reform planning codes to speed up the process of releasing and developing land for industry and housing (NHS 1991b), or how to expand the role of local government and regional organisations in the making of urban policy (ALGA 1993; WESROC 1994).

It is from these sorts of questions that the current debate over 'urban futures' is changing the way Australian cities are analysed and challenging some of the key assumptions of 'economic rationalism', particularly its insistence on the benefits of less, rather than more, government activity. The debate covers a wide ground, surfacing in consultants' reports and research sponsored by Federal, State and local governments, the more traditional arenas of academic and professional exchange, and in the ongoing deliberations about reorganising planning and housing functions in all levels of government. In the best traditions of Australian thought, it also draws eclectically on a variety of European and North American literatures. All up, its vigour and breadth mark this debate as a promising return to the kinds of concerns about cities which have always surfaced at times of profound change. What remains to be seen is whether it will generate and sustain any comprehensive reforms to the basic physical and social structures of the Australian city.

The Turn to Efficiency

If reshaping Australia's cities is emerging as a general policy interest, those initiatives must eventually answer to the most powerful criterion of them all: their contribution to the productive efficiency of the nation. Under this rubric, governments must be small, tightly run organisations. Shrunk in size, they aim to make markets work better, thus maximising the rule of individual choice, all the while becoming more market-like and more 'customer-driven' themselves, for instance, by charging 'users' for their services. 'Efficiency' is a shorthand term for a fixation on cost-effectiveness, doing better with less, not interfering with market mechanisms, and ensuring that anything private actors can do 'better' is left to them. And the principle of 'efficiency first' is rarely open to question: much of the urban critique, let alone the attempts to produce urban policy, operates within the constraints of what it defines as possible.

Of course, challenging the dictates of efficiency is a tricky business. I certainly do not mean to discredit 'efficiency' per se, rather the definitions of efficiency that dominate current policy. The meaning of efficiency is not always clear within documents setting out government policy. Efficient in what ways? To what ends? How is efficiency measured? Does efficient mean cheap? Is the cheapest way of delivering a government service (be it providing health care or building roads) also the most effective way? The most equitable way? Which is more important?

Versions of efficiency clearly vary. Definitions of 'best practice' in Mr Kennett's Victoria differ in important respects from those pursued in Canberra or in the other States, just as different arms of the same government might have to deploy different tests of efficiency in determining what might be done and how. The 'human service' departments, for instance – health, family and community services, or education – cannot easily shoehorn their program outcomes into the same measures of performance as those used by departments providing a more easily quantifiable output. Does the 'efficient' use of resources in health, for example, measure the public and human value of a particular program, or its cost-effectiveness, or a combination of both? How do you 'cost' public health or community development as an 'output'?

As Peter Saunders (1994:106–8) points out, it is unlikely that cost-efficient and effective solutions will always be the same. Also, because different programs deal with issues which relate to each other – public transport and traffic management, for instance – a focus on short-term efficiencies in one program may adversely affect the efficiency or effectiveness of another or even create new and costly problems for another public authority. A case in point is the de-institutionalisation of mentally ill people: this may be a cheaper and possibly more effective form of treatment, but it makes for dramatically increased demands on other programs, from public housing and community medical facilities to social welfare and policing. Public authorities, after all, are not private businesses. They have social and cultural purposes, they must cooperate rather than compete, and their performance cannot be measured in the same way, because 'the market-disciplined pursuit of profit cannot sufficiently motivate the kind of performance, or the range and distribution of services, that the public wants' (Stretton 1987:86).

So it is the empowerment of particular versions of efficiency that matters, especially the way those versions stress short-term over long-term imperatives and seek immediate financial savings rather than a more imaginative redeployment of public resources. To take just one example: is it always more efficient to close public schools and sell the land for an immediate cash return, when there may be a need for another community facility in the same area now, or even a decade down the track? Would it be better, in some cases at least, to invest some money in rendering under-used schools into more flexible institutions, able to become community centres, places for elderly citizens, creches or health centres, in line with changing local needs?

If a public service – say public transport or public housing – exists for reasons of equity, because we believe that a decent society must provide basic transportation and shelter for everybody, what is the best way to measure its long-term efficiency? Is it best to cut it to the bone and restrict its use to those who can't afford anything better? Or is a more general service ultimately more efficient because some of the people who use it can help pay for its maintenance? Or because more people using the public service might create more competition and bring down the costs of private alternatives? To take another case: privatising a public activity, say building roads, might save money now. But might it also mean that governments will eventually have to spend more money inspecting and policing the standards of the service provided by private operators, in the interests of public safety and stricter design standards? As Beilharz, Considine and Watts (1992:151) suggest, 'since the 1980s, the discussion of problems to do with efficiency has been truncated by the identification of "efficient" with "cheap"'. And what is cheap now may prove remarkably inefficient in the long run, if governments simply have to spend more money later, or if the public (especially wealthier citizens) lose trust in the ability of governments to provide worthwhile services and take their money out of public institutions.

All of this turns, of course, on an even more basic question: how do we define an 'efficient society'? I would argue that public values like distributive fairness and social justice should be a central part of that definition. So efficiency should be defined as 'allocative', not just 'productive', measured not just by how efficiently we produce wealth or goods but how efficiently and fairly we allocate them. Do public services reach those who need them most? Do policies contribute to public trust in government and a sense of shared citizenship? Do tax policies and funding programs redistribute resources and promote a real equality of opportunity?

This approach to efficiency does not mean freezing social or economic policies in a time-warp or ignoring dramatic changes in national and international economic conditions. In some instances, the efficiencies being proposed are probably warranted, and may improve the effectiveness of some public services. If resources are finite, governments will have to make hard decisions about what gets funded. If something can be done more cheaply and more effectively by bringing in the particular expertise or resources of a private firm, fair enough. Nor does this rule out correcting and adjusting policies in line with changing definitions of need or 'best practice'. As Hugh Stretton (1987:53) suggests, 'new kinds and conditions of both public and private enterprise, new patterns of trade between them, should all be open to consideration on their merits, with reference to the ultimate social purposes which economic policies are supposed to serve'.

There, perhaps, is the rub: 'ultimate social purposes'. Those have not disappeared, of course. Current Federal urban policies do attempt to exert a social purpose at odds with the individualism of the free marketeers: the task is 'guiding and, where necessary, constraining the market's operation' because 'our goals and aspirations as citizens can never be wholly met through the market's unfettered operations' (Brian Howe, quoted in Orchard 1992:23). Howe (quoted in Campbell 1991:1) has also stressed the importance of 'civic culture' and 'a balanced realisation of both social justice and economic growth'. In the various States, bringing private-sector firms into urban programs is a way of meeting government housing and planning objectives, especially as the flow of federal funds becomes increasingly uncertain. Through advantageous relationships with private firms, including joint venturing, Labor and Liberal governments alike are able to undertake large projects while staying within the tighter restrictions on their capacity to borrow money.

Still, for all the talk of happy unions, these are more often marriages of convenience, based first of all on State governments' need for cash (Badcock 1986; Hamnett & Parham 1992). And there is the constant danger that 'joint ventures' will effectively use public money to subsidise private-sector profits with a nebulous promise of 'future development and jobs' rather than to provide specific returns to the taxpaying public in the form of affordable housing or high-quality community facilities. The contrast between Melbourne's Bayside and Angliss projects is a case in point: as Joan Doyle (1993:52–3) argues, the Angliss project, initiated largely by the Victorian Ministry of Housing, 'involved a high degree of public accountability, clear guidelines and explicit contracts to encourage real investment by the private sector', while Bayside, a private-sector initiative, was much more speculative and unspecific, part of 'the packaging of the city with a view to making it attractive to international finance markets'.

However useful the more flexible financing of urban development might prove to be, and however expert State and local governments become at balancing smaller budgets with growing demands on their services, the most powerful undertone in contemporary urban and public policy is continuing constraint. 'Adjusting the boundaries' between the private and public sectors usually means the latter giving away more and more of its previous ground. As Rob Watts (1993) argues, public activity is severely truncated by the distorted view that the private sector is always more efficient and effective than the public sector. Urban policy is trapped by a refusal to allow that there are some things – building expensive infrastructure, or providing affordable housing and land – which governments may well do much better than private businesses. Instead, governments must abandon the field, manage and facilitate economic change, following behind the rationalisers and the privatisers with a few targeted social programs. In terms of urban planning and urban deprivation, as Clive Forster (1986:10) puts it, government 'appears to be expected to have little part to play in the process of fighting poverty other than by keeping out of the way of attempts to attract investment and growth'.

Long-term or value-informed social objectives which do not look immediately cost-efficient are in constant danger of being marginalised. Everything must refer to short-term gains in productive efficiency. Urban programs, for instance, must create productive, not 'just' equitable, cities (Orchard 1993). Cities must be machines of comparative advantage, contributors to the competitive edge. Even preserving heritage or enhancing culture and lifestyle become 'active agents in the economic development process' (Neilson & Spiller 1992:11) in order to escape [from] the trap of 'mere' good intentions. The South Australian Planning Review (1992:9), for example, suggests that the 'essential character of Adelaide . . . should be preserved and put to economic use', while the National Housing Strategy's final agenda for action approvingly quotes a Canadian planner's conviction that liveability 'will be the ultimate competitive weapon for cities in the future' (NHS 1992:19).

Policy language is forced into a cul-de-sac of fine adjustments and marginal increments: 'rather than justifying radical changes to the form of Australian cities, the infrastructure cost savings argument calls for smarter urban management and fine tuning which will yield savings at the margin without compromising lifestyle choices' (Spiller 1992:3). Urban problems are simplified into matters of administrative flexibility and efficient management. Blair Badcock (1991) cites the example of streamlined development controls in local planning to challenge the expectation that administrative reform can generate a 'better city' by itself. Of course, focusing on administrative shortcomings makes it far easier to render solutions in terms of small-scale, cheap measures: marginal adjustments, better coordination, research programs and 'facilitations' (House of Representatives Standing Committee 1992:xiv–xxi).

At the same time, urban problems are pacified: there may be a few concerns, but there is no crisis. The National Housing Strategy (1991a:xiv), for instance, assures us that 'Australia does not have an overall housing "crisis"'. Moreover, '[i]f Australia succeeds in catching up with "world best" practice in terms of productivity, there should be no "housing crisis" (in terms of significantly worsened housing affordability) between now and the year 2006' (NHS 1991a:xiii). Maybe so, but some Australians are experiencing a housing crisis, which some of the government's macro-economic policies are making worse.

The experiences of struggling mortgagees, and especially the thousands of low-income households paying private rents they can barely afford, might be expected to provoke a more challenging response than 'crisis, what crisis?' Nor is a policy dedicated to avoiding a 'significantly worsened' outcome the stuff to stir the blood. We are very close here to such pallid rationalisations as 'the poor will always be with us' and to definitions of 'good management' as holding the line on existing social divisions, rather than actually confronting them.

This pacification of the problems also relies on consensus as an achievable objective of urban programs. All that we know about the power of different groups of people to form 'consensus' quietly slips away, to be replaced by a wishy-washy pluralism of 'community desires' and 'choices'. The South Australian Planning Review (1992:x) even makes the rather breathtaking claim that its urban program reflects 'a broad historical consensus amongst the people on the need for fairness'. In my research (1993b) on the relationships between consultation and local activism in working-class suburbs like Adelaide's Elizabeth, there is strong evidence that these people do not feel part of a 'consensus' on Adelaide's future, even if they have been consulted. What worked in this community was a very different kind of consultation, based on empowerment and advocacy, not securing the agreement of local people to some fictional 'consensus'. The demands which emerged out of the Elizabeth–Munno Para Project were often explicitly redistributive and posed direct challenges to the way resources like education, health facilities and employment are allocated within Adelaide. A pacifying approach to urban problems cannot handle those kinds of claims.

In the same way, potentially conflicting policies – heritage preservation or urban redevelopment, a central city focus or development at the fringe, 'quality' housing or affordable housing – float free of their social and political context (Bagguley et al. 1990:147–52). These programs stem from the attempts of different groups to secure their version of the 'community interest' at the centre of urban policy and present their particular interests as universal ones. While different versions of the general good are not always mutually exclusive, they can clash, as in the way that the claims of inner-city gentrifiers can contradict the interests of low-income renters in cheap, older housing. The questions must always be: whose views of the urban future are empowered and whose demands are incorporated within public policy?

Policy documents also tend to generalise the effects of urban problems across the social and physical landscape of the city: '[w]e are starting to pay, socially, environmentally and economically, for our poorly managed urban growth' (DHHLGCS 1993:4). Maybe 'we' are, but it should be fairly obvious that some are paying a much higher price than others. Generalising urban problems might foster political accept-ance, but what it abandons is the insistence that a long-term response to those problems might actually involve changing the distribution of the costs and benefits of economic growth. For instance, will different people gain from the economic recovery in the same proportion as they have lost from the economic adjustments and recessions of the last two decades?

Recent urban policy initiatives – from Building Better Cities (BBC) and the NHS to State government metropolitan schemes and local government strategic planning – are ultimately constrained within the narrow range of possibilities allowed by the fixation on short-term efficiencies. Even more interventionist programs like BBC seek, at best, 'a sophisticated form of instrumentalism' (Badcock 1993:79) in which immediate efficiency goals override normative goals like social justice. Of course, the critique of current programs must be sensitive to the specifics of Australia's management of economic and political change. Australia is neither Thatcher's Britain nor Reagan's America, and the retreat into smaller government has involved struggles within and between political parties and competing government departments.

Yet the ground rules for public intervention in private decisions have clearly changed. If public policy comes to mean not unduly interfering with market mechanisms, then the socially responsible commitment to protect disadvantaged citizens from the consequences of their lack of private resources is harder and harder to maintain. More and more 'choices' depend upon our financial muscle as private individuals. The rights that come with wealth and social status overshadow and threaten those that come from common membership in a society. Apart from something called 'the community' or 'the electorate', there are few places where individual citizens might seek collective solutions or practice collective responsibilities. Instead, citizens must be able to operate efficiently within the marketplace and make the 'lifestyle choices' appropriate to their income from a range of efficient and competitive private providers. Those who have the income might do just fine, if private providers can and do meet their choices, and if they are aware of the range of choice, and if they have easy access to a number of providers to choose from, and if those providers are self-regulating and accountable in terms of standards, safety and quality. Even for the relatively wealthy, the job of being a mobile maximiser is not an easy one.

Of course, there is another kind of citizen, those 'truly needy' people who consume public funds. Because they use resources which might be directed elsewhere, they must make do with the 'hard choices' of a thoroughly efficient compassion. Fortunately, the nation can still save money, through more and more expert welfare targeting. Unfortunately, there is little evidence that targeting actually reduces the extent of poverty: 'it is outcomes that matter rather than the structure of the mechanisms used to produce them' (Saunders 1994:49). What matters is the amount of money we spend reducing inequality, not just how efficiently we spend it. In the rush to make Australia efficient and competitive today, we are left to hope that the nation will become more generous in the quality of its public care tomorrow. But for now, at least, our brave new Australia rewards some, but only by punishing others.

A Polarising Future?

Will the fixation on smaller government and efficiency deliver Australian cities to a 'Los Angeles' future of increasing social polarisation? So long as the task of confronting social inequality is written out of national economic and social policy, it is at least a possibility. The tendency for inequality to slide out of the language of urban policy, in favour of 'diversity' or 'lifestyle choices', is hardly encouraging in that regard. The potential for policies devoted to privatisation and cutbacks to widen existing social divisions should be clear from the British and American experience, even if historical and political differences should make us wary of simply transposing such trends on to Australia.

Here, as in other nations, it is clear that whatever economic growth occurred during the 1970s and 1980s coincided with increasing income inequality, in part because the shift of private investment offshore, into capital-intensive activities like mining, or into property and financial speculation, compounded the effects of restructuring and labour-shedding on employment (Saunders 1994:139–46). While the social wage policies of the Hawke government protected Australians on very low incomes from the general fall in living standards during the 1980s, the losers were not high-income earners, but the lower- to middle-income bands, especially households dependent upon the kinds of full-time, skilled and unskilled, manufacturing work devastated by the restructuring of industry (Raskall 1993). Australia has distributed the costs of structural change and recession somewhat differently from other nations. But the potential for increasing divisions between haves and have-nots is real enough.

One facet of that polarisation could be a severe generational inequality in the distribution of housing and secure employment, as the groups who benefited from the relative affluence of the 1960s and 1970s protect their advantages against newcomers. Changes in urban policy may exacerbate these trends. In housing, for instance, attempts to shift the burden of financing infrastructure in new suburbs from governments to developers and ultimately to home buyers might reduce burdens on public expenditure, but only by penalising new buyers relative to old and substantially increasing the 'entry price' for home ownership.

Another polarising force is what Glenda Laws (1989) has termed the 'uneven development' of the welfare state. In effect, the commitment to cutting and privatising produces two 'welfare states'. In Australia, the difference between them is not based on their universal or selective coverage, since few of our welfare programs are truly universal, but on the different status of the beneficiaries and the relative rigour with which eligibility and proper use of the funds are policed (Jamrozik 1983). One welfare state provides poor people with services of marginal concern to the well-off (public housing, unemployment benefits, or rental assistance, for example). It is strictly targeted, means-tested and policed. The other, even if not fully universal, is expected as a right and is much less vulnerable to restrictions on eligibility or proper conduct (family allowances or aged pensions, for instance). Another way of picturing the difference is to imagine the degree of 'social humiliation' (home visits, requirements to attend counselling and other therapies, control over personal spending, and so on) and identification of the individual as 'needy' which different kinds of welfare produce (Esping-Andersen 1990:23–6).

Another facet of current or proposed welfare policy which can only increase the degree of social polarisation is the subjection of more and more public services to privatisation or user-pays principles, while giving the truly needy a bit of money so they can participate in the market too. The pretence that increasing the importance of private means in fulfilling human needs is a way of providing 'choice' is one of the more disturbing defences of the push for smaller government, because it represents first and foremost an investment in inequality. People get the choices they can afford, and the market responds by catering far better to those with money than those without. The wealthy get choice, the poor get a basic – probably very basic – standard. The 'capacity' catered to best by the market is the capacity to pay. Nor should the 'goods' in question be reduced to the same common denominator of 'who pays, wins'. It might make little real difference if the market ranks the quality of restaurant meals by ability to pay. But should the quality of education, or health care, or water, be ranked the same way?

In this context, too, if 'public' begins to mean 'basic' or even 'sub-standard', then any person who has the choice is likely to seek privately-provided options instead, further draining public systems of resources, common usage and a broad base of political support. As those who can pay desert public provision, the principle that only the market provides quality goods becomes self-fulfilling. Any public system or institution which cannot attract private resources will eventually serve only poorer people, leaving it politically marginal, ever more vulnerable to further cutbacks and less and less able to 'compete' for 'clients'. Redistributions from rich to poor within systems like schooling also become less generous, because the systems have less money to shift around. Poor people, and the places they inhabit, will be left with residualised services or the crumbling remains of general programs.

These are the very same people, of course, who are least able to compensate for lower government spending with their own resources. Nor can they pay the kind of rates and charges that might allow local government to pick up some of the burden. Local service providers face great demands at the same time as their own funds are cut or the bureaucracies which provide the money insist on greater control over how it is spent. Certainly, programs which address specific disadvantages (like the Disadvantaged Schools Program) are welcome, but if there is less and less money being spent, this can only mean holding the line on what is already a severely unequal situation. There are real concerns, too, about how an emphasis on low-cost, delivery-oriented welfare removes the incentive to make the increased participation or even em-powerment of beneficiaries a central part of the welfare process.

Perhaps the most powerful force increasing social and spatial divisions within our cities is that the rise and fall of people and places is ever more dependent on the experiments of powerful, private decision-makers in stock markets, credit agencies and large companies. By opening the nation to these experiments, through rapid deregulation and the dis-mantling of protective instruments like tariffs, governments increasingly allow investors, speculators and corporate boards to deliver the verdict on local fortunes. People, and the places they inhabit, win or lose according to their contribution to the balance sheets of multinational corporations and global financial markets.

The rapid economic adjustments and deep recessions of the 1980s and 1990s might have been inevitable: it is inconceivable that Australia could somehow stand apart from global forces and the imperatives of corporate financial power. Yet the specific forms of the social and political management of economic adjustment are not inevitable.

Governments draw the boundaries between national and global economies, and they take decisions about how global economic forces 'work through' a nation's economy. The Australia we are making now is the product of decisions and interests, not immutable destiny: 'the State continues to be at the heart of current forms of urban politics, as organiser of new forms of investment, market regulation, new forms of control and policing and as disorganiser of old forms of welfare provision and social collectivity' (Savage & Warde 1993:187).

Clearly, the management of restructuring, especially in Federal policies for economic growth and employment, involves political determinations which have tended to throw the heaviest burden of adjustment on to particular industries and regions. This has left these places with often terrible choices and uncertainties. To survive, older industrial towns and suburbs, along with declining rural areas, must rethink their relationship to mobile investors and producers. They must reshape their physical organisation and make themselves more attractive to the key players in international finance markets.

In the now derelict landscapes of long-boom Australia, for the places built around iron and steel, cars or textiles, producing a future depends on the ability of local governments or development boards to turn their hand to the task of 'adjusting' to a harshly competitive landscape. Perhaps these places, and the people who live in them, will have to change. But it is surely cruel to expect them to do it on their own, with few returns from the very efficiencies, productivity gains and cost savings they have helped produce. As the polarisations outlined above persist into and through the economic recovery, some of the people and places on the wrong side of the line will fall further and further behind. And I think we have yet to fully comprehend the possible consequences of allowing the nation to split in two.

The Urban Village Solution

If this sort of polarisation is a possible outcome of an efficient Australia, we might expect something more compelling from a supposedly reforming government than a resigned adaptation to necessary adjustments, a promise to more efficiently manage an increasingly unequal nation, or quibbles over whether what is happening is a crisis or not. In the specific area of urban policy, there are certainly attempts to undertake more direct salvage operations among the wreckage left behind by restructuring: the Kelty report on regional inequalities, BBC funding for disadvantaged areas, local social justice and welfare projects, and direct funding to local governments for capital works and job creation. Even here, though, reform generally comes down to demonstrations and spot projects which can only try and solve some of the local consequences – dilapidated public housing, decaying infrastructure, backlogs of inadequate sewerage, roads or schools – of more general financial stringencies.

Those implementing urban policy within government know how difficult more interventionist programs would be in a political environment dominated by the compulsion to cut public expenditure. One problem, clearly, is the lack of political support for versions of efficiency which focus explicitly on social justice or long-term distributive implications. Another, though, is the trajectory of the urban debate itself, especially the tendency to seek a safe haven in more expert technical design or in small-scale physical responses to fundamental social and economic problems. Michael Dear (1989:460) has warned that 'the planner's ability and responsibility to forge substantive visions of the urban future have been all but forgotten in the rush to become "technocractic facilitators"'. While this is a characterisation of an American planning system that is rather more defensive and myopic than its Australian counterpart, I would argue that many proposals for urban Australia have made a similarly soft landing, in easy options like physical determinism and a rather romantic nostalgia for 'the kind of local feeling and interaction associated with centuries of tradition in villages' (Newman & Kenworthy 1992a:50).

The re-emergence of 'urban village' models is part of this trend in planning. The village is partly a physical model of small-scale, medium-density 'walking neighbourhoods', but it also functions as a metaphor for 'community spirit'. Newman and Kenworthy (1992b:33) provide an appealing description of 'high-density, mixed-use development, clustered around rail stations, with generous open spaces and a high-quality public realm'. But what are the problems addressed by this kind of village development? Automobile dependence and suburban sprawl, certainly. Yet references to equity or increased justice are sparse or vague, even if improved public transport and services closer at hand would significantly help some disadvantaged people reach the jobs or facilities they now need to reach by car.

The overwhelming impression of the urban village, though, is its strong focus on aesthetic and design issues, on shape and form rather than substance. Villages may have benefits for poorer citizens, but they do not seem centred on their experience or expectations of the city. This impression of proposals for more 'compact cities' is not helped by a recent description of medium-density housing projects in Australia (Judd 1993). Despite claims about the greater affordability of medium-density housing, just two of the twenty-one attractive developments surveyed in the book offer even reasonable access to people on low incomes, while to afford a home in more than half of the estates people would need at least 'upper-middle' incomes. Such evidence surely begs the question of just who a better city based on medium-density housing is better for.

There is no doubt that a more design-conscious planning is an advance over one which ignores the impact of physical form on residents' enjoyment and use of homes, streets and neighbourhoods. Stretton (1987:145-9) urges us to remember that criticising the idea that environment determines behaviour does not imply that any old building or town plan will do. Nor does a critique of the attempt to create community – perhaps by conscious attempts to design neighbourhoods which foster rather than inhibit interactions between different kinds of individuals and groups – imply that planners should therefore ignore their responsibility to provide new developments with adequate meeting places and community facilities, especially where the residents will be unable to provide such things on their own account. Yet if there is no prior commitment to tackling the basic causes of inequality, these design initiatives can do little more than alleviate some of its symptoms or, by giving poorer people a better standard of resources, provide them with the material for a bit of self-help and self-determination. This does not mean that the quality of planning and building doesn't matter because the poor will still be poor. What it does mean is that so long as the poor remain poor, the quality of planning and building is only a start and not an ending.

In inner and middle suburbs, particularly those undergoing gentrification, identifying 'mixed-use village precincts' often means preserving and enhancing particular local features which bring people together in public: markets, street cafes, parks and so on (Victorian Department of Planning and Development 1993). In disadvantaged areas, especially working-class outer suburbs, however, the 'urban village' approach may involve substantial disruptions to the local physical and social landscape, as in some of the projects funded by the BBC program.

One aim of these demonstration projects, especially those in Elizabeth–Munno Para in South Australia or Inala–Ipswich in Queensland, is to provide funds for a better integration of the various local welfare and health services. Few would deny that these suburbs need money spent on such facilities. Nor would many criticise another BBC goal: the more coherent development of new areas, in part by coordinating land release with the extension of sewers and public transport routes (Spiller 1992). All fine and good. Yet while the information pamphlet on these projects (DHHCS 1992b) insists that there is no plan for a 'wholesale redevelopment of Australian cities', they do appear to mean something like that for disadvantaged outer suburbs.

The BBC program is promoting a 'renovation agenda' (Peel 1993b), in which public housing estates are being refurbished, with private developer involvement, and the houses mostly sold to owner-occupiers. Other funds are being used to improve local roads, parks and shops.

There are real and valuable gains from these projects, perhaps especially the increased opportunities for home ownership provided by new low-deposit schemes. Providing a greater 'mix' of housing opportunities and reducing the amount of public rental housing will also help reduce the burdens that high concentrations of disadvantaged tenants place on local government and service providers. There will be more people able to provide a bit of financial help to local schools and charities, fewer people absolutely dependent on hard-pressed welfare agencies. And because the new or renovated housing is cheap, an area like Elizabeth may well end up with the kind of social profile it had before job loss and short-sighted changes in public housing policy made it poor: a mix of working families and single people, older folk and newcomers, tradespeople, labourers and local professionals, public housing tenants and mortgagees, and new Asian and European migrants alongside the migrants of the 1950s and 1960s.

Yet the generalisation of this 'renovation agenda' to all of Australia's depressed areas is a troubling prospect, ignoring for the moment what it would cost. For one thing, these projects may have very disruptive consequences for some residents, because all rely on a substantial replacement of the current population by a more 'diverse' one. South Australia's Rosewood Village, for instance, links a changed tenure mix (which will displace about 14 000 public housing tenants into home ownership or other suburbs) with 'a friendly, village-like atmosphere' and a 'genuine community spirit' (SAHT 1993). In similar vein, plans for urban renewal in the more down-at-heel parts of inner Brisbane promise 'vibrant urban centres', 'new attractive residential environments' and a 'broad social and demographic mix' (Brisbane City Council 1992:10–11). Achieving mix, in both cases, will mean uprooting a good proportion of those residents who lack the protection of home ownership. And given their local focus, we need to ask if the loss of rental housing in these areas will be matched by new rental construction close by. If not, the choices of those who are being displaced are, in fact, being reduced.

While these projects address some of the problems associated with the concentration of disadvantage, they do little to address disadvantage itself, and particularly the ways in which people become disadvantaged. This disruptive renovation helps the 'locality' but not all of 'the locals'. Essentially, it changes the physical distribution of people who will, for the most part, remain poor. Without schemes to create jobs or provide more generous welfare payments, changed location may not help and may end up detaching some people from the networks of solidarity and support which hold poor communities together. What happens to the people who leave these areas? Where do they go? Are they better- or worse-off? What is the impact of sudden population transfers on existing services like refuges and community centres? Will the new population want or support those services? Will the relocated poor find the same kinds of services in their new environment? Will those who get to stay in the area become the submerged and ignored rump of a more 'normal' locality? The South Australian Housing Trust is surveying relocated tenants and studying the local consequences of the Rosewood develop-ment, but it is significant that these social implications were really tackled only after the project commenced.

Through these disruptive renovations some of our suburbs may become more socially heterogenous. That might mean, with a bit of luck, that some of the people who are now disadvantaged will shop at slightly nicer shops, be closer to a slightly better hospital and see their kids attend slightly better schools. Hopefully, that won't induce better-off people to desert the public facilities and seek the exclusive havens of private ones. Working against the social forces which divide our cities is a decent social objective, and it has some practical merit. But if a better urban future rests on long-term solutions and more challenging visions of what might be, the physical dispersal of the poor through a series of urban villages can only ever be a half-measure.

Without that more challenging vision, the transformative capacity of urban reform is more and more compromised. Better cities, urban villages and strategic visions may promise new beginnings for a few suburbs, and they may deliver improved living conditions to a few of the people who need them. But they are also running against more powerful trends which are stripping those same people of jobs, security and opportunity.

Deregulation, privatisation and increasingly regressive taxation schemes like dividend imputation and negative gearing have been pushing money up the social ladder for well over a decade, while the bulk of ordinary Australians see their wages buy less and less, their assets and their skills devalued and their kids struggling towards adulthood in a harsher and harsher world. That is the Australia that cutbacks and meanness and greed are helping to produce, and the only political alternative seems to be more of the same, if a little more quickly. The urban policy programs of the 1990s might be a brave effort to preserve a few scraps of social justice in a leaner and meaner Australia. But the kind of localised better city they produce may well exist alongside another city, a place of insecurity and redundancy for those who must move out, to make way for other people's future.

Rethinking the Urban Future

Where might we go from here? Perhaps the starkest dilemma is how to think about social justice as social inequalities seem to inexorably widen all over the world. Fortunately, there are more possibilities than problems in the urban debate. The realities that have for years pressed hard on workers and residents in disadvantaged communities are filtering into the language of research and, to an extent, government policy. Certainly, we must recognise and endorse those aspects of current urban policy and planning which are keeping principles like social justice alive in public debate. We should also resist the temptation to respond to privatisation and cutbacks with a defence of the public sector 'as it used to be'. The structures of public provision forged in the more prosperous 1960s and 1970s may well need reform. In public housing policy, for instance, the point is to defend people's right to decent and affordable housing whatever their economic situation, not to defend a particular housing form (Forrest & Murie 1988:236–47).

As ever, a key factor is the broader context in which urban projects are conceived. At this time, that must mean a confrontation with inequality: with the traumatic effects of job loss and entrenched unemployment, with the penalisation of people and groups trapped in poverty, with the legacies of neglect and marginalisation which scar many people's lives. This is urgent, I think. If whole groups of people fall out of networks of social support and citizenship, it will be very difficult to bring them back. As a first step, money and effort should flow into those local institutions – neighbourhood houses, training programs, health centres and so on – which are doing the hard day-to-day work of basic support, keeping people active and engaged, teaching them to read and write, advocating for and with them, maintaining a bit of hope and a bit of self-esteem.

In the longer term, building fairer cities will rest on a reconceptualisation of efficiency and 'good policy'. Abandoning 'the market' and 'economic development' is hardly an option in an established capitalist economy. Instead, our task is to articulate a concept of efficient development which centres on questions of who gets what, and which takes the social and distributional outcomes of growth as a primary test of adequate economic performance (Stilwell 1993b).

In the American context, Sharon Zukin (1991:275) has argued that policy should focus on the public, not just the private, value of economic activity, because this 'mandates a discussion of development goals on the basis of citizenship rather than ownership' and generates 'a politics that emphasises local continuity, a social return on investment to citizens rather than shareholders' financial returns, and obligations on businesses to put down roots'. This focus on local outcomes and activism is a common feature of recent urban theory, with some arguing for a 'decentralist continuation of modernity' through locally relevant social protest and action (Cooke 1990:179) or a 'repoliticisation of social life and control' in local communities (Hedgecock, Hillier & Wood 1991: 223). Others counter that a local or particularistic focus must complement, rather than replace, national commitments to fundamental social change (Duncan & Goodwin 1987), especially when the forces which effect individual localities are increasingly global in nature (Cooke 1989). In this regard, Zukin's (1991:273–5) model of an 'alternative market culture', which combines national and local economic development goals with a commitment to respect the future of all citizens and all communities, is a useful middle ground.

In building that kind of culture, one of the hardest problems is coming up with mobilising definitions of equality and justice, especially when there are good reasons to suspect that the 'universalising' strategies of 'justice' and 'citizenship' which prevailed in the past were biased towards specific class, cultural and gender experiences and tended to exclude or attempt to assimilate many people who could not or did not share those experiences (Young 1990:156–91). The point, as Nancy Fraser (1989:63) stresses, is not to overthrow humanist and inclusive ideals, but to make claims 'in the name of the rights traditionally recognized but not generally realized in modern Western culture'. Or, as David Harvey (1992:598) argues, we need to speak about abstract concepts like justice as ultimate goals: 'justice and rationality take on different meanings across space and time and persons, yet the existence of everyday meanings to which people do attach importance and which to them appear unproblematic, gives the terms a political and mobilizing power that can never be neglected'.

Our best bet might be to reformulate the idea of 'social justice' along the lines suggested by Iris Young (1990) as a combination of more equitable income distribution and more widespread access to the power of self-determination. In this formulation, social justice cannot be realised until inequalities are understood to include social and cultural as well as economic power: injustice stems from the relative inability of disadvantaged people to take action, make meaningful decisions, and have those decisions valued and listened to. Distributive justice and social justice, in these terms, must occur together. Some of the principles behind recent urban policies, like the emphasis on public participation and community development, lead in this direction. But to mobilise more generally, I think those principles will also have to find room for the expectations embedded in everyday meanings of social justice, which will generally demand changes in the distribution of wealth and power. People have every reason to ask what social justice means when their lives are still ruled by constraint and when the places they live in are still badly off compared to the suburbs of the well-to-do. If the same people keep winning, and the same people keep losing, then social justice is further away than ever.

These are all speculations, and they depend first and foremost on a general acceptance that the ultimate problems of our cities stem from social inequality. That will also mean recognising the continuing – and perhaps increasing – salience of class position in determining people's life chances. Class is not a lifestyle choice, or a market niche. Like gender, race, or disability, it is a fundamental experience of limits and barriers in everyday life. And it is up to governments to address and dismantle those barriers.

The urban debate itself might provide some of the materials for these mobilising arguments. Fears that our cities are becoming 'Los Angeles' may lack precision, but they can nonetheless be a useful tool. The urban debate, new and old, has always been about alternative societies, not just alternative urban designs. 'Los Angeles' raises the spectre of social disintegration, and shows the enormous costs we will all bear if we persist in excluding more and more of our fellow citizens from a decent existence.

Most important, reinventing Australia must involve finding a place for those who have suffered the most from what Australia is becoming and who have paid the price – without compensation – for an efficient future. The first question to be asked of any plan, any design, any policy, must be who wins and who loses. Ultimately, we must be willing to spend more of our money on resuscitating other people's fortunes, rather than on simply securing our own. These are challenges way beyond the scope of planning departments, housing authorities or social justice teams. They go to questions about values and choices in public culture, about the balance between public responsibility and private freedom which constitutes shared citizenship. Most of all, they ask whether Australians want to live with the possibility of increasing social polarisation, or do something about it.

CHAPTER 3

National Urban Policy in the 1990s

Lionel Orchard

Since 1990 cities have returned to the national policy agenda after a long absence. Not since the heady days of Whitlam and the Department of Urban and Regional Development (DURD) has a national government seen it necessary to develop explicit policies and programs for the cities. This chapter analyses the national ideas and policies of the 1990s and some of the debates about them against the background of the recent history of national involvement in urban policy and the broader direction of public policy in contemporary Australia. In particular, the relation of the general debates about economic rationalism to the contemporary developments in national urban policy are explored.

National Urban Policy: 1968–1989

The story of national urban and regional policy from the late 1960s to the late 1980s can be divided into three main phases: a 'social demo-cratic' phase under Whitlam; what can be loosely called a 'libertarian' phase under Fraser, and a 'corporatist' phase under Hawke.

The Whitlam urban program was conceived in an era when there was general confidence in the capacity of government to undertake reform. There was broad agreement about what was wrong with our cities and what needed to be done. While many bemoaned the 'great Australian ugliness' of the suburbs, no one seriously challenged the Australian preference for house and garden and the fringe urban growth that resulted. Neither did they challenge the preference for home owner-ship. In general, solutions were conceived that worked with those preferences rather than against them. In particular, many thought that services and employment should be redirected to the newer outer suburbs away from inner suburbs and central business districts. We should take the 'city to the suburbs'. We should also redirect some of the growth of our big cities to new, smaller cities in regional Australia. In this way, the most serious inequalities and structural problems in Australia's cities could be addressed. The overall vision was regionalist and interventionist. Regional development within and away from the big cities required strong and active government.

The urban policies and programs developed within DURD between 1972 and 1975 reflected this broad perspective. DURD sought to reform what were broadly recognised as ossified State bureaucracies by offering State governments federal money (grants and loans) for urban programs as part of a new, cooperative federalism using the powers conferred by section 96 of the Constitution. Planned urban development was pursued through public land development on the fringes of the capital cities – the land commissions – and through publicly sponsored encouragement of new regional cities. The deprivations of the outer suburbs were addressed through area improvement initiatives, decentralisation of employment and service provision, and the establishment of new institutional structures to help achieve that by regional organisations of councils. Federal grant-giving was extended to local government to help it address the increasing demands being placed upon it particularly in the growing outer suburbs of Australian cities. A sewerage backlog program gave grants to the States to deal with this mainly outer-suburban problem. In all of these policies, the problems were dealt with where they occur – the 'city went to the suburbs'. The rehabilitation of inner-urban housing in Glebe (Sydney) and Emerald Hill (Melbourne) was also sponsored by DURD. This work reflected the new idea that inner-city housing should be preserved and rehabilitated. It also meshed well with the regional vision by standing in the way of normal processes of redevelopment and freeway provision focused upon central business districts. DURD also sought to reform and coordinate urban investment and administration across all levels of government – Federal, State and local – through a 'national urban and regional strategy' and an 'urban and regional budget' (Lloyd & Troy 1981a).

Many of the DURD reforms had a stormy passage while the experience with them has been patchy. Many of the simple reforms, like aid to poor western suburbs by way of area improvement schemes and direct Federal grants to local government, have been successful. The direct grants to local government have been ongoing. Inner-city rehabilitation projects in Glebe and Emerald Hill were important demonstrations of what could be achieved. There was some success in making State urban policy and administration more sensitive to social needs.

Nevertheless, many of the more fundamental reforms did not get very far. Public enterprises for urban land and new city development ran into many problems, some highlighting the hostility to urban reform in some States, some showing flaws in the design of the programs themselves, and some showing the difficulties of ventures whose success could only be measured in a long-term (30- or 40-year) perspective. There have been some successes in these areas though. Albury–Wodonga has survived as the 'national growth centre' even though its rationale has changed from comprehensive public development to encouragement and facilitation of private investment in the centre. Public-land banking is now an established activity of all State governments even if the direct public role in land development is not widely supported.

DURD's efforts to exercise some overall influence on national economic policy and the location of public and private activity within Australian cities are still remembered with some hostility. This work involved DURD in bureaucratic warfare with other Commonwealth and State agencies, particularly Treasury. Some early headway was made. In the longer term, however, this aspect of DURD's work metamorphosed into the fiscal managerialism and expenditure cutback of the Department of Finance.

The DURD experience has been the subject of intense criticism and debate on all sides. Many policies central to the Whitlam/DURD vision and designed to be of direct economic and social benefit to people – like the development of regional growth centres and the establishment of land commissions – did not produce the results hoped for and left a general cynicism in urban policy circles about a strong public presence in new urban and regional development. Many thought that these failures were due to the urban reforms flying in the face of economic forces and trends. For example, many argued that the idea of new regional cities underplayed the role of large cities in fostering high levels of economic growth and a more efficient economy.

Nevertheless, there is no doubt that the DURD years represented a sea-change in the way cities and their problems were viewed. Permanent changes came about as a consequence of ideas and policies developed within DURD. Some of the ideas meshed in interesting ways with the new 'libertarian' emphasis on smaller government and less regulation that emerged with the election of the Fraser government. Three urban policies of the mid-1970s reflected this reconciliation of libertarian thinking with urban reform: 'urban management', urban consolidation and planning code reform emphasising performance rather than prescriptive criteria. Just as the Whitlam ideas reinforced one another, so too did the three new arguments.

DURD's ideas about the reform of urban planning away from physical land-use considerations towards greater concern for the social and economic factors shaping cities was the key idea behind 'urban management'. But, in many ways, 'urban management' was a drastically reduced view of urban planning from that imagined by the early 1970s reformers, particularly in terms of the use of public power and investment in planning new urban development. By the mid-1970s the quest for smaller and more efficient government began to dominate Australian public policy. 'Urban management' reflected this quest in urban policy. Urban managers sought to coordinate the major providers of urban services – for example, water, sewerage, transport, education, health, housing – in order to save public resources and so that the social and environmental implications of urban development could be better monitored. This is where urban management joined the idea of urban consolidation. Better management of cities led to a general questioning of the ongoing growth of Australian cities and to a greater hope that denser housing might lessen the need for new, fringe-urban development. Because of increasing constraints on public finance, the Whitlam/ DURD focus on better planning of outer-suburban areas became, in the hands of 'urban managers', a general critique of the ongoing expansion of our cities and a defence of urban consolidation. Lastly, it was widely argued that the way urban development was regulated through planning and other requirements produced socially undesirable consequences in terms of urban design as well as more costly urban development and housing than would occur through more flexible regulation.

Urban management, urban consolidation and performance-based planning codes became the new conventional wisdom in Australian urban policy in the late 1970s and, as we shall see, lay behind many of the ideas for national urban policy in the 1990s.

Many argued for the re-establishment of a conscious national presence in urban and regional policy when the Hawke government was elected in 1983. These pressures were resisted because of the perception in the new government of the need to distance itself from any taint of the Whitlam years. The Hawke government was also intent on dealing with more pressing economic problems, in particular high levels of unemployment and the general need to restructure key industries in the Australian economy.

Nevertheless, some of the Hawke government's policies reflected Whitlam ideas, while the pursuit of planning code reform and denser housing was continued. The Whitlam influence was probably most evident in the way that the new government used local government to deal with the problem of unemployment. Tom Uren, Whitlam's Minister of Urban and Regional Development, was appointed Minister of Local

Government in the early Hawke governments. The Community Employment Program, established in 1983, dealt with unemployment problems by sponsoring a range of local projects upgrading social and community facilities. It owed much to the area-improvement ideas developed in DURD. Later, a Bicentennial program provided Federal finance to local government to generally upgrade and provide a range of new 'showpiece' facilities of use to local communities. Early in its first term of office, the Hawke government established a National Inquiry into Local Government Finance with Professor Peter Self as chairperson. It reported in 1985 and recommended continuing Federal financial sharing to local government on an equity and needs basis.

The 'Green Street' project, foreshadowed in the last days of the Fraser government, was formally established in 1983. It was the vehicle at the national level for pursuing urban consolidation and planning code reform. Demonstration projects were sponsored around Australia with the aim of showing higher-density housing in a more positive light. It also commenced work on a national model planning code for residential development based on performance criteria.

The Revival of National Urban Policy in the 1990s

Urban and housing issues really began to attract strong national attention again in 1989. In response to escalating house prices, particularly in Sydney, the Hawke government convened a Special Premier's Conference on Housing, the Housing Summit, in March 1989. It recommended action to release Commonwealth land for housing and improve land supply in each of the major cities, and to accelerate the reform of planning and building regulations and approval processes. Some of these initiatives built on policies already in train in the area of regulatory reform. They were rationalised as supply-side responses to the problems of high housing costs. The 'Green Street' Project was given a further impetus. Its work on the development of model planning codes culminated in the release of the Australian Model Code for Residential Development (AMCORD) in 1989 and Guidelines for Urban Housing (AMCORD URBAN) in 1992.

By mid-1989 Brian Howe (Minister for Social Security and Minister assisting the Prime Minister for Social Justice in the Hawke government) was signalling the need for the government's social justice agenda to be extended to the cities. Howe argued that urban policy should be better integrated with social and economic policy, paying particular attention to infrastructure problems, the need for more environmentally and energy efficient cities, and the need for better coordination within and between governments.

After the election in March 1990 the political will to develop new approaches to urban and housing policy produced a number of initiatives. An 'Urban Futures' conference was held in April. It explored key economic, environmental and social changes in Australia as they affected cities (Wilmoth 1990). A research program to explore the implications of these changes was established, the results of which were published in 1991 and 1992. The National Housing Strategy was established in June 1990 with a broad mandate to look at housing affordability, finance, supply, location and choice. It too has published a range of reports on these issues culminating in a final report proposing an overall strategy in December 1992 (National Housing Strategy 1992b).

Urban consolidation and the 'compact city' provide two key foundations of the revival of national urban policy in the 1990s. These ideas have been around since the late 1970s in one way or another, particularly in urban policy at the State government level. The 1990s policies and programs at the national level represent their coming of age.

A range of demographic, social, economic and environmental arguments underpin the case for denser, more compact cities. The ageing of the population and the declining average household size produce the need for a more diverse range of smaller houses in denser urban settings. The social and environmental problems of urban sprawl and the car reliance it produces contrast with well-serviced inner suburbs losing population. The demand for new urban growth is high – an additional 1.2 million dwellings will be required over the next ten years – but the economic resources to adequately build and service it are increasingly scarce. (For a summary of these arguments, see DHHCS 1992a:2–8.) The economic defence of the compact city also reflects the widely held view that investment in cities and their infrastructure represents unproductive and wasteful investment that would be better directed to other areas of the economy, particularly at a time of stagnant economic growth (Frost 1991b:163; Newman 1992). Finally, there has recently emerged a moral and communitarian defence of the denser city built on the argument that well-serviced medium-density housing can encourage greater 'incidental contact' between neighbours and thereby build a healthier sense of moral responsibility: 'Unless we can be prised out of our domestic fortresses – and our cars – to eat together, to chat together, to stroll together, we are unlikely to rediscover the joys of being a community' (Mackay 1993).

Other advocates of the 'compact city', like Peter Newman and Jeff Kenworthy, argue that Australia's low-density cities are over-reliant on the private car as a means of transport and are very energy-expensive as a consequence. The need to provide freeways and other facilities for the car is very destructive of community structures. On the other hand, higher-density housing makes public transport more viable and may help lessen the influence of the private car in shaping our cities. Denser 'urban villages' and regional centres connected by light rail systems will help us 'win back the cities' from the private car as well as help achieve better balance between the location of home and jobs (Newman & Kenworthy 1992b).

National urban thinking in the 1990s also reflects general scepticism about government involvement in urban development. Two examples illustrate this. Many view the direct public provision of infrastructure in Australian cities as inefficient and wasteful. They argue that this approach has perpetuated the problems of ongoing urban sprawl because of the subsidies built into infrastructure pricing. Wider adoption of market principles in infrastructure provision through 'user pays' and other schemes is seen as the main alternative even though there is some concern about their equity consequences (Kirwan 1991b). The second example relates to urban land policy. Government involvement in urban land markets has, in the past, been justified as a means of achieving better urban planning and the important social objective of cheaper land prices. Now the convention is that public land-banking and development are inefficient, tie up valuable public resources for too long, and do not achieve prices significantly below those in the private market. Social objectives are better achieved through the taxation and social security systems rather than 'interfering directly in the workings of the land market' (Industry Commission 1992).

The 'Better Cities' program is the main practical result of the resurgence of national interest in urban policy. Negotiated in 1991–1992, a number of projects have been established under this program. They aim to demonstrate how higher-density, planned urban development integrating housing, services and employment will help the three aims of economic efficiency, environmental sustainability and social justice in Australian cities. The means of achieving these objectives are through 'area strategies' – facilitating change of a strategic kind which demonstrates the virtues of new approaches at a scale large enough to be visible. A number of common themes are evident in the projects sponsored under the program – the development of more coherent regional centres involving retail, service employment, cultural facilities and housing; upgrading of and extensions to railway services, particularly in outer-suburban areas; renewal and upgrading of old public housing estates integrating medium-density redevelopment and involving the sale of public housing into home ownership; inner-city housing redevelopment and renewal on underutilised and disused sites many of which are in public ownership; and infrastructure improvement and upgrading. Over $800 million will be spent through the program over five years. One of the key aims of the program is to improve the management of change in Australian cities. This has gone with a more flexible approach to Commonwealth/State relations emphasising a range of processes and outcomes to achieve the objectives of the program rather than rigid Commonwealth control over the States (DHHCS 1992a; Neilson & Spiller 1992).

Overall, national urban thinking in the 1990s suggests that a range of new economic, social and environmental pressures and changes in our cities and housing system require a range of new responses. The main motif is the idea of the 'compact city' although ideas about more productive and efficient cities also inform the recent national interest in the future development of our cities. Ideas for more compact and productive cities have much in common. Both defend the need for denser urban development, better integrated with public transport and other strategic infrastructure investment. Both emphasise the need to provide a more supportive regulatory framework and generally less regulation to encourage better urban development in Australia. The main difference is that whereas the 'compact city' view justifies these things on primarily social and environmental grounds, ideas for the 'productive city' justify them on primarily economic efficiency grounds.

Social Democracy Strikes Back

After three years of development of national urban policy and the generation of an unprecedented amount of applied policy research, by 1992 criticisms of the direction and detail of the national effort to reform the cities had emerged. The debate takes place in two main areas. The first centres on urban consolidation and the 'compact city' as general frameworks for shaping national policy for the development and growth of Australia's cities. The second concerns the question of the role of government in urban development and the cities generally.

The limits of urban consolidation and the compact city are slowly being recognised in the national urban policy debate. It has long been argued in Australian urban policy circles that a simple emphasis on increasing the density of housing will not achieve very much in terms of limiting the need for new urban development in Australian cities. The reasons were well articulated by Peter Harrison in a famous paper published in 1970 (Harrison 1970). Harrison placed the question of housing density in the broader perspective of overall urban density. His first point was that since housing consumes only between a half and a third of the land area of a modern city, increasing its density will not result in limiting the spread of the city to any great extent. Secondly, he pointed out that as western cities increase in size, their overall population density actually falls because they encroach on more uses less directly related to the urban population – conservation areas, international airports and other broadacre uses. Harrison concluded that: 'All the symptoms suggest that these non-residential space demands are increasing at a greater rate per thousand of population than the residential areas and are the major contributors to urban spread. Until it can be shown to be otherwise, why pick on housing?' (Harrison 1970:3.6).

Harrison's argument lent support to the decentralist, 'city to the suburbs' strategy. Given the limits of the denser city argument, planning for new urban growth was essential. This did not mean that medium density did not have a role to play in the development of Australia's cities. Some defended the Australian suburb as reconciling private and public life in a progressive and egalitarian way while also defending the need for medium-density housing to serve diverse and changing social needs (Stretton 1970).

Many of these arguments have resurfaced in the 1990s. Brian McLoughlin provides an important technical analysis of the relations between residential housing density and overall urban density, showing that 'heroic assumptions' about increases to the former do little to affect the latter and are therefore not likely to dramatically curtail the land needs for new urban development on the fringes of our cities. Urban consolidation is a smokescreen for other problems, particularly the general constraints on public funds for the necessary infrastructure and other supports for new urban development. It helps to legitimate the lack of attention to the needs of new urban communities and may be producing considerable social, economic and environmental costs in the longer term (McLoughlin 1991).

Patrick Troy has also recently subjected the propositions underlying urban consolidation to critical scrutiny and found them wanting in many ways. Increases in residential density will not achieve land and infrastructure savings for the reasons adduced by Harrison and McLoughlin. There is little evidence of spare infrastructure capacity in established suburbs and, if there were to be increased levels of redevelopment, pressures on important elements of the infrastructure system in these areas may lead to problems. For example, road congestion may worsen. Social facilities in these areas are also older and therefore may need significant upgrading to address the new needs being asked of them. Many of the studies purporting to show the savings in infrastructure costs through urban consolidation do not acknowledge the amount of upgrading that infrastructure may require in these areas in order to cope with high levels of new development. There is also a wide preference for the detached house on its own allotment despite the demographic shift to smaller households, a fact supported by the many recent studies of housing preferences in Australian cities. There is no evidence that housing will be cheaper as a consequence of urban consolidation while denser housing, far from reducing environmental stress, will add to it in all sorts of ways: waste disposal, water runoff, and sound insulation present more problems as housing density increases. Overall, urban consolidation is motivated by the constraints on public funds for new urban development. It threatens reduced housing standards for lower-income groups, and therefore a more inegalitarian society (Troy 1992b).

As Chris Maher has recently noted:

> The policy of consolidation is . . . a simplistic solution to a deceptively complex problem . . . There must also be real concern that the types of measures presently being promoted will have by far the greatest impact on those groups and localities least able to protect themselves. Measures which are ostensibly based, in part at least, on notions of social justice may themselves become a part of a redistributive process which further disadvantages those whose choices, in both housing and location, are limited, while leaving virtually unaffected those whose economic and political power enable them to resist such changes. (Maher 1993:822)

On moral and communitarian grounds then, the defence of the denser city fairly soon runs up against the different sense of community and morality engendered by the low-density city built upon home ownership, detached housing, the quarter-acre block and the egalitarian values which underpin them.

The implications for urban policy of the environmental agenda have also been the subject of much recent debate. Some support the need for change but argue that it should be incremental and pay attention to the value of existing urban structures. More comprehensive approaches to city planning and infrastructure provision will be required in order to adequately shape the future development of cities for environmental reasons. There is also a need to balance arguments for smaller cities for environmental sustainability reasons with a recognition that larger cities have high economic productivity (Urwin & Searle 1991).

Some critics view Newman and Kenworthy's arguments with incredulity. For them, the account of cause and effect underlying the argument is very simplistic, unhistorical and determinist. The basis of comparison is between the higher-density European city served well by public transport and involving low petrol consumption with the Australian pattern of low-density cities, car reliance and high petrol consumption. Some argue that the European pattern is the product of a number of things, in particular high petrol costs and strong policies for urban containment. In Australia, without European policies of containment, the most direct way to achieve better use of public transport and higher residential densities would be to increase petrol prices, restrict road building and increase public transport speeds. And the best way to increase the speed of public transport is through traditional 'heavy' rail trains rather than through 'novel forms of public transport' like light rail (Kirwan 1992b).

Other critics argue that Newman and Kenworthy ignore the role of public transport in encouraging the development of low-density residential areas in Australian and North American cities. They extrapolate too directly from an assessment of petrol use in Australian cities to an argument that urban densities must be increased. They assume that changes to urban structure can be quickly effected and are costless. They also ignore the egalitarian nature of the Australian housing system and the likely undermining of that equality through a strong pursuit of denser, more expensive housing. There are other ways of achieving the environmental improvement that Newman and Kenworthy seek, for example, through strong decentralisation away from the big cities and strong regional centring within them. Both would probably reduce travel while allowing the Australian preference for low-density housing to be maintained (Troy 1992a).

The hostility and scepticism about the role of government in urban development in the current national debate has also not gone unchallenged. For example, many defend the role of government in managing urban land markets, especially given the importance of land markets in determining overall housing prices in various cities. A recent housing cost study concluded that: 'a government role in the provision of land is not just desirable but obligatory . . If the availability of raw land indeed determines relative house prices, it is strongly indicated that governments should ensure that adequate land is provided to prevent super profits being appropriated by owners of raw land; to maintain supply; and to keep prices down across the city' (Hamley 1992:23).

More generally, critics set the new principles of greater efficiency, less subsidy and a greater private role in infrastructure provision alongside the equity and efficiency benefits of the traditional reliance on public provision paid for through taxes and services charges (Kirwan *et al.* 1992). The new approach reflects the reality of the limits on public finance and government action in contemporary Australia. Many argue that Commonwealth fiscal policy in the 1980s has dramatically curtailed the capacity of State and local governments to adequately finance urban services. In order to achieve good budget outcomes (in some cases, budget surpluses), the Commonwealth has constrained State government funds in various ways rather than raise taxes. As Burke and Hayward note, the Commonwealth has: 'displaced the burden of expenditure restraint on to the States. This has been achieved by reducing significantly Commonwealth net payments (grants and advances) to the States while simultaneously reducing the States' global borrowing limits so as to prevent the States from borrowing more to make up the revenue shortfall' (Burke & Hayward 1990:132).

Other national economic policies have also had a severe impact at the State government level, the most dramatic and significant being the failures and bailouts of various State banks that resulted from competition in the deregulated financial environment. Some argue that all of these changes are gradually shifting the dynamic at work in Australian politics. Crises and limits on the capacity of State and local governments to deliver services are the direct result of decisions of the national government. But the political odium is being felt most severely by State governments, not their national counterparts (Hayward 1993).

Some advocates of the compact city accuse the social democratic critics of cynicism about the possibility of any change to the structure of our cities (Newman, Kenworthy & Vintila 1993). Nevertheless, what is really at issue in this debate are rival views about good urban policy. For social democrats, rather than emphasis on the virtues of the compact city, we need greater public planning and market management to ensure that affordable, well-planned urban environments emerge. The chief barrier to this is not entrenched community support for the wrong kind of urban environment but rather national economic policies which make good urban development increasingly difficult to provide. Another reconciliation of social, economic, environmental and moral argument suggests that the Australian pattern of low-density urban development should not be abandoned, just better planned and resourced.

Onward to the Productive City: Rival Views

Greater scepticism and the declining national enthusiasm about the compact city and urban consolidation, together with the ongoing economic constraints at all levels of government, have recently produced a shift in the national urban policy debate towards the idea of the 'productive city'. Two major national reports reflect this shift (House of Representatives 1992; Industry Commission 1992). The environmental and social rationale for urban change is gradually being displaced by arguments linking urban policy and change more closely to processes of economic restructuring in contemporary Australia. Cities are increasingly viewed from the perspective of whether they do or do not facilitate economic efficiency and growth. It seems likely that the 'productive city' may become the new holy grail of national urban policy in Australia.

There are two broad views about the productive city in recent Australian debates: one suggesting that the processes of economic change in the modern economy are producing a fairly open range of urban and regional possibilities, the other focusing on the economic benefits of big cities and the need to develop policies to encourage greater economic growth and efficiency within them.

The first view is expressed in essays by Peter Hall (1992) and John Brotchie (1992). In a world context, Hall discerns a pattern of urban deconcentration and reconcentration. There are great forces pushing for population dispersal from big cities. Hall argues that urban policy can positively hitch itself to this change and quotes the example of the new towns in Britain after World War II. As a consequence of these processes of concentration and deconcentration, what we now have is an increasingly complex urban system but one in which location and its attributes matter to people. We are moving from an urban system with 'fixed' locational requirements to a much more fluid one in which 'created' attributes are more important. This reflects the economic change from the dominance of secondary manufacturing industry to a service and information economy with more open locational require-ments. A 'created city' which attracts investment from new 'footloose' industries is one in which infrastructure will be very important. 'Urban quality' and 'urban image' are becoming increasingly important in the attractiveness of cities to investors and people more generally. Such qualities are created by planners and civic leaders (Hall 1992). Some of these arguments were anticipated in a contemporary overview of British urban policy (Donnison with Soto 1980).

In terms of the Australian urban policy debate, Hall's arguments suggest a range of possibilities. If he is right about metropolitan concentration leading to eventual dispersal, how should urban policy respond to it? There seem to be a number of responses, all of which can co-exist: regional development on the fringes or in proximity to big urban agglomerations; planning for more rapid dispersal to new regional centres attractive for a variety of reasons (e.g. tourist develop-ment on the Gold and Sunshine Coasts); and the renewal of old urban fabric. Which of these should get the most attention is the interesting and important question.

Brotchie's essay on the recent changes to Australia's cities reflects many of Hall's themes. The trends in the Australian urban system include the increasing dominance of service-based employment in cities, the increasing dispersal of economic activity within cities, and a general unravelling of the close relationship between the economic efficiencies which come from urban agglomeration and concentration. Economic activities can be dispersed over much wider areas but still achieve the agglomeration efficiencies because of advances in telecommunications. These changes also mean that old ideas about optimum city size are breaking down. Incomes used to increase and costs decrease with increased city size, but income per capita has shown decreasing variation with city size over the last decade. The variation of net income per capita is not large over Australia's major cities, while future increases in costs could shift the optimum back to smaller cities. Brotchie notes that 'the reducing urban scale effects on household income may be an indication of the increasing integration of urban systems through telematics and improved transport systems' (Brotchie 1992:16).

Brotchie draws a number of policy implications from this analysis. First, there is a need for consolidation of activity patterns and services but not necessarily dwellings. Second, the increments to urban growth in our cities should be focused to achieve maximum benefit. Demonstration projects may help show the benefits of this focusing of effort. Third, the breakdown between income and city size 'provides the opportunity for growth in non-metropolitan centres, where essential trip distances are less, and housing and infrastructure costs are also reduced, and a further range of lifestyle and environmental choices is available' (Brotchie 1992:23). Hall's and Brotchie's analysis and sentiments are well-reflected in Kirwan's recent call for a national settlement strategy and a national regional policy in Australia. Action is 'needed to focus and contain future urban growth, to stimulate alternatives to the dominant capital cities – especially Sydney and Melbourne, where there is a severe risk of diminishing returns to scale – and to encourage new centres of urban growth to increase their productivity' (Kirwan 1992c:200).

The second view about what the 'productive city' requires in Australia is reflected in an essay by Kevin O'Connor and in the rationale for the Building Better Cities program. O'Connor's essay focuses on recent economic trends in Australian cities. His basic message is that since Sydney and Melbourne are the focus for most of Australia's existing linkages into the world economy, the development of these two cities should be facilitated in order that a 'productive' Australian economy emerges, particularly one that is internationally competitive. Nevertheless, the cost structures of Sydney and Melbourne (as reflected in office rents, industrial rents and housing prices) are high by comparison with other Australian cities. This needs to be addressed if their ongoing development is to proceed well. In particular, there should be additional national financial assistance for infrastructure development in Sydney and Melbourne. O'Connor briefly addresses another response to encourage the development of an internationally competitive economy in Australia: fostering the development of smaller urban centres on the grounds that the equity and environmental consequences of ongoing growth in Sydney and Melbourne are too large and might weaken the national economy due to the perpetuation of high cost structures. He quickly dismisses this option by arguing that all other urban centres lack the necessary foundations and prerequisites to maintain 'international best practice' in advanced manufacturing and services (O'Connor 1992).

The BBC program reflects this emphasis on the big cities, albeit beyond just Sydney and Melbourne. The BBC rationale includes arguments that agglomeration efficiencies of spatially concentrated labour forces help labour mobility in a period of economic change while the quality of the urban environment is very important to provide the basis for new investment. There is a close relationship between city form, its culture and services, and economic innovation. The BBC program sponsors projects which assist the process of change while helping provide the necessary urban framework for new investment (Neilson & Spiller 1992).

These two views about the productive city are in many ways quite narrow in their focus and emphasis – the productivity and efficiency of cities as it relates to formal economic measures of cost, price and growth. There are other views about the productivity of cities emphasising material standards of living and the contribution made by the public and household economies to these standards. For example, comparison of the Australian and Japanese economies in formal terms shows the Japanese superiority, but a wider comparison of the standards of living in Japanese and Australian cities shows the Australian superiority in terms of housing costs, disposable income, and the capacity for flexible and cheap accommodation to economic and social change (Castles 1992 cited in Stretton 1993). It all depends on what you count as productive – high levels of economic growth in the formal economy, or the different but essential role played by the three economic realms to the quality and productivity of economic and social life in any society: private, public and household. This view challenges the conventional wisdom that low-density Australian cities are economically unproductive, as much as it does the idea that the 'productive city' should only be thought about in terms of formal measures of efficiency and growth. But it seems unlikely that such arguments will be taken seriously, given the ongoing hegemony of economic rationalism in Australian public policy.

Productive Cities and National Urban Policy

National urban policy has now entered a new phase. In 1992 several major reports were published and major policy reviews of urban and regional development and urban design have been established. All promise to take the debate about the foundations and practice of urban policy in new directions. One of the reports – the House of

Representatives Standing Committee for Long-Term Strategies: Report on Patterns of Urban Settlement (HR 1992) – reviews the present debate about the cities and puts forwards a framework and ideas for future national urban policy. This section critically reviews this report, so this account of the recent national urban debate is selective. Nevertheless, the House of Representatives' report is important as one of the few attempts by the national parliament to take a general look at the cities. While it is somewhat removed from actual policy development within the national bureaucracy, it is a free-standing overview of the state of play in the early 1990s and it will at least partly shape national urban policy in the future. For these reasons, it deserves close scrutiny. A more comprehensive review of the current national developments for the cities and regions must be left for another time.

The House of Representatives' report makes a number of major points. First, urban consolidation is a limited basis upon which to build a national urban policy. While there is clearly a role for denser, smaller housing forms to serve a range of new needs, consolidation within the existing urban fabric of cities will only house about one-third of urban growth, with the remaining two-thirds occurring on the urban fringes. There won't be substantial space savings because residential uses consume only a small part of the land area of the modern city, while the cost savings derived from urban consolidation in terms of investment in urban infrastructure have been exaggerated and are uncertain (HR 1992:xii–xiii).

Second, the report defines the key influences on Australia's urban system as we head into the twenty-first century. They include economic restructuring, technological change, the transition to an information economy and the ageing of the population. A number of implications of these trends for the Australian urban system are drawn. There will be a further enhancement of Sydney and an increased population along the eastern seaboard that gradually moves to the north. Brisbane may emerge as Australia's second-largest city in the twenty-first century. Within cities, there will be greater dispersal of economic activities. Cities will become multi-centred with a corresponding reduction in the role of the old central business districts.

Third, the report defines a new policy agenda post-urban consolidation to take heed of the changing economic and social pressures on the Australian urban system. The report advocates a policy agenda with a number of dimensions: better coordination and planning between levels of government, and greater emphasis on urban management and more flexible policy responses. There is a case for greater reliance on taxation and pricing policies to shape urban and housing preferences but 'Until pricing systems are better developed it is best to continue to fix costs through regulatory and policy means which push in the same direction as the market is eventually expected to travel' (HR 1992:141). A national perspective on urban and regional development and a national settlement strategy should be developed. The latter should include 'a nationally coordinated program for the development of key productive infrastructure such as the integration of urban transit networks for the movement of export freight' (HR 1992:xvi). The report recommends inter-governmental coordination and better planning in a whole series of areas including the integration of Commonwealth location decisions, land release programs and national highway provision with State planning strategies, inter-governmental coordination to facilitate better regional development, and the identification of the most environmentally sensitive sites in urban growth areas with a view to determining those that should be protected from development. It also recommends that infrastructure adequacy and management and land-banking be researched.

Balancing regional needs as different regions rise and fall due to economic change is identified as a particularly important task. The main policy issue raised by the report in relation to this is the question of how public finance should be directed to deal with these changes – on the existing fiscal equalisation basis whereby the smaller States and cities get more assistance per capita, or on a more equal basis whereby Victoria and New South Wales receive more than they do now? The report calls for major reviews by the Commonwealth Grants Commission's fiscal equalisation formulae addressing 'the efficiency and equity in the delivery of services in a national context' and the States' formulae 'because there is evidence that they do not always accurately express the operations of cause and effect when assigning funds to the alleviation of social problems' (HR 1992:xvi). For example, the report mentions the subsidies which flow to States based on the number of aged inhabitants, but suggests that the number of unemployed may be just as important in determining subsidy flows (HR 1992:46).

Overall, there is a refreshing willingness shown in the House of Representatives' report to subject the ideas underlying the recent resurgence of national interest in cities to detailed scrutiny. The report finds them wanting in all sorts of ways and suggests that we should be sceptical of grand visions seeking to turn the structure of our cities around in the short term. Urban consolidation comes in for this criticism in particular.

However, the report is aware of the need to articulate some overall framework within which a national urban and regional policy can proceed. In general, the report calls for the replacement of the 'urban consolidation, eco-city' vision with a 'productive' city vision. Given the Keating government's likely focus on micro-economic reform and the quest for greater efficiency in the Australian economy, we are likely to see national urban policy move increasingly down this path.

While there are some overtures to the arguments for public intervention in the report, most of the emphasis is on providing a supportive framework for the economic changes that are taking place in contemporary Australia. There is not much in this report about the virtues of a social democratic urban policy in which economic change is balanced against the social needs of cities and their residents, and government action is employed to ensure that balance. It seems that social needs are still to be made to adjust to the imperatives of the economy. The only thing that has changed are the reasons for the adjustment – national efficiency rather than social and environmental imperatives. Overall, the strategy articulated in the report echoes the 'level playing field' arguments made in so many other areas of national policy in the 1980s: 'A national strategy does not in itself imply significant bureaucratic intervention in the development of regional economic strategies; it may well be that a national/regional economic strategy entails the removal of fiscal equalisation and greater regional differences in factors such as wages' (HR 1992:146).

The questioning of the existing redistributive basis and the emerging defence of the need for more equality in Federal financial allocation to the benefit of New South Wales and Victoria, and the disadvantage of the smaller States, raises important urban policy questions. The argument is linked with O'Connor's view that efficiency criteria should become more important in the allocation of Commonwealth finance to the States, so that Sydney and Melbourne, as important centres for the emergence of the new information and service economy, get a bigger share of the national public budget. This would enable the more adequate provision of the necessary infrastructure to support the process of economic change in those cities. Such arguments are reinforced (if a little muddied) by the call to direct national infrastructure investment away from the 'rust-belt States' (Vic., SA, Tas.) towards high-growth States (NSW, Qld) (MacDermott 1993).

Nevertheless, it is not clear that the principles of equity in public finance and the urban imperatives of greater efficiency in the national economy go together in quite the way that O'Connor and the House of Representatives' report imply. As already noted, other analysts of the urban implications of the service and information economy – like Peter Hall and John Brotchie – suggest that locational choices for this economic activity are much more flexible and 'footloose' than traditional manufacturing industry. Indeed, Hall suggests that the international experience with the location of such activity is in small cities in environmentally attractive locations that do not suffer the problems of congestion and pollution of big cities, even though these smaller centres may be within the orbit of bigger conurbations. The other side of the story of the emergence of the service and information economy is that older manufacturing industry is on the decline in all Australian cities, and that there will need to be a range of policy responses to deal with the social and economic problems caused by those changes. Two responses could be that more effort is made to spread the 'footloose' service and information industries around Australian cities of all sizes, and that the public finance necessary to support those industries should similarly be spread around. Indeed, an argument could be made that the current bias in Federal financial allocations to the smaller States meshes well with the urban policy objectives of encouraging the development and adjustment of Australia's smaller cities, particularly those in the 'rust-belt' States.

Also, it is not obvious why national urban policy should be built on the idea that the further growth of Sydney and Melbourne should be encouraged, given the urban problems they now suffer. For national urban policy to become fixated with the emerging conurbation on Australia's eastern seaboard, and particularly the needs of Sydney and Melbourne, is dangerous for a number of reasons – it is likely to reinforce the concentration rather than offer some means to check it, and it is likely to mean that Australia's other cities will be seen as backwaters undeserving of the benefits of new public or private invest-ment. Such a scenario would mean that the tension that Leonie Sandercock identified between 'economy' and 'community' in the urban problems left by the structural changes in the Australian steel industry in the mid-1980s (Sandercock 1986) could manifest themselves throughout the Australian urban system beyond the eastern seaboard. All of our cities represent economic and social investment which we should do our best to manage and guide in the national interest. The emerging emphasis on developing 'productive' cities on the eastern seaboard has the potential to skew national urban policy away from a more balanced assessment of the problems and potential of the whole Australian urban system.

In summary then, it is not clear that the policy implications of the 'productive city' are as the House of Representatives' report defines them. Another reading of the recent debates about 'productive cities' in Australia suggests that a much more open range of urban possibilities could accompany the change to the service and information economy. Such economic activity is increasingly footloose and has no particular locational requirements except that services and infrastructure should be of good quality. The implication is that the growth derived from the information and service economies could be spread around a bit so as to effectively utilise the good urban fabric of Australia's existing cities. We should not simply assume that such activity is best located on the eastern seaboard. There are different locational advantages throughout the Australian urban and regional system which could be exploited in different ways. The role of urban policy in such a scenario will surely be important and could involve many social democratic urban policy principles: regional planning within and without cities, strong urban planning to guide and shape urban development, and generally stronger management of land and housing markets through land-banking and other policies. Such policies will only emerge through thinking about good urban policy on its own terms and not just as the new 'productive' city is said to demand policy change.

It is curious that a report, which spends so much of its time challenging the urban determinism that has underlain so much of the recent advocacy of urban consolidation and the 'eco-city', should then smuggle in another set of arguments about the 'productive city' that are said to require a particular urban policy direction. The adoption of the O'Connor view in the House of Representatives' report is another reflection of the limits to public resources for urban development in contemporary Australia. The increasing limits on the role of government will inform policy for the 'productive city' just as much as it did the arguments for urban consolidation. This time though, the issue concerns how public resources should be distributed between cities and regions, not just within them.

However, the report's critique of urban consolidation and focus on policies for the 'productive city' tends to lose sight of how we are to effectively plan, guide and pay for that bulk of new urban development which will continue on the fringes of our cities. As the report acknowledges, 'Governments are trying to reduce expenditure on infrastructure, but, in succeeding, they may be placing a significant long-term burden on the community' in terms of future needs for new and renewed infrastructure (HR 1992:127). But nowhere in the report are these issues really explored. I think the hope is that greater levels of private finance can be mobilised to provide the necessary infrastructure and urban supports for the 'productive economy'. Despite the rhetoric, the 'productive' city is going to be an increasingly privatised and unequal one. The idea of equality is only employed in this report to challenge the existing distribution of public finance through the Federal system. Nowhere is there any effort to raise the question of the overall size of the public economy and the fact that, as noted earlier, the 1980s have seen a sea-change in national fiscal policy whereby the State governments, which carry the burden of the responsibility for urban infrastructure provision, have been massively disadvantaged by the national quest for a smaller Australian public sector and Commonwealth budget surpluses.

Conclusion

Much has been said over recent times about the way in which national policy-making in contemporary Australia is being shaped by the 'economic rationalist' doctrine. Critics argue that the nation-building capacities of national government have been profoundly curtailed in the 1980s and early 1990s as a set of arguments defending negative liberty, free markets and limited government have gained ground in national policy-making. Social democratic 'nation building' and public direction of the national economy have given way to policy prescriptions which say that private markets must be extended and government reduced if the health of the Australian economy is to be restored. The practical influence of these ideas on the shape and direction of state action in contemporary Australia has been profound at all levels of government. At the national level, some have suggested that the service and 'doing' departments have been fundamentally constrained by the central economic agencies, with their control of the purse strings and their emphasis on managerialism (Pusey 1991). National economic policies have also had a dramatic impact on State governments (Hayward 1993).

Critics argue that alternatives to economic rationalism should emphasise the cooperative basis of social and economic life and the much more 'open' quality of the relationship between theoretical concepts and the real world. Public policy should pay greater attention to the historical, cultural and moral dimensions of economic life. More practically, the modern economy should be seen as a mixture of market, public and household activity, each realm contributing to economic and social productivity in its own way.

In important ways, the debates about national urban policy in Australia over the past twenty-five years reflect this wider debate about social democracy and economic rationalism – or better, the libertarian defence of market choice and limited government – in national policy. Three visions for the future of our cities can be discerned in the national urban policy debates in Australia over the last twenty-five years: the 'social democratic' city in the 1970s; the 'compact city' which first emerged in the late 1970s; and the 'productive' city which emerged in the late 1980s. In comparing the ideas 'then and now', the clearest difference is over the meaning and purpose of 'reform'. In the 1970s reform was based on the significant extension of the role of government and the public economy in Australia's cities to achieve a variety of social-equity and market-shaping objectives. In the 1980s and 1990s reform has focused on streamlining and decreasing the role of government and the public economy in Australia's cities, rationalised on social, environmental and, increasingly, economic efficiency grounds.

The debates of the early 1990s about urban consolidation, the 'compact city', infrastructure, urban land and the 'productive city' all ultimately turn on the conflict between adjusting urban policy to the imperatives of the private economy versus a restated defence of the need for a more autonomous urban policy, addressing questions of equity and good management in our cities. Should the government role in urban planning and urban markets just be about providing the strategic context and regulatory framework for private economic growth? Why should it not be about the direct intervention many commentators now see as essential in order that our urban and regional system develops without excluding more and more groups from the benefits of our cities?

The new reconciliation of market and government in the work of the Keating government does not hold out much hope for a more interventionist and broadly based urban and regional policy. The Prime Minister recently acknowledged that markets are a limited means of social organisation: 'the market is a dumb mechanism. It does not establish priorities, it does not assert social goods, it does not assert the social value of some institutions over others . . . The market does not – and never will – protect the weak from the encroachments of the strong' (Keating 1993).

The role of government is usually defended in response to these failures of the market. But the government role in this Keating view is a rather limited, 'hands-off' one. Government must continue to be taken 'out of publicly owned enterprises – where appropriate – to introduce private sector disciplines and efficiencies. But where government does have a fundamental role is in managing the process of change in all its facets' (Keating 1993).

In 1993 three new national reviews of urban and regional issues were established to define new directions for urban and regional policy: the Australian Urban and Regional Development Review, the Task Force on Regional Development, and the Task Force on Urban Design. The first two of these reflect the emphasis on managing economic change to ensure that barriers to greater economic growth and efficiency in the cities are tackled. Exactly what policy directions they will produce is still a little unclear. Indeed, the multiplicity of national reviews and task forces may mean the splintering of any coherent agenda. Nevertheless, there is little doubt the social democratic view that good urban and regional policy depends on much more active government has been placed on hold one more time.

CHAPTER 4

Households, Consumerism, and Metropolitan Development

Patrick Mullins

A valuable though unintended consequence of the important debate now under way on the future of Australian cities, particularly on how to plan metropolitan areas, is the way it has highlighted how little we know about the role played by households in urban development. Surprisingly little is published on the household's place in urban social structures, both in Australia and elsewhere, and even less is available on the way households act as a force to help form and transform cities and towns. With the household being the major institution upon which 'social' (as against 'economic' and 'political') aspects of urban growth and change are based, knowing little about this institution inevitably thwarts a fuller understanding of urban development and this, in turn, blocks the formulation of more adequate urban planning.

Such ignorance is particularly disconcerting at this time because the current debate on Australian cities cites the actions of households as a major cause of today's urban problems. This is especially apparent in the urban consolidation debate, where advocates of the policy are expressing alarm at the continuing movement of large numbers of households to the metropolitan fringe and at their disinterest in living in well-established, well-serviced, but depopulating, inner and middle suburbs. The result is a worsening urban sprawl, one said to be increasingly wasteful of land, infrastructure, and other resources, and with fringe households also being more reliant than other urban residents upon the ownership and use of private motor vehicles they are also said to be contributing disproportionately to a rapidly worsening metropolitan air pollution and traffic congestion.

This chapter explores what seems to be a fundamental but unacknowledged reason for the continuing concentration of households at the metropolitan fringe, and the relative decline of inner and middle suburbs. This is consumerism, the obsessive desire to devour more and more goods and services, and an ideology said to be central to a rapidly expanding global culture (Bocock 1993; Sklair 1991). Since the household is the principal consuming (and income-pooling) unit, an understanding of the link between households, consumerism and residential mobility/development seems necessary if we are to understand why Australian metropolitan households are disproportionately preferring to live at the fringe than elsewhere in the metropolitan area.

There is some risk in proposing this argument since consumerism has not been incorporated into the current debates on metropolitan Australia, with government-initiated research and policy such as the National Housing Strategy – which have led the debates (Alexander 1994) – focusing solely on the way households attempt to satisfy housing and related *needs*. Issues raised include those of housing affordability, housing access, and locational disadvantage, with housing cost being cited as the principal reason for the flight to the fringe: home ownership, the preferred housing tenure in Australia, is said to be cheaper there than elsewhere in the metropolitan area (Burgess & Skeltys 1992; Burke & Hayward 1990).

Yet, in focusing solely on households' efforts to satisfy housing and associated residential needs, this government-initiated work, in conjunction with academic research, has neglected wider consumption-related factors which may have significantly contributed towards current residential structuring. In particular, there is a failure to draw attention to the way households strive to satisfy *wants/desires* as well. Goods and services are now increasingly being consumed for fun, enjoyment, pleasure, recreation and leisure, and it is a consumption which is quite different from that required to satisfy needs. Consumerism, then, is the component of contemporary culture identifying the desirability and necessity of satisfying wants/desires by consuming as many goods and services as possible.

The major thrust of this chapter can be summarised in the following way: a disproportionate number of Australian metropolitan households have moved to the metropolitan fringe because it offers them, relative to their social circumstances and to the opportunities available to them if they lived in inner and middle suburbs, greater consumption opportunities for satisfying both *wants/desires* and *needs*.

The failure of government-initiated research, and related academic work, to incorporate the consumerism question into current debates is surprising because a relationship between consumerism/consumption and residential mobility/development has long been recognised for the cities of the developed world. This relationship has been defined particularly in terms of suburbanisation, the dominant residential form of the post-1940s period and one characterised by low-density housing, the continual outward expansion of the urban fringe, and the mass consumption of consumer durables (Bocock 1993; Lee 1993; Sayer & Walker 1992; Walker 1981; for Australia, see Whitwell 1989). The decades from the early 1970s have, however, seen a marked expansion in the availability of goods and services for satisfying wants/desires, with gentrification (discussed below) being perhaps the most striking example of the new residential forms accompanying this consumption (Bocock 1993; Hamnett 1991; Savage *et al.* 1992; Sayer & Walker 1992; Sklair 1991). Thus, not only has consumerism long had a marked effect on Australian metropolitan residential development, but this effect has changed somewhat over the last couple of decades as the pattern of consumption has changed.

The rapid residential expansion of the metropolitan fringe, and the accompanying relative decline of inner and middle suburbs, is of course not new. This has been going on since the 1940s (Maher 1982), although current concerns seem to be responses to fears about growing costs of metropolitan expansion, particularly in the two largest metropolitan areas, Melbourne and Sydney. In addition, marked changes have forced planners, critics, and urban analysts to reconsider the manner in which Australian metropolitan areas are expanding.

In exploring the alleged link between consumerism and the residential mobility/development of contemporary metropolitan Australia, the chapter is divided into four main sections. The first three provide necessary background for exploring this link, with the first briefly summarising urban consolidation and its related policies; policies trying to change the historic pattern of Australian residential development. The second section defines the basic concepts employed in the argument. The third section provides an empirical sketch of the current Australian metropolitan household, and the last section examines the link between households, consumerism, and the contemporary pattern of Australian metropolitan residential development.

Urban Policy and Residential Life

Urban consolidation and related policies will, if successful, have a profound impact on housing and residential life. A low-density city based on single-family detached housing will be replaced by a city of somewhat higher housing density, and the ultimate goal is to reduce urban costs by constraining metropolitan expansion. The achievement of this goal, in turn, will hopefully lead to a more efficient use of metropolitan land and infrastructure, a reduction in environmental damage, a decline in urban inequality, and an urban form more congruent with the coming twenty-first century (Alexander 1994; Neilson & Spiller 1992).

Planned actions associated with these policies include those aiming to slow the rate of population growth at the fringe, those attempting to increase housing densities, and those to encourage more people to live in inner and middle suburbs. Particular effort will be made to establish 'urban villages': compact residential areas located around major employment centres, because these will enable households to use public transport to commute to and from work and other important locations. This means, in turn, that households' reliance on private motor vehicles will be reduced and this will help limit the environmental damage wrought by this form of transport. Higher housing densities will also, it is implied, encourage closer contact between households, both for reasons of sociability and for mutual assistance; goals considered desirable in these hard times as governments try to cut welfare expenditure in their efforts to reduce taxes. In conclusion, all of these proposals are to be placed within a wider metropolitan policy devised to stimulate economic growth, increase social justice, achieve ecologically sustainable development, and develop more liveable cities (for summaries, see Alexander 1994; Maher 1993).

Though widely acclaimed as a policy, urban consolidation has received some sharp criticism, particularly over the reliability and meaning of the data used, and whether a number of the goals posed are achievable or even desirable (McLoughlin 1991; Troy 1992b). Yet, despite the debates, we still do not know why so many households prefer the fringe to other residential locales, and any further evaluation will require more detailed information on households since it is the actions of households which are critical to this process.

Not only would household data help explain the housing and residential decisions of households, but they will aid understanding of more general assumptions about contemporary metropolitan residential life. Most notable is the claim that the households living on the fringe are socially isolated compared with those residing in other parts of the metropolitan area. While fringe households certainly reside at a distance from many other urban residents, and from a number of necessary resources and facilities, it is questionable whether spatial distance in itself is the cause of social isolation. In fact, the argument is a form of environmental determinism; an ideology claiming a change to built form will bring changes to people's behaviour and social circumstances, and it is a notion long bedevilling urban policy and planning.

Seeing whether fringe households are socially isolated necessitates an understanding of households' social circumstances, particularly their social class, gender and ethnicity, and then comparing these circumstances with those of households living in other parts of the metropolitan area. What seems clear is that social circumstance, not geography, creates social isolation, with geographic isolation being a symptom rather than a cause of the problem. Thus, to remove the social isolation experienced by fringe households it is necessary to remove the social circumstances causing the problem. In fact, there is considerable evidence to show that the socially isolated are concentrated in inner-city areas of many developed societies, not at the fringe, and there is little to suggest that this inner-city location has any positive effects in alleviating these households' social isolation (Wilson 1987). All of this again underlines the need for detailed household data.

Defining Households and Consumerism

To understand the link between households, consumerism and residential development, and to achieve this understanding with reference to the growth of the Australian metropolitan fringe, it is necessary to define the central concepts involved in such an analysis. Three main concepts are considered: 'household', 'household and residential organisation', and 'consumerism'.

The Household

The limited empirical interest shown in households seems an unintended consequence of the way empirical research has been drawn to the 'public' and dominant worlds of the formal economy and of state-based politics, and turned away from the 'private' and subordinate world of household and residential life (Calhoun 1991). The result is not only limited information on households, but a restricted conceptualisation as well, and this has occurred despite the central economic, political, and social role played by households. In the specific case of economic development, for example, Snooks (1994:37) has shown how 'Australian economic development since 1860 has been dominated by three roughly equal sectors – the household, public, and private sectors'.

The household is an income-pooling and consuming unit, and it is the social group immediately responsible for ensuring people's survival and well-being (Marsh & Arber 1992; Pahl 1984; Redclift & Mingione 1985; Smith & Wallerstein 1992; Smith *et al.* 1984. For Australian discussions, see Snooks (1994) and Ironmonger (1990)). 'The "household" [is] the social unit that effectively over long periods of time enables individuals, of varying ages of both sexes, to pool income coming from multiple sources in order to ensure their individual and collective reproduction and well-being' (Wallerstein & Smith 1992:13). Mainly formed of people related by marriage and/or kinship, households are continually transformed following economic and political changes, and as individuals pass through the life cycle.

Five major sources of household income can be discerned (Wallerstein & Smith 1992). The first, wage labour, has historically been derived from male employment, although major changes in the capitalist world economy over the last twenty or so years have brought the marked involvement of women, both in developed and developing countries. The second source emanates from the way households make or provide and then exchange goods and services, with the work done involving both men and women. The third is rent, ranging from the renting of rooms to boarders, to interest-bearing deposits in banks. The fourth source is transfers of income, including government benefits, and gifts received from family. The fifth comes from subsistence work, including food preparation and the day-to-day production of goods and services by households for household consumption, to hunting, fishing and other forms of food gathering, as well as home production, again for household consumption. Though more commonly associated with the work of women, subsistence income is derived from the labour of other household members as well.

While the proportions of income secured from each of these five sources varies over time and between and within countries, it is a cash income – particularly in the form of wages – which is of pre-eminent importance today. Cash enables households to participate in mass consumption and so fulfil the wants/desires expressed by what Sklair (1991) calls the 'culture ideology of consumerism'; an ideology rooted in an expanding global culture and one central to the lives of the peoples of the developed world and now increasingly to those of the developing world as well. Mass consumption essentially had its beginnings in the 1940s, and is only possible through cash transactions, which means that non-cash income, particularly that derived from elaborate subsistence activities, has declined in importance, even in the developing world where non-cash income still contributes to the bulk of household income (Wallerstein & Smith 1992).

In the case of Australia and other parts of the developed world, the rolling recessions of the last twenty years have brought a dramatic change in the sourcing of household income (Pahl 1984). There is now a marked struggle for a cash income, and this is reflected in perennially high rates of unemployment, the rise of two-wage income households, the slow decline in male employment, the marked growth in female employment, and the sharp increase in government transfers, notably in the form of unemployment benefits (Esping-Andersen 1990, 1993; for

Australia, Snooks 1994). Again, cash income is critical because it is the only legal avenue for purchasing the goods and services demanded of a life overwhelmed by a desire to consume. Theft is the alternative, and this may partly account for the marked rise in property crime in the developed world over recent years.

Very little detailed data is available on household consumption patterns, although there is a scattering of information on, for example, gender differences in this consumption (Brannen & Moss 1987). But we know little about the overall process, specifically how households and different household members obtain and consume goods and services from income derived from various sources both inside and outside the household.

Impinging upon households' efforts to obtain cash income, to pool income, and to buy necessary and desired consumption items, is the pervading power of the formal economy, coming notably from dominant classes, and of politics, notably from the state. The different relations urban households have over time with dominant classes and with the state, and the impact these relations have on households' ability to obtain and pool income and then consume various goods and services, have been sketched broadly for a number of cities in a number of countries by contributors to Smith and Wallerstein (1992). The contributors show the way household structures and the actions and activities of households change as wider economic and political circumstances transform cities and societies.

Household and Residential Organisation

To clarify the place of households in urban development it is also necessary to understand their location in the wider residential context, for in sharing a residential area households share common interests, meaning that they form distinctive locally based social structures which, for present purposes, can be called 'household and residential organisations' (Mullins 1987, 1988, 1993). These organisations are politically important because they form the social bases from which households act to protect and improve household and residential life. When necessary, households will come together to formally organise groups to lead urban movements; to lead actions over consumption items, whether these be those defined as needs or as wants/desires (Castells 1983).

'Community' (or 'urban community') is the term invariably used to identify and define this social structure of households, and thus the social base for urban actions/urban movements. Unfortunately, this is a very crude term whose ambiguity recommends its removal from the social sciences, and in its place should be a concept: an unambiguous term identifying and defining the social world of households and residential life.

'Community' is ambiguous because, in practice, it is used to refer to a number of different and contradictory social situations/social structures (Mullins 1987). Most frequently it is employed to refer to a tightly knit and largely localised way of life, one which is rare today, but which was apparent in the past (e.g. with feudalism), and which is still evident in the rural areas of developing countries. Second, 'community' is used to refer to any collection of people sharing a common geographic area: neighbourhood, suburb, collection of suburbs, village, small town, and even city. This diversity of meaning, then, again makes 'community' a meaningless term. Third, it is employed as a synonym for 'society' and, once more, this shows how no separate social structure called 'community' is identified. Finally, it is used to refer to a diverse number of different social groups, from collections of professionals (e.g. 'a community of lawyers') to groups of intimates (e.g. 'a community of friends'). Thus, since it is being used in all these diverse and ambiguous ways, 'community' cannot then be employed as a social science *concept*, and it is therefore of very little – if any – value in contemporary urban research and urban policy/planning.

Equally seriously, 'community' has long been used ideologically, for it idealises a tightly knit, localised way of life, one contrasting with what is regarded as the antithesis of 'community': a loose-knit and socially distant form of residential life, one claimed to be riddled with social problems and said to typify the contemporary urban world (Bell & Newby 1972). This usage is ideological because closely knit social networks are thought to offer greater social advantages, particularly for intense sociability and for the social support contained therein, even though there is little evidence to suggest that this is the case. Moreover, the rigid forms of social control typifying communal societies are considered ideal mechanisms for limiting social disorder and maintaining social stability, and the widespread mutual dependence thought to exist in communal relations are seen to offer the contemporary state an opportunity of withdrawing welfare benefits and placing even more responsibility for social support on relatives, friends and neighbours.

In the case of urban Australia, the little empirical information on 'community' that exists suggests that household and residential life is, and always has been, loosely knit (Bryson & Thompson 1972; Mullins 1981b; Richards 1990); a structure shared with the cities of other developed countries (Wellman & Wortley 1990). Contacts between households are friendly and cordial but they are also socially distant. The 1990 Brisbane Household and Residential Area Study, for example, conducted by myself and a colleague, found 'good neighbours' to be those who are defined as friendly, and helpful when necessary, but who keep to themselves and do not intrude in day-to-day household life (see also Richards 1990).

Unfortunately it is impossible to provide support for, or to dismiss, this ideological use of 'community' because of the lack of evidence. The alleged value of living in tightly knit collections of households versus other social arrangements is not clearly known. Indeed, 'community' seems to have, by contemporary standards, a number of undesirable features, because communal societies have been shown to be parochial, socially rigid, repressive, and undemocratic; features clearly identifying harsh mechanisms of social control and the way people's lives are ascribed at birth (Kymlicka 1989).

What is even more disturbing is the lack of information on the range of different types of household and residential organisation, including knowing the social advantages and disadvantages of each. Thus, we are clearly not in a position to identify 'community', or any other form of household and residential organisation, as being more or less desirable than any other, and so we lack an adequate data base from which to plan contemporary household and residential life. Moreover, this tendency to distinguish between 'community'/'lack of community' is part of a wider, unfortunate tendency within the social sciences to see life in dualities (e.g. developed/underdeveloped, capital/labour, public/ private) and, in the case of urban research, Beauregard (1993) has recently made a welcome attack on this long-lasting and persistent tendency. Research which is guided by conceptual dualities cannot identify variations or nuances and subtleties of social life.

The long history of ambiguity and ideology surrounding 'community' led sociologists in the 1970s to abandon it as a sociological concept, and those who have persisted with it have had little success in reforming the term (Davies & Herbert 1993; Keller 1988). Ironically, this jettisoning occurred at a time when the applied social sciences, notably social policy and social work, were making increasing use of the term, mainly in relation to 'community development' and 'community organising' (Day & Murdoch 1993).

Therefore, if 'community' is to be a concept and thus of use to the social sciences, it must have a precise and unambiguous meaning. In these terms it seems most appropriately applied to the communal life of many pre-capitalist societies (e.g. feudal Europe) and to the rural life of many developing countries. More importantly, if we are to understand household and residential life in contemporary cities and towns, we need to formulate a concept which would identify this social structure (Cohen & Fukui 1993). Once this is done, we would then be in a position to undertake precise empirical research, including being able to study successfully the link between households, consumerism, and residential mobility/residential development.

Consumerism

The third concept requiring clarification is 'consumerism'. This is the overriding obsession with the consumption of goods and services, specifically those providing fun, enjoyment, etc., and it is an ideology said to have become the central life-interest of the peoples of the developed world, and now increasingly those of the developing world as well (Bocock 1993; Featherstone 1991; Rojek 1993; Sklair 1991). 'The culture-ideology of consumerism proclaims, literally, that the meaning of life is to be found in the things that we possess. To consume, therefore, is to be fully alive, and to be fully alive we must continuously consume' (Sklair 1991:41).

Similar claims have been made by other writers, notably those from the relatively new and rapidly expanding fields of cultural sociology/ cultural studies (Bauman 1988; Bourdieu 1984; Bocock 1993; Harvey 1989; Savage et al. 1992). However, Sklair comes from a totally different intellectual tradition – the sociology of development – and his thesis on 'culture ideology of consumerism' is, interestingly, directed at the Third World, not the First World where consumerism is most developed culturally and socially. Sklair sees consumerism's intrusion into the Third World as being intricately linked to global capitalism, with its accompanying shifts in culture, politics and social life more generally. 'The culture-ideology of consumerism is, as it were, the fuel that powers the motor of global capitalism. The driver is the transnational capitalist class. But the vehicle itself is the mighty transnational corporation' (Sklair 1991:42).

Evidence provided by Sklair on consumerism's place in the Third World includes the rapid growth of fast-food chains, the Cola wars (between Coca-Cola, Pepsi Cola, and indigenous colas), the Nestlés breast-milk substitute scandal, and the rapidly growing consumer demands for pharmaceutical drugs, clothing and personal effects, motor vehicles, and electronic goods. In all of this, the media and the advertising industry come to reinforce consumerism.

Paradoxically, consumerism is an obsession from which few people wish to escape. The overwhelming bulk of the population – whether rich or poor, in developed or developing countries, employed or unemployed – seem to grasp consumerism with great enthusiasm and to define the quality of their lives by their consumption. Wallman

(1993:66), for example, quotes a 1980s study of unemployed men and their families in a part of Scotland with a very high rate of unemployment, and where the lives of the people are defined by their consumption; by their expenditure on 'appropriate' goods and services. For the unemployed men, employment is now no longer the source of their identity, and this shift for them reflects a wider change in terms of the growing importance of consumption as the principal source of people's identities (Bocock 1993; Lunt & Livingstone 1992). Households, then, increasingly pool income, from whatever source, to satisfy the wants/desires defined by the culture ideology of consumerism.

With consumerism markedly affecting the lives of even those on low incomes, the definition of poverty, at least in developed countries, must be reassessed. The underconsumption of wants/desires must now also be stressed, with the poor being those unable, relative to the non-poor, to satisfy the cultural goal of consuming wants/desires, and not simply needs (Cheal 1990; Preteceille & Terrail 1985).

Such is the overriding power of consumerism that it is frequently difficult to mobilise people to counter its negative consequences, in particular to slow down the continuing exploitation of non-renewable resources (Sklair 1991). The counter-culture, as the social movement leading this opposition, has become marginalised or absorbed into mainstream social and political life. This can be seen in Australia, for example, in the way the counter-culture based in northern New South Wales has apparently been absorbed into the consumerism of that region's tourism industry.

Even goods and services defined as necessities, such as dwellings and transport, have come to express the cultural ideology of consumerism. A house and a car are now important not just as shelter and as a means of transport, but for cultural reasons as well; for what they say about the consumer; for their symbolic value (Featherstone 1991). The house, the car, and other consumer goods have increasingly become expressions of the people who consume them, with goods and services now being valued not simply for their usefulness, but for their symbolic value as well. Consumption, then, defines the person, irrespective of whether there is any truth in the symbolism expressed.

It is perhaps surprising that consumerism as an ideology, and consumption as a social activity, have expanded so significantly over the last twenty years considering how this period has been a time of rolling recession and high unemployment. In Britain, for example, the rate of home ownership increased dramatically during the 1970s and 1980s (Saunders 1990), and although home ownership has remained unchanged in Australia, households at younger ages are now buying dwellings, a trend linked to new opportunities for pooling cash income, particularly in the form of two income earners, and because of easier access to credit (Neutze & Kendig 1991).

Households and Australian Metropolitan Development

The contemporary Australian metropolitan household appears to be a modified version of one formed during the economic boom of 1860–1890 and institutionalised by the state during the first decade of this century; an institutionalisation occurring after the hardship of the 1890s Depression (Castles 1985, 1988). This institutionalised household foundered in the chaos of the 1930s and 1940s, but was reconstructed with modifications over the economic boom of 1945–1971; the era in which consumerism took hold. The rolling recessions of the last two decades, in conjunction with other economic and social changes, have brought a new household structure.

Wages have always been the most important component of the income-pooling activities of Australian urban households. Until recently, this came overwhelmingly from male wage labour, at least when compared with European households, and it was a dominance partly resulting from the ready availability of high wages which enabled men to become the household's sole wage earner. It may also have been because male-led trade unions defined wage labour as white male work, with women and non-whites largely being excluded, or at least marginalised, from this income source. This pattern was institutionalised by the state in 1907 through the Harvester judgement (Castles 1985, 1988).

The high wages men earned enabled households to achieve a relatively marked degree of self-sufficiency and a high standard of living. This was clearly aided by a history of full employment and low taxes, and today Australia has the third lowest taxes of all OECD countries. With the development of import-substitution manufacturing from the 1930s/1940s, wage income became even more significant.

Australian urban households have, of course, derived income from other major sources as well, perhaps the most important until the 1940s being a highly developed domestic economy which has been called 'the urban peasantry' (Mullins 1981a, 1981b). Women were overwhelmingly responsible for producing this income, as well as income from other subsistence activities. Also, and in contrast with many European countries, the Australian state has been a more limited source and so Australian households have received far less income from here, notably during the welfare era of 1945–1975 (Castles 1985, 1988; Esping-Andersen 1990, 1993).

The greater significance of wage income among urban households from the 1860s seems to have been important for the early growth of mass consumption in Australia, this being reflected in the early high rates of home ownership, the early and rapid establishment of suburbs, the early and high rates of car ownership, and the way in which import substitution manufacturing from the 1930s/1940s came to produce consumer goods for local consumption. Therefore, although consumerism in Australia essentially had its beginning in the 1940s, the form of household necessary for this activity – a household with a high cash income – was long established in Australian cities. Thus, from the 1940s households became eager participants in mass consumption, a participation significantly extended after the 1970s as new goods and, particularly, services became available (Whitwell 1989).

Over the last two decades important changes have occurred in the structure of urban households: they have got smaller, there are more aged households, and fewer have dependent children. Table 4.1 shows a marked increase in one-parent households, and in sole-person households; changes associated with broader social alterations occurring over the last twenty-five years, such as easier divorce, more people choosing not to marry, more choosing not to have children, an increased acceptance of alternative households, and new social arrangements more generally.

At the 1991 census, one-parent families formed 10 per cent of Australian households, these being the most socially deprived of all households, while sole-person households comprised an extraordinary 20 per cent. Nuclear families (the traditional household) comprised 40 per cent, and couples made up 25 per cent. More generally, three-quarters of all these households were family households, with the rest being non-family households; most being people living by themselves.

Table 4.1 *Changes in Australian households, 1976–1986*

Household type	Percentage change 1976–81	1981–86
Couple only	+11.3	+ 8.7
Couples plus dependent children and/or other kin	+ 3.2	+ 4.4
One parent, plus dependent children and/or other kin	+43.2	+12.2
Related adults	+11.2	+22.3
Total family households	+ 8.5	+ 7.4
Non-family households	+32.1	+18.0

Source: Australian Bureau of Statistics Census 1986 – Australian Families and Households, Catalogue No. 2506.0.

There are also differences in the household structure of different cities, thus reflecting broader urban differences. Table 4.2 presents the household structures of Australia's five metropolitan areas – cities of 1 million or more – as well as three cities of more than 100 000 people. The latter are included because they identify differences in urban household structures between themselves, and between them and the five metropolitan areas. Canberra is a rapidly growing government centre with a population of 300 000; the Gold Coast is an even faster growing tourist city of about the same size; and Wollongong is a slow-growing industrial centre of 240 000. While all eight cities have similar percentages in family and non-family households – though Wollongong has a somewhat larger concentration in the former, and Adelaide and the Gold Coast have slightly more in the latter – there are differences within family households, particularly in terms of the three smaller centres, and between these and the metropolitan areas (table 4.2). The Gold Coast (especially) and Adelaide have more couple-households and fewer nuclear (two-parent) families, a pattern reflecting these cities' older populations. Indeed, with a larger aged population it is perhaps surprising that the Gold Coast did not have more people living by themselves, although it did have the largest percentage of group households, these probably being young adults sharing dwellings (table 4.2). Canberra is also somewhat distinctive, having proportionately more living in nuclear-family households, and the smallest proportion of one-parent family households.

These differences reflect variations in urban form. While the five metropolitan areas are similar cities, the Gold Coast, Canberra, and Wollongong are quite different. The Gold Coast is a rapidly developing city with a large transient population, and it also appears to have the most socially polarised population, while Canberra seems to have the least polarised. The Gold Coast has the highest rate of unemployment, the lowest income, fewer in the labour force, a different class structure (mainly because of a large *petite bourgeoisie*), a larger female population, fewer ethnic differences, and fewer children. Canberra has the lowest rate of unemployment, the highest income, more in the labour force, more children, and a distinctive class structure (specifically a larger middle class). Wollongong also has high unemployment, relatively few in the labour force, and a somewhat larger working class. These differences reflect differences in these cities' economic bases, and these in turn suggest differences in household structure and in the way households pool income and consume goods and services.

Although unemployment rates have increased sharply over the last two decades, cash income is now more crucial than ever before because of the increased demands to consume. Yet, the way cash is obtained and

Table 4.2 *Households of metropolitan areas and three selected regional cities, 1991*

Household type	Sydney	Melbourne	Brisbane	Perth	Adelaide	Gold Coast–Tweed Heads	Canberra	Wollongong
	%	%	%	%	%	%	%	%
Family households								
One parent family	9.6	9.3	10.0	10.0	9.9	8.9	10.5	9.8
Couples only	21.8	21.4	23.0	23.1	24.7	29.9	20.5	23.9
Two-parent family	40.4	42.1	40.9	40.1	37.0	32.7	44.2	43.1
Two+ families	1.1	0.9	0.7	0.4	0.5	0.7	0.5	0.9
Other family	1.7	1.6	1.6	1.4	1.3	1.4	1.0	1.1
Total	74.6	75.3	76.2	75.0	73.4	73.6	76.7	78.8
Non-family households								
Group	5.4	4.8	5.2	5.1	4.3	6.5	6.0	3.3
Sole person	20.0	19.9	18.6	19.9	22.3	19.9	17.3	17.9
Total	25.4	24.7	23.8	25.0	26.6	26.4	23.3	21.2

Source: Unpublished 1991 census data.

pooled is different now from the immediate past. Males no longer hold such a pre-eminent position as wage earners – indeed their participation rate has declined – and women are now significantly involved. The other principal source of cash income is the state, this being in the form of various social security payments, while minor sources of cash income include activities such as garage sales and the marketing of illegal drugs. However, it is difficult to find information on how cash obtained from these illegal sources – this informal economy – fit household income-pooling and consuming activities, although Pahl's (1984) British study has shown how those households most involved in the informal economy (e.g. in subsistence activities) are also those most involved in the formal economy (e.g. most likely to be employed). Such resource-rich households, then, appear to be those with the greatest opportunities to consume.

Households, Consumerism and Residential Development

Before exploring the link between households, consumerism, and fringe residential development, it is worth reviewing the reasons proffered for this development and, concomitantly, the relative stagnation of inner and middle suburbs. Distinction is made here between subjective reasons – those stated by households or individuals – and objective reasons – those derived inductively from a variety of non-subjective data.

The principal objective reason given for the movement to the fringe, which was cited at the outset of this chapter, is housing cost (Burke & Hayward 1990): it is said to be cheaper to buy a house at the fringe than elsewhere in the metropolitan area. There is need, however, to clarify this reason by examining house prices over time, particularly for the period since the 1940s (a time when fringe expansion became marked) for this will allow us to see whether fringe housing has always been cheaper. Unfortunately there is limited data available, although Badcock (1992) provides information on average house prices for eight groupings of Adelaide suburbs for the years 1970 and 1988. He showed that the most significant change in house prices occurred in the inner city. In 1970, the house prices here, and in four other of the city's eight major residential locations, were below the Adelaide average. However, by 1988 average house prices had increased markedly in inner Adelaide, to the extent that it had the second highest house prices in the city. Thus, while house prices were shown to be generally lower at the fringe than elsewhere in Adelaide, they were also relatively low in inner Adelaide in 1970, and in two of the five middle-suburban areas in both 1970 and 1988, suggesting that these were places also with relatively affordable housing.

Of course, house price in itself is not an adequate indicator of the total cost of living in a particular suburb or group of suburbs. What is needed is a measure of total cost and, in these terms, the urban consolidation debate – specifically discussions revolving around locational disadvantage – seems to suggest that life at the fringe is more expensive than life in inner and middle suburbs, relative to households' income, and their access to other resources. Since fringe households have relatively low incomes and are geographically more isolated from necessary resources and facilities, they are said to experience a higher cost of living. This suggests, then, that any gains fringe households may achieve from relatively low housing costs come to be lost from the higher overall costs of suburban living. Unfortunately, there appear to be no adequate comparative data to confirm this supposition.

In contrast with the objective data, subjective reasons for the growth of the fringe are couched primarily in terms of housing preferences. Like Australian urban households generally, there is a clear preference for the ownership of a detached dwelling (Stevens, Baum & Hassan 1992; Wulff 1993), a preference which includes mention of the residential area as well (Burgess & Skeltys 1992). Residential mobility to the fringe, then, is not just linked to housing cost but also to issues such as house design and the quality of life offered by the residential area as a whole, particularly its environmental attributes and its scenic attractiveness. In all of this, access to services and employment are of secondary importance and are not the critical issues frequently assumed (Alexander 1994; Burgess & Skeltys 1992; Maher *et al.* 1992). Similarly, the 1990 Brisbane Household and Residential Area Study, mentioned above, found 'housing' covered an array of issues, some being dwelling-specific and other ones focusing on the residential area as a whole. Greatest satisfaction was expressed by those whose housing and residential goals were most closely realised, relative to the constraints placed upon them by their cash income.

These subjective data, then, suggest that there is something about the combined character of a house and residential area which attracts households to the fringe and other households to other residential areas. This 'something' seems to be 'lifestyle', and since contemporary lifestyles are disproportionately based on the consumption of more and more goods and services, consumerism can therefore be said to be integral to this process. Residential mobility is thus not just a response to housing needs – relative to cost – but to satisfying the wants/desires evoked by the culture of consumerism as well. Those residential areas offering households the greatest opportunities to satisfy both needs and wants/desires, relative to cash income, are therefore those towards which households are most likely to gravitate. Conversely, those residential areas offering fewer opportunities for households to satisfy both needs and wants/desires, again relative to cash income, are those most likely to be avoided. Thus, low- and middle-income households who numerically dominate the metropolitan outskirts go there because it is easier to satisfy their basic needs and wants/desires in these locations.

The evidence of consumerism in contemporary societies is clearly evident in the ever-increasing mass consumption of consumer durables, including a growing commodification of goods and services once produced in the home, from food preparation to leisure/recreation (Sayer & Walker 1992; Walker 1981). Thus, today Australians spend considerable amounts of time in consumption for enjoyment, with about 20 per cent of waking hours being devoted to entertainment and leisure (Castles 1994). Associated with this trend is the growing role played by advertising and the media in promoting consumption; in expressing the cultural goal of consumerism.

In the urban studies literature, post-1970 consumerism has been subsumed in a clumsy and frequently unintelligible way under the term 'post-modernism' (Harvey 1989; Savage & Warde 1993; Savage et al. 1992; Soja 1989; Zukin 1991), with the most dramatic non-residential indicator of this process being the very rapid expansion of infrastructure of consumption. This refers to physical and social edifices built to aid consumption, and six major forms of infrastructure can be discerned.

First, there are the new shopping towns/plazas/malls/hypermarkets, most of which are concentrated on the metropolitan outskirts, and they are places which highlight the way shopping is now an 'experience' and not just a necessity (Shields 1989). Second, there are 'consumption compounds' and 'festival places': large urban precincts specially built to enable residents and tourists to buy and consume fun goods and services which are on sale. They range from Sydney's Darling Harbour and Brisbane's South Bank Parklands to Movieland and Dreamworld along the Brisbane–Gold Coast corridor. Third, there is the growth of cultural centres, specialised consumption compounds which produce 'high culture'. They draw a growing body of consumers and are increasingly developed from cultural policy: state planning for both 'high culture' and for other forms of 'culture' as well, such as 'community arts' (Bianchini & Parkinson 1993). Fourth, there has been a spectacular growth in restaurants and takeaway food establishments, places partly responding to changes in household structure, and partly to the increased desire to consume food for pleasure, with fast-food restaurants being particularly closely tied to residential development. In Brisbane they are disproportionately concentrated on the southern metropolitan outskirts. Fifth, there are major events, like the Olympic Games or Indy car races, which are held at particular periods and are intended, among other things, to capture the consumption dollar. Finally, and perhaps most dramatically, there is the growth of tourist cities and towns; centres catering specifically for people to visit so they can consume some of the great range of goods and services on sale (Mullins 1991). It is extraordinary to find Australia having three (21 per cent) of its fourteen largest urban centres (those of about 100 000+) being tourist cities, with two – the Gold Coast and the Sunshine Coast – being specially built for this purpose, and the other – Cairns – being transformed over the 1980s from a commercial centre. The Gold Coast is now Australia's eighth largest urban area and it is likely to displace Canberra to become the seventh largest within the next few years. This marked presence of tourist cities and towns suggests, then, that consumerism holds a significant place in the country's society generally and in its urban system in particular.

Although these six forms of infrastructure are the most dramatic urban expressions of contemporary consumerism, the dwelling and the residential area are the spatial and social locations of most consumption since the household is the major consuming unit. Where suburbanisation has, historically, most clearly shown the link between consumerism and residential development, gentrification is its most spectacular contemporary expression. This is a process whereby dwellings formerly occupied by the working class are refurbished for sections of the middle classes; classes that have grown rapidly over the last few decades (Savage et al. 1992; Smith 1987). Refurbished dwellings are sold as new housing to these middle-class consumers, and to other households whose lives are oriented towards living in the inner city in order to devour the many fun goods and services available there. Accompanying these residential changes is a commercial redevelopment, where old inner-city shops and warehouses are transformed into new establishments selling the goods and services so desired by gentrifiers, as well as by consumers living elsewhere who visit the area to buy what is on sale. This newly built environment of refurbished housing, of specialty shops, eating places, theatres, museums, art galleries and so on, comprises a new and unique *infrastructure of consumption*, and one clearly symbolising the culture ideology of consumerism. The level of capital invested, the nature of consumption, the distinctiveness of the gentrifiers, and the physical and social transformation of residential areas all come together to make gentrification a physically striking process.

Of course, gentrification is (essentially) a small-scale inner-city phenomenon and contrasts sharply with the extensive residential life of the metropolitan fringe; a life claimed here to be influenced by consumerism as well, though in unspectacular fashion. There are, however, new fringe residential developments which parallel, and are as spectacular as, gentrification. Having similar levels of consumption (although what is consumed is different), these places include canal estates – like those on Brisbane's northern and south-western fringes – and walled estates like Sanctuary Cove on Brisbane's southern outskirts and the northern outskirts of the Gold Coast. The consumption undertaken by the people living in these places is more expressive than that of gentrifiers – with their boats and golfing – and they lack the intellectually based 'cultural capital' of gentrifiers (Bourdieu 1984; Savage *et al.* 1992). Yet, like gentrification, these fringe residential developments are also new (post-1970) and thus express a new link between consumerism and residential development.

For the rest of the metropolitan fringe, the unspectacular link with consumerism is the result of relatively low household income. But consumerism is still expressed here, notably through the interior and exterior house designs, however modest. The contemporary kitchens reflect the way the production/provisioning of meals is now increasingly for enjoyment, rather than simply for satisfying biological needs. Bathrooms are now also places for 'experiences', with spa baths and other accoutrements, rather than simply for daily ablutions. Living areas are increasingly set aside for entertainment and other leisure pursuits, and outdoor dwelling space is being used more and more as the location for sports and leisure equipment, ranging from swimming pools to tennis courts, and from gardens of native trees to gazebos (Savage *et al.* 1992). And beyond the dwellings is the largest concentration of the most modern of the infrastructure of consumption: the shopping towns/ malls/hypermarkets, the fast-food chains, the theme parks, the sports/ leisure/entertainment centres, and other places selling fun, leisure, recreation and relaxation.

Thus, it is a combination of new housing at the fringe and the surrounding residential area which reflects a congruence with the contemporary consumerism demanded by fringe households. In contrast, old inner and middle suburbs are – except for gentrified areas – overwhelmingly places responding to consumption needs of the past, and are areas which are in social and physical decline, or, at best, transition. The housing is old and small according to standards dictated by consumerism, with many of the houses being subdivided into flats, and the interior designs are frequently seen as inadequate for contemporary household activities. Bathrooms, kitchens, living areas were designed for an era long past and they lack the facilities for a life oriented towards consumption. Bathrooms may still be out the back, cooking facilities may be too inadequate to produce the 'right' meals, there may be no garage to house the one or more cars owned by each household, bedrooms may be regarded as too small and lacking desired facilities (e.g. en suites), and there may be an insufficient number of 'appropriate' rooms. All of this may lead to criticisms of life in these suburbs. Indeed, the Brisbane Household and Residential Area Study found residents of inner and middle suburbs being more likely to complain about their area, including criticism of those who shared their location. And those households who planned to move intended to relocate to the fringe because of the benefits perceived by life in this location.

Thus, many older residential areas – those of the inner and middle suburbs – come to express negative images for many metropolitan residents; they symbolise the past rather than the contemporary period, with its focus on consumption. Of course, inner-city gentrified areas evoke quite different images and they do this because of their social and physical transformation; their past has been removed. The old dwellings, the housing of the past, have been vigorously scrubbed and refurbished to remove all signs of earlier occupancy, with new bathrooms, new kitchens, new outdoor spaces, new residential areas being built to allow, encourage, and predispose consumption. Into these houses go a new population, a select and tiny fraction of the high-consuming new middle classes (Savage *et al.* 1992). This marked physical and social transformation, then, creates a new image – a post-modern image, an image of consumerism – and it is an image contrasting sharply with those old, neighbouring residential areas in the inner city.

In summary, then, consumerism is closely linked to all contemporary residential developments, whether at the fringe or elsewhere, and this is an association which has taken different forms. The most dramatic is gentrification, because it involves the redevelopment – the total transformation – of some old inner-city residential areas, and it is the dramatic nature of this development which has disproportionately caught researchers' attention. In contrast, new and rapidly expanding fringe residential areas, though far larger and involving many more households, have drawn relatively little research attention from those interested in the link between consumerism and residential development. This is because the association is comparatively modest due to households having middle to low incomes. Yet, greater attention should be given to the fringe since its association with consumerism dates back to the 1940s, and because some components of this development are as striking as gentrification, notably canal estates and walled suburbs.

It is also important to recognise that the link identified between consumerism and contemporary residential development may parallel other major socio-spatial changes which are currently occurring in Australia. In particular, there has been, and continues to be, a massive movement of households to the northern and western parts of Australia; a socio-spatial shift representing the largest internal migration in Australia's history. One result is a new and unique urban region in south-east Queensland and far northern New South Wales, and the role of consumerism is evident here not only in the tourism of the region, but the way the internal migrants appear to have relocated for both work-related reasons and for consumption-related reasons.

It is also worth noting the way contemporary Australian urban policy is partially responding to the demands of the culture ideology of consumerism. The policy promoting the (apparently now defunct) Multi Function Polis (MFP) involved not only attracting residents by offering employment and entrepreneurial opportunities, but proffering opportunities for households to consume goods and services which provide fun: with sports, food, cultural activities, and so on. Therefore, where MFP policy is (at least implicitly) cognisant with the power of consumerism, urban consolidation and its related policies seem to lack this awareness, suggesting that their success will be constrained by a failure to recognise the power of consumerism.

Conclusion: Some Policy Implications

In summary, although the analysis given is partly conceptual and partly inductive, and needs more detailed data, it does suggest a link between consumerism and contemporary residential forms. While this link is most apparent with gentrification and striking fringe developments like canal estates, it is also evident among the low- to middle-income households who populate the fringe. What now needs to be done is to consider policy implications arising from this analysis and relate them to concerns raised in the urban consolidation debate.

The analysis suggests a fair degree of flexibility for contemporary urban policy/planning, so long as households can satisfy the cultural demands of both needs and consumerism. First, the goal of establishing medium-density housing at the urban fringe to constrain an ever-expanding metropolitan fringe is achievable so long as increased density does not infringe on consumption and other lifestyle goals.

Second, efforts to increase public transport patronage, following the creation of polynucleated employment and residential centres – at the fringe and elsewhere – should also be acceptable to households, again, so long as households' cultural expectations (their desire to consume) can be realised. And this will include the opportunity to consume cars for both symbolic and transport reasons (which may not be acceptable to many planners).

Finally, the major hurdle is getting more households to move to inner and middle suburbs. The only way this will be achieved is to redevelop the area; to renovate it so as to make it congruent with households' cultural needs. Gentrification has clearly shown how expensive this task will be, and so it is unlikely that middle- and low-income earners, who have relatively little choice about where to live, will be able to afford to buy new/refurbished housing; the costs of redevelopment will price them out of the market. If a range of households are to be attracted to these areas, then some form of government assistance will be needed, but because of costs and government efforts to cut expenditure this is an unlikely scenario. Moreover, it may be difficult to overcome the negative sentiments many urban residents feel about the inner city; sentiments appearing not only to be directed at residential areas, but at the Central Business District as well. The CBD, with its concentration of economic and political power and its built environment symbolising this power, may not be particularly attractive to the majority of the population. While some sections of the middle classes are very positive about life in the inner city, there is little evidence to suggest that this sentiment is held universally; the continuing depopulation of inner and middle suburbs seems to provide confirmation of this sentiment.

The purpose of this chapter has been to open out the debate on why households live in some, rather than other, residential areas, specifically why they have flocked, and are continuing to flock, to the metropolitan fringe, and vacating the inner and middle suburbs. The chapter suggests that the culture ideology of consumerism is the principal fuel behind the drive to the fringe, relative to households' income, and therefore any attempt to plan future housing and residential development will need to consider this cultural goal.

PART TWO

Current Policies and Options

CHAPTER 5

The Battle for Balmain

Tim Bonyhady

For over twenty-five years, Balmain has been a testing ground for a new inner-city politics characterised by the prominence of environmental and planning issues, the rise of Independents as a political force, and a commitment to open government and public participation unprecedented in Australia (Power 1969; Jakubowicz 1972; Balmain Residents Case 1975; Johnston 1979). The most notorious battles have been within the Australian Labor Party where in the 1970s branch-stacking reached new heights for this old Labor art form. In seven years the local branch grew from 70 to 700 (Wheelwright 1983). But the local council has also been the scene of major conflicts, initially over the introduction of new industries into Balmain, then their containment and now their replacement. Central to all these changes have been Balmain's new middle class who began 'gentrifying' the peninsula in the early 1960s, before this term was coined in England let alone used in Australia.[1]

The most recent conflict has involved five sites, covering 23 hectares or 7 per cent of the peninsula, which once made Balmain a centre of Australian manufacturing. The only one still operating is the Caltex plant at Ballast Point – the company's largest oil and grease plant in Australia. Ampol turned its old headquarters on the edge of White Bay into just a distribution point for its refinery in Queensland before closing it down altogether in 1993. Unilever moved its adjoining detergent plant to the Macarthur Growth Centre in the late 1970s and

---

1 The term 'gentrification' appears to have been coined by Ruth Glass (1964:xviii). According to Zulia Nittim (1980:232) it was first used in Australia when R.E. Pahl visited Sydney in 1970.

closed its soap manufactory – once the largest in the southern hemisphere – in 1988. Chemplex's plant at Iron Cove, the site of the first industrial production of chemicals in Australia, shut down in 1989. The adjoining Balmain Power Station stopped producing electricity in 1972 and was decommissioned in 1976 (Cardew & Rich 1982:124; LC 1990a:66, 107, 120, 145, 149, 150, 157).

The redevelopment of these five sites could improve the amenity of Balmain by ridding the peninsula of contaminated industrial land and creating new access to Sydney Harbour. But if the developers have their way the five sites will bring another 3000 people to Balmain. If the same happened on the other 40 hectares of industrial land in Balmain expected to come up for rezoning in the next few years, the peninsula's population could rise from 15 300 to 26 000. The problem with these increases is not the number of people. Like most of Australia's inner suburbs, Balmain's population has been steadily declining. But because occupancy rates have also fallen, the developers would need to build on a scale out of all proportion to the existing environment. The redevelopments would also radically increase the number of cars in Balmain which in 1971 stood at just 0.66 vehicles per household but by 1986 had increased to 1.04. Instead of 7850 cars there could be 12 500 (Commissioners of Inquiry for Environment and Planning 1991:65; LC 1992a:3).

The conflict over the five sites has been unprecedented, even in Balmain. While commentators in the early 1980s were quick to warn that government could not radically increase the densities of Australia's inner cities without significant opposition from existing residents (Sandercock 1983:6), no one could have predicted what has happened since the owners of the five sites asked Leichhardt Council to rezone them in 1989. So far the council's planners have prepared two reports on the rezonings, the State's Commissioners of Inquiry for Environment and Planning have conducted a public hearing, and a planning consultant has held a series of workshops. The five sites have also gone twice to the Land and Environment Court and twice to the Court of Appeal. The State government has appointed a planning administrator for Balmain and made a special State Environmental Planning Policy and a Regional Environmental Plan in order to get its way. Still the five sites have not been rezoned.[2]

This latest 'Battle for Balmain' has become a *cause célèbre* because the dispute has gone on so long and involved so many parties. No less

2 For a very different interpretation of this conflict, see Michael Bounds (1993a, 1993b:14–18).

significant has been the adroitness with which all sides have presented their actions as if they were of larger consequence, exploiting the tendency to see anything which happens in Balmain as of more than local interest because it is one of Australia's few iconic suburbs. Not least, there has been the failure of the State government to impose its will when the environmental planning system in New South Wales is notorious for the government's power to get its way. While it is not unusual for the State to fail once, for it to lose twice, two years apart over the same sites, is something even the New South Wales Forestry Commission has avoided despite its long record of breaching environmental laws (Bonyhady 1993:ch.5).

Yet are the five sites of more than local significance, as has generally been accepted? For example, Sandra Nori, the residents' greatest supporter in State parliament, claimed in 1991 that 'what the Government was trying to do on the Balmain peninsula was really only a forerunner for the rest of the inner city' (NSWPD 23 Feb. 1991:105). A feature article in the *Sydney Morning Herald* characterised Balmain as 'the proving ground for the entire [State] strategy for Sydney's growth into the second decade of the next century'. According to the newspaper, what happened in Balmain would demonstrate the government's capacity to curb 'the westward sprawl of the city down the basins of the Hawkesbury and Nepean rivers, [by] recycling hundreds of hectares of inner-city industrial land across five suburbs and three councils, levelling the docks and the silos and the tank farms for housing' (*SMH* 23 Feb. 1991:41; Bounds 1993a:7, 10; Bounds 1993b:17).

These claims ignore the fact that few suburbs can match Balmain's capacity to defend itself against unwanted development. Even if the residents achieved all their aims for the five sites, this success would be unlikely to deter the State government from supporting similar high-density proposals for suburbs such as Pyrmont and Surry Hills because it would not expect the same degree of opposition.

The suggestion that what happens in Balmain could affect the urban fringe is equally unlikely – an example of the success of the State government in presenting its intervention as if its sole concern were 'urban consolidation'. So seductive is the prospect of stopping Sydney's sprawl that the government's claims have generally been accepted without scrutiny. Yet even the most intense development of every industrial site in inner Sydney could not achieve the government's goals, as these sites could not accommodate all the people who move to the urban fringe each year. The nexus between the density of residential development and the extent of urban sprawl is also particularly weak when inner-city redevelopment is for the upper middle class. As Sandra Nori put it in 1992, 'How many people going out west will turn around and say I'm going to pay more than $500,000 to live in Balmain?' (*SMH* 19 Sept. 1992:3; *SMH* 22 Feb. 1992:7; NSWPD 6 May 1992:3664).[3]

A better starting point is to view the conflict over the five sites as primarily a competition between private interests. On one side have been local residents eager to protect if not enhance their amenity and property values by keeping the densities of the redevelopments as low as possible and forcing the developers to part with as much land as possible for public open space. On the other side have been the owners of the five sites anxious to develop as much of their land as intensely as possible. Many of the residents are successful professionals, unusually adept at promoting their own interests. The developers include Caltex, Kerry Packer's Chemplex and the New South Wales Electricity Commission.

This conflict between powerful private interests has gained a public dimension partly because each side has had its cause taken up by government. While Independents have controlled Leichhardt Council, they have upheld the local interest in trying to preserve Balmain from over-development. The State government has been an obliging servant of big business while pursuing its own self-interest in minimising its loss from the Balmain Power Station, which has proved so badly polluted that it will cost more to clean up than the land can be sold for once it has been decontaminated. The result has been no ordinary test of the power of local residents, developers, councils and State governments. The strongest of the residents' groups and the most defiant of councils have opposed the largest of corporations and the least tractable of State governments.

This characterisation of the conflict over the five sites does not fit neatly within the various theories of the role of government in the urban arena. One theory has government as an instrument of capital. Another conceives it as 'relatively autonomous' – usually but not always representing the interests of the dominant class. A third has it as an arbiter between capital and socialism or private property and social justice (Sandercock & Berry 1983:xi; Badcock 1984:chs.3, 9; Forrest & Burnley 1985:5–6; Forrest 1985:183). While government undoubtedly fills all these roles at different times (McLoughlin 1992:13), the five sites suggest another possibility with the different arms of government acting as both agents of and arbiters between different fractions of capital.

Local councils and State governments frequently assume these oppositional roles, particularly over the redevelopment of old industrial

---

3 Only apartments at Ballast Point and on the waterfront on the Power Station and Chemplex sites will probably cost $500 000. Elsewhere they will probably start from $250 000.

land in inner-city suburbs. As in Balmain, most of these sites are contaminated and, because of the costs of clean-up, their owners are especially prone to devise vast projects which display little or no concern for their impact on their surroundings. Consequently, local residents and councils are quick to oppose them; State governments – whether Liberal or Labor – have been quick to take special measures to see they proceed. The result, almost always, is conflict, often extending over several years.[4]

The Rights of Property

When the owners of the five sites began asking Leichhardt Council for permission to redevelop their land, they had no right to a rezoning. As part of what, on paper, was a radical change to land ownership in New South Wales, first the Local Government Act in 1945 and then the Environmental Planning and Assessment Act (EPAA) in 1979 treated the framework governing the use of land as a matter of public policy, not individual entitlement. Hence the owners of the five sites could not even formally apply to turn their land to new uses prohibited by the existing planning schemes.[5] Nor could they formally appeal to the Land and Environment Court if the council refused their requests.

Nonetheless, the developers, residents, Leichhardt Council and State government all assumed that the site-owners were entitled to some form of rezoning. Their assumption – articulated most clearly by the Commissioners of Inquiry in 1991 – was that the sites were too important to remain dormant and that their owners had a right to develop them (Commissioners of Inquiry for Environment and Planning 1991:1, 20). If the council refused, the State government could impose its will on Balmain. Unlike the land owners, the Minister for Planning could direct the council to make new environmental plans. So long as the sites were of regional significance the Minister could 'call in' development applications from the companies and, after holding a public inquiry, approve

4 The Mobil site at Pulpit Point in Hunter's Hill and the North Shore Gas Company site on Wollstonecraft Bay at Waverton are two other recent examples of this type of conflict in Sydney. See North Shore Gas Company v North Sydney Municipal Company 1991; Harris 1991.
5 In 1989 the Greiner government introduced Part 3, Division 4 of the Environmental Planning and Assessment Act which provides that developers may appeal to the Land and Environment Court against refusals by councils to spot-rezone for medium-density residential housing. But this mechanism for developer-initiated rezonings has not come into effect because parliament disallowed the necessary regulations.

them without any rezoning. Alternatively, the Minister could rezone them by making a regional plan. The Minister could even strip the council of its powers by appointing a planning administrator or authorise the redevelopments by special legislation (*LC* v *Minister for Planning* 1992).

Whereas the Environmental Planning Act was premised on councils making comprehensive plans for their areas after examining the interrelationships between different forms of land use, each of the developers wanted 'spot zonings' covering just their own sites. These rezonings, which typically are the obverse of planning, have become the norm in New South Wales. Each year about 80 per cent of rezonings have been of this type, leading to an extraordinary mosaic of plans in most municipalities. A survey prepared in 1987 found that thirteen councils had over 100 local plans; three had between 150 and 200; one had over 200. In 1991 three councils had over 200 local plans. Only five had prepared comprehensive documents (Auster 1984:347–53; Jonathon Falk Planning Consultants 1987:199; Ryan 1987:199; *New Planner* 1991:10).

While a majority of the Leichhardt Council opposed the developers' plans for their sites, the State government's powers prompted the council to embark on the rezoning process by exhibiting draft plans for each site, starting in November 1989. The usual practice is that these plans represent the council's vision of the best use of these areas. But the plans exhibited for the five sites simply reflected the developers' aspirations as the council made clear at the time, declaring that its preparation and display of the plans should not be interpreted as indicating that it approved their contents. The council adopted this approach in order to demonstrate its ambivalence about the developers' plans though, as its planners subsequently emphasised, this process also allowed local residents an early, 'unfiltered' opportunity to participate in the rezonings (*SMH* 25 Aug. 1990:7; Coker 1991:8–9).

By April the State government was impatient with the council which was among the slowest in Sydney to make planning decisions. One reason for the council's slowness was its commitment to open government. Another was the difficulty of making so many planning decisions in Leichhardt because the municipality was in flux – no longer blue-collar industrial, not yet completely gentrified-residential (Leichhardt Public Inquiry 1990/1991:16, 26). But still the council had become notorious for how long it took. As Ian Kiernan quipped at the time, when people asked him about his solo yacht trip round the world, he replied that it was the most exciting thing to happen to him. The second most exciting was to get a development application through the Leichhardt Council (*Glebe* 13 Mar. 1991:13).

The State government's problem was that, for all its powers, it knew that its intervention could delay rather than accelerate the rezonings. One possibility considered by the Department of Planning was to take control of the sites from the council by preparing a regional environmental plan. Another was to second one of its officers to the council in order to help it to complete a report on the rezonings. Whereas an extra planner could enable the council to finish examining the sites in six weeks, a regional plan would take much longer and 'lead to considerable animosity between the council and the Government which in turn could lead to even longer delays'. While the department recognised that there was 'no guarantee' the council would support the rezonings, it believed that 'all indications' were 'positive' (*Balmain Association (BA)* v *Planning Administrator for the Leichhardt Council* 1991a:615, 622).

Eleven days later, the council imposed a moratorium on all rezonings in Balmain so that it could prepare a new plan for the entire peninsula – a process which would freeze development of the five sites for up to a year. While the State government promptly accused it of being obstructionist, the council had good reason to take this step because of the significance of the five sites within Balmain: 1500 local residents had called on it to do so. Only a dearth of resources had stopped the council preparing such a plan earlier. Having resolved to prepare a comprehensive local plan in 1986, it had done nothing because other issues were more pressing (*BA* v *Planning Administrator for the Leichhardt Council* 1991a:615, 624; NSWPD 12 Sept. 1990:7050, 21 Feb. 1991:10, 21 Mar. 1991:1567; Coker 1991:8–9).

Hard Ball

Approval of major redevelopments is ill-left to the faint-hearted. Bluff and bullying are commonplace. If owners of large industrial plants do not threaten to take up their bat and ball and go interstate or overseas, they threaten to upgrade their plants, blighting the neighbourhood for years. The Electricity Commission and the owners of the Ampol and Unilever sites could not play this game because they had closed down their operations. But Chemplex could as its chloroflurocarbon plant at Iron Cove was still intact. So could Caltex because its plant was in full production.

According to the planners who acted as consultants to Chemplex, redevelopment of the company's site had become less attractive because of the increasing difficulty of finding sites for chemical plants, new restrictions on the disposal of contaminated waste and the falling property market. By their account, Chemplex's use of its existing site was not only authorised by its current zoning but the company was also entitled to extend its operations. If it did so, peak traffic from its plant would rise from 30 to 570 vehicles an hour, including 190 trucks – much more than if Chemplex were allowed to turn its site over to residential development. The State government might also be unable to redevelop the Balmain Power Station because of the need to maintain a buffer between industrial and residential land (Planning Workshop 1990; *Glebe* 25 Apr. 1990:3).

These claims were not entirely unfounded. As demonstrated by Chemplex's abandonment of its plans to establish a new plant in Newcastle, the company was finding it harder to find new sites for its operations and Sydney's Castlereagh Waste Depot had stopped accepting all contaminated soil. But, as the council's planners advised the council, the decline in the property market was of little account since the redevelopment of Chemplex's site would take at least two to three years and the market might have improved by then. More significantly, Chemplex's plant was in breach of its 'industrial waterfront' zoning because it did not require a waterfront location. While Chemplex could still seek approval to extend its plant, it could not be confident of obtaining the consent of either the council or the Land and Environment Court (Leichhardt Town Planner 1990).

Local residents showed their disdain for the company's threat when a crowd of 700 packed the Balmain Town Hall in support of the moratorium. But three Labor aldermen still switched their votes. After watching Chemplex operate next to Balmain High School for thirty years, Bill Brady declared that the council should not miss this opportunity to get rid of it. On the basis that there was a 'real possibility that further delay' would lead to 'an upgraded chemical plant' next to the school, the council exempted Chemplex from the moratorium. Within a fortnight, Caltex announced that it also was considering upgrading its plant so that it could use it for another ten years (*Glebe* 23 May 1990:3, 6 Jun. 1990:1 and 13, 13 Jun. 1990:7; *BA* v *Planning Administrator for the Leichhardt Council* 1991a:615, 623).

The council's exemption of Chemplex was not enough for the Minister for Planning, David Hay, who was under no immediate political constraints in deciding what to do about the five sites. The local member was an Independent, the former Olympic swimming champion Dawn Fraser, who had taken Balmain from the Labor Party with a 22 per cent swing in 1988, relying on little else than the slogan 'Our Dawn, Our Balmain'. At the next election Balmain was likely to be combined with part of the adjoining seat of McKell, held by the Labor Party's Sandra Nori. If the State's electoral commissioners made this change, the new seat would be a contest between Fraser and Nori. The Liberal Party could not win – hence local opinion in Balmain was of little or no consequence to it (*SH* 27 Feb. 1991:30; *WSC* 6 Mar. 1991:4; *SMH* 6 May 1991:6).

Hay could not have been more eager to help the owners of the five sites. Over a period of eight days in late May to early June he saw the developers' representatives three times. While in Cairns, the developers briefed him by telephone on the latest actions of the council. According to an internal company memo, the Minister advised Caltex that it should 'make very clear to the residents' that, if its land were not rezoned, it would carry out its threat to expand its operations at Ballast Point. At another meeting Hay dismissed the council's actions as 'ridiculous'. In mid-June he directed the council to submit draft plans for all five sites within five weeks (Hay 1990; *BA* v *Planning Administrator for Leichhardt Council* 1991a:615, 622; NSWPD 21 Feb. 1991:106; *SMH* 22 Feb. 1991:5; *TM* 22 Feb. 1991:26; *Glebe* 27 Feb. 1991:6).

What They Didn't Know

The last twenty years have been rich in talk of informed consent, not just in the medical arena. While New South Wales has been quicker to embrace environmental impact assessment and environmental studies than any other part of Australia, the gap between rhetoric and practice has been vast. Not only have most of the studies been superficial but even the most limited investigations have been sacrificed in the State government's enthusiasm to facilitate development. Hay's deadline of five weeks made a mockery of informed decision-making, particularly when the need to clean up the sites before they were redeveloped meant that no building could start for at least a year (*SMH* 18 Oct. 1991:1; Smyth 1992:16).

Leichhardt could have only complied with Hay's deadline if its planners had reported on the sites in less than three weeks. Even with the help of the officer from the State department who began working with them in late June, the council could have only provided recommendations, not reasons. Consequently, the council's chief planner, Allan Coker, sought an extension from Hay's department which indicated that it might give the council 'some latitude' provided the planners made 'a concerted effort' to report within the five weeks (Leichhardt Metropolitan Town Planner 1990; *Glebe* 27 Jun. 1990:6; LC 1990a:9). By often working until midnight, the planners finished in nine weeks – a remarkable achievement given their report ran to over 200 single-spaced pages.

Because the planners reported so soon, there was much they did not know about car-parking and traffic – the issues of greatest concern to local residents. Even though the planners had shown the foresight to commission a major traffic study from consultants at the start of the year, it was only half ready. Even more significantly, the State's Roads and Traffic Authority failed to comment on the rezonings. Because only it had the power and money to act on the consultants' report, the planners were left with a series of proposals for how traffic could be discouraged or controlled but no idea whether they would be acted on – something they only acknowledged at the end of the year (LC 1990a:17; LC 1990b:2).

The planners were none the wiser about contamination of the Ampol, Unilever and Caltex sites, having received no information from either their owners or the State Pollution Control Commission. While an initial study by consultants employed by Chemplex revealed that its site contained 'a wide range of heavy metals, organic pesticides, and isolated areas of PCB contamination, petroleum hyrdocarbons, and high sulphur/acid producing soils', the planners did not know whether a clean-up could make it fit for residential development. A report submitted to the Pollution Control Commission by consultants employed by the Electricity Commission showed that PCBs at the Balmain Power Station were at levels far above those set for residential land and open space. Again the planners had received no advice as to whether this site could be contaminated. But as they advised the council, neither this ignorance nor the contamination of the land precluded the council from rezoning the five sites (*SMH* 20 Jun. 1990:7; LC 1990a:11, 60–1, 93, 134–6, 156, 158, 177).

What They Couldn't Do

The impotence of planners is notorious. They sometimes can stop things but rarely start them. Their plans are usually no less dependent on developers than on other branches of government. After analysing land-use controls from Broadmeadows to Berwick in 'Shaping Melbourne's Future', Brian McLoughlin concluded that local planning works when the interests of all parties coincide! Otherwise he found that planning fails, particularly if developers do not cooperate with local councils (McLoughlin 1992:223).

Leichhardt's planners grappled with the limitations of local government as part of examining how the council could acquire part of the five sites as parkland. Because Leichhardt was among the Sydney municipalities with least open space per head of population, the council had strong reason to do so. Three of the sites were also particularly suited for open space because they included long stretches of foreshore. The State government had already identified Ballast Point as suitable for a park in its regional environmental plan for Sydney Harbour. The planners recognised it would be a 'magnificent' addition to the public domain (LC 1990a:36, 167).

While the council had the power to buy the five sites, they were far beyond its budget because of the way in which land is valued when it is resumed. Instead of the price being fixed according to the existing zoning, the land is valued according to its 'highest and best' use which would give its owner the greatest possible return. According to this system, the zoning of an area such as Ballast Point as industrial is irrelevant; so is the fact that Caltex had no right to have it reclassified. The valuation is based on the land being residential. On this basis, Ballast Point could easily be worth $25 million. Caltex gave it a boom-time valuation of $50 million (EPAA 1979a:s.27; LC 1990a:36, 167; LC 1990b:36; Commissioners of Inquiry 1991:60; *Glebe* 1 Aug. 1990:2, 15 Aug. 1990:11; Leichhardt Assistant Treasurer 1991).

Yet even if the council could have acquired Ballast Point for its unimproved capital value of $5 million, or $200 for each ratepayer in Leichhardt, the council would have been unable to raise this sum because of the State government's controls over its finances. The council's loans were controlled by the Minister for Local Government who allowed them to be used only for essential road and sewerage works. Its power to impose special rates again required ministerial permission (Leichhardt Assistant Treasurer 1991).

While the council was eligible for a grant from the Department of Planning's Sydney Regional Development and Open Space Fund, the State government refused because of its commitment to redevelopment of the site and its own budgetary constraints (*Glebe* 1 Aug. 1990:2, 15 Aug. 1990:11).

The council's only other option was to exercise its power to require developers to meet new demand for open space generated by their projects. When the council had tried to use this provision in 1981 to increase the proportion of open space in Leichhardt – which was one of the lowest in Sydney per head of population – two assessors of the Land and Environment Court had held that the council could not require developers to satisfy a higher standard than existed in Leichhardt. This decision was not binding so far as other cases were concerned. It was flawed by the assessors' failure to reason to their conclusion. If followed it would also have had the unfortunate result of perpetuating existing inequalities between different parts of Sydney. Even so, the planners advised that Leichhardt was bound by this decision and hence could demand no more than the existing standard of 1.7 hectares per 1000 people (*Revay & Scott* v *LC* 1981:625; Pickles 1983:14; LC 1990b: 26, 29, 83, 90).

The planners also warned that this power was dependent on the intensity of the redevelopments – an awkward nexus. If the council allowed the site-owners to develop their land more densely and hence bring more people to Balmain – something the council did not want to do – it could require them to dedicate more land as open space. The bulk and scale of the development would be greater, there would be more traffic but there would also be more parkland. If the council forced them to develop the land less intensely, the site-owners would have to provide less land. On one set of figures, low density development, covering half of each site, could result in as little as 17 per cent of the sites becoming open space. High density could result in 42 per cent becoming parkland (LC 1990a:35–41; LC 1990b:44, 82).

Beyond Science

The notion of planning as a political matter is a commonplace. In *Ideas for Australian Cities* Hugh Stretton explained how values could not be avoided even by traffic planners whose work appears most mechanistic. Whether deciding to put a premium on cost or speed or fixing a minimum standard of transport safety, planners could not be neutral. According to Stretton, no planning information was 'more political – and moral or immoral – than the traffic planner's choice of what to feed into his computer'. Planners, he declared, could not escape making value judgements even though many of them denied the politics of their work, insisting on 'posing as neutral, technical, unbiased servants of the people' (Stretton 1970:271–6).

Nothing had changed in Leichhardt twenty years later. When the planners prepared their first report on the five sites, their premise was that they were professionals offering 'an objective and balanced appraisal' rather than making value judgements or implementing the wishes of their political masters. When they listed the 'diverse groups' with an interest in their report, they put the council last each time. As the planners defined it, their report sought 'to balance the needs and expectations of . . . residents, developers, State Government and the Council' (LC 1990a:1, 3).

The planners' assertion of neutrality was hardly surprising given the pressure that they were under from the competing interests. 'Objectivity' was a way for the planners to distinguish themselves from the parties – to try to avoid being seen as biased, even corrupt (LC 1990b:2). But despite their assertions, the planners inevitably brought their own values and assumptions to their task including not just their sense of what was important but also their sense of what was possible. Their invocation of 'balance' was no less political, for all its connotations of fairness and equity. The only way in which the planners could take account of the different interests was to reach a value judgement to give equal or different weight to them.

In practice, the planners did not weigh all the competing interests which they identified. Most of their report was devoted to the competition between the residents and the developers. On the one hand, the planners recognised that since residents 'have to live with the effects of change', they should be able to 'contribute to the processes which bring about change'. On the other hand, they emphasised that developers, 'confronted with the *daunting* tasks of planning, financing and executing development projects', should 'receive reasonable returns on their investment' (emphasis added). While they could not meet the 'full expectations' of both groups, the planners believed that they could produce 'a reasonable outcome' between the two extremes (LC 1990a:193, 194).

The planners were equally alive to the policies of the State government – particularly its commitment to urban consolidation. One reason was that they implicitly accepted consolidation as an appropriate response to 'population decline in the established suburbs, the rising costs and constraints of fringe development, and the desire for more efficient use of urban land and infrastructure'. Another was that the planners believed that it would be futile to do otherwise because their plans 'would be unacceptable to the State government and ... the Minister would amend them accordingly' (LC 1990a:10, 191, 193).

The council was absent from this calculus, as the planners themselves acknowledged when they declared their aim was to offer 'a higher level of amenity and environmental quality for residents, viable margins for developers, and a plan which compl[ied] with State Government policies and directions'. Apart from recognising that residential redevelopment of the five sites would increase both its rate base and its obligations, the planners acted as if the council had no interest in the rezonings. While the planners may have taken this approach partly because the council had no clear policies on the rezonings, they also seem to have seen the council in their own self-image, as a neutral arbiter between opposing forces (LC 1990a:3, 190).

Turning Values into Numbers

The numbers employed by planners are sometimes pseudo-science embraced by a profession eager to demonstrate that it deals in more than subjectivities. Sometimes they are a device for avoiding having to consider the merits of particular projects. But they are not simply a vehicle for obfuscation and laziness. They are also a way of implementing political decisions and achieving environmental and social goals – an essential means of translating the subjective into the objective by giving form to values.

The most notorious numerical standard has been the requirement that developers provide 7 acres (now 2.83 hectares) of open space per 1000 people. Having been fixed in England in the early 1900s for recreation grounds for children, this standard was adopted in Australia because Brown and Sherrard set it in their text on town and country planning which was the bible of most Australian planners after World War II (Brown & Sherrard 1951, 1969:145; Shiels 1989:12; Roberts 1992:17). Its continued application on the urban fringe of Sydney has simply been a consequence of maintaining the status quo. A report to the Department of Planning in 1989 acknowledged that 2.83 hectares was 'arbitary' but declared that in 'the absence of any more definitive figure' it was 'an appropriate standard which should continue to be used' (Commissioner of Inquiry for Environment and Planning 1989: 84–5).[6]

A similar problem was highlighted by Leichhardt's planners when they looked to set floor space ratios which would control the density of the redevelopment of the five sites by fixing the maximum amount of floor space that could be developed as a ratio of the area of each site. In searching for an appropriate standard, the planners examined one of the State government's policies for urban consolidation which set ratios of 0.5:1, 0.8:1 and 1:1 for 'low', 'medium' and 'high' density town-houses. While as planners they had no reason to expect anything else, they were still disappointed to find that there was 'no statistical or research basis' for the State government's numbers (LC 1990a:40–1).

In recommending their ratios, the planners had to decide whether the five sites should be developed at lower, similar or higher densities than the rest of Balmain. Because they approached this issue on the basis that traffic and noise in the area were already operating at 'marginal', if not 'unacceptable' levels, the planners might well have concluded that the density of the redevelopments should be kept as low as possible. Instead they leaped to the premise that a 'fair' approach was that the redevelopments should not be at a 'significantly higher density' than the rest of Balmain. When the planners recommended ratios for the sites, their object was to achieve 'a level of development . . . commensurate in . . . density, scale and bulk with the existing pattern of development on the Balmain Peninsula' (LC 1990a:27–8).

6 The position may be changing now as a result of the work of Manidis Roberts, see *Revcourt Pty Ltd* v *Wingecarribee SC* 1993.

The planners fixed these limits by initially setting 'gross floor space ratios' which applied to the whole of each site and then converting these proportions into much higher 'nett floor space ratios' which applied to the land remaining after the developers had dedicated their open space (LC 1990a:103, 175, 187). While the planners initially attributed their adoption of this process to legal advice, it seems to have rested simply on their sense of fairness to the site-owners. The planners knew that developers generally avoid having to dedicate any of their land as open space by making payments meant to be the monetary equivalent of the land but in practice set much lower. Because developers then not only make this saving but also enjoy their floor space ratio over their entire plots, the planners believed that the site-owners should enjoy at least this benefit when required to dedicate land (LC 1990a:103; LC 1990b:48).

The flaw in this approach was that it gave the developers a bonus without regard to the environmental consequences, jeopardising if not contradicting the planners' own premise that the five sites should conform to the existing landscape of Balmain. The problem was that their 'gross' ratios of 0.7:1 for Caltex, Ampol and Unilever and 0.8:1 for the Balmain Power Station and Chemplex already allowed medium-density development according to the State government's figures and were significantly greater than the existing density of about 0.5:1 in Balmain. When these 'gross' figures were converted into 'nett' densities of around 1:1, they permitted development at densities twice as great as those which already existed.

Far from striking a balance between the residents and the developers, these recommendations also gave the developers most of what they wanted for the Power Station, Ampol and Unilever sites. They were closer to the residents' proposals in relation to the Chemplex and Caltex sites, cutting the Chemplex proposal down from 346 to 268 units and the Caltex proposal from 163 units to 104 units of the same size. But even so, the result on Ballast Point would have been five- or six-storey towers when most of the surrounding buildings were one- or two-storey houses (*SMH* 18 Aug. 1990:9; *AFR* 20 Aug. 1990:45).

Developers' Heaven

When State governments strip local councils of their powers, the administrators and commissioners who take over have the same autonomy as the councils they replace. But they also have a job to do. When Sir Robert Askin sacked the Sydney City Council in 1967 the commissioners' planning meetings took an average of three minutes. At one meeting they approved 1.2 million square metres of office space. In all, development approvals increased 1000 per cent. When the Victorian government dismissed the Melbourne City Council in 1981 the commissioners issued a record number of planning permits in their first four months in office. The Chief Commissioner proudly declared, 'We have got to the point now where the Planning Department is almost waiting for the next applicant to come in the door' (Saunders 1984b:102; Ashton 1993:92–4).

Hay intervened in Balmain after the council had considered its planners' report, a week after receiving it, before 500 residents whom even the State government acknowledged were 'overwhelmed by the voluminous apparently complex nature of the report' (*BA* v *Planning Administrator for Leichhardt Council* 1991a:615, 626). The council's dilemma at this meeting was acute. If it ignored the confusion among its constituents and submitted draft plans for each site, Hay would probably take no further action against it, but if it began by holding a public hearing as requested by local residents, Hay would intervene. The council also knew that if it submitted its plans, Hay could probably alter only their details, not their substance. If Hay took over the rezonings, he could do what he liked (EPAA 1979b). After Labor's Kate Butler broke Caucus to side with the Independents, the council voted 6–5 to hold a public hearing. A week later, Hay appointed Sean O'Toole, an Assistant Director of Hay's own department, as planning administrator for Balmain (Minister for Planning 1990; Government Gazette 1990:7841; *Glebe* 29 Aug. 1990:1 and 2, 5 Sept. 1990:1 and 2, 12 Sept. 1990:5, 26 Sept. 1990:2; *SMH* 1 Sept. 1990:9).

O'Toole promptly rescinded the council's decision to hold a public hearing but otherwise began as if he were not a ministerial appointee. Emphasising that he had received no directions from Hay or the Director of Planning, O'Toole announced that he would not rezone the sites until he had received the second stage of the Balmain traffic study and more information about contamination of each site. While limiting participation to invitation only, he convened a series of workshops on each site as well as more general issues such as open space and traffic. As a council of one, he held meetings twice a month, inviting the residents to attend and speak in accordance with the council's usual practice. At a public meeting at the town hall, he dwelt on the 'agony' of his decision, the difficult position in which he had been 'put' and his 'hopes' that he would reach the 'right' conclusions (*Glebe* 12 Sept. 1990:2 and 12, 19 Sept. 1990:2, 26 Sept. 1990:2, 31 Oct. 1990:5, 12 Dec. 1990:1; *EH* 15 Nov. 1990:7; BA 1991).

This process took three-and-a-half months when the council had expected its public hearing to take five weeks. When the council's planners presented O'Toole with a new 150-page report in December, the traffic study was finished and the Roads and Traffic Authority had commented on the draft plans for the rezonings. The State Pollution Control Commission had also advised that contamination would not pose 'a long-term restraint' to redevelopment of the land since sites of a 'similar nature' had been rehabilitated to 'accommodate unrestricted residential use'. But this 'opinion' was unsupported by any evidence except for the Balmain Power Station. Because the consultants employed by Monsanto, Caltex, Ampol and Unilever had not submitted their reports, the commission had not assessed the contamination of the sites (LC 1990b:94).

The planners' conclusions were much the same as in their first report. Once again they started from the premise that the sites should be developed at densities in keeping with the land which surrounded them. Again they jeopardised this goal through the generosity of their recommendations. While they repeated their original proposals for the Ampol, Chemplex and Caltex sites, they upped the floor space ratio for the Unilever site by 0.1 because its owner wanted a different mix of residential and hi-tech industry. They similarly increased the ratio for the power station site having reassessed its topography (LC 1990b: 50–4).

These increases were not enough for Sean O'Toole who, far from deferring his decision in keeping with his original commitments, took one day to recommend further increases for all five sites over and above those recommended by the planners. In doing so, O'Toole fell just 0.1 short of the developer's proposals for the Unilever and Caltex sites. He gave Kerry Packer, Ampol and the Electricity Commission exactly what they wanted. Because of the difference between gross and nett floor space ratios, these changes radically increased the site-owners' freedom – entitling them to develop their land to a bulk and scale out of all proportion to the surrounding land or any other developments in the rest of the peninsula (LC 1990b:50–3; *Glebe* 12 Dec. 1990:1, 32).

Yuppie Trotskyites and Left-wing Communists

One of the functions of local councils is to defend the interests of their constituents – if need be in the courts. Members of councils dismissed by State governments have occasionally tried to stop this usurpation of their powers. When the Unsworth government sacked the Sydney City Council in 1987 only special legislation stopped the Lord Mayor, Doug Sutherland, claiming a breach of natural justice (*Local Government Bulletin* 1987:9). But until 1990 local residents had never defended their elected representatives in this way. Either they had presumed that such action would be futile or they had lacked the means or enthusiasm to resort to litigation.

When Hay appointed O'Toole, the Leichhardt Council did nothing. According to the local newspaper *Glebe*, a majority of councillors were pleased not to find themselves out of office and anxious not to give the State government any new reason to act against them. The Local Government Association was equally 'wimpish' according to one of its own vice presidents, Alderman Peter Woods of Concord. Far from defending Leichhardt because Hay's intervention raised issues of consequence for all councils, the association's president, Frank McKay, applauded Hay's restraint and implicitly criticised the council's slowness to make planning decisions. When the association's board met a fortnight later, it simply reminded Hay of its policy that the State government should hold public hearings before appointing administrators (*SMH* 3 Sept. 1990:3, 15 Sept. 1990:28; *EH* 6 Sept. 1990:4; *Glebe* 12 Sept. 1990:4, 19 Sept. 1990:2).

Any possibility of the council challenging Hay's decision depended on Leichhardt's next Mayor. The two candidates were the ALP's Bill Brady and an Independent, Larry Hand. Politicking before the election was intense for a job with an allowance of just $22 000. After Labor's Kate Butler again defied the ALP by supporting Hand, the ballot was tied six each. But on a draw from a hat, Brady became Mayor. Far from taking to the courts, he was keen to cooperate with O'Toole because he believed that the rezonings were inevitable and would benefit Balmain by ridding it of Caltex and Chemplex (*SMH* 6 Sept. 1990:9; *Glebe* 26 Sept. 1990:7, 3 Oct. 1990:2).

The only other possible source of opposition to Hay's intervention was local residents, particularly those who owned houses near the five sites. While their concern for Balmain was far from simply financial, they had more to lose than their elected representatives because their investments were at risk. They also had more to gain if they could minimise traffic in the peninsula and secure a significant part of the five sites as public open space. Three of the residents who campaigned most actively against the rezonings lived in Wharf Road, the harbour-side street which runs from Birchgrove Park to Ballast Point.

These local campaigners were as quick to invoke their property rights as the developers. They believed that they should prevail because they represented the owners of 'billions of dollars of real estate' covering two-thirds of the peninsula, whereas industry owned just one-third. Privately they boasted that Louisa Road – another bastion of opposition to the developments – contributed 5 per cent of Leichhardt's rates. If they could not force the developers to cede their land free of charge, they did not want to pay to buy it, suggesting that instead of trying to impose a general levy to acquire Ballast Point the council should charge pensioners rates (*Glebe* 1 Aug. 1990:2; Styles 1991).

When the residents went for advice to Ted Mack, the doyen of local government and Independents in politics, he counselled that the State government could be beaten if residents, the council and the local member of parliament worked together. The problem in Balmain was not only that the council had acquiesced in the State government's actions but that Dawn Fraser had also tacitly accepted Hay's inter-vention. In what she later recognised was a 'naive' response, Fraser attacked the council for its failure to 'deal reasonably quickly with routine development applications' and vied with Hay in his invective against the residents. Whereas Hay dismissed them as 'yuppie Trotskyites', Fraser dubbed them 'left-wing communists' (*SMH* 1 Sept. 1990:9; *Glebe* 5 Sept. 1990:2; *EH* 24 Jan. 1991:1).

The only avenue for the residents was the law. They were entitled to resort to the Land and Environment Court because the Environmental Planning Act had overturned the notorious requirements of 'standing', allowing any member of the public to sue. But the residents still needed to raise the money to exercise this right. Apart from paying their own lawyers, they had to consider their obligation to pay the State government's costs if they lost. Their solution was to bring their action through the Balmain Association, a residents' group formed in 1965 which was incorporated and hence provided a shield against personal liability. Although the residents could also have relied on this shield to avoid paying their own lawyers – the Balmain Association had assets of only $12 000 – they felt obliged to pay them.

The residents set about raising the money to challenge O'Toole's appointment by forming a new organisation which they misleadingly called the Balmain Development Trust, like a progress association of the 1950s, in a crude attempt to disguise their protectionist purpose. At the same time, the residents pursued the council's original intention of securing a new plan for the entire peninsula – establishing an 'Urban Ideas' competition with prizes totalling $10 000 for the best proposals to maintain Balmain's 'village environment and diverse socio-economic community'. In doing so, the residents ensured that they would not be accused of simply taking a spoiling role. Apart from defending the council's powers, they assumed its functions (*Glebe* 12 Sept. 1990:4, 19 Sept. 1990:1, 7 Nov. 1990:6; *EH* 21 Feb. 1991:2).

The Balmain Development Trust could only be so ambitious because of Balmain's taste for conspicuous consumption. The trust began with a $100-a-head dinner in the Wentworth Ballroom at Sydney's Sheraton Hotel. The keynote speakers were two Balmain celebrities – the playwright, David Williamson, and the ABC's Robin Williams. Two hundred and forty people attended, yielding a profit of $12 000 (*SMH* 6 Sept. 1990:9; *Glebe* 12 Sept. 1990:4, 19 Sept. 1990:1, 14 Nov. 1990:18).

As a result, the trust organised similar entertainments at Parliament House with the help of Sandra Nori, who made the most of Dawn Fraser's failure to represent local interests. After a $60-a-head lunch in December, Nori hosted another $100-a-head dinner in February. In between, the trust pursued more plebian methods of fund-raising by holding stalls, running raffles and door-knocking. In all, it raised $66 000 in three months. After expenses, it was left with $42 000 (*EH* 24 Jan. 1991:2, 21 Feb. 1991:2).

By the time the residents launched their action in December 1990 the council could have initiated the case itself with the help of the Local Government Association which had become a much keener defender of local government following the election of Peter Woods as president in October. Apart from providing the council with an opinion from a Queen's Counsel that the State government's actions were invalid, Woods offered to raise money from councils across the State to challenge Hay's intervention. But Bill Brady still did not want the case to proceed. Relying on advice from the council's own solicitor that the case could not be won, he not only declined Woods' offer but also asked the Local Government Association not to support the Balmain Development Trust. According to the Mayor, he was 'on the side of the poor bugger in Leichhardt battling away at three jobs to try and pay off his mortgage, not the millionaires in Louisa Road' (*EH* 21 Feb. 1991:2; *SMH* 14 Jan. 1991:4, 23 Feb. 1991:41; *TM* 14 Jan. 1991:16; *SH* 17 Feb. 1991:120; *WSC* 27 Feb. 1991:64; *Glebe* 13 Mar. 1991:14).

The result was a remarkable case in which residents sought to defend their council against State intervention but the council acted as if the case were of no significance to it. When the council was forced to become a party since its powers were in question, it did not oppose the Land and Environment Court dismissing the residents' action and took no part in the argument although its solicitor was present throughout the hearing. The only order it sought was that the residents pay its costs. In case the court refused, the council asked the Minister to pay, emphasising that it had never 'countenanced the actions of this residents' group' because it believed that Hay 'as Minister, had the prerogative to appoint the planning administrator' (*BA* v *Planning Administrator for Leichhardt Council* 1991b; *Agenda* 1991a:3–4; *TM* 21 Feb. 1991:10; *WSC* 27 Feb. 1991:64).

While Justice Cripps dismissed the residents' action in January, the Court of Appeal overturned his decision within a month, restoring the council's resolution to hold a public hearing and ordering the State government to pay the residents' costs (*Agenda* 1991:3; *Glebe* 16 Jan. 1991:7, 27 Feb. 1991:7; *WSC* 10 April 1991:3). According to the court, the council's right to hold a public hearing prevailed over the Minister's right to require the council to submit its environmental plans. The Minister had also flouted the rules of natural justice in appointing O'Toole. While Hay blustered about the possibility of taking the case to the High Court, this decision put an end to the litigation because the State government could not be confident of gaining leave to appeal from the High Court and it had little chance of success when the Court of Appeal had unanimously held against it on two counts (*BA* v *Planning Administrator for Leichhardt Council* 1991b; *BA* v *Planning Administrator for Leichhardt Council* 1991a:615; *SMH* 26 Feb. 1991:6; *WSC* 27 Feb. 1991:64; *Glebe* 20 Mar. 1991:5).

This decision was dismissed by Leichhardt's Labor aldermen as a matter of interest to 'only a small proportion of residents', just 'millionaire's row'. By way of contrast, the local *Glebe* greeted it as a 'Victory to the People' in which 'a group of residents had taken on Kerry Packer, Caltex, Ampol, the Electricity Commission and Unilever – and, to everyone's amazement, won' (*Glebe* 20 Feb. 1991:1; *EH* 21 Feb. 1991:2, 7 Mar. 1991:6). Who was correct? If the rezonings had been just a concern of a few, 1500 residents would not have called on the council to impose a moratorium on the rezonings. Nor would 700 residents have packed the town hall to urge the council to maintain its ban. Yet without the wealth of Balmain the litigation would never have occurred. Like all campaigns, this 'Battle for Balmain' also depended on a small group of activists. In the way of residents' groups since the late 1960s, almost all were women. They liked to present themselves as powerless. When quizzed on the Balmain Development Trust, Susan Frisoli replied: 'Shall we reveal ourselves as a public servant, a nurse, a chef and a mum?' (*EH* 21 Feb. 1991:2). They equally could have been described as a barrister, an architect and a member of the Broadcasting Tribunal.

A month after this victory the Balmain Development Trust revealed the results of its planning competition which was judged by a panel led by the designer of new Parliament House in Canberra, Romaldo Giurgola. Rather than displaying the best entries in Balmain as a matter of just local interest, it began by exhibiting them at the Sydney Opera House as a matter of metropolitan significance. Peter Thompson, the presenter of AM on ABC's Radio National, announced the winners. Another Balmain resident, Ian Kiernan of Clean Up Australia, was the principal speaker. Consistent with the trust's brief that the plans show an understanding of Balmain's 'sense of place', the enhancement of the peninsula's 'village' atmosphere was central to two of the three winning designs (*Glebe* 13 Mar. 1991:6, 13; *WSC* 13 Mar. 1991:3; *Agenda* 1991c: 10–11).

Because it had won in the Court of Appeal, the Balmain Development Trust was able to pay both the $10 000 prize money for this competition and meet almost all its legal expenses of $72 000. But it still suffered a shortfall because the State government was only obliged to pay costs on a 'party–party' basis which are always much less than full costs and enabled the residents to recover little more than half their fees (Bonyhady 1993:77). Had the residents lost, their position would have been far worse. Even without paying the costs of the State government and the council, they would have needed $38 000 over and above the $44 000 they had already raised. Instead of the relative ease of raising money for a live issue, they would have been trying to pay for a lost cause. As the trust's Helen Styles observed, they would have been selling lamingtons for the rest of their lives (*Glebe* 20 Feb. 1991:1).

Play It Again, Sam

When the residents won in the Court of Appeal, their solicitor predicted that, instead of 'ad hoc planning or looking at the peninsula site by site', there would be 'an integrated approach' to the entire area. After its competition, the Balmain Development Trust approached all the site-owners about changing their plans in accordance with the winning entries. One of the winning teams approached the Electricity Commission (*WSC* 20 Feb. 1991:1; *EH* 14 Mar. 1991:2). All were disappointed. When members of the public win in the courts, government usually re-takes its decision paying greater regard to the proper procedures (Bonyhady 1993:ch.5). After losing in the Court of Appeal, Hay was as anxious as ever to see the sites rezoned. In mid-March he issued a new direction giving the council fourteen weeks to submit local plans for the five sites (*BA* v *Planning Administrator for Leichhardt Council* 1991a:635; *LC* v *Minister for Planning* 1992:402, 404 and 1993:306, 320).

This restoration of the council's powers was something Bill Brady still did not want. His solution, reached after discussions with Hay, the developers and Helen Styles, was to ask the State's Commissioners of Inquiry to examine the rezoning of the five sites. According to Styles this decision meant that the council had finally 'accepted responsibility for planning the Balmain peninsula'. Brady thought it the best way 'to get rid of' the five sites. Either way, it was an expensive decision because the council had to pay $40 000 for the work of William Simpson and Mark Carleton, the two commissioners (*Agenda* 1991b:3; *SMH* 6 Mar. 1991:14; *AFR* 20 Mar. 1991:41; *Glebe* 20 Mar. 1991:1, 5).

While the great claim of these commissioners was their independence (Commissioners of Inquiry 1991:4), they did not enjoy the same security of tenure as judges. After their first chairman, John Woodward, recommended against the Greiner government's proposed Castlereagh freeway in 1990, the government did not reappoint Woodward when his seven-year contract came up for renewal.

Because the norm has been for the commissioners to support the State government's proposals, the council might have looked elsewhere for someone to hold their public hearing. In 1986 when Labor was still in office, one observer noted that there was 'a remarkable unanimity of opinion between the Commissioners . . . and the Minister for Planning and Environment' (Ashton 1993:113). When Simpson and Carleton reported on the five sites at the end of July 1991, already five weeks after the deadline set by Hay, they began by submitting their findings to the Minister for Planning even though they had been employed by Leichhardt Council and the Environmental Planning Act required them to furnish their report to the council (EPAA 1979a:s.68(2)).

In compiling their report Simpson and Carleton started from a different premise to that of the council's planners. Instead of arguing that the five sites should be developed at the same densities as the rest of Balmain, the commissioners looked on the sites as 'an opportunity for an increase in density to accommodate the demands for more housing in the Peninsula'. Even so, the only site on which the commissioners differed from the planners in December was Ballast Point, where they suggested a floor space ratio of 0.8:1, not 0.7:1. This identity of conclusions suggests that the ratios recommended by the planners would not have achieved their object of making the five sites consistent with the rest of Balmain. Unlike the planners, the commissioners acknowledged this fact (Commissioners of Inquiry 1991:2, 67–8, 73).

The other significant difference between the planners and the commissioners involved the developers' obligation to dedicate part of their land as open space. Whereas the planners had opted to apply the existing standard of 1.7 hectares per 1000 people within Leichhardt, the commissioners rejected this standard as inappropriate for an area such as Balmain which was among the 'most deficient in open space' in Sydney, isolated from other parkland because it was a peninsula and likely to be subject to a significant increase in population. Their solution was to accept that councils could not improve the lot of an area but to redefine the relevant testing ground as Balmain rather than all of Leichhardt because, conveniently for them, the existing standard in Balmain was 2.1 hectares. This standard allowed the commissioners to recommend 6.9 hectares of new open space – a significant area when the five sites covered only 23 hectares (Commissioners of Inquiry 1991:118–19).

By then, Balmain had a new local member and the State a new Minister for Planning. Dawn Fraser's defeat in the May 1991 election was partly due to her initial stance over the five sites. Although she tried to restore her credentials as a representative of local interests – sitting with the residents in the Land and Environment Court, joining them as they celebrated their victory in the Court of Appeal with chardonnay – Sandra Nori easily won the new seat of Port Jackson which was created out of Balmain and McKell. In Manly, David Hay lost to the Independent, Dr Peter McDonald, who was able to paint Hay as an opponent of community interests because of his intervention in Leichhardt. With his defeat, the National Party's Robert Webster became Minister for Planning (*SH* 27 Jan. 1991:30; *SMH* 6 May 1991:6; *Glebe* 29 May 1991:5).

Brady intended to act on the commissioners' report as his last act as Mayor before quitting local politics rather than risk defeat at the next council election. Because the issues had 'been around for so long and debated so much', Brady argued that there was no reason for the council not to meet Webster's new deadline of 9 September 1991. Brady also knew that he had the numbers. While the council was split, his casting vote would ensure that it adopted the commissioners' report. But the other six aldermen claimed that they did not have time to digest the commissioners' report and, in any event, the issue should be left to the new council, enabling local residents to express their views on the rezonings at the poll on 14 September. By boycotting the council's meetings, denying it a quorum, these aldermen prevented the issue being decided (*Glebe* 7 Aug. 1991:8, 14 Aug. 1991:2, 28 Sept. 1991:3; *SMH* 27 Aug. 1991:6).

The election was a triumph for candidates opposed to the redevelopments who won three-quarters of the vote, a further demonstration that their stance had the support of much more than 'millionaire's row'. All but one of the aldermen who had opposed the site-owners' plans were re-elected. The four new Labor councillors were led by Kate Butler who had been the one Labor member of the old council to vote for the initial moratorium and the public hearing. Helen Styles, the spokesperson of the Balmain Development Trust, was also elected. The new Mayor was Larry Hand (*Glebe* 13 Mar. 1991:1, 18 Sept. 1991:3, 25 Sept. 1991:6; Origlass 1991).

When the new council met to consider the rezonings it opted to embark on a new program of community workshops which would see the sites rezoned in three months in accordance with local opinion (*SMH* 1 Oct. 1991:6; Origlass 1991). The only dissentient was Helen Styles who argued that 'the residents' fight to have a say in the planning process' was 'being threatened by the council shirking its role as decision-maker'. She proposed that the council accept the commissioners' recommendations except for Ballast Point which should become four-fifths open space (*Glebe* 23 Oct. 1991:9, 30 Oct. 1991:9, 27 Nov. 1991:8).

Hand hoped that, as new Mayor, he would be able to open a dialogue with Webster, the new Minister. But Webster refused to meet him. According to the Minister, the council was obliged to accept the commissioners' report 'in toto' even though their findings were purely recommendatory and the State government did not always implement their advice.

The council set about drawing up its new plans by employing Richard Smyth, a former Director of the Department of Planning. His brief involved none of the claims to neutrality of either the Leichhardt planners or the Commissioners of Inquiry. Instead his task was to articulate and press the residents' interests, more or less in keeping with the concept of the 'advocate planner' first developed in 1965 by Paul Davidoff of the City University of New York (Davidoff 1965:331–8; Blecher 1971). The one difference was that Davidoff expected advocate planners to work exclusively with the underprivileged: ghetto dwellers, welfare mothers and militants. Smyth worked with professionals, blue-collar workers and pensioners in relation to the Power Station and the Chemplex, Ampol and Unilever sites. The Caltex group needed even less empowering – they all came from Balmain's already powerful middle class.

Apart from reporting on what the residents wanted for each site, Smyth's task was to justify as much open space and as low densities as possible. He did so by attacking the approach adopted by both the council's own planners and the Commissioners of Inquiry of giving the developers the benefit of floor space ratios calculated over their entire sites and then converting them into much higher 'nett' ratios over areas which they retained after making their dedications of open space. Smyth argued that this process gave the developers an unwarranted benefit because their dedication of open space was a matter of statutory obligation. Why, he asked, should developers be rewarded for something they had to do? He also argued that this bonus was undeserved because those who would gain most from the new open space would be the future residents of the five sites. Since this open space would help to sell the sites, there was no reason for the council to reward the developers for what was in their own self-interest (Richard Smyth Planning Consultants Pty Ltd 1991).

Smyth advised that, by denying the developers this bonus, the council could reduce the scale of the developments by 30 per cent. The only problem was that, because their projects would then bring fewer people to Balmain and their obligation to dedicate open space was tied to this increase in population, the developers would have to provide a much smaller area (Richard Smyth Planning Consultants Pty Ltd 1991). Leichhardt's planners subsequently estimated that the council would either have to forsake almost one-third of the open space it otherwise would have received or pay $17 million to buy it (LC 1993:32–4). But Smyth argued that the loss of this land was of little account because the developers had designed their schemes so that the open space would be of much greater benefit to the new residents of the five sites than Balmain's existing residents. On this basis, the council adopted Smyth's recommendations and finally submitted local plans for four of the five sites to Webster in February 1992. The only site it deferred was Ballast Point, which the council argued should continue to be used for manufacturing by Caltex until there was public money to buy it for inclusion in Sydney Harbour National Park.

Meanwhile, Webster intervened again. While his department suggested that he appoint another administrator (*LC v Minister for Planning* 1992:402, 405), he decided against doing so because the council had just been elected with a new mandate. Instead he tried a combination of a State Environmental Planning Policy and a regional environmental plan which together empowered him to implement the government's urban consolidation policies without council approval. The State policy was in force from November 1991 – a consequence of it not being subject to any statutory requirement of public consultation. The regional plan was slowed by the requirement that the government exhibit a draft plan for public comment. Consequently, it was not until late February 1992 – four months after Webster decided to take over the rezonings – that he implemented the recommendations of the Commissioners of Inquiry (EPAA 1979a:ss.41, 47).

The differences between the plans submitted by the council and those gazetted by the State government would have been significant even if the council had submitted a plan for the rezoning of the Caltex site. Because the council deferred its decision about this site on which it might otherwise have allowed 160 dwellings, the differences were profound. Whereas the State government's plans allowed 1027 dwellings, the council's plans permitted only 688 dwellings. Where the State government had made no provision for 'affordable dwellings', the council provided for one-quarter to one-third of each site to be given over to pensioner and public housing. Where the State government had set aside an average of just 19 per cent of the sites for public open space, the council demanded 32 per cent. According to the council's calculations, the owners of the five sites would be $30 million richer under the State government's plan. If they developed their land themselves, they stood to make an extra $60 million (LC 1992a:1–4).

By then, the State government's intervention had become an issue of much more than local interest because its new plans allowed the government to approve the redevelopment of any site over 1 hectare from Kiama to Port Stephens, and the government had demonstrated its intention to exercise this power by identifying several sites in areas outside Balmain (*Australian* 19 Oct. 1991:55; *Glebe* 30 Oct. 1991:9, 11 Dec. 1991:5, 18 Dec. 1991:3, 26 Dec. 1991:3; *SMH* 3 Dec. 1991:6, 4 Dec. 1991:6, 15 Feb. 1992:9, 22 Feb. 1992:2; NSWPD 6 May 1992:3662; *LC* v *Minister for Planning* 1993:306, 330). When Webster refused to compromise despite opposition from councils across the State, Peter Woods of the Local Government Association established a fighting fund to help Leichhardt challenge his actions. Whereas only Liverpool Council had helped the Balmain residents to pay for their case – giving them $1000 because it recognised that their action was of general significance to local government (*Glebe* 20 Feb. 1991:3, 27 Feb. 1991:7, 22 May 1991:6; *SH* 5 May 1991:11) – councils proved much happier to assist their own. A record 65 per cent responded to Woods' call, donating $45 000 to Leichhardt which received another $4000 directly from other councils. A ball at the Apia Club, a very different venue to the Sheraton, raised $6000. After the council had helped the Balmain Development Trust to meet the $2500 still owing from its case, local residents gave the council another $9000 (*Glebe* 30 Oct. 1991:9, 11 Dec. 1991:5, 5 Aug. 1992:3, 9; *SMH* 4 Dec. 1991:6, 19 Sept. 1992:3; LC 1992b; Environmental Services 1993).

This financial support was critical because Leichhardt was taking an even greater risk than the Balmain Development Trust in challenging the State government's regional plan. Whereas the residents knew that if they lost they would not have to pay the government's costs because of the corporate shield provided by the Balmain Association, the council did not enjoy this immunity. Its case was also even more expensive: $95 500 for the Land and Environment Court where Chief Judge Pearlman ruled against it in September; another $45 000 (making a total of $140 500) for the Court of Appeal which unanimously reversed Pearlman's decision in December. Because of this victory, the council did not have to pay the State government's costs. But like the residents it still had to pay for upholding the law. Because it recouped only one-third of its expenses from the State government, Leichhardt Council was left $28 000 out-of-pocket, even after taking into account the $65 000 it had raised (*SMH* 4 Dec. 1991:6, 19 Sept. 1992:3; *AFR* 11 Dec. 1992:37; Environmental Services 1993).

The Distribution of Power

The State government's second defeat in the Court of Appeal was unprecedented. Two-and-a-half years after it first intervened it had still not got its way. Each of its mistimed interventions had delayed the rezonings by a year. Had Hay given the council twelve weeks to hold a public hearing and consider its findings, as well as allowed it to explain itself before appointing O'Toole, he would have won in the Court of Appeal in February 1991. Had Webster delayed perhaps a month in 1991, giving the council a reasonable opportunity to comment on his draft regional plan, Leichhardt would probably not have pursued the case as far as the Court of Appeal, let alone won there in December 1992. Why did the State government make these mistakes?

One explanation for the government's blunder in 1990 is that it did not expect to be challenged. The Planning Department, in the way of powerful government instrumentalities, was accustomed to cutting corners and rarely being called to account. It probably figured that rather than resenting Hay's intervention, a majority of aldermen would be so grateful that Hay had not dismissed them that they would not defend the council's loss of powers. It probably never even contemplated that local residents might act on the council's behalf. As Sandra Nori put it: 'When the administrator was appointed to the Leichhardt Council, no one imagined that the Balmain community would be able to raise the thousands of dollars required for the matter to go before the court' (NSWPD 1992:3661).

This explanation does not account for the State government's mistake in making its regional environmental plan because, having learned from its first defeat, the Planning Department recognised the risk of further litigation. What else then can account for what transpired? One explanation is the uncertainty of the law. The Ministers' initial victories in the Land and Environment Court indicate that there was at least some basis for justifying his interventions. Another possibility is ineptitude caused by loss of senior staff. After the residents' victory in the Court of Appeal, Peter Woods declared that Hay had been poorly advised, pitying him for having been 'briefed by amateurs' (*BA* v *Planning Administrator for Leichhardt Council* 1991a:615, 622; *SMH* 21 Feb. 1991:4).

The State government's defeats were, however, also a result of the Court of Appeal upholding the original objects of the Environmental Planning Act to reduce the role of the State government in planning decisions by increasing public participation and empowering local government (EPAA 1979a:s.5). By amending the Act in 1985, as well as by introducing special legislation to approve such favoured projects as the Harbour Tunnel and Darling Harbour, the Wran government had undermined these goals (Ryan 1987:330). So had the Greiner and Fahey governments, by making a series of State Environmental Planning Policies which took decisions away from local councils or reduced their discretion. The court's decisions went a small way to restoring the original distribution of power – recognising that members of the public and local government were entitled to a significant voice in planning decisions.

As the president of the Court of Appeal, Justice Kirby, observed, 'participatory democracy' was the key issue in the first case (*Agenda* 1991b:3). The State government was caught by a provision allowing councils to hold public hearings on draft local plans. While this provision was intended to be a token gesture, creating the possibility for consultation while conferring no rights on members of the public, it formed the basis of the court's decision that the Minister had been unreasonable in giving the council just five weeks to submit its plans. During argument, Justice Kirby remarked that while democracy was 'sometimes inconvenient', it was preferable to executive power being wielded without public participation. According to the court, 'any reasonable administration of the Act' had to 'take account of the delays . . . inherent in procedures established by Parliament for consulting the public about environmental decisions that may affect them' (EPAA 1979a:s.68; *BA* v *Planning Administrator for Leichhardt Council* 1991a:615, 628–33; *AFR* 1 Feb. 1991:37; BA 1991).

In the second case, the State government was caught by a provision which required the Director of Planning to consult with affected local councils when preparing draft regional plans. The government's normal practice had been to allow two to three months for this process. The Court of Appeal held that it was not enough for the government to have given Leichhardt three weeks without explaining its criteria for taking control of particular sites, the scope of its intervention or the consequences for local plans. Drawing on a series of cases in which the courts had decided that 'consultation' was 'no empty term', 'never to be treated perfunctorily or as a mere formality', the court held that 'proper consultation . . . required that the Council know what was proposed before it was expected to give its view and that the Council be given a reasonable opportunity to state its views' (*LC* v *Minister for Planning* 1993:336, 338).

While both these decisions were purely procedural – the court did not question the State government's ultimate power to intervene – at some point procedural requirements may become so onerous that they have substantive consequences, resulting in negotiations, compromises and changes in position. Some indication of this can be seen in Balmain where, following the State government's second defeat in the Court of Appeal, Robert Webster finally met Larry Hand for the first time and established a consultative committee including representatives not just of the council and the Department of Planning but also the local community and chamber of commerce, the Housing Industry Association, the Water Board, the Roads and Traffic Authority and the

State's new Environment Protection Authority which had been so wayward in responding to the council's requests for information.

This consultative process has been brought about at extraordinary cost for all parties – not just the residents and developers but also the Leichhardt Council and the State government. The litigation has cost the State government several hundred thousand dollars because of its defeats. All the site-owners and the council have incurred significant consultants' fees. Both the council and its staff have been diverted from their ordinary job of running Leichhardt. Bob Ell's Leda Group, the only specialist developer which bought most of the Unilever site in 1989, has incurred vast holding costs (*Glebe* 21 Nov. 1990:2).

Even so, the outcome of this new process remains uncertain. It could still come to nothing as the State government could try again to impose its will on Balmain and succeed in satisfying its legal obligations at its third attempt. But if the new uses of the five sites are worked out through the consultative committee, the costs of the dispute will have been worth it because of the significance of the five sites within the peninsula. If there is any spill-over to other areas, this 'Battle for Balmain' will have been even more worthwhile.

CHAPTER 6

State Planning Operation

Raymond Bunker

This chapter concentrates on recent planning initiatives in South Australia. It goes beyond official publications to review, comment on and provide a critique on those developments. In doing so it seeks to place them within a wider, if more superficial, appreciation of current trends in State urban planning operations generally. A major linkage is made between these two dimensions by analysing the concept of strategic planning which is a common ambition of all State operations, and a prominent and distinctive feature of the South Australian current experiments.

Setting the Scene

There are some background assumptions and interpretations that should be outlined. While government policies and actions of all kinds and all levels impact on urban conditions, the States build and operate the cities. Commonwealth policies and actions, whether targeted on urban issues or unintended in their urban impacts, have great influence. They tend to be more abstract in their character and effect. State policies involve constructing the built environment of the cities, operating it and servicing its people, so that they are a mixture of the abstract and the physical. Local policies are mainly physical in their orientation and impact and considerably influence the character of the street and the suburb.

A few more impressions: financial resources are more available at Commonwealth level, but there the expertise and insight into urban conditions is uneven, and badly dislocated periodically by changes in personnel, programs and ministerial responsibilities (Bunker & Minnery 1992). State skills are reasonable but often badly organised, and not conspicuously innovative as a general rule. Local government resources and roles are changing. There is increasing recognition of the important role that local government plays in urban affairs, but that acknowledgement has a long way to go on the part of all parties, and is hindered by the erratic and eccentric performance of some local councils.

In the urban scene, strong individual preferences by households for detached dwellings, pleasant surroundings and home ownership continue to be asserted (Stevens, Baum & Hassan 1992). Economic conditions and changes of recent times have increasingly threatened and affected the fulfilment of these desires. The collective expression and planning for these perceptions, needs and preferences in terms of suburban development still tends to be unimaginative despite the efforts of programs like Green Street and AMCORD.

The content of metropolitan plans has traditionally been concerned with organising land use, patterning open space, identifying centres of commercial activity, safeguarding residential amenity, organising orderly and timely expansion of the metropolitan area, and accommodating the use of the car. The implementation of many of these proposals has tended to be weak at the metropolitan scale (McLoughlin 1992) reflecting either inadequate administrative and political power or picking the wrong targets, emphases and priorities, or a combination of both.

Organisationally, urban planning in State governments is linked from time to time with different parties, usually transport, housing, land development, environment or local government. Such partnerships depend on the importance and association of particular issues at any time, and on ministerial/faction perceptions and alignments in terms of the allocation of portfolios. Planning operations are only occasionally seen as an important factor or contributor to many resource allocation decisions or to pricing of public goods and services, except in relation to capital works programs and major projects. This may change with the recent Industry Commission Inquiry into pricing and taxation measures as they affect urban development (Industry Commission 1993).

Finally, urban planning is one of the few State government operations with contact with local councils, the community and sections of private industry. Hence while planners can be accused of a 'municipal dog-catcher to philosopher-king' syndrome, there is also the occasional opportunity to use communication, liaison, interaction, coordination, and packaging skills of the highest order.

Impetus and Agenda

Over recent years there has been a considerable critique levelled at urban planning in the States of Australia, particularly directed at metropolitan planning. This has basically come from two sources. One is from those involved in planning themselves, and is addressed to questions of urban form, structure and function. Brian McLoughlin has recently completed a research program in Melbourne where he sought to 'study the effectiveness of land-use planning in achieving its own stated aims about land-use configurations' (McLoughlin 1992:232). He came to the conclusion that they had been relatively ineffective at the metropolitan scale. In Sydney, Jim Colman has reviewed the environmental problems arising from its post-war growth and commented on '[t]he extraordinary paradox . . . that this same period has seen three metropolitan plans prepared and pursued by successive governments, ostensibly to ensure that the city's growth did not get out of hand' (Colman 1991:30).

In Western Australia, Yiftachel and Kenworthy have concluded that recent metropolitan planning operations in Perth have been 'unable to effectively control the form, structure and function of the metropolitan region' (Yiftachel & Kenworthy 1992:137).

Another kind of critique comes from others interested in more general constructs of public policy affecting cities. They are well represented in this book, by contributors such as Mark Peel, Patrick Troy and Blair Badcock. Here the argument is that urban conditions, spatial characteristics, and arrangements of built form do express, reflect, compound or condition issues of efficiency, equity and environmental character. If that is so, then those connections and relationships need to be more powerfully expressed and used.

Against that background it is possible to review briefly recent documentation about planning systems and urban planning in each of the States, draw out the concerns raised and the issues and problems addressed. An inventory of this kind would include:

• disquiet with traditional content and ideology of urban and metropolitan plans
• the urgency of economic restructuring and creating employment
• concern for areas and populations of perceived disadvantage, but without, for example, consideration of the gendered division of urban environments
• attempts to better associate and integrate the people, skills and resources affecting urban conditions
• more attention to abstract values on which urban living and communities are based – sustainability, efficiency and equity, but difficulty in expressing them in urban plans

- the notion of 'strategic planning'
- more attention to implementation
- attempt to effect better relationships between capital city planning, and the general pattern of urban settlement in the State
- more concern with waste management and disposal, pollution and natural resource management, personal security and energy conservation
- more appreciation of rural-urban fringe planning issues as distinctive challenges
- financial stringency, sometimes desperation, and re-assessment of the public economy of cities
- the place of major projects in strategic planning, and assessment of their impact
- public involvement and participation; vision-building
- attempts to develop partnership arrangements between spheres and agencies of government: this often involving recursive and iterative styles of operation
- judgements as to whether threshold or gradualist changes to the planning system are required
- content still focused on containment, intensification of activities, centres, open space and exhortations about public transport
- little sign of relating changing urban communities and their needs to altered kinds of residential environments – apart from increased densities and 'village' structure
- innovations and differentiation in urban infrastructure provision and pricing
- integration, association and facilitation of building and development assessment procedures
- attempts to develop a 'whole-of-government' approach to urban conditions.

There appears to be an uneven engagement by each State with this inventory of issues, and less commonality of approach than in earlier days when, for example, Toni Logan and Ian Alexander were able to identify three generations of post-war metropolitan plans in Australia (Alexander 1986). States appear to be responding to their own particular circumstances in a more differentiated fashion.

Urban Planning: Current Initiatives in South Australia

In the 1980s there was growing criticism in South Australia about the Adelaide metropolitan plan and the planning system (Forster 1984; Badcock 1989). The plan had been put together in the late 1950s and released in 1962. This Metropolitan Development Plan was a competent document for its time, but it was dominated by concepts reflecting the long boom, such as the arrangement and separation of land uses, strong and unilateral assertions of residential character and amenity, and the enshrinement of these in statutory form. It tried to act both as a metropolitan plan and a fairly detailed structure for local planning. It attempted to be both an instrument of development control and a fundamental statement of metropolitan character. It was revised unevenly and indiscriminately, largely at the initiative of local councils (Bunker 1989b). Nevertheless, there were still some solid accomplishments. They included great attention to residential amenity, and the development of an urban development program to manage and coordinate the servicing and extension of the metropolitan area – an effective management device which began to become an end in itself rather than a means to an end.

Likewise the planning system came under attack. It was perceived by many as bureaucratic, complex, confusing and negative. Quixotically, attempts to by-pass the system by fast-tracking some major projects had less success than if they had gone through the normal processes. After John Bannon won the general State election in November 1989, he launched a Planning Review in April 1990 to draw up a new metropolitan plan expressing a 'community-shared vision', to formulate an improved planning system, and to do both with a maximum of community consultation and involvement.

One important feature of the Planning Review was that most members of the team working on it were largely unfamiliar with metropolitan planning. This had important consequences in adding new dimensions and initiatives to the somewhat outworn perspectives and practices that had prevailed. It also helped to explain why some important issues were not sufficiently appreciated or addressed in the formal two-year process of the Planning Review. For example, the importance and largely diffused nature of suburban employment was not adequately understood and encompassed. Neither were transportation issues and methods of implementation of the plan sufficiently addressed. On the other hand, the strategic planning process for Adelaide was seen as essentially dynamic and evolving, and the fact that some of the people in the Planning Review team are now in positions of responsibility filling out and implementing the planning strategy for Adelaide, means that a final evaluation and critique of the outcome of the exercise must wait for some years.

Certainly the concept of strategic planning was adopted wholeheartedly by the Planning Review. The first of the three final reports released in July 1992 was concerned with the overall character of the proposed new planning system and concluded: 'The central recommendation of the Planning Review is that a new method of dealing with urban development is required, which applies policy derived from strategic planning to government agency actions, control of public and private development and involves the community through information exchange and education' (Planning Review 1992b:1).

Following the principle of discussing planning ideas and issues in plain English, the Planning Review published on one map what the elements of a planning strategy for Adelaide might comprise. It had the title 'Visions of Adelaide' in the draft planning strategy for Adelaide, which formed the second of the three final reports of the Planning Review (1992c), and appears here as figure 6.1. The strategy starts with statements of values, expressed and articulated as a result of extensive public involvement in the review process. It then goes on to a series of analyses and propositions about Adelaide concerning living, economic activity, use and conservation of natural resources, access, heritage and design. A series of strategic statements about how to deal with these are then advanced in the document for discussion and adoption. Inevitably only some of these are shown in figure 6.1, but three different kinds of examples can be given. The first is the statement that the rate of growth of Adelaide to the south should be slowed down over time. This represents a change in direction from that articulated as long ago as 1975. In April of that year, the then State government and Common-wealth government had jointly noted that in terms of land availability there were no substantial impediments to continued growth to the north and south of Adelaide, and that even growth would facilitate choices concerning housing and location by the metropolitan population (Bunker 1978). In a sense the later urban development program operated on that premise. The proposed change of direction is a pivotal strategic decision.

A second example of a strategic planning statement is not shown in figure 6.1, but is an important and immediate part of present urban policy. This concerns '[t]he staged redevelopment of older public housing estates in the north, north west and inner south' (Planning Review 1992c:25). This involves large tracts and estates of public housing built in the 1940s, 1950s and 1960s in the middle and outer suburbs of Adelaide. Most of these areas are in accessible locations, frequently on large blocks, with undifferentiated family housing, often constructed of basic materials. Selective redevelopment, rehabilitation, construction of smaller scale and aged persons' housing, street closures and realign-ments, landscaping, and some sale of houses and land are all measures being used to upgrade, diversify and provide affordable housing in good locations well provided with infrastructure and services.

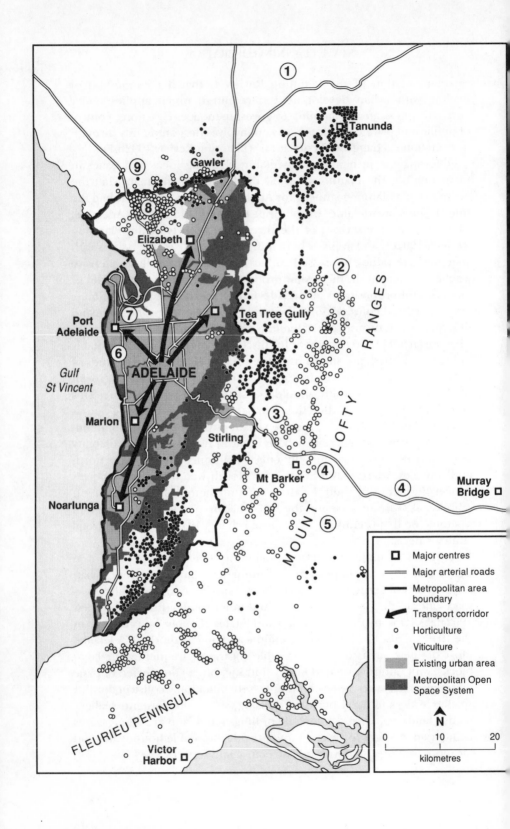

(1) Protection of viticulture a priority

(2) Integrated land and natural resource management throughout the Mt Lofty Ranges

(3) No expansion in hills area within Water Supply Protection Zone. Urban growth restrained due to environmental imperatives

(4) Population increase in longer term

(5) Hills areas outside the Water Supply Protection Zone to experience some urban development with modest expansion of hills township boundaries

(6) Transport infrastructure upgraded in north-western area

(7) MFP urban development and industrial area revitalised

(8) Stormwater management linked to urban revitalisation

(9) Horticultural areas preserved

Major tourism focus on coast, city and hills

Development in Fleurieu Peninsula focusing on retirement and tourism centres

Firm decisions on land use will have a 10-year time horizon

Slower growth in southern sector through the 1990s and beyond due to environmental and land-use imperatives and more limited employment prospects

Noarlunga Centre priority development as focus for southern region

Emphasis on improved design and character retention in all redevelopment

Transit link between major centres. Improved cross-suburb transport for local trips

Elizabeth a major priority for centre development as focus for northern region

Northern sector focus for Adelaide's long-term growth

Figure 6.1 *Planning strategy for metropolitan Adelaide*
Source: Planning Review 1992c. *Planning Strategy for Metropolitan Adelaide,*
Planning Review, Adelaide.

A final strategic initiative is to remove separate planning and development control over the central city area from the City of Adelaide. This is meant to associate and integrate the central city more closely with metropolitan planning. There have been a number of examples where city policies have not adequately reflected their influence on matters of metropolitan significance. Conversely, the City of Adelaide has taken initiatives in housing, urban design, townscape and heritage preservation which are useful and relevant to inner suburbs in particular.

Strategic Planning

It is appropriate to turn to the concept of strategic planning, so powerfully expressed in current Adelaide urban policy, and also appearing in all recent State pronouncements. It has also attracted the attention and the endorsement of the National Housing Strategy (NHS 1992b).

However, the term 'strategic planning' is used indiscriminately. Its use ranges from merely changing the label on conventional urban planning, to an attempt to use it as an instrument and a lexicon for quite radical changes in the culture and processes of urban development and governance. Even when the process is defined (Planning Review 1992c; Hayes 1993), there still remains the crucial test of competent conceptualisation and application to any given planning situation.

Nevertheless, references to the virtues of strategic planning abound in recent planning reports in every State and, as will be seen, in some legislation. Its character is grounded most firmly theoretically and methodologically in the seminal work of Friend, Jessop and Hickling over the years (Friend & Jessop 1969; Friend & Hickling 1987). In these terms, it means a comprehensive view of the issues attending urban conditions, selection as to their particular importance, and combining this with the degree of power and influence available to address them, using a variety of direct and indirect instruments. It forms a dynamic process of selecting leading variables, arranging and arraying their associations and relationships, and progressive, and increasingly informed use of them. It involves a definition of the different types and degrees of uncertainty attending strategic choices, and how to handle them. This obviously has to combine learning, adjustment and implementation with a long-term and fundamental view about where the city is heading.

As has been noted, the draft planning strategy for metropolitan Adelaide (Planning Review 1992c) starts with statements of values, expressed and articulated as a result of extensive processes of public involvement in the review process. In these processes 'workshops addressed ideas and issues not in traditional categories such as employment, economic development, environmental management and social justice but by referring to visions of a productive, sustainable, fair, accessible, affordable and healthy city' (Department of the Premier and Cabinet 1993:15).

The third of the three final reports consisted of a draft of proposed planning legislation setting up a new system of planning (Planning Review 1992a). In May 1993 this legislation was passed, with some changes, and became the Development Act which came into force in January 1994. Section 22 of the Act provides for a planning strategy for development within the State. Subsection (8) defines the strategy as 'an expression of policy formed after consultation within government and within the community and does not affect rights or liabilities'. Under the legislation the strategy is the responsibility of the Premier who reports on it annually to parliament.

Section 23 provides for development plans which are to promote the provisions of the planning strategy and provide the basis for decisions concerning proposed development. The present Development Plan, which still largely reflects the long-boom conditions mentioned previously, and also acts as a statement of property rights, is to be progressively enlarged and enriched so that the built environment and urban development reflect the ambitions of the planning strategy. The development plans provide development guidelines and outline the built environment and communications that reflect, express and partly implement the planning strategy. Everything depends, of course, on what the character of each of these plans is, how their relationship is pursued, and how successful they are. There is both some irony and some optimism in the fact that some of the senior people involved in the Planning Review are now responsible for the further developmental work needed to pursue and implement its recommendations.

The Making of Adelaide's Metropolitan Strategy: Contribution of Area Plans

There are a number of ways in which progress is being made on the development of the planning strategy for metropolitan Adelaide. For example, figure 6.1 shows Elizabeth and Noarlunga centres as priorities for further development and focus of the northern and southern regions respectively. During 1993 much work was done in developing analyses and proposals about how this might be accomplished. The Elizabeth–Munno Para social justice project, mentioned extensively in Mark Peel's chapter, has opened up new processes and approaches of consultation and public involvement. This exercise followed on from a Commonwealth Local Area Research Study. It has demonstrated the need in this area for the 'investment of resources into education, training, health, and community development, and not just physical facilities' (O'Donovan & Ferretti 1993:7). But, because of their illustrative value, it is useful here to review the preparation of so-called area plans.

Despite the encouragement of urban consolidation, the planning strategy recognises the continued primacy of metropolitan growth by extension to the north and south. It has become urgent to prepare better statements and programs about what kind of urban space this might be, and how it might be provided. This work would also test some development principles espoused by the Planning Review, and correspondingly change and better define the draft planning strategy to take account of local issues.

Table 6.1 and figure 6.2 are taken from David Ellis' paper on metropolitan strategic planning presented in Adelaide (Ellis 1993). Table 6.1 shows the responsibility for managing development, the instruments available and who wields them. Figure 6.2 briefly outlines the character of the area planning process. Putting all these together establishes further dimensions for the planning process and hopefully, improves and enriches the urban environment in its widest meaning. What are some of these desirable dimensions and outcomes?

Briefly table 6.1 and figure 6.2 demonstrate again the importance of directing planning resources and energies to areas undergoing rapid change, and involving more than one council area. The process must be dynamic, evolving and interactive, with outcomes and outputs of various kinds. In doing this local councils, business interests and the community at large must be involved. Finally, the table and figure suggest that the ambit of urban planning must be widely drawn. For example, natural resource management is of vital concern. In the north, stormwater management and the future of market gardening operations, which are of great economic significance in the area, are of paramount concern. Market gardening in the area is drawing on increasingly saline and restricted groundwater supplies. In the south, groundwater supplies are not so depleted but need to be husbanded and augmented. Here the future of the wine-growing and tourist areas of the Southern Vales is of central concern. Figure 6.3 from *Choices for the Future* depicts some of these natural resource management and agricultural issues in the northern Adelaide area plan. Its preparation has involved a large number of parties including Commonwealth participation in some of the area planning and community welfare aspects.

This northern area planning exercise represents a partnership between State and local government in particular, which extends and

Table 6.1 *Responsibility for managing development*

	Federal	State	Local	Private
Urban planning	minor	major	major	minor
Grants	major	medium	minor	none
Providing services	minor	major	major	major
Pricing	minor	major	medium	major
Control	none	medium	major	minor

Source: Ellis 1993. Metropolitan Strategic Planning.

Working relationships

• State and local government partnership on key urban issues

• support local government regional processes through State government coordination of services, plans and funds

• integrate the large number of separate planning initiatives (Economics and Social Strategies, ILAP, LARP, staging plans, etc.)

• focus for community involvement in planning

Outputs

• resolve key issues and actions

• change and better define the planning strategy for local issues

• define key policy changes (the Development Plan)

• define key action plans or projects that need a joint approach

• define key staging and servicing needs and integrate State and local government service provision

• generally improve the quality of urban areas through environmental and design improvements

---

Figure 6.2 *Area planning*
Source: Ellis 1993. Metropolitan Strategic Planning.

reflects a general memorandum of agreement signed by the State government and South Australian Local Government Association in 1992 concerning the roles and relationships of the two levels of government. Four local councils constituting the northern area were heavily involved in the drafting of the northern area plan and their chief executive officers formed part of the steering committee. Different conditions and issues in the south, and lessons learnt from the northern

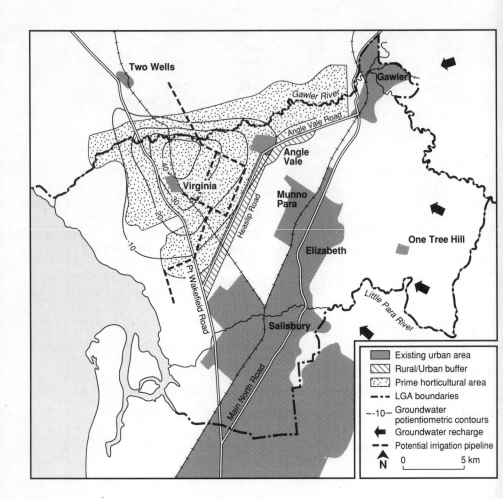

Figure 6.3 *Agricultural development issues in northern Adelaide*
Source: Office of Planning and Urban Development, South Australia, 1993.
Choices for the Future, Area Planning in Northern Adelaide, Adelaide, SA Office of
Planning and Urban Development.

exercise, mean a somewhat different process is being followed there. It involves, for example, agreement between the State government and councils in the southern area. This could express an understanding about the principles underlying future development of the south, for example, on the difficult question of appropriate infrastructure provision for sewage treatment and disposal. An agreement of this kind was signed in February 1994.

Other Strategies

One of the difficulties in the work of the Planning Review was the government's lack of interest in and attention to economic affairs and what this might mean for urban development and change. South Australia had been reasonably successful in the 1980s in winning a number of competitions useful to the State economy, such as the Formula 1 Grand Prix, the submarine contract and participation in frigate-building. However, there had been little sense of urgency in re-orienting and strengthening the State's limited economic base in the changing conditions of the 1980s. It took a forthright report from international consultants Arthur D. Little in August 1992 called 'New Directions for South Australia's Economy' to make the case for urgent economic, financial and institutional reform. When this report was combined with a full realisation of the extent of the State Bank disaster, and the resignation of John Bannon as Premier, the new Arnold government initiated a number of measures to bring the situation under control. This included the development of an economic plan to be linked to and to enrich the draft metropolitan strategy. The first of these plans produced on an annual 'rolling' basis was released for public discussion in October 1993, described as a 'strategic plan rather than a prescriptive one' (Economic Development Board 1993:i). At the same time a social development strategy was prepared with a similar intention, and was also released in October 1993 (Arnold 1993b). South Australia was suddenly awash with strategies.

Significantly, the Arthur D. Little Report recommended reform of the public sector in order to 'play a facilitative role in economic development'. What this meant was not apparent, but the new Arnold government seized upon this proposal as part of its management of the ballooning State debt. Premier Lynn Arnold established a new portfolio of Public Sector Reform, held by a senior minister, Chris Sumner. Premier Arnold presented an interim economic statement in April 1993 called *Meeting the Challenge* (Arnold 1993a). As part of this he announced a restructuring of the State's public sector, and the reduction of 3000 full-time jobs from those paid from the public purse.

These economic and political changes merged with the ideas and impetus coming from the Planning Review. The final report of the Planning Review emphasised that strategic planning and thinking needed organisational and cultural changes in government. It maintained that 'more than anything else it is the culture, perspective and operational style of organisations and their staff which needs to change' (Planning Review 1992b:45).

So these three streams of economic and social strategic planning, of public sector reform, and of the development of the draft metropolitan strategy and embryonic planning system continue to grow, but have yet to carve out a united and common confluence and course to the sea. One part of that, however, is the association of these same issues and influences in the area planning exercises, and the attempt to integrate them there.

What do all these changes mean for urban planning? They mean that urban planning is partly caught up with the changes and partly in the van of them. These ideas, influences and events are still evolving, working out, connecting or changing course and emphasis. The change of State government from Labor to Liberal as a result of the December 1993 election means the new government's emphasis on economic growth and different views about the role of the public sector will also change the character of the new planning system. The draft metropolitan strategy has already been modified by the new Liberal government to reflect a change in emphasis towards economic development and private sector involvement. Submissions on the new strategy were sought by March 1994.

The Transformation of Urban Institutions

The organisation of public administration to address urgent problems of shifting composition and changing political emphasis more adequately is frequent, familiar and overdone. It almost invariably occurs when there is a change in government, sometimes when there is a change in leadership of a party, and occasionally when a government is re-elected. Richard Crossman gave a revealing comment on these processes in relation to planning and urban development when he became Minister of Housing in the 1964 Wilson Labour government in Britain. His diary commented on his rebuke from his Permanent Secretary, Dame Evelyn Sharp, when he unconsciously demolished the whole basis of her department and his then ministerial effectiveness by agreeing to separate planning from housing: 'in her view – which I now suspect is correct – it's quite impossible to give physical planning, the land policy, to a new Ministry without giving it all control of housing' (Howard 1979:27).

Admirers of Sir Humphrey Appleby will be glad to hear that Dame Evelyn managed to rescue Crossman and herself from 'my stupidity and ignorance' and 'saved physical planning for us' (sic).

In South Australia, Premier Lynn Arnold's economic statement of April 1993 outlined a streamlining of public administration by a reduction in the number of departments from thirty to twelve by mid-1994, and a decrease in the number of statutory authorities. While a reduction in the number of government agencies does not necessarily increase efficiency, effectiveness and productivity, the South Australian changes did have the logic of new large groupings of functions which reflect the portfolios held by each minister. A new Department of Housing and Urban Development was one of the first of these new large consolidated departments and was formed on 1 July 1993. It combined the former Office of Planning and Urban Development, Local Government Relations Unit, and Department of Recreation and Sport with two statutory authorities: the South Australian Housing Trust and the South Australian Urban Lands Trust. These latter are brought more closely under ministerial control. This separates planning from environment with which it has been partnered organisationally over the last decade. The new Liberal government initially kept these arrangements, but has now modified them.

The role, organisation and coordination of public activity require fairly structured and formalised decisions, structures and processes. Yet within the enabling legislation authorising the use and deployment of public power, there is often much room for initiative, manoeuvre and constructive engagement. As has been seen, the new Development Act in South Australia has purposes which include the establishment of objectives and principles of planning and development, the construction of a system of strategic planning governing development, and the creation of development plans. What this means precisely, and how it is done provides the opportunity for a burst of creative activity in the next few years.

Two new independent statutory authorities are created under the new legislation, although they modify similar institutions that have been functioning for over ten years under the Planning Act of 1982. The new Development Policy Advisory Committee is established to 'advise the Minister on any matter relating to planning or development that should, in the opinion of the Advisory Committee, be brought to the Minister's attention' (Government of South Australia 1993:s.9[1][a]).

The other authority, the Development Assessment Commission, can similarly 'report to the Minister (on its own initiative or at the request of the Minister) on matters relevant to the development of land' (Government of South Australia 1993:s.11[1][b]). In addition, while the

Commission essentially exercises development control powers, experience has shown that successive decisions about particular classes and types of proposed development can become important policy constructs. An example of this kind of process is where medium-density housing is being placed in old suburbs, with planning and design challenges about the use of space, noise abatement, remediation of contaminated land and air quality.

Both these authorities will continue to be made up of part-time members representing different areas of expertise and interest. They are given secretarial support and infrastructure by the Department of Housing and Urban Development. This model of enlisting relevant resources and expert contributions from the community while providing administrative support is one that is likely to grow in the light of the need for better connection with the community and the increasing scarcity of expert resources in the public service. It represents a change from these functions being provided by professionals working from within departments of state.

There are also opportunities for innovation presented by informal arrangements, able to operate without formal foundation or legislative authority. These have existed from time immemorial. One of the most recognisable would be the inter-departmental committee, constituted to carry out specified tasks involving several agencies, and sometimes more formally constituted on a standing basis. While some of these are reasonably successful, they can also be the burial grounds for difficult issues for a variety of reasons, including ministerial apathy or unacceptance, bureaucratic infighting, or lack of attendance or substantial contribution by its members.

An example of this kind of informal arrangement is the joint City of Adelaide–State Forum set up in South Australia in October 1992. This was seen as a facilitating body to help the association and integration of planning policies and development control functions of the central City of Adelaide with those of the metropolitan area. The City of Adelaide had had its own separate planning system under the City of Adelaide Development Control Act of 1976, but as has been noted, this ended under the new Development Act of 1993.

The State Forum was set up to report to the minister about measures considered necessary to integrate strategic planning and development policy concerning the City with the draft metropolitan strategy resulting from the Planning Review. It was also asked to consider appropriate day-to-day development control mechanisms which separated them from policy issues. As an immediate priority, the Forum was asked to report urgently to the minister on the City of Adelaide's townscape proposals in terms of the above, which it did by Christmas 1992. It finished its work in October 1993.

The Forum was an informal body that had few rules, and it could be abolished instantly. It operated through the support and trust of its members, political support of different kinds, and perceived perform-ance and value. It evolved into a more structured format as the new Development Act came into force, with a new City of Adelaide Develop-ment Plan Committee being formed as a sub-committee of the Dev-elopment Policy Advisory Committee. As such, the Forum provided a useful and flexible process for working out new arrangements and understandings, following which it was discontinued.

How Widespread and Universal?

This chapter started by hypothesising that a number of conditions, circumstances and characteristics of urban planning in the States may be changing. It then concentrated on how part of that suggested agenda may be operating in South Australia, and what forms that is taking. It is now appropriate to go back from that singular experience, and speculate on how far those influences as illuminated in South Australia might be apparent elsewhere. As part of that this chapter provides a short commentary on what is happening in each mainland State insofar as this can be discerned from official pronouncements.

In New South Wales, as in South Australia, there has been a recent process of reviewing what changes might be needed in the planning system, and in updating the metropolitan strategy. The results on both these matters are likely to be less far-reaching. A *Discussion Paper on Modernising the Planning System in New South Wales* prepared by the Department of Planning and a technical committee of planners was issued in late 1991. There is likely to be little fundamental change to the system. While there are some proposed changes in the responsibilities and relationships of State and local governments, these are likely to be governed more by a new Local Government Act than new planning legislation. The discussion paper also proposes broader and more flexible types of land-use zoning, and calls for broader and more visionary styles of planning, especially strategic planning.

It is understood that the new metropolitan strategy, when approved by the government, will be extended to include the Illawarra and Hunter Regions to the south and north. The 1968 Sydney Region Outline Plan made similar proposals. There are attempts to build more of a whole-of-government approach into the revised plan. An integrated transport strategy is to be part of the update, and a task force involving all major government agencies is involved in reviewing the 1988 strategy, *Sydney into Its Third Century*. There is an independent advisory committee.

None of these operations is as radical as the South Australian proposals. They are generated largely by planners, of different kinds, whereas the South Australian exercise involved new personnel in leading positions from outside the existing system, and very extensive involvement of the Premier, Cabinet, reference groups and the community as the process continued. On the other hand, the South Australian system had further to come.

In Victoria, the Kennett government has begun to reduce the role and significance of the public sector in a more direct and peremptory way than in South Australia. There is also action on the cumbersome and expensive development approvals system, and a call for much larger local governments, somewhat euphemistically described as 'larger politico-economic units at the sub-State level', as a necessary condition for the lasting improvement of the planning system (Minister for Planning 1993:13). Improvements sought include increased speed in determining planning applications; a reduction in the number of residential zones in the metropolitan area from about 150 to about 10 as soon as possible; 'a generally similar process . . . for commercial and industrial zones . . . [with] councils to take the lead in applying the zones'; and the use of population targets for metropolitan municipalities in conjunction with the zoning adjustments and changes (Minister for Planning 1993:13).

The metropolitan strategy *A Place to Live, Urban Development 1992–2031* is to be revised, partly to incorporate the new population targets. As a recent review of that 1992 document commented, it is difficult to see how that strategy reflects the planning intentions of the current Victorian government (Batten, Fincher & Gleeson 1993). In the terms of the analysis of this paper, the 1992 strategy was prepared with extensive public consultation, did place Melbourne's development within the growth of the total Victorian urban system, and was more sensible than before about the role of various major suburban and provincial centres. It is also an interesting if somewhat confused attempt to argue that its pursuit of economic development is consistent with 'the emphasis through this strategy . . . on . . . planning for ecologically sustainable development' (Government of Victoria 1992:59).

Recent trends in Victoria suggest that planning reforms will mean the demise of the Cain brand of compulsive corporatism in planning by government, but will not lead to the clearer definition of the scope and purposes of metropolitan strategic planning advocated by McLoughlin (McLoughlin 1992). That is not to question the importance now placed on improving the speed, certainty and performance of the local approvals system, and the valuable work on energy conservation, good design, safety and security, and the search for better management of natural resources in the urban setting.

Queensland is in a state of flux. This is reflected in the uncertain, confused status of the Stimson Report on the development, growth and management of Brisbane City, presented to the then council in September 1991. The report has been neither endorsed nor rejected. Its proposals regarding the role and status of various types of suburban centres are contrary to the larger regional planning exercise called 'South East Queensland 2001', initiated towards the end of the Brisbane City exercise. A draft document from this latter project, called *Creating Our Future*, which 'encapsulates the main outcomes and recommendations of the SEQ 2001 Project', was released in 1993. It was prepared by a Regional Planning Advisory Group, a loose coalition of State government agencies, the then Commonwealth Department of Health, Housing, Local Government and Community Services, local councils, and relevant professional, interest and community organisations. This exercise was initiated by the State government but local government appears to be playing a strong role. The outcome is a broad preferred pattern of urban development co-existing with an analysis of environmental constraints. *Creating our Future* suggests the preferred regional growth pattern be given refinement and detailed development by sub-regional structure plans. These appear to be 'bottom-up' sub-regional strategic plans prepared by regional organisations of councils. *Creating our Future* suggests that: 'Statutory planning will occur through the use of Strategic Plans, development control plans, and Local and State adherence to the agreed Regional Framework for Growth Management and State Planning Policies' (SEQ2001 1993:42). The State government is reviewing the Local Government (Planning and Environment) Act and the Local Government Act.

In Western Australia the recent story starts with new legislation in 1985 aimed at simplifying planning administration and improving the efficiency of the planning system (Yiftachell & Kenworthy 1992).

Following this, a five-member review group led by Max Neutze examined the performance and outcomes of the corridor plan for Perth which had become government policy in 1973. This group reported in 1987 (Review Group to the State Planning Commission of Western Australia 1987). Following the receipt of public submissions on their report and further studies, 'Metroplan' was released in 1990, replacing the corridor plan as the metropolitan strategy for Perth. Many of the principles lying beneath the preferred strategy indicated in the 1987 report were used in Metroplan. But its proposals for stronger containment of urban growth were modified to facilitate some element of continued corridor growth, including the addition of a fifth north-east corridor (Yiftachel & Kenworthy 1992). The new planning approach is broader in scope than the 1987 review, carries a wider range of policy measures, and stresses the continuing and adjusting nature of the metropolitan planning process (Stokes & Hill 1992).

Metroplan is a more ambiguous and less explicit document than previous metropolitan strategies for Perth. For example, it simultaneously advocates decentralisation and the strengthening of central Perth, suburbanisation and consolidation, public transport and continuing substantial road construction, environmental protection and assertive urban conditions. It is full of interesting ideas and well-argued contentions, but is short on choices, priorities and decisions like so many contemporary metropolitan plans. It is widely viewed in Perth as a weak compromise between persistent economic pressures from above, demanding optimal conditions for investment, and growing community pressure from below, resisting development, particularly round established residential areas.

Conclusions

This somewhat discursive chapter began by outlining a broad and undifferentiated agenda of metropolitan planning issues which could be detected or surmised from recent reports, plans, processes and policy pronouncements. There appears to be an uneven engagement by each State with this inventory of issues and less commonality of approach than in earlier days. But there is a search for both more imaginative and feasible forms of urban development and planning placed within a wide interpretation of what comprises urban policy. This is most quixotically expressed in the term 'strategic planning', and its large number of different interpretations.

There followed a detailed description and interpretation about how South Australian events of recent years reflected or subscribed to parts of this agenda. In particular, the chapter described how the concept of strategic planning has been pursued and is still in the process of full articulation and development. A fuller interpretation and commentary on that experience will have to wait a couple of years. The Planning Review of 1990–1992 did not complete a system or a plan: it launched a process whose outcomes cannot yet be fully defined or described and which will undoubtedly be modified by the new Liberal government.

A few final observations. All States have been experimenting with different methods of community involvement in developing urban plans and legislation. Local government has generally been seen as a more active partner and contributor. The difficult economic fortunes of

Victoria and South Australia and changes in leadership are affecting urban conditions and policies in those States. Commonwealth involvement has been of varied value in these new kinds of operations. There still remains the need for more consistent and constant involvement in urban-related programs on the part of the Commonwealth, and more importantly, consideration of the urban impacts of policies pursued in terms of its broad constitutional responsibilities.

CHAPTER 7

Planning in a Multicultural Environment: A Challenge for the Nineties

Sophie Watson and Alec McGillivray[1]

'In those Local Government Areas in which immigrants are concentrated, Local Government's response to immigrant needs has, with a few exceptions, been slow and uneven. Many Local Governments recognise this and generally perceive the problem to be sourced in financial constraints.' This evaluation of immigration and local government budgets (Cutts 1992:xii) is supported by the concurrent evaluation of immigration on State government budgets: 'the present financial capacity of State governments is not adequate to provide education, housing and other services on the scale needed by many immigrants if they are to be fully integrated into Australian society' (Mathews 1992:xxiv). At a higher level, the Commonwealth government and its policies of fiscal restraint are blamed. Yet it is recognised by both documents that immigrants from non-English speaking backgrounds (NESBs) contribute more to government budgets than they claim back.

This purely financial outlook is a common rationale for limited action on social or urban issues, including planning which addresses multicultural issues. Making sure migrants, new and old, receive a 'fair go' is more often seen in the light of the goals of a democratic, interesting, vibrant country. While Australian popular opinion varies, often in direct relation to the strength of the economy, some level of immigration has been accepted by both parties. As Ian McAllister writes, 'Publicly at least, immigration is not on the elite agenda' (McAllister 1993:176). Across the governmental spectrum, there is general support for most aspects of multiculturalism, and the successful evolution of a multicultural society.

1 We would like to thank Joy Llewellyn-Smith for her contribution to this research.

This view was also reflected by everyone contacted and involved in the research which informs this chapter.

The focus of the research was aimed more narrowly, engaging in debates less often undertaken. Urban issues at the local level were examined and strategies for better response to NESB migrants were investigated. To date there has been no specific attempt, at a policy or theoretical level, to unravel the extent to which urban policy in Australia responds to the different needs of this population. While some of the positive strategies we find or recommend are limited by financial constraints, some are not. The perception of lack of funds as the source of slow and uneven responsiveness is limiting.

To get at the issues, the problems, and various attempted or successful planning and service provision strategies, the project undertaken was a qualitative one with the focus on interviews. Forty local government planners, social planners, community workers and migrant resource workers, and migrant representatives were interviewed individually and in groups. Most interviewees were from Fairfield and Penrith, with some representatives from neighbouring areas as well as several key Statewide agencies concerned with migrant issues, such as the Ethnic Affairs Commission (EAC). Context was also provided through a content analysis of planning documents and the coverage of migrant issues in the local media. (For more on the media and migrants consult Bell 1992 and Coupe & Jakubowicz 1992.) The interviews worked from a set of twenty open-ended questions on urban policy, multiculturalism, perception, and 'fit' of the suburban environment as well as the adequacy of consultation and service provision to migrants. While most questions were directed at all forty of the interviewees, some were tailored to the position of the people being interviewed. Planners and ethnic community officers faced the same questions, and the difference in response was one of the more interesting findings.

The focus of the research was on public sector policies: first, because Federal, State and local governments set many of the parameters within which private developers and organisations must operate; secondly, because it was outside the scope of the study to do any extensive interviewing of private sector players given the limited resources. This is not to suggest that private interests do not play a very critical part nor to suggest that the private sector or the market does not limit what is available and therefore defines demand. Some of these issues were touched on, but the focus remained on public planning responses to migrants and difference. (An 'in progress' description of the study can be found in the *Australian Planner* July 1992:78–80.) This chapter is one of several papers reporting on the results of this research. The others are a paper on housing, a more theoretical and critical paper on contested space and perception (Llewellyn-Smith & Watson 1992) and a forthcoming paper on planning and the politics of difference. The questions grew out of earlier work on women's housing issues and concerns about the responsiveness of Australian planning to difference (Watson 1988).

Western Sydney

The geographic focus of research is on an area that still shows a high degree of suburban physical homogeneity despite a decade, and often more, of in-migration of various diverse ethnic groups: groups that do not always live in ways traditionally planned for. By this is meant that migrants, particularly from non-Western countries, are often not used to the numerous regulatory processes involved in construction, the rigid separation of land uses, the low-density and inward-looking private nature of housing and space, the family arrangements prescribed by the housing stock, and the sometimes confusing layout of the 'city beautiful' neighbourhood unit plan that remains the template by which land is subdivided and developed. Yet in some localities there is adaptation going on. So Western Sydney provides the information needed to start to evaluate how, or if, urban policies are confronting diversity and change.

In particular, Fairfield and Penrith were looked at in detail. Fairfield was selected since it has the reputation of being one of the most multi-cultural local government areas in Sydney, stemming from a history of migrant settlement through a concentration of migrant reception hostels and the propensity for migrants to locate close to family and same-group populations. In 1991, 47.9 per cent of the population were born overseas, and there was a total of 109 language groups in the locality. There is also evidence of some change to the physical make-up of the area, with Cabramatta assuming a very ethnic-specific identity (Vietnamese). Penrith, in contrast, is a country town which has expanded and been subsumed into the Sydney region over the last decade. Despite the 13 per cent of migrants born overseas, there is little visible impact on the environment apart from the expansion of a fairly conservative form of subdivision development. It is interesting to ask if there are strategies and lessons that the latter can learn from the former.

Planning, as a key component of urban policy, is clearly political and works within certain constraints. There is a bureaucratic, social, legal, and council 'status quo' that tends, in many cases, to define existing processes and dampen the responsiveness to change new initiatives. Yet faced with the fact that the suburban environment is accommodating an increasingly diverse group of inhabitants and, indeed, has historically been more diverse than recognised, traditional planning must be revisited and questioned. As one planner in Fairfield said: 'We may have written the [land use and building] codes to reflect an Anglo-Saxon view of life.' Even within this notion, one type of the Anglo-Saxon view of life is constructed. In terms of service provision, a cultural planner noted, 'There is a real push to mainstreaming in Australia. The problem is it assumes people have equal abilities to compete, to articulate their needs.' They do not. This has to be accepted first and foremost. The profession no longer rests on the 'firm' public good foundations that were once taken as given. Also open to question is how reflective of, and responsive to, diversities are the channels to power and decision-making. Planners and service providers do or should have the training, the influence as information conduits, and opportunity through their role as facilitators and educators to work on both these questions within the broader arena of public debate.

But in pushing more progressive ideas, they are often, as John Forester phrases it, 'planning in the face of power' (Forester 1989). Before examining the problems we have found and the strategies of intervention that are being tried and which are working in the planning and physical environments, it is helpful to look first at the social environment that these are part of. Ruth Fincher's 1991 review of the literature on the impact of immigration on urban infrastructure concludes that immigrants' demands on the physical and social fabric of cities seem little different from those of the Australian-born population of the same ages and income levels. The interesting question is why this is the case, given a higher unemployment rate among migrants, the need in most cases for further or even initial language training, the various difficulties of settling in a new country and culture, and often a history of very different living conditions, ranging from a lifelong reliance on domestic help to a decade or so in a refugee camp. Does the lack of demands for services reflect a reluctance to make demands on what is available: a reluctance to counter the dominant cultural forms of provision for fear of being seen as a drain on resources and thus fuelling the fires of racist antagonism? A migrant worker put it most forcefully in an interview: 'the big barrier to implementing mainstreaming is racism, people not acknowledging that there are particularly cultural barriers [to multiculturalism]. My concern is who is going to check that ethnic communities are not again missing out.'

Contentious Sites

As mentioned, much of this debate is played out in the larger arena of public policy or sociological study, rather than with a local level planning focus. Some cultural differences and needs however have created controversy in the Sydney suburbs, and it is through these that some underlying political and sometimes racist forces are brought to light. One of the most contentious is the location of religious places of worship, so much so that in New South Wales the State government set up an interdepartmental committee chaired by the Ethnic Affairs Commission to examine planning for religious developments. In several local government areas Muslim or Hindu communities have either established in existing residential areas, or submitted a development application for, a mosque or temple. In some cases, a number of individuals have come together to acquire a site on which a residential dwelling or warehouse is currently located. In the instances examined the course of events is as follows: the local Muslim or Hindu community begins to use the building/s as a place of worship. As time goes on, more and more people visit the site until, on certain festival days like Ramadan, very large numbers of people arrive. This causes traffic and noise problems for the local residents who alert the local council. The planning officers visit the site and inform the group that it can no longer be used as a mosque or temple unless certain regulations are complied with.

In many cases, either at the end of the above stage, or in initial applications, site selection for places of worship causes conflicts. The architectural forms proposed are distinct and the patterns of usage are different from the Christian norm. Parking becomes an issue because of regional drawing power and poor public transport. It is also argued that the noise impact is greater since mosques and temples are used as social meeting places as well as places of worship. Still much of this conflict can be argued not on racist grounds, as one planner said, since most people would not like a church going up beside their house either. Nevertheless, newspaper articles reveal that some local politicians have not been embarrassed to express racist attitudes: 'the temple will not be an asset. There are no Vietnamese people living there. You are hoping to put in a complete foreign body in anticipation of people coming to use it' (*FA* 3 Mar. 1987:4). It is the Anglo-Australian body in danger of contamination. Or there is the case of an application to increase the height of a mosque spire at Smithfield that was refused 'on the grounds that it was likely to spoil the amenity of the area' (*FA* 21 Nov. 1989:11). 'Amenity', a somewhat ambiguous planning term referring to the visual landscape as well as more conventional variables, is often used to defend the way things are at present.

A second area of contested sites is a number of council-provided social clubs, particularly senior citizen clubs, where long use is seen to denote ownership. In one case, a group of Anglo-Australian senior citizens felt it was legitimate to keep a local club for their exclusive use. According to the president of the club, the rooms had been used by this group exclusively for fifteen years: 'Last year the Spanish senior citizens began using our rooms, and wish to use the inside toilets. This is not possible without allowing access to our private lounge room, the heart of our organisation, which contains all our records, private furniture and other material' (*FA* 18 Aug. 1987). Again, the metaphor of the body as sacred is evoked. Similar cases can be found in other publicly owned social and sporting clubs. What is important to recognise here is that planners often face a reluctance, by either a majority or a vocal minority, to accommodate change; the NIMBY (not-in-my-backyard) syndrome. Michael Dear (1990), in writing about this reluctance, states: 'Opposition arguments, after the initial angry phase, usually express three specific concerns: the perceived threat to property values, personal security, and neighbourhood amenity'.

A third area of contested sites is in the domestic/public interface. This is where migrants use domestic residences, in areas zoned residential, for commercial purposes. This may represent a genuine misunderstanding about the regulations, or may be an attempt to cut costs or to avoid compliance with employment regulations. The following were examples given in the interviews:

> I went out to have a look at this house and the guts had been ripped out of the house. How the roof stayed up I will never know. This guy had stripped the internal walls out, and it was only a conventional roof, to employ women from round and about his home to come in and do this sewing so he could produce a lot more. So he was starting his factory, unbeknown to anybody, in the middle of a residential area. And that was his means of cutting his price. Because he wasn't paying the necessary factory fees and everything else that the government requires, and he was doing it at night, and he had even developed to a stage where he had four shifts going. Women would come in and they'd work for the length of time he employed them and before they were finished, the next lot were waiting to slip into the seat while it was still warm to carry on. They were turning out clothes like sausages.

And another comment: 'They either know the rules and conveniently forget them, or they are totally oblivious that there are rules in relation to planning.'

Apart from the problems of employees working in unsuitable conditions, noise, pollution, parking problems and other such effects, the power supply is often put under stress: 'Poor old Prospect County Council are now having to go out to a lot of the areas and put in additional transformers to cope with the power supply demands. And it grows.' Rather than ignoring the problem, or forbidding home industries, Fairfield Council has tackled this issue head on – both in terms of providing more information to migrants and allowing home industries to be registered where certain conditions are met.

These examples illustrate some of the constraints the profession of planning works under: financial cutbacks in the form of fiscal restraint and conservative spending policy; political decision-making that can be influenced by racist attitudes, either held by a councillor (as one planner regretfully noted, these attitudes are not the sole property of Anglo-Australian councillors) or as the result of a desire to appease a significantly large or vocal group of her/his constituency. And, finally, the very real threat that change can pose in the mind of a home owner or renter, or those of the dominant class/gender that is not receptive to seeing things change. But while 'planning organizations are, of course, constrained, the planning process also recreates relations of political power' (Forester 1992:8). Some redistributive and advocacy planning work is a facet of every public sector planner wanting to avoid socially unnecessary distortions. Once planners can anticipate how 'the organizations with which they work render citizens powerless, they can begin to respond' (Forester 1992:79). And it is these organisations that we turn to, to look for ways local government planning responses to migrants can be faster and more even.

Housing and Urban Form

City shape is the stage upon which human relations are enacted. Every physical plan affects the city form and in turn this has economic and social implications. The physical spread of the suburbs of Western Sydney creates issues and problems common to all residents. Distance dislocates people from family, friends, services and facilities, and separates service- and care-givers from a section of the population in need of some form of assistance. The separation of residential and other activities is magnified for residents of new estates in the outer suburbs. Poor public transport turns a physical separation of residential and other uses into social isolation for those least likely to have access to a car: women, children, adolescents and the elderly. For migrants, one has to add to the lack of public transport the difficulty in understanding complicated timetables written in English or reading streets signs and the difficulty of orienting oneself in a homogeneous landscape; as one interviewee reported: 'uniformity is a danger, because you don't know where you are'. Such problems could be easily solved by putting key signs in several languages where appropriate.

Suburban public space is geared to traffic and generally unused or underused boulevard sidings, school playgrounds, and active recreational facilities such as soccer fields, cricket ovals, and baseball diamonds. These spaces are restricted to certain users or do not have appeal for social intermixing. As a migrant resources centre coordinator notes: 'the

Anglo-Australian leisure culture has not been related to festivals [and socialising] in the park or street parties. It is much more an individual one-on-one, *let's go to the beach*, type'. Again, careful recreational planning initiatives could create spaces that were more flexible and amenable to a range of different uses, such as shaded places for sitting and chatting, areas for badminton and bowls, tables for chess and so on.

Yet the Western suburbs, where many of these problems are the greatest, are the suburbs where housing is least expensive in the Sydney metropolitan region. They are the areas where new housing estates are being developed which is reflected in the percentage of first-time home buyers. And home ownership has been found to be as strong, if not stronger, a desire among migrants as among the Australian-born since it is perceived to represent greater security and personal control (Kee 1992). For these budget-conscious buyers or private renters there is a choice, as one Fairfield engineer points out: 'There are standard cluster homes, standard town-houses, standard 600-square-metre blocks, standard quarter-acre blocks.' But the emphasis is still on 'standard'. As another interviewee said: 'It would be really surprising if they [NESB] weren't used to different forms of housing. So far our response has just been that the Australian private sector provides housing of various sorts and anyone who wants to live here has to fit in as best they can'. Although the private housing building market is responsive at the middle and upper ends, for those that have less money there is little choice. Barbara Gapps of Fairfield City Council writes:

Fairfield continues to be one of the most interesting and dynamic Local Government Areas in Western Sydney and home to a diverse range of non-English speaking communities. Its human faces, dress and special places of worship and culture reflect its diversity. Its housing, however, is distinctly Australian. Despite the fact that many people in Fairfield may not be dreaming of the quarter-acre block, the challenge to change house design is one I believe we have not yet faced.

In the private and the surrounding public space there is a sameness of form.

In the public sector a problem arises with the size of most Housing Commission dwellings. As one migrant worker explained:

Asians often have more than three children. Even if you have three children or four children you can squeeze into a two-bedroom flat. And when you apply for housing, the department will put your name on the list according to the size of your family. If you have three children, then you will go to four, if you have four then you will have to go to five. But the Department of Housing doesn't have many of those. Mostly two- and three-bedroom houses that's all. And if the Asian family apply for that one they say 'no, you have to wait for four bedroom'. They have to wait five or six years . . .

On the other hand, Fairfield and other councils have tried to address the desire that many migrants have for sharing their residential space with other family members in the form of granny flats or other extensions or additions. These are the provisions for dual occupancy.

Another important migrant housing issue is migrants' relationship with lending institutions. Here it is a question of lending institutions needing to be aware of different cultural practices and to find ways of either providing accessible information as to their practices or becoming more flexible in their own rules – which is difficult, given their responsibilities to the shareholders. First, many Asian families are reluctant to place their money in a bank and are therefore disadvantaged when attempting to borrow money. Second, Asians group together and practice Tonti – a group mechanism for borrowing money without interest. A building society manager explained:

> They have their deposit but it's not in the bank and that's maybe due to the mistrust of financial institutions but also the way that they lent money between each other and between their families in Vietnam. They all contribute and if one wants to buy something they all pay. And then they'll get the money back when they need to buy something themselves. But it's very difficult for a lending institution to be able to justify those savings. This is the main difficulty we have in lending to the Asian community. Because we can't see that it's their money. A lot of our loan applications get declined because of that reason because we can't verify it.

And:

> It's very difficult to get that message across to the community, that 'please trust us, save your money in a bank, because then we can help you with a loan'. Otherwise they don't get a loan. You wouldn't accept the deposit was under the mattress. If you did, they would have to be able to justify where it came from by way of the savings – by their income, what they've earnt, their expenses, etc. If on paper their income is $2000 and their expenses are $1800 per month and the net income is $200 a month and they walk in with $50 000 cash, it doesn't tie up.

A Vietnamese interviewee described the Tonti as follows: 'We have thirty people in a group and we decide which amount that everyone has to put in every month, say $300. From thirty people, they can have a turn to get the whole money each month. So, one by one they get the money.'

Rethinking Planning

Some of the problems that migrants face derive from the two 'cultures' of planning revealed in this study. The first culture is the Australian conceptualisation of physical planning and its continued dominance of local government planning. Observations and interviews conducted during this research have reinforced the position of such commentators as David Wilmoth that, 'Unlike urban planners in USA, Asia and even UK, Australian urban planning has clung to its land use planning and development control core, a peculiarly defensive response' (Wilmoth 1987:138). The high-powered and economically significant issues centre on physical planning: physical infrastructure, negotiations with developers over financing of some public services through the New South Wales Environmental Planning and Assessment Act section 94 contributions, the enforcement of building codes, and the allocation of land. Within the process, certain norms and standards have been built up that assist in this type of planning and are legitimised by their formal or informal enactment in codes and processes. John Toon writes of these public spaces and building form standards: '[they] are coming under increased scrutiny in terms of their continued relevance to the communities they serve. The conventions which have distributed community space to particular user groups are now regarded as just that – conventions' (Toon 1987:6). Or at least they should be. Undue limits on what people can do on their private land and 'unjust' space allocation on public land are something to be guarded against. Simply, 'racism enshrined in law serves as the model for citizens to follow' (Tatz 1972:13).

The problem is that physical planning culture tends to see planning solely as plans, with the officially or culturally codified two-dimensional elements that implies. Patrick Troy points to planning's achievements: 'It took planning powers to put an end to socially unjust speculative subdivision by ensuring that roads and services were built at the subdivider's expense. Sewers before settlement – now taken for granted – is one of the most dramatic changes brought about by planning in the postwar period' (Troy 1987:27). Yet these goals and focuses sometimes skew the direction of planning, and the separation of social planning and physical planning make altering this skewed focus difficult. Rather than physical planning being conceived as the provision of land, housing, roads, and urban infrastructure for clear social ends, physical planning sometimes becomes an end in itself. In *Out West* Powell (1993) details the West's growth and historical lack of services. Jill Lang, in a review of the provision of social infrastructure, writes: 'Because of section 94, social planning in many of the fringe local councils is concerned only with obtaining contributions from developers in new release areas. There is little ongoing commitment to integrating social issues into town planning decisions' (Lang 1990:93). This was also the overwhelming view of this type of physical planning given by the second culture of planning, the social planners and service providers.

Consultation and the gaining of input on social and migrant needs 'come in as an afterthought'. 'Social planning input is vital from day one but other people's jobs are easier if it is not included.' Migrant workers are there to deal with those who are not able to 'fit in'. The view of these interviewees was highlighted by the response of many of the planners dealing with the physical and land-use side of issues that there were no specific migrant problems that they could think of.

This is a relevant finding, but it is important to note some positive things being done in this field. The better integration of a multiplicity of concerns will take time and work, including, as a number of respondents pointed out, better integration within the tertiary-planning school curriculum. Today, as Forester notes, 'the planner or admin-istrator who fails to appreciate institutional constraints will overreach and underachieve – and will be ineffective, if only because time and resources are always scarce, organisationally allocated, forcing bounds upon the practitioner's analysis' (Forester 1989:7). Within constraints that often include political and/or popular opposition, physical planners are introducing dual occupancy; consolidating, loosening and sometimes simplifying zoning regulations; expanding what is considered under section 94 contributions; and, in some instances, such as Fairfield, introducing progressive policies dealing with home industry. Specifically, there is a noticed desire to promote a built form that increases options in house forms and to foster small-scale businesses to lessen unemployment and promote growth. The chief planner at Fairfield indicates decisions are even being made on what building and space allocation codes are tied to relatively non-contentious variables, such as climate, public health, and privacy and shading, and which are socially constructed and a detriment to multicultural change. With a few exceptions, and with mixed degrees of commitment, there does seem to be a willingness to begin questioning conventions. Yet often the planners interviewed, particularly those in Penrith, took a while to get to this point of recognising that 'in the physical planning sense I don't think that we have really got to a point of thinking about special migrant or ethnic groups'. Another stressed that 'if you are getting a shift in the . . . ethnic make-up of the place where you haven't encountered that before – there's nothing to draw on from the past – then it becomes a very difficult exercise'. Difficult but important: and less difficult if done through consultation.

Further, places of worship are being secured, sometimes with innovative planning such as shared parking between facilities if holidays and worship times do not conflict. A NSW Department of Local Government worker regrets the combative position now taken from the beginning of the applications for places of worship. This forces the issue to the State level, where resolution should be at least attempted carefully at the local level. Migrants are doing some of the housing developing. This (hopefully) leads to planners recognising that difference is out there, and that they do hold ethnocentric norms: '[a development was] not really Ordinance 70 problems, just floor plan design that we didn't see as the normal way to do it'. A recreation and cultural service manager who was interviewed (a position that has a little of both planning cultures in its mandate) states: 'I am aware that communities of different types of backgrounds are starting to spring up. I think it is incumbent on us as providers of a range of services that those needs are identified and taken on board.' The eighty employees in his locality are being used as sources to explore different needs. Finally, a park in Mt Druitt is being converted. Community tree planting and public involvement is resulting in more representative land allocation.

There is still a need to better facilitate an understanding of the planning process so that meaningful input of a multicultural perspective can be achieved. There is an ever-pressing need for explanation of how to use the services of local government and other organisations through the provision of information in major community languages using the ethnic media and other points of contact. There must be an increased flexibility in the subjective assessment of the merit of projects, large and small, submitted for approval. It is here, on the process side of the equation, that the culture of service provision and social planning can shift to better interact with physical planning. Seeing things as a process, interviewees tended to reveal that they did not tie things as closely to geographic representation. Yet migrant problems and preferences were recognised by respondents and, if they were presented as important in geographic allocation and development decisions, could well carry more influence. Unfortunately, many of the local planning departments in Western Sydney have no social planner or only one, who invariably has not been through the same training and education of most land-use planners. In most cases they come from a different work background, which has more in common with the community or social service sector. In councils where there are no social planners, the social/community perspective and responsibility are left to the community development officers within the council: 'In effect what happens is that the social planners pick up the negative fall-outs'.

With financial resources looking to remain modest, it is up to both planning 'cultures' to work more closely at the beginning of the process to deal with change. On this we can report some headway: the above examples, the knowledge on the part of physical planners that the infor-mation was with their planning counterparts (now for the next step), and a migrant worker who regularly checks development applications from migrants that have been turned down to question decisions. This double check can help divide the ones that are being turned down for reasons that are 'legitimate' (e.g. the construction as proposed is not appropriate for the NSW climate) and those that are not (e.g. those designs that do not conform to what are perceived as normal). Allbrook and Cattalini (1988) discuss some of these strategies in the larger policy debates in *Community Relations in a Multicultural Society*.

The Power of Information

The source of much of a planner's power is derived from information. In the interviews, many respondents did seem to be waiting on the 1991 census data to see how the populations in question were changing (some results were provided earlier). It is the planners' role to try to understand the heterogeneous make-up of the population. Statistical information is available on gender and age, household structure, housing structure, home ownership and percentage of income spent on housing, income and job status, level of education, some information on health, country of origin or ethnicity (often grouped into NESB and ESB), proficiency in English, religion, reason for immigration and status, and by other variables, all of which can be combined in various configurations. Service provision is most strongly based on these criteria. Pockets of 'isolated' NESB populations can be found, community workers can be hired with language proficiency in areas of need, and migrant provision can be located based on findings such as these. Here funding was the critical element most noted by those professionals interviewed. There was not enough. A second key point that the range of variables, the service providers, the migrant access planners and others pointed to was that migrants, even when disaggregated, are not a homogeneous group. Large variations on all of the scales listed above as well as some that are not measured, like status of family in the departed country, are also important. Heterogeneity has to be taken on board.

Physical planning, especially for new release areas, is based on a more limited set of data based on household size and age of recently developed areas as well as of the broader population. Yet these statistics often mask variation and support the construction/planning of a set and known number of land uses and housing forms. Models of development need to be worked out that also support the planning of a wider variety, or at least a more adaptable set of subdivisions. Planners spoken to recognise the homogeneity of housing form and land subdivision, but do not seem to be taking a next step. One of the easiest ways of doing this is through the use of the social planners at the beginning of the planning process to address issues. This can introduce an element of creativity and local adaptation of the conventions that often are solely relied on to lay out new release areas. Such elements as the desire for 'traditional' shopping streets, corner stores for the many groups that like to shop daily, intimate parks and pockets of commercial areas to sit and play chess, badminton courts in recreational halls, all will emerge as new forms are tried. Norms can be questioned and developers pushed to be more creative, particularly since physical design would be considered as in a 'dialogue' with planning conventions. Across the board, formal and informal measures of communication and information sharing between facets of community, planning and developers are needed.

One of the key areas where information sharing improvement is needed is not between the planners, or between the planners and council, but between local government in total and the migrant community. Certain information documents, particularly information on what local government does and how it works, are needed in a number of languages. When enquiries are made, extra effort needs to be put in to bridging difference; often harder than it sounds for overworked clerical and reception staff. Lists of volunteers, employees and politicians who are willing to do translation for enquiries could be compiled. Such details as the fact that some communities, such as migrants from Arabic countries, do not have the same understanding of community services emerge. Gender issues, such as Arabic women's relative exclusion from the public sphere, need also to be taken into account. Information collection and dissemination is a hard enough task with the English-speaking, Australian-born population; it must be looked on as a 'rewarding challenge' to improve it with the migrant community. As one community worker in Penrith said: 'Lack of community awareness of cultural differences . . . leads to fear on the part of older Australians. Community workers need resources to break down the barriers on both sides.'

Finally, some of the roles of planners, as we see them, need to be stressed. Planners must facilitate change and interaction. While service providers and social planners should continue to lobby for more needed resources, thought must also be given to how more can be done with less. On top of an already full workload, this is not easy. The physical planners must, for their part, also take up the role of facilitator. Needs and demands of migrants, general services, and other elements must be incorporated into plans and codes in order that the private developers will also work towards change. Here again, information needs to be passed on to other parties and coordination engaged in. Physical planners can discuss with developers the numbers of migrants that will probably move into a new area, and their possible needs as different from the 'normal' house plan.

Conclusions

Migrants now make up a significant percentage of the populations of Western Sydney, yet the fabric of this largely suburban region has not changed markedly. The implication for urban policy is that past practices may not always be appropriate in the future. We have found reasons both in the reluctance to change heretofore unchallenged space allocation and development conventions and an information divide between physical and social planning, and between local governments and some community needs and desires. We have also found some strategies to help. Most important, questions must be raised, even if the answers are not clear. Urban policy makers and planners need to be aware of some underlying status quo assumptions that guide urban policy and planning, and the implications for the way in which these restrict a realisation of cross-cultural difference.

CHAPTER 8

Local Government and
the Urban Growth Debate

Renate Howe

The perception of local government as the third and least relevant tier of government in urban planning is changing. The expansion of the role of local government in social and physical planning in the 1980s has led to a revolution in Australian town halls and the emergence of a more complex pattern of partnerships between governments, infrastructure authorities and the private sector. These changes are a response to the impact of global forces on Australian urban development which have resulted in dramatic population and economic changes in local areas. The relationship of global/local change is the essential framework for any meaningful analysis of local government and the urban debate.

Australia is not alone in experiencing change in inter-government relations as a result of world-wide trends in globalisation and inter-nationalisation:

> throughout the world, there are a series of changes taking place which impact on regional and local governments, forcing them to adapt their behaviour and to change their relationship with other levels of government vertically and horizontally ... Some of these changes are political ... some are social – greater migration, and social segregation of cities; but the major driving force has undoubtedly been that of economic change. (Goldsmith 1993:683)

World-wide trends in the trade of agricultural and mining products, the shift in the location of industrial/manufacturing activities, the growing importance of the financial and service sectors, the dominance of multinational interests and the communications revolution have especially impacted on Australian local communities. The urban impact of these changes has not been a return to the traditional urban patterns of the post-World War II decades – suburban development of capital

cities, especially Melbourne and Sydney – but has rather been influenced by the changing geography of employment opportunities,
demographic changes and a remarkable fluidity in growth and decline
patterns. Four of the country's seven fastest growing urban areas are in
Queensland, while Perth on the west coast was the fastest growing capital
city in the 1986–1989 period (Maher 1993:797–801).

The ability of local government in Australia to respond to these
changed urban patterns of development has been limited by its small
size, the lack of inter-government coordination (especially between State
and local governments) inherent in the federal system and by its own
structures and practices. Thus, rather than enhancing the potential of
governments to expand their policy purview, the structural position of
the 'local State' in Australia has tended to restrict policy development
(Wanna & Davies 1992). In international terms Australian local governments are smaller, less powerful and more easily dismissed than
equivalents in any other country. Although local government has been
recognised as the gatekeeper for Australian urban development
(AURDR 1994) this role has been limited by the lack of capacity, both
financial and administrative, to develop a policy framework. The extent
to which inter-government cooperation is achieved and the extent to
which local government structures are reformed, will determine its
future influence.

In the review of current metropolitan strategic planning which I
undertook in 1992 at the Urban Research Program, it was clear that the
strategic planning process was slowly recognising the need for a more
coordinated approach between levels of governments and the
importance of local government in developing and especially in
implementing strategy plans (Howe & Norman 1992). In South Australia
the Final Report of the Planning Review recommended a broader
framework for local strategic planning 'to allow local government to
inform strategic decisions at the metropolitan level' (20:20 Vision 1992).
In New South Wales a discussion paper released by the Department of
Planning emphasised the need for local plans to address strategic
decisions by State governments and the Commonwealth government
(Modernising the Planning system in NSW 1991). The National Housing
Strategy identified as a major priority the need for improvement in
strategic planning processes, especially liaison between the three tiers of
government (NHS 1991b).

Generally, metropolitan strategic planning undertaken by State
governments has ignored local government. Of the three priorities of
metropolitan strategic planning in the 1980s identified in the URP study
– coordinating urban fringe development and infrastructure provision,

encouraging urban consolidation and controlling suburban retail and commercial centres – there has been most success with the development of urban management systems to coordinate fringe development and infrastructure provision in capital cities. In New South Wales, Victoria, South Australia and Western Australia, local government has joined with Federal and State governments, infrastructure authorities and the private sector in regulating development on the fringe of cities (Howe & Norman 1992:3–11). However, a report on the influence of local government in these urban management systems recommended that local government could play a more central role especially by collecting local and regional information, monitoring the extent to which funding met identified local or regional needs and by coordinating urban development with the provision of human services (Lang 1991).

> Local Government has considerable potential to develop integrated approaches to urban development and restructuring. This potential is made more realistic because Local Government carries out almost all building and development approvals in all States, as well as being responsible for local strategic planning, which allows it to shape investment patterns. It is also a significant provider and coordinator of urban infrastructure. (NHS 1991b)

If local government is to expand its role in urban management systems and strategic planning more resources are needed; the NHS recognised this, recommending that the Federal government provide financial assistance to local government to establish the data systems necessary for modern urban planning. However, strategic planning resources within local government have been meagre and unco-ordinated and 'it is rare for strategic planners to work from a vision of desired outcomes for a community and then develop a corporate approach across the multiplicity of council functions' (Crofts 1992).

The URP study also found that urban management systems related to fringe development and infrastructure provision had not been used to monitor the other strategic planning objectives of urban consolidation in established urban areas and controlling the location and size of retail and commercial developments and district centres. On these important and contentious issues in the urban growth debate, local government has been marginal to the strategic planning process in metropolitan areas.

The most significant developments in inter-government coordination have taken place in Federal government attempts to introduce more uniform yet less prescriptive standards into the statutory planning system. Especially significant are direct federal/local inititiatives in which the State government is either not involved or plays a marginal role. Some examples are programs to encourage a uniform approach to building and planning codes. In February 1992 the Local Areas Review Program (LARP) released a *Better Approvals Practices Manual* as a tool for councils to use in assessing their approvals systems. The Australian Model Code for Residential Development (AMCORD) is based on a performance standard rather than a prescriptive approach to development while the Review of Residential Regulations (RRR) is an attempt by the Federal government to facilitate reform in local government regulatory practices. The Integrated Local Area Planning (ILAP) program, the direct funding of some projects through the One Nation Capital Works program and the Building Better Cities program, which has as one of its objectives the encouragement of government coordination, are other programs in which Federal and local government can have a direct relationship. It would seem that the model of federal/local programs that has been developed in the social (especially the Home and Community Care program) and cultural sectors, where there are a plethora of specific purpose grants for local projects, is increasingly being applied to urban development.

These developments reflect concern by the Federal government that money filtered through the States is not getting to local programs and that therefore direct dealing with regional or local levels of government may improve the implementation of policies. An investigation of local government financing is one of the first projects of the Australian Urban and Regional Development Review. The impact of new Local Government Acts passed in 1992 and 1993 by all State and Territory governments (except the ACT) on relationships between the tiers of government cannot yet be assessed, but all are characterised by a move to greater responsibility and accountability and allow the development of Partnership Agreements between local and other levels of government (Wensing 1993).

There have been positive and negative responses from local government to these changing relationships. Devolution of responsibility to local government from State governments and Federal government is not always accompanied by devolution of power and resources. Local government is also concerned that direct funding of specific programs limits local government initiative and policy potential (Munro 1993). Nevertheless, the broadening of local government responsibilities and coordination initiatives have been important factors in influencing organisational changes at the local level, the most significant being (inward) re-organisation within local government structures and (outward) the increasingly cooperative relationships between councils, especially the formation of Regional Organisations of Councils (ROCs).

The latter development is especially significant, as the overwhelming characteristic of Australian local government has been the number and diversity of municipal governments, with approximately 810 councils and shires throughout the nation ranging from small rural shires to large metropolitan councils. Historically, there have been few successful attempts at amalgamation of local governments in either metropolitan areas (with the exception of the Brisbane council amalgamations in the 1920s) or in country areas. There has been a plethora of regional authorities of varying powers and effectiveness that have emerged from time to time, with the most complete attempt to develop a regional structure during the Whitlam Federal government in the 1970s (Troy 1978). Local government itself has generally opposed amalgamations and regional bodies imposed by other tiers of government. The need to develop more comprehensive policies as national and international changes impact at the local level is changing the culture at town halls towards relations with neighbouring councils, leading to the bottom-up formation of ROCs.

Although the impetus for regional cooperation has often been driven by the search for efficiency of service delivery (collecting the garbage or sharing computers) rather than strategic planning and policy considerations, this is now changing. A study for the Municipal Association of Victoria (MAV) identified the pressure for Victorian councils to enlarge their role in response to the economic growth or decline of a local area. 'The prospect of rapid population growth as in Werribee, or of decline as in Moe, have clearly motivated councillor commitment to local economic development. The decline in manufacturing, as in the City of Melbourne, or the threatened decline of a major retail precinct as in the City of Malvern, have also encouraged a more interventionist approach' (Munro 1993:3).

In this MAV study the issue of scale was identified as integral to confronting issues of economic growth or decline and the constraints of municipal fragmentation were seen to be best overcome by participation in a regional body. ROCs have quickly developed network and lobbying functions. The executive director of the Outer Eastern Municipalities' Association (OEMA), representing seven Melbourne municipalities, identified the lobbying functions of the association as more important than resource sharing between councils. 'There has been a large growth in regional organisations just in the past few years so while they might have had a down time in the 80s they are gaining strength now . . . Regional organisations have the ability to get a better deal for their communities in areas they are not directly responsible for . . . such as employment and education' (Rance 1992).

Two of the larger and more effective ROCs have survived from the regional government initiatives of the Whitlam years – the Western Region Council in Melbourne and the Western Sydney Regional Organisation of Councils (WESROC). The Western Region Council has been effective in developing policies to tackle the economic collapse of Melbourne's western suburbs while WESROC recently produced a study 'Consolidating for People' outlining the lack of coordination of medium-density development with social infrastructure and human services in this fast-growing metropolitan region (Gooding 1990). In Adelaide, cooperation between the City of Adelaide, Enfield and Wood-ville in industrial planning has been achieved through the Northern Regional Organisation of Councils (NOROC) which emphasises co-operation and partnership. The challenge of economic growth or decline is an impetus for ROC formation in metropolitan and rural areas and has contributed to overcoming the hostile attitude of Australian local government towards regional organisation.

Peak local government groups have supported the Federal government's Integrated Local Area Planning program and in general have supported a regionalism strategy (ALGA 1992), although the State municipal associations are not always as enthusiastic. In Victoria, the six metropolitan ROCs have no formal relationship with the MAV which, while supporting regional organisations in principle, recognises the potential of the ROCs 'as an alternative political power base' for local government (Munro 1993:7).

A more important priority for peak local government bodies at State and federal level has been the encouragement of a 'micro-economic reform agenda' for local government which emphasises an overhaul of town hall bureaucracies and the introduction of corporate management structures such as the replacement of town clerks and city engineers by chief executive officers, the development of new work methods and procedures and the contracting out of traditional services. It is these issues which tend to dominate local government organisations and conferences rather than issues of regional linkages and cross-sectoral coordination as a means of more meaningful participation in strategic planning processes.

Are the ROCs a significant development with the potential to enable local government to have a more effective role in strategic planning? Their size, power and funding varies considerably. Most have no guaranteed core funding and depend on the financial contributions of cooperating councils although in the future they may seek to be eligible for Federal government financial assistance grants. Many have no paid executive officer and depend on attracting outside research grants for important studies and data gathering. So far neither State nor local governments have been prepared to devolve significant powers or financial resources to ROCs. At the State level there is little recognition of ROCs by relevant State government departments or statutory authorities. Both State government and Federal government departments have defined their own regions creating 'an overlapping web of committees and regions in which councils are changeably located . . . Strategic economic planning and coordination is currently ill-developed at local and regional levels . . . Responsibility is fragmented between a variety of separately funded bodies and services, statutory and community-based' (Munro 1993:4–5).

The ROCs are an encouraging development in terms of fostering inter-government cooperation but are not having a significant impact on the limiting structural position of the 'local state' in terms of influencing the global and national changes affecting Australian regional economies and the shape of urban development. It is problematic that the ROCs could form the basis for the development of the Regional Development Corporations advocated by Peter Self in chapter 11. The strengths of the voluntary system of regional organisation are rather in advocacy and lobbying other tiers of government and providing a forum in which issues of regional concern can be discussed, but 'the fact remains that such voluntary bodies do not have the mandate to effectively manage the growth and development of the wider regional areas' (SEQROC 1993(1):47).

The Taskforce on Regional Development (headed by ACTU secretary, Bill Kelty) has also recommended forms of regional organisation in which the role of ROCs would be problematic (*Developing Australia; A Regional Perspective* 1993). The Kelty taskforce found problems 'relating to the definition of a region, the structures within a region and a region's relationship with the three spheres of government'. The taskforce report exposes the rivalry between Regional Economic Development Organisations (REDOs), which dominated submissions to the taskforce, and the local government ROCs. The composition of REDOs varies between States – in South Australia they represent local government, industry and community groups; in New South Wales, Regional Development Boards are appointed by the State minister and have no local government representation; in Victoria, REDOs are a small-scale initiative of the State government and it was in this State that ROCs made the most substantial submissions to the taskforce (Taskforce on Regional Development 1993(2)).

There is strong resistance among REDOs to local council involvement in economic development decisions which affect urban growth and the peak organisations believe that 'an effective relationship can only rarely be established between a council and the private sector in promoting economic development and even argue that regional organisations need to be autonomous and seen to be independent of councils' (Munro 1993:16). It is not entirely clear that the Kelty taskforce report supports this view; the recommendation for REDOs to be the basis for new regional structures does not spell out their nature and composition. Reference is made to the incorporation of existing structures and the need to encourage councils and shires 'to work together in regional groupings' noting the submission of the Queensland Local Government Association that 'various areas of government funding should be moved to the regions to give them more say in the allocation of resources . . . local government could play a more effective role in coordinating and integrating programs from each sphere of government at a regional level' (Taskforce on Regional Development 1993(1):68). It is possible that the establishment of REDOs and their capacity to enter into regional agreements in relation to development proposals could give a major impetus to the establishment and upgrading of ROCs, allowing local government to influence regional economic development planning and coordinate urban development with human services.

The Vulnerability of Local Government

The repositioning of the Australian economy in a global context has especially impacted on the capital cities. Global and international pressures have been very intense for central city governments trying to reverse decay and population drift to distant suburbs.

Central city government has 'never sat comfortably in the structure of local government' (Lennon 1993), and there are tensions between ALGA and the capital city councils. The search for a suitable city government model in the 1980s has been fraught with tensions between State governments, central-city councils and surrounding inner-city councils. In the struggle for political control of the central city, powers have been removed from councils, and administrators and planning committees appointed. Factional politics have prevailed with a rapid succession of Lord Mayors and councillors sitting in council chambers. Fiascos over the election of Lord Mayors of Melbourne led the *Age* to regularly dub Melbourne's city government 'clown hall'. The 1993 Conference of Capital City Mayors was told that, during the 1980s, central-city governments in Perth, Adelaide, Melbourne and Sydney were ineffective in preventing the demolition of historic precincts and buildings, the over-supply of commercial buildings, the flight of retailing and jobs from the city and inner suburbs and a steady population drain from central and inner-city areas (Lennon 1993). This failure occurred despite the resources of central-city governments which have the largest planning departments in local government and in Brisbane and Hobart are larger than State government planning departments.

The problems of central-city government magnify the dilemmas for local government of managing urban change. It is central-city and inner-suburban councils, for example, that are important in approving and monitoring urban consolidation projects, especially location, accessibility and suitability of infrastructure (see Lionel Orchard's comments in chapter 3). If the population drain is to be halted, the Conference of Capital City Mayors was told that inner-city and central-city councils should be working harder to target residential markets and that 'if higher residential densities are to be successful it also means that the councils should be far more innovative and participatory' and that a 'joint partnership' approach with State governments was needed (Lennon 1993). Yet the trend is away from such a 'joint partnership' ideal; even the most powerful of local governments have been unable to resist the strength of State governments in conflict over planning issues. State governments have appointed administrators to replace central-city councils in Melbourne and Perth. In Sydney, planning powers were taken away from Sydney City Council in 1988 and given to the Central Sydney Planning Committee (CSPC). The sacking of the Melbourne City Council, the appointment of commissioners and the redrawing of boundaries was undoubtedly hastened by the plotting and intrigue in the city, but was also a response to a review dating from 1991 on the need to recast the government of central Melbourne, 'an area administered by eight municipalities and a myriad of Victorian Government departments and agencies. There are effectively ten planning agencies within a 5-kilometre radius of the GPO' (Gettler 1993:6). Planning authorities in the Sydney CBD include the Darling Harbour and Sydney Cove authorities, the City Council, the CSPC, the Heritage Council, the Land and Environment Court, the Department of Planning and the Minister for Planning.

The lack of legal autonomy makes local government vulnerable to sacking by State governments and to having decisions overturned by State planning ministers, usually on the grounds of the larger economic development needs of the State. In the inner Melbourne suburb of Richmond, the deputy mayor complained when the State Planning Minister overturned a decision of the council to refuse a permit for a large knitting mill because the council had put the views of residents before economic considerations. 'This is happening more and more but local government should have its own integrity . . . It's a bit like someone reaching 21, becoming a fully fledged adult and having the parent rush in and interfere. Local governments are mature enough and experienced enough and have the local knowledge to make decisions' (Cook 1993).

This is not a view that State governments share. As Tim Bonyhady points out in chapter 5, the parochialism of local government is usually given as the reason for the removal of planning powers. Increasingly State ministers and planning departments act as de facto local councils in relation to a range of planning matters. When approval of projects worth more than $20 million and employing more than twenty people were designated to be approved by the NSW Minister for Planning instead of local councils, the reasons given included the time taken in decision-making and the influence on decision-making of local interest groups. State governments are able to exploit uncertainty as to whether local government has the capacity for informed urban policy-making and planning in today's complex city. A recent analysis of the development of the highly successful Southbank area in central Melbourne described the approach of Melbourne City Councillors as 'parochial' as 'the respective councillors tried to protect their constituency and not the interests of Melbourne as a regional, national and international centre', and concluded that 'cross-sectoral coordination would be most enhanced through the creation of greater or regional councils which would better define common needs and opportunities and provide valuable input into the coordination and development process' (Siebert 1993:13).

Certainly the strategic capacity of local government has improved enormously in recent years with better managerial skills and more professionally trained staff. However, as the Australian Local Government Association (1992:4) draft discussion paper on *Towards Integrated Local Area Planning* notes, 'the complex interplay between elected members and senior managers which characterises Local Government' and 'the sheer amount of work involved in effective strategic and corporate planning will require additional resources'. There is also a problem in the uneven distribution of planning expertise nationally, regionally and within cities which affects the ability of local government in the most vulnerable areas of economic and population change, to develop urban management policies. The development of the Gold Coast in Queensland, Australia's fastest growing area of urban settlement (Maher 1993:799), has largely been the responsibility of a former rural shire council, the Albert Shire. The city of Cairns in North Queensland is another fast-growing urban area. The sections of the city where most urban development is taking place is under the control of the Mulgrave Shire – again, a former rural local council. These small units of government have had to adapt to the complex and rapid development of the areas for which they are responsible. The candidates for election as Gold Coast mayor in 1994 included a 'campaigner for nude bathing who has a charge for prostitution pending, a television and music hall entertainer and a marketing consultant whose penchant for self-promotion seemingly knows no bounds' (Meade 1994). Allowing for media exaggeration, the quality of some candidates offering to lead the second largest local authority in Australia (after Brisbane) with an annual budget over $200 million must be a concern.

> Planning, and especially regional planning, represents an area of traditional policy neglect in Queensland. This is explained in part by a unique division of powers in Queensland such that local authorities rather than the State government have the major responsibility for land-use development and physical services. Local government jurisdiction in planning poses a challenge for the State in how best to strategically manage regional growth, while at the same time respecting local authority autonomy.(Caulfield 1992:2)

The response of the Queensland Labor government to this dilemma was to set up the South East Queensland (SEQ) 2001 project, representing State, Federal and local governments, the private sector and community groups to report on government options. The project's draft document on growth management, *Creating Our Future*, argues that the growth of the area 'transcends existing institutional boundaries' and that 'a regional approach to growth management and coordination are needed'. The document argues that the achievement of cooperation between State government and local authorities on regional development objectives will not be easy because 'the development of a model which is not cumbersome and which is based on cooperation will require significant commitment to the negotiation and achievement of shared and often long-term outcomes' (*SEQ2001* 1993:41).

A Regional Coordination Committee, representing the three levels of government with community involvement through a Regional Non-Government Sector Committee, is recommended as the new body to take on the implementation of the growth management plan. Resources would be made available to the Regional Co-ordination Committee through a special unit of the State government's Housing and Planning Department. The debate about the appropriate form of government for the SEQ sector is of great significance, especially as urban development continues in previously rural or semi-rural areas and where a model of effective regional government is an increasingly urgent need.

Closer to the People?

Closeness to the people is the great justification of Australia's small units of local government. But who are the 'people' local government is closest to? Tim Bonyhady's chapter provides case studies of the conflict between residents and local government in Sydney over council decisions related to urban growth. There are, of course, other examples where residents' groups and local councils have been as one, usually to fight State government planning decisions such as the Merri Creek powerline in Melbourne or commercial development in North Sydney.

> The growth agenda is intensely political and community activism wide-spread. This activism is not always apparent but is most easily identified in the establishment of voluntary groups. In Brisbane these groups constellate around two broad types. The first is the developer lobby – business and associated groups who stand to benefit from the intensification of land use through increased investment and population growth. The second type represents a coalition of resident, environmental and welfare groups, more concerned with quality-of-life issues and possibly alternative routes to growth. (Caulfield & Davies 1992:3)

These groups are usually represented among the councillors themselves. Representation on local councils has changed considerably in the 1970s and 1980s, with far more women and resident groups now represented than in the past, although in many crucial urban and regional areas of Australia the traditional dominance of male developers and local business interests prevails. Although this is the most accessible level of government, restraints of time and money limit the extent to which many population groups in local communities can undertake this demanding and time-consuming voluntary job. The dominant Anglo-Celtic ethos of Australian local government is evidence that ethnic populations and cultures are marginal at this level of government. Local government has not had a participatory image, with many cities and shires run by benevolent dictators disguised as town clerks and shire secretaries (Munro 1993). In more recent times, the corporatisation of structures and the increase in professional staff has also had the effect of marginalising elected councillors and community groups.

There is wide-spread criticism of the inflexible way that local government is perceived to have implemented urban planning and a growing demand for more flexible controls and more pro-active planners. Although planning processes in most States allow for formal objections to the granting of permits, such participation is seen as a middle-class prerogative which comes too late in the planning process, making it possible to at best modify rather than prevent developments. This disquiet was expressed at a recent Royal Australian Planning

Institute workshop held in Canberra, one of the current urban growth areas.

> The continuing growth of Canberra together with a relatively new style of 'local' government has presented both the government and the community with some 'teething' problems. Planning issues such as redevelopment of existing residential areas and the planning of future growth areas already require careful consideration. The message from the workshop is that a more collaborative approach is required during the early stages of the planning process if the long-term interests of the community are to be met. (RAPI–ACT 1993:2)

Statutory consultation requirements also focus participation on small-scale developments making it difficult for objectors to get into the debate about the big picture while the large developments have, as has been noted, become a State government responsibility (Munro-Clark 1992). In a recent article, Judge McClelland of the Land and Environment Court of New South Wales – established in 1976 'to make provision for maximum feasible participation by the community in a wide range of areas' – expressed his disenchantment with the court and its failure to ensure third parties the right of appeal argued on merit. Instead, the State government has ensured the powerlessness of third parties and the court on important urban development issues (McClelland 1992:7). There are similar complaints in relation to planning appeal courts and tribunals in other States where large projects have generally been removed from the consultation requirements of the planning system. 'The delays, costs and risks of public participation, rather than its benefits as an end in itself or as a management strategy, seem to be the prominent considerations' (Painter 1992:21).

The movement away from consultation is in part the result of conflicting priorities in urban development between State and local governments, made more intense by the openness of local government to popular pressure and aspirations (Saunders 1984) and the inequitable power of some municipalities within cities. Brian McLoughlin's study of the history of strategic planning in Melbourne identified the eastern suburbs as the most powerful sector in the city (McLoughlin 1992). These suburbs have successfully delayed the implementation of urban consolidation policies in their municipalities and have been the source of most resident appeals to the Victorian AAT Planning Division against multi-unit developments (Howe & Norman 1992). The power of this sector was underlined when planning code amendments relating to multi-unit developments were recently gazetted minus four proposed mandatory elements covering building envelopes, open-space car-parking and privacy. 'This move would have pleased most councillors, particularly in the politically influential middle-ring eastern and south-eastern municipalities, where governments win and lose elections. They had lobbied strongly against these mandatory requirements and won' (Kilgour 1994:7).

The northern and western suburbs of Melbourne are the source of very few appeals against such developments, not necessarily because residents are satisfied with the form of urban development in their communities, but because neither the planning system nor local government is facilitating the expression of their views (Logan 1984). Community interests that can easily access local government and participatory planning processes exacerbate inequity in cities. Mark Peel in chapter 2 includes a discussion of the powerlessness of outer-suburban working-class suburbs over planning decision-making and the implications of this powerlessness as Australian cities become more socially and spatially segregated and inter-suburban conflict increases.

Most of the current organisational reform program of local government is focused on efficiency and service delivery rather than on encouraging more equitable forms of commmunity participation. In early 1993 the Tasmanian State government reduced the number of local councils from forty-five to twenty-nine without community consultation. The Victorian State government has embarked on an even more ambitious program. Victoria has the largest number of municipalities (over 200) and the Kennett Liberal government is, through the Local Government Board established under the new Local Government Act of 1992, pressing ahead with an extensive program of municipal amalgamations. The government initially targeted the regional areas of Victoria as appropriate for amalgamations – Geelong, Ballarat, Bendigo and the Latrobe Valley. A Geelong Super Council, covering six former local government areas, has been established as well as a Surf Coast Council which includes most of the local government areas along the Great Ocean Road. More recently, the Victorian government has turned its attention to the metropolitan area where it has implemented a large-scale program of amalgamations.

The influence on Victorian government policy of a report on local government reform prepared by the conservative think-tank, the Institute of Public Affairs, which recommended a population target of 100 000 for viable municipal areas is evident (IPA 1993). While acknowledging that local government is 'an important instrument for the expression of local aspirations, concerns and priorities' the focus of the report is on the efficiency of local government. 'This focus reflects a widespread concern, both in the business community and amongst ratepayers generally that local government is too receptive to pressures from relatively small but politically influential interest groups. Implicit in this concern is the belief that, for local government to perform its proper role, it needs to be more efficient and more accountable' (IPA 1993:1).

Whether the Kennett government has thought through the political and constitutional issues of the proposed local government changes is not clear. As has been argued, one of the main reasons that State governments have been wary of viable regional groupings of local councils in the past has been their potential to threaten the power of the State. Although the Kennett government has not set out to empower local councils this could be the long-term effect of the amalgamations (Munro 1993:6). It is possible that the State government plans to prevent this by exploiting the weak constitutional position of local government and replacing elected local councils with State government nominated commissioners. At the time of writing, nominated commissioners control the Geelong Super Council, the revamped Melbourne City Council, and all other amalgamated councils.

The increasing practice of appointing commissioners to replace elected councils is part of the erosion of local democracy which has followed in the wake of contemporary urban change. Local democracy is also threatened in those areas of urban growth which do not easily relate to traditional suburban local government areas. Some of these expanding urban regions have similar characteristics to those identified by American journalist, Joel Garreau, in his analysis of 'edge cities' as the increasingly dominant urban form in America, developing around transport interchanges, usually freeway intersections, and including large-scale retail and commercial as well as residential developments. 'Edge cities' are mixed-use developments, not suburbs, combining residences, employment and shopping and developing new institutions to create community. Garreau documents the private-enterprise governments of edge cities, 'the shadow governments' which are replacing local government, once the cornerstone of American democracy.

> These shadow governments have become the most ubiquitous and largest form of local government in America today . . . In their various guises shadow governments levy taxes, adjudicate disputes, provide police protection, run fire departments, provide health care, channel development, plan regionally, enforce aesthetic standards . . . These shadow governments have powers far beyond those ever granted rulers in this country before . . . nevertheless, the general public almost never gets the opportunity to vote its leaders out of office, and rarely is protected from them by the United States Constitution. (Garreau 1991:185)

Garreau's discussion of Southern California, where he identifies the largest number of edge cities, includes an interview with the executive director of the Southern California Association of Governments, the nation's largest planning agency. Interestingly, the director focused on his concern about the loss of a sense of community in these new urban developments, the loss of a sense of citizenship. 'He yearns for a mayor and city council', precisely the kind of ruling structure that edge cities rarely have (Garreau 1991:286).

Proposals to introduce American participatory structures, such as the initiative and referendum, have been met with caution in Australia as this process has been used so successfully to entrench urban social division (Franklin 1992:62). As Sophie Watson and Alec McGillivray point out in chapter 7, Australia needs more responsive forms of democracy to address the diversity and complexity of modern Australian communities, forms which overcome the limitations of local government but which avoid the private and exclusive nature of American 'shadow governments'. Such issues have not been a priority either in the increasing practice of appointing non-elected local government administrators or in the non-representative nature of mooted regional organisations. While acknowledging 'the Club-like operation of many councils', Angela Munro believes that elected local councils 'are the body corporate of the community – the expression of community aspirations, concerns and priorities' and have the 'untested potential' to contribute to macro-urban policy through regional groupings of councils or through State and national organisations (Munro 1993:16).

Conclusion

The urban growth debate has highlighted the need for 'new institutional arrangements to implement strategic planning priorities'. Two of the most thorough and recent metropolitan strategic planning exercises, the *20:20 Vision* study in South Australia and the *SEQ 2001* study in Queensland, emphasised this need, as has the Kelty report. These responses have been influenced by the impact of globalisation on jobs and economic well-being at the local level which has exposed the inadequacies of existing governmental institutions and strategies in matching the development of economic structures (Goldsmith 1993:684). At the same time, the need for fiscal restraint has focused attention on the inefficiencies of inter-government relations and the limited capacities of Australia's small local authorities.

The impact on local government has opened up opportunities where there is a wide recognition of the need for a more coordinated planning approach and 'a mature relationship between the respective spheres of government wherein roles and responsibilities are negotiated and clear' (Ohlin 1992:1). On the other hand, central–local conflicts are everywhere in evidence. 'In an intergovernmental environment, consultation with local authorities is especially important. The managerialist aspects of corporate government, however, are likely to encourage central control of the planning policy agenda. Both are necessary for improved urban outcomes, but it remains to be seen how these potentially conflicting processes can be reconciled in practice' (Caulfield 1992:4).

Although the trend has been to the growth of State planning powers at the expense of local government, the dominance of strategic urban planning by State governments could be weakened in the future by the privatisation of the large infrastructure authorities, contracting-out of services, the development of partnership agreements, the move to more flexible planning systems and the increasing involvement of the Federal government in urban and regional issues. As a medium-term strategy, the encouragement of councils to be more accountable to their communities, to cooperate in regional organisations, and to make available more resources to develop and implement metropolitan strategies would strengthen the local response to urban change. In the long term, the challenge for political institutions to respond to economic change – especially the rates of growth and decline across communities, regions and metropolitan areas – and be relevant to new forms of urban development and an increasingly diverse population, has implications for the place of locality in the Australian federal system.

CHAPTER 9

Towards More Equitable Cities: A Receding Prospect?

Blair Badcock

The pursuit of social justice via the various urban programs of both the Commonwealth (Building Better Cities) and the States has been compromised well into the 1990s by the accelerated restructuring of the Australian economy and the high unemployment that will persist in its wake. The likelihood is that whilst recovery is now underway, even the more optimistic forecasts of economic growth (3–4 per cent) will not create enough jobs to lower unemployment much beyond 5 or 6 per cent before the end of the decade. According to a recent report on the medium-term outlook for the economy prepared by the Economic Planning Advisory Council (EPAC) (1993), this would still leave between 140 000 and 220 000 long-term unemployed out of work by the year 2001, and pockets of 'hard-core' poverty and inequity within the cities. The federal Labor administration has to bear a major part of the responsibility for this given the policies pursued throughout the 1980s, not the least being the over-reliance on monetary stimuli at the expense of fiscal measures.

This claim is followed through in the second section of this chapter by examining some of the income and wealth effects in the markets for labour, housing, and public services that I believe will make for a more rather than less unequal Australian society. In the face of stubborn structural unemployment, and given expected household formation rates, all three tiers of government will be increasingly hard-pressed to reconcile expanding service needs in the cities with their diminished fiscal capacity in the 1990s.

In the third section of this chapter consideration will turn to the 'urban' strategies promoted by both the Commonwealth and the States to address the market-based inequalities found in the metropolitan areas, including housing and transportation policies, and funding options. As well as highlighting the contradictory nature of present government policy, consideration will be given to some of the structural impediments to more equitable cities in the 1990s. One of the consequences of so wholeheartedly opening up the Australian economy to global forces in the 1980s is that the scope for efficacious urban and regional policy is somewhat diminished. In the 1990s the essentially palliative nature of urban policy will be even more apparent than it was twenty years ago when David Donnison was moved to ask:

> What kind of city or urban region would provide the richest array of opportunities and choices, particularly for those towards the bottom of the distributions of income, education, housing and political power? The main programmes required to extend or redistribute such opportunities are, I believe, national in scope, and town planners cannot do much about them. They include policies for full employment, for industrial relations and civil rights, for social security, rents and housing. (Donnison 1973:648)

Background to the Argument

While there is mounting evidence from overseas to suggest that the restructuring of urban labour and housing markets under a regime of 'flexible accumulation' is making for divided or dual global cities (Castells 1989; Fainstein, Gordon & Harloe 1992; Sassen 1991), it is also possible to argue that such divisions have been a long-standing feature of Australia's largest cities. Sydney, Melbourne and Adelaide certainly exhibited the degree of socio-spatial polarisation in their housing markets that is now attracting attention in global cities like London, New York and Tokyo (Stilwell & Hardwick 1973). However, the important difference is that the spatial segregation by class in Australian cities occurred under a Fordist regime of capital accumulation when the manufacturing sector dominated the urban economy.

It has also been suggested that the patriarchal nature of industrial capitalism is reproduced in cities in the form of a gender division of space between the city centre and suburbs (Saegert 1980). Whilst Australian feminists like Harman (1988) and Fincher (1990) find Saegert's idealisation of distinctive zones of production and control as opposed to reproduction somewhat overdrawn, there is no doubt that gender relations constitute an important independent source of inequality in cities (England 1991). But how will organisational and regulatory changes within the spheres of economic activity and work change the mappings of gender in Australian cities? Will the growing flexibility in the types of work performed, in the gender mix of the paid workforce, in the scheduling of the working week, and where work is located (i.e.

mixed-use zones) eventually remove any remaining separation between the zones of production and reproduction in cities?

One of the aims of this chapter is to try and decide how processes associated with global economic restructuring and the shift to service economies will affect Australian cities in the future. Will it make them more or less equal with respect to class and gender, and what are the implications for the growth of our cities and urban management?

It is difficult to make a case for more equitable cities in a future where the pressures of urban growth and demand for housing and services in our cities show no sign of abating, yet where workforce restructuring, growing long-term unemployment, and shrinking resources in the government sector threaten to create a permanent underclass living precariously at the margins of Australian society.

The seeds of this dilemma lie with the state's response to restructuring: too often in the last decade Commonwealth policy has been counterproductive by working to heighten Australia's vulnerability to destabilising forces within the global economy. The human costs of blind adherence to undiluted market theory during the 1980s will persist, perhaps most visibly in the disconcerting juxtaposition of affluence and destitution in the public spaces of Sydney and Melbourne, throughout the remainder of the 1990s (Peel, chapter 2). The domestic policies pursued by the federal Labor governments under Hawke and Keating are implicated at two levels: firstly, at the level of economic management where spending priorities or taxation policy, for example, will continue to compromise the urban development or social justice strategies of the States; and secondly, within the realm of urban policy itself. Indeed, there has been a clear shift in Commonwealth priorities from a 'needs' based orientation in the late 1980s, to a 'productive and efficient cities' agenda which promises to dominate well into the 1990s (Orchard, chapter 3; Badcock 1993).

Despite the reform of income support and the real growth in employment achieved during the first three terms of the Hawke government, structural inequalities remained as deep-seated and geographically localised as ever at the end of the decade (Stilwell 1989). Indeed, the closeness of the vote in the federal elections at the beginning of 1990 confirmed just how disaffected the traditional Labor vote within the neglected suburban heartland had grown (Sulzberger 1990). Yet worse was to come: at the time of writing (midway through 1993), structural unemployment has a more tenacious hold on the Australian workforce than at any time since the Great Depression, and seems likely to persist at unacceptably high levels to the end of the 1990s (EPAC 1993).

Arguably, the revival of interest in urban issues on the part of the federal Labor government was politically motivated (Badcock 1993). Taking care to distance himself from Whitlam's unfinished agenda, Brian Howe, the Minister of Health and Community Services, called for a more integrated approach to urban labour markets, affordable housing, and energy-efficient transport policies to help overcome some of the more glaring disparities in suburban living conditions (Grattan 1989:13). On the other hand, Treasurer Keating developed his own analysis of Australian urban problems and gave an indication that once the public account was in balance he would be prepared to make good the shortfall in capital funds denied the States in previous years (Burrell 1989:8).

By the second half of the 1980s most of the States had already inititated major reviews of metropolitan strategy which canvas a variety of urban forms, housing and transportation options, and funding arrangements that hold the key to more equitable cities (Orchard, chapter 3). When a number of Commonwealth agencies belatedly followed up these issues they expressed differing views about the balance to be struck between efficiency and equity, and questioned some of the long-held assumptions underlying location policy (Industry Commission 1992; HRSC–LTS 1992). But given the severity of the economic downturn in the early 1990s and its expected aftermath, these policy debates within the government bureaucracies tend to be somewhat academic. The funds presently available for urban-oriented programs simply do not begin to match the backlog of needs emerging in communities worst hit by restructuring in the 1980s.

However, in arguing that the combined weight of structural adjustment and a contracting public economy are working to frustrate the urban strategies of the States, one should not overlook the magnitude of the task before them: over the next decade 1.2 million dwellings, or the equivalent of four cities the size of Adelaide, will be added to the stock of urban capital in Australia (Neilson & Spiller 1992:2).

Moreover, the centre of gravity of urban growth in Australia is shifting geographically. In the last twenty years almost three-quarters of the nation's population growth has occurred outside Sydney and Melbourne. On present trends there will be fifteen Australian cities with populations in excess of 100 000 by 2001 (in 1966 there were only eight). And perhaps of greatest import: the redistribution of this growth is such that Queensland is expected to overtake NSW and Victoria as the largest State within the next forty years or so. Accordingly, while Sydney and Melbourne grew by about 10 per cent between 1981 and 1991, the corresponding growth rates for Brisbane and Perth were 30 per cent and

27 per cent respectively (ABS 1993). Meanwhile, Queensland's Gold and Sunshine Coasts both reported growth rates for the decade of 70 per cent, which has lifted the Gold Coast with about 310 000 residents to seventh position in the metropolitan league table.

Transformations in the Labour, Housing, and Services Markets

The processes that ultimately determine whether or not future urban development in Australia is likely to lead to more equitable cities are embedded in the separate markets for labour, housing, and services.[1] These markets have been transformed to varying degrees by the restructuring of the Australian economy and changes to the regulatory environment during the 1980s. The sectoral shift from manufacturing to services will continue into the 1990s (table 9.1); and together with the changing composition of households seems likely to further polarise the social structure of Australian cities.

While much conjecture remains about the nature of 'social polarisation' within the advanced economies (Pinch 1993), and its mapping in cities (Castells 1989:203–7), the complexity of the underlying processes certainly belies the clear-cut distinction implied by the terms 'dual city' or 'divided city'. These processes include: 'deindustrialization and increasing levels of unemployment; the bifurcation of rapidly expanding service sectors into high-paid and low-paid jobs; the increase in temporary and part-time work; changes in family structure such as the increase in lone-parent, lone-elderly, and dual-income families; the continuing economic and social marginalization of ethnic minorities; and the "residualization" of State welfare services' (Pinch 1993:779).

These are the key dynamics changing the social tapestry of 'post-industrial' societies like Australia. As they unfold, in all these societies they are threatening to permanently marginalise sectors of the traditional blue-collar workforce and young people leaving school without marketable skills in the advanced service economy. Governments are challenged in the short-run to compensate the communities in our cities that are bearing the brunt of rapid social and economic adjustment, and in the longer run to manage these processes in the labour market to ensure that they do not create an 'underclass' of people who are willing but unable to work.

1 There are some social costs that are extra-market 'in the sense that even by redefining property rights and removing market rigidities, their impacts would still not be fully captured by market values; social isolation in urban fringe areas, lack of effective choices, restricted physical movement and the generalised malaise experienced by marginalised groups like unemployed and homeless youth are cases in point' (Berry 1992:37).

Table 9.1 *Impact of employment change on Australian State and Territory capital cities,ᵃ 1981ᵇ–1991*

	Australia		Sydney		Melbourne		Brisbane		Perth		Adelaide		Canberra		Hobart		Darwin	
	1991 wkfᶜ	% change 81–91	1991 wkf	% change 81–91	1991 wkf	% change 81–91	1991 wkf	% change 81–91	1991 wkf	% change 81–91	1991 wkf	% change 81–91	1991 wkf	% change 81–91	1991 wkf	% change 81–91	1991 wkf	% change 81–91
Expanding sectors																		
Finance, property, business services	788 283	48.3	240 997	42.0	168 405	47.0	69 976	59.7	59 916	46.1	49 717	49.8	15 009	96.0	7 273	21.3	3 465	61.2
Community services	1 261 261	34.3	262 745	26.6	231 605	27.1	106 949	50.6	95 576	36.1	93 000	22.4	28 715	26.8	16 722	15.0	7 223	36.4
Recreation and personal services	496 172	50.8	109 376	37.8	80 203	46.1	36 651	66.4	34 588	60.1	30 229	45.8	9 363	57.5	6 256	21.0	3 413	98.3
Moderate growth sectors																		
Wholesale and retail trade	1 337 246	22.2	303 405	14.4	261 890	21.3	120 158	34.8	97 769	26.0	84 431	9.4	18 972	45.4	12 994	4.4	6 325	45.6
Public administration and defence	402 410	13.8	77 266	1.4	67 028	4.1	35 891	26.1	24 782	32.6	23 370	6.5	37 800	16.0	6 255	13.3	5 537	4.2
Construction	421 174	5.8	94 672	11.4	69 624	8.7	37 443	21.9	29 688	-1.7	22 669	1.7	7 109	39.0	3 960	-19.5	2 039	-26.1
Stalled growth sectors																		
Communications	116 977	-6.8	29 477	-7.7	26 989	5.7	10 379	-7.2	7 170	-6.0	6 664	-15.4	1 891	17.7	1 354	-29.2	577	-21.6
Mining	86 607	-2.7	4 385	-3.0	2 607	11.4	2 547	-19.3	6 849	43.5	1 739	-8.6	186	0.5	301	126.3	520	85.1
Transport and storage	325 453	-1.3	84 815	-8.1	58 849	-3.6	30 455	13.8	22 341	2.4	16 408	-3.9	3 952	43.0	2 401	-15.1	1 948	21.0
Contracting sectors																		
Electricity, gas, water	91 553	-27.1	19 010	-33.4	13 527	-39.3	5 541	-27.5	5 556	-9.9	4 839	-31.2	489	-32.3	1 522	-28.7	374	-53.3
Manufacturing	933 652	-16.2	219 016	-25.7	234 965	-23.0	73 586	3.4	53 573	-7.4	67 621	-16.7	4 798	31.1	7 826	-13.1	1 679	15.0
Agriculture, forestry, fishing	320 563	-15.5	9 981	-8.2	9 982	1.1	5 913	26.7	6 083	-10.6	3 753	-13.3	518	-18.4	1 156	10.5	294	-13.0
Non-classified	26 124		5 503		5 718		1 971		2 266		2 386		902		444		162	
Not stated	501 860		102 453		92 273		37 546		34 269		35 475		9 530		5 580		2 865	
Total employment (1991)	7 109 335	13.0	1 563 101	7.6	1 323 665	8.5	575 006	31.2	480 426	24.2	442 301	12.5	139 234	38.0	74 044	6.6	36 421	21.8

Notes: a Metropolitan Statistical Division or District.
  b The 1981 figures have not been cited due to space limitations.
  c wkf = workforce.
Source: Australian Bureau of Statistics, Census of Population and Dwellings, 1981 and 1991.

Labour Markets

Two main constructs have been developed to describe the impact of occupational change on the structure of the workforce in advanced economies (Pinch 1993). One emphasises the relative decline of middle-income occupations – 'the disappearing middle' – in conjunction with an expansion of high-paying and low-paying jobs at each end of the occupational hierarchy. Reich (1991) postulates that economies dominated by advanced services are regrouping around three main functions: the solving, identification, and brokering of problems ('symbolic analysts'); the provision of personal and community services ('in-person servers'); the production of intermediate and final goods ('routine producers'). The effect of these shifts on workforce structure has been likened to an 'hour-glass' and is said to best describe present experience in the United States, Canada and Australia (Gregory 1992).

The other construct focuses on a segment of the labour force that has been increasingly marginalised by a succession of recessions during the last decade or so. Many of the long-term unemployed who have fallen out of the labour market in the United States (Wilson 1987) and Britain (Pahl 1984) now constitute an 'underclass' which, according to Pahl (1988), is reshaping the class structure in the likeness of an onion. Ethnic minorities and women are grossly over-represented in all the advanced economies in the layers forming the base of the onion.

Both these representations of society in the advanced economies postulate that individuals and households at either end of the class spectrum are moving further apart in terms of their job status and security, wage levels, and fringe benefits in the workplace. An analysis of shifts in the distribution of earnings during the 1980s confirms that wage inequality grew in twelve OECD countries, with the United Kingdom and the United States experiencing the most pronounced polarisation (OECD 1993:157–84).

In Australia, as average earnings fell in real terms during the decade, the dispersion of earnings between 1980 and 1991 has left men in the lowest decile group 7 per cent worse off, and men in the highest decile group 5 per cent better off. There was no change in the real value of earnings received by women in the lowest decile group over the same period of time, though those in the highest decile enjoyed an 8 per cent improvement (OECD 1993:163). Significantly, Australia, Canada and the United States were the only countries within the OECD to record falls in the real value of the bottom earnings decile during the 1980s (OECD 1993:176). Comparatively speaking, the dispersion in earnings is mild in Australia and these data make no allowance for social security payments.

Broadly speaking, therefore, this 'fanning' in the pattern of Australian earnings in the 1980s and first part of the 1990s presages a more, rather than less, unequal society in the future if the trend is maintained. Labour market adjustments together with evolving household structures are making for greater social fluidity within the strata forming middle Australia. The impact of the changing division of labour on the household as an economic unit will be quite selective according to whether or not, and how many, members are actively employed, and their occupational background(s). Not only are households affected by the shifts occurring in the sectors of the economy depending on the training and skill levels of their members, they are also vitally affected by whether or not women in the household are in the paid workforce (Mullins, chapter 4).

By the year 2006 almost 60 per cent of women are expected to be in paid employment. The ratio will exceed two out of every three women of working age, largely due to the increased participation rate of married women (NHS 1991:93). Many of the women entering the paid workforce are being absorbed within the services sector where, until the early 1990s, job growth has tended to outpace other sectors of the economy. Because of the preponderance of part-time jobs, a noticeable gap is growing between the small number of women in the well-rewarded upper echelons of the advanced services, and the rest who typically receive low wages and poor fringe benefits (EPAC 1993).

While these trends relating to the rise in paid female employment will continue to stratify household incomes in Australia, of greater concern for our cities in the immediate future is the emerging economic dichotomy between households with no one in the paid workforce, and those with two or more wage earners. The disparity between 'one- or two-parent non-earning households with dependent children' and salaried couples without dependants will be even more dramatic. Of course, as the level of economic activity recovers in the mid-1990s, many of the families with no wage income at present can expect that at least one of the household heads – probably the female partner – will re-enter the paid labour force, if only on a part-time or casual basis.

A recent forecast indicates that by the end of the decade, one-quarter of all Australian workers will have casual jobs (Milburn 1993). With a superfluity of labour throughout the remainder of the 1990s, the wage levels and conditions of workers in the secondary labour market may be progressively eroded. On the other hand, the increase in the relative demand for highly educated workers in technologically progressive industries, and with it productivity-linked remuneration, shows no signs of abating (OECD 1993:175–77). Thus there is a strong likelihood that the dispersion of incomes taking place in Australia (OECD 1993) will be translated by the housing markets of our largest cities into even more polarised urban structures in the decades ahead.

Housing Markets

Australian conditions, where housing markets are subject to only the mildest forms of regulation, tend to reproduce and even amplify the economic differences generated in the labour market. This arises firstly from the housing subsidies that different tenures attract; and secondly from the spatial transfers of wealth that occur across urban and regional property markets. Thirdly, changes to the structure of housing provision underway at present in Australia are inherently regressive: as the subtle shift from public housing to welfare housing gathers momentum in Australia, the State housing providers are set to become the poor relations of the housing system.

Naturally, the demand for low-cost rental housing – private or public – is closely linked to conditions in the labour market (Burbidge & Gondor 1992; Yates & Vipond 1991). Thus, even though public rental housing has grown from 270 000 dwellings in 1984–1985 to 360 000 in 1990–1991, the expanded stock – up from 4.7 per cent to 5.6 per cent – has not kept pace with the waiting lists during a decade of mounting structural unemployment. It seems, therefore, that despite the recent efforts of the States to broaden the forms of social housing available and spread public tenants throughout the community – partly at the prompting of the Commonwealth – the problematic 'high rise' and 'fringe' housing estates are unlikely to be rebuilt before they are structurally unsound.

Flood (1993) has recently updated an earlier study of Australia's housing subsidy system undertaken in 1984–1985. Apart from the contribution of increased rent allowances to some alleviation of after-housing poverty, he concludes that the flow of housing subsidies still fails the test of tenure neutrality. According to Flood (1993:22–4), the indirect aid provided to home owners through tax expenditures continues to greatly benefit those in the highest income decile.

In addition, Yates (1991:35) estimates that the imputed rent associated with home ownership contributes significantly to the redistribution of household income: the 27.3 per cent of households who were renting had no increase in their average incomes; the 29.9 per cent who were buying had their income decreased by $41 per week (in 1988 values); and the 42.8 per cent who were outright owners had their income increased by an average of $137 per week.

In Australia, the owner-occupied dwelling stock accounts for almost two-thirds of all private sector wealth (Dilnot 1990). Hence, the amassing of household wealth hinges crucially upon whether the dwelling is rented or owned. And while there has been much debate about the distribution of capital gains and tax benefits within owner-occupation with respect to class position, it is now apparent that when the succession of homes owned during the housing career is considered the concentration of housing wealth tends to match the occupational mobility of the household members (Badcock 1994). Furthermore, all the indications are that inheritance will help to consolidate these existing concentrations of housing wealth even while some of the acquired equity is dispersed downwards as part of a bequest (Badcock, forthcoming).

The Market for Collective Services

For well over a decade, fiscal policy in Australia has been guided by the credo that 'economic growth came to a standstill because public consumption was a drain on private production' (Smith 1988:28). In retrospect, much Commonwealth economic policy has proven contradictory and self-defeating: financial deregulation created the preconditions that led to the squandering of capital by the money markets; especially tight monetary policy at the beginning of the 1990s choked off any remaining business investment that might have been planned; budget surpluses in the late 1980s were ultimately achieved at the expense of public sector employment (with the 'lagged' retrenchments contributing to the size of the welfare 'burden' in the 1990s). Having subdued inflation by 1992–1993 without a commensurate lift in private investment, the Keating government now appears resigned to unprecedented levels of unemployment to the end of the decade.

Real cutbacks in State finances (Wilmoth 1990) flow on into physical and social services where once again, due to the unequal needs and fiscal capacity of local authorities, particular sections of the community have suffered disproportionately (DHHCS 1992d; Jackson & O'Connor 1993). The service standards on older suburban housing estates, for example, often fall far behind community-wide benchmarks as local authorities concentrate on providing basic services to recently completed subdivisions (DHHCS 1992d:23). Inevitably, the reduction of Commonwealth and State outlays in recent years has put even more pressure on outlying suburban councils trying to cope with the specialised needs of very young, fast-growing communities (Jackson & O'Connor 1993:93).

As part of the strategy to cope with falling revenue, the States have embarked on the selective privatisation of collective consumption (public transport, education, and health). While the impact of deteriorating public services and 'user-pays' levies falls right across the community, the residents of the poorest suburbs often lack the discretionary income to ensure the continuing viability of some activities on a 'fee-for-service' basis. The cutbacks in the education sector have had an even more debilitating effect coming on top of the steady drift of middle-class children to the private-school sector since the early 1970s.

Impact of Structural Adjustment on Australian Cities

The flow-on effects of the radical program of structural adjustment within the Australian economy will continue to be felt during the remainder of the 1990s. Even though private sector output is beginning to pick up, the rate of labour absorption coming out of the 1991–1993 recession appears unlikely to match that achieved after the 1975 and 1982 downturns (Burrell 1993:17). Moreover, the projected change in regional rates of industry protection envisaged during the mid-1990s will continue to impact selectively and unevenly in different sectors of the economy and therefore upon different metropolitan areas and regional centres. According to Taylor (1992b:10), virtually all districts of Melbourne, together with centres like Geelong, Ballarat, Bendigo, and Albury–Wodonga, parts of western and southern Sydney, and Adelaide, face even more severe falls in protection than was accommodated in the 1980s, threatening another 219 000 jobs.

However, in the 1990s the regional incidence of unemployment in Australia is no longer synonymous with the restructuring popularly depicted as 'de-industrialisation'. The current recession has created levels of unemployment in the retirement and recreation centres along the eastern and western seaboards of the continent, sufficient to move Taylor (1992a:20) to question 'whether tourism and recreation offer a stable foundation for future employment growth in Australia'. Only southern New South Wales and the ACT have really escaped the employment consequences of the current recession, largely due to the direct and indirect employment effects of the Federal government, thereby 'cocooning Commonwealth decision-makers within a daily urban environment divorced from the labour market problems that preoccupy much of the rest of the country' (Taylor 1992a:15).

Even in those urban labour markets enjoying net job growth, there tends to be a spatial mismatch between the shrinkage and mushrooming of employment at a sub-regional level. During the relatively prosperous middle years of the last decade, for every job created in Melbourne's industrial west, forty jobs (net) were being created in the east: 'The east and south have experienced significant levels of new office and factory construction and manufacturing employment even when these activities have been in overall decline' (Victorian Ministry of Planning and Environment 1987:13).

On the other hand, there has been no such compensatory job replacement in those suburbs where retrenchment has been concentrated in traditional sectors like 'textiles, clothing and footwear' – over half of Melbourne's TCF workers live in three metropolitan regions. Similarly, there has also been a noticeable shortfall in new employment opportunities in suburbs zoned for manufacturing and industrial housing in the post-war years (Broadmeadows and Dandenong in Melbourne; Bankstown and Liverpool in Sydney; Elizabeth in Adelaide). Male blue-collar workers in their forties and fifties have been the main victims of job-shedding in the 1980s and 1990s, and even with retraining and/or relocation some may never work again. Typically, many of the newly created jobs in the suburbs are associated with the rise of sub-assembly and packaging tasks, with fast-food services, and as part of the emerging 'back office' phenomenon. While women are being absorbed in disproportionate numbers in these expanding producer services, including in so-called 'pink-collar' occupations, these are mainly poorer quality jobs.

The growth of producer services and allied functions in banking, finance and business helped to stabilise, if not enlarge, the employment base of the central areas of Australian cities in the 1980s. Sydney, especially, gained from the positive employment effect of financial deregulation and the internationalisation of banking in the second half of the 1980s (Murphy & Watson 1990). The surge in high-paying occupations in the office core fed the demand for nearby housing and inflated inner-area house prices which had already been stimulated by gentrification in Sydney as well as in a number of other Australian cities. Since the late 1970s there has been a noticeable steepening of the price gradient for residential land in cities like Sydney, Melbourne and Adelaide (figure 9.1). There are two important effects: real wealth is transferred from outer-area to inner-area home buyers (Badcock 1992); the traditional supply of low-cost housing in the inner areas of Australian cities will continue to diminish except in those few pockets of cities like Melbourne with considerable pre-existing public rental stock (and only then in the future if there is a determination to prevent it being sold off).

This evidence suggests that the changing division of labour, together with evolving household types, will continue to modify patterns of access to housing, and the class and gender composition of some suburbs in Australian cities over the next two or three decades. Yet regardless of the occupational and housing mobility of individual households, the net effect of these shifts transmitted through the housing market will be to sharpen the existing disparities between the poorest and wealthiest suburbs. Characteristically, the suburbs in Australian cities at the far ends of the class spectrum also tend to be the most apart geographically.[2]

'Stressed out' Communities

The severity of the economic downturn in the early 1990s was such that there are now households sprinkled through most middle-class suburbs in Australia that have had to come to terms with dismissal and unemployment for the first time in their lives. Nonetheless, apart from some isolated business failures and the withdrawal of children from private schools, the communities in which they live escaped the recession largely unscathed. Not only are middle-class suburbs inherently more resilient with their social and physical infrastructure in good condition, and possessing the local institutions and voluntary organisations with reserves to draw upon, but they have few households where all wage earners are out of work.

By contrast, it is impossible for those from comfortable middle-class backgrounds to relate to the transformation that has taken place in the shared experience of 'solid' working-class communities from Blacktown to Broadmeadows, and Werribee to Whyalla, during the last decade (Peel 1993a). These are communities that simply had the misfortune to concentrate a blue-collar workforce that in large measure has now outlived its usefulness. The compounding effect of recession in 1982–1983, and again in 1991–1993, has run down household savings, closed local businesses, and threatens to exhaust local government reserves.

Household indebtedness has reduced the capacity of stressed communities to underwrite public services, while stagnant or even falling house prices have eroded the rate base of some local government areas (Badcock 1992; Gondor & Burbidge 1992). Tragically, this haemorrhaging by the worst-hit urban communities has coincided with a tightening of Commonwealth and State outlays in key human service areas like health and welfare, education, housing, and public transport. All these cumulative financial pressures have taken their toll on families (Edgar 1992), and increased their susceptibility to stress-related illness (Glover & Woollacott 1992).

Illustrations of these effects are well documented in the series of case studies of disadvantaged communities prepared by the Department of

---

2 The adjacency of classes that one finds in Sydney's federal electorate of Wentworth, for example, or the north and south of Fitzroy (Melbourne), or between North Adelaide and Hindmarsh in Adelaide, is very much the exception in Australian cities.

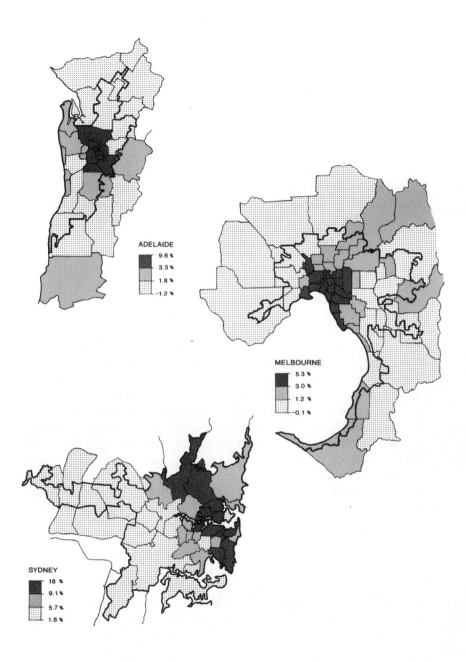

ADELAIDE
9.8 %
3.3 %
1.8 %
-1.2 %

MELBOURNE
5.3 %
3.0 %
1.2 %
-0.1 %

SYDNEY
18 %
9.1 %
5.7 %
1.8 %

Figure 9.1 *Annual percentage change in median dwelling prices (constant) 1974–1990*
Note: Sydney 1976–1990.

Health, Housing and Community Services (DHHCS 1992d). While both urban and rural communities are well represented, it is significant that all the capital city study areas fall into the category of metropolitan 'fringe' sites, viz.: Liverpool Shire (NSW), Berwick City and Werribee City (Victoria), Elizabeth and Munno Para Cities combined (South Australia), Swan Shire (WA), and Caboolture Shire (Queensland). These Local Area Research Studies emphasise that where communities hardest hit by structural unemployment are also located in the outermost parts of the metropolitan region their residents may be burdened by additional hardships. For example, inadequate 'pivotal' access services like public transport and child care are singled out for special attention by Victoria's Social Justice Consultative Council (SJCC 1992:7).

Metropolitan Strategy and Redistribution

How should the Commonwealth and States respond to the apparent prospect of an ever-widening gulf between communities within the largest cities, especially when the demand for further urban development and housing shows no sign of slowing during the next generation? The Commonwealth's urban program really fails to follow up the recommendations of the Local Area Research Studies on Locational Disadvantage (DHHCS 1992d) in any meaningful way. In large part the concern for social justice that featured in the early statements accompanying 'Building Better Cities' has been overtaken by the costs of urban expansion, and a striving for efficiencies insofar as they can be achieved through the improved operation and management of our cities (Badcock 1993). The main thrust of 'Building Better Cities' (BBC) is directed to demonstrations of 'best practice' in growth corridors and improvement areas at the expense of concentrating scarce resources on the neediest communities.[3] The only BBC area strategies that devote a significant share of their funds to ameliorating local conditions are Adelaide's Elizabeth–Munno Para and Brisbane's Inala–Ipswich Corridor.

The Contribution of 'Building Better Cities' to More Equitable Cities

The Commonwealth will provide $816 million over a five-year period for the area strategies nominated by the States (DHHCS 1992a). At best, the Commonwealth's contribution is 'top-up' funding. In the case of the

---

3 See Fincher (1991b) for a critical discussion of the difficulties inherent in programs that focus exclusively on designated communities.

South Australian projects the BBC contribution forms 8.4 per cent of the total funding ($192.75 million) for the Elizabeth–Munno Para Area Strategy, 14.6 per cent of the indicative funding ($274.7 million) currently allocated for the North-western Crescent Strategy between 1991–1996, 40.5 per cent of the funds ($9.9 million) available for the Inner Western Area Strategy, and 27 per cent of the $31.45 million for the Southern Areas Area Strategy.

However, even where the BBC area strategies succeed as demonstration projects there are grounds for doubting whether the funds will be available to extend their lessons more widely as part of a concerted metropolitan strategy. Two cases underline this point. Firstly, at the same time as the Commonwealth is attempting to demonstrate the feasibility of refurbishing some of the extensive tracts of dilapidated public housing in parts of Elizabeth–Munno Para (Adelaide) and Inala, Carole Park and Riverview (Brisbane), it is drastically reducing the access of the State's housing ministries to capital funds. The larger irony is that the greatest scope in the short-term for innovative housing mix and wider housing choice within Australian cities lies with the public landlords since they own much of the dwelling stock most in need of redevelopment.

The second illustration of the real limits that exist to the wider application of these BBC area strategies relates to the provision of 'affordable' housing as part of the different inner-area improvement schemes: Sydney's Pyrmont–Ultimo; Inner Melbourne and Rivers Area; Brisbane's Inner North-eastern Suburbs; East Perth; Adelaide's Mile End site. These schemes include sizeable tracts of unencumbered, even unpriced, land such as disused government sites. It is doubtful whether private developers could assemble similar sized tracts of well-located land and bring housing onto the market within the price range of households with modest incomes. Residential reinvestment and house price inflation prompted by gentrification has been so thoroughgoing in the heart of Sydney, Melbourne and Adelaide over the last two decades (see figure 9.1) that developers of affordable town-housing, like the South Australian Housing Trust, have been progressively priced out of the inner-city property market (Badcock & Browett 1992).

In turn, the fixed investment associated with these BBC demonstration projects will be capitalised into nearby property values, further raising inner-city housing prices and putting additional pressure on remnant housing stock. It is unrealistic, therefore, to expect much expansion of affordable housing in the inner areas of Australian cities, even with public participation helping to subsidise the lower-priced dwelling units in joint venture developments (Sant & Jackson 1991).

State Spending Priorities

The uneven impact of economic restructuring poses a policy dilemma for State governments: on what, and where, to spend the significantly reduced funds in the cities? Should they compensate the 'losers' via local job creation and by providing public housing and improved community infrastructure, or stimulate development that promises to create new kinds of employment and housing catering for 'winners'? The proposals for Sydney's Darling Harbour and Pyrmont–Ultimo, Melbourne's Docklands, Jolimont and Bayside, Adelaide's MFP and East End Market precinct, and Brisbane's waterfront raise this dilemma. The redevelopment of Pyrmont–Ultimo is expected to increase the resident population by about 17 000 and boost the workforce from 14 000 to 50 000 (DHHCS 1992a). But these will be mostly office jobs in knowledge-based and information processing activities. There is a stark difference between the beneficiaries in the alternatives posed above – both entail redistribution of public resources, one progressive and the other decidedly, though plainly not intentionally, regressive.

The Distributive Effects of Urban Consolidation

There are a number of common threads running through the strategic planning reviews undertaken by several of the States in the early 1990s (*Urban Futures* 1992). They were framed in the context of a growing inability – or disinclination – on the part of the States to finance either the projected demand for infrastructure in the new suburbs, or a program of asset replacement in the older established suburbs. Together with evidence indicating that household formation rates will continue into the early decades of the next century (though households will be older, smaller, and support fewer children), these concerns have prompted 'general support for urban consolidation in official structures' (Jay 1993:41–2).

The OECD (1988) predicts that the number of Australians over 65 years will rise from 1.9 million in 1990 to 4.3 million by 2030 (an increase of 126.3 per cent). One in four of these Australians will exceed 80 years of age. However, 'it is not the ageing of the population that is going to add proportionately most to the demand for housing but the extraordinary growth in the "middle-aged and childless" group' (Kirwan 1991c:17). Modelling done on behalf of the National Housing Strategy (1991a) suggests that two-thirds of all households in the 25–35 age range will be without children by 2006.

Notwithstanding the argument that the post-war suburban bungalow is more adaptable than one gives it credit for (Burke & Hayward 1990:145–6), Australian cities are the built form equivalent of a monoculture. The answer, according to Stretton (1989b:246–7), is not the 'landless housing' advocated by many cost-cutting committees, but 'more medium-density housing for the rising proportion of small households . . . at any levels of income and private motoring . . . who want small house and garden forms'.

As the Australian population 'greys' at least some parts of the purpose-built suburbs from the 1950s and 1960s will need to be reconditioned as growing numbers of the 'very old' in their eighties stop driving cars. Too many of the amenities and services, not to mention the convenience as well as the comparative shopping, have been regionalised in centres that can only be reached by private vehicle. Even with help from family and friends, community buses, domiciliary care and the like, the 'very old' will be isolated from too many of the necessities of life.

Ideally, this 'replacement' stock for the independent elderly should take the form of medium-density town-housing clustered around suburban rail and bus stations. But already the granting of 'dual occupancy' rights (Eccles 1991) and attempts to rezone suitable nodes within the middle-distance suburbs have encountered formidable resistance from established property interests (e.g. Willoughby on Sydney's North Shore, the areas around the Marion shopping centre in Adelaide, and Camberwell Junction in Melbourne's eastern suburbs). Because of this, at present the greater proportion of the medium-density stock in our cities is being constructed in the new, outermost suburbs: Blacktown, Bankstown, Fairfield, Sutherland and Gosford accounted for 44 per cent of medium-density completions in the Sydney region in 1991–1992. This is inappropriate to the needs of the elderly pensioners and, due to the inadequacy of public transport in the outer suburbs, perpetuates car-dependency.

Further, as more medium-density housing is approved for development in the growth areas of our cities, lower-income households may find that they are denied the one attraction that has traditionally drawn them outwards – space. As Yates & Vipond (1991:246) note, in the past households which needed low-cost housing basically chose between a crowded, possibly poor quality, dwelling in the inner city, or a house on a block in a new suburb without jobs or services. As block size falls below 300 square metres, and the amount of medium-density housing rises in new subdivisions, lower-income families may well find that they forfeit space as well.

Moving the Urban Workforce

The mismatch between employment and housing, and the difficulty of providing financially viable public transport services to far-flung suburban communities is another of the problems confronting strategic planners at the State level. So even though the decentralisation of office activity to nodes like Box Hill and Waverley enables Melbourne households to live further afield in outlying areas, 1986 estimates show that working residents exceeded local jobs in the outer zone by 41 per cent, and in fringe areas by 78 per cent (Brotchie 1992). Likewise, the imbalance alluded to above between the concentration of new jobs in the south-east and the residential distribution of the workforce in Melbourne is reproduced to some extent in the Adelaide metropolitan region, where much of the new housing development is being channelled in a southerly direction along the coastline.

What Brotchie (1992:18–19) also found was that the dispersal of employment within Australian metropolitan regions helped to reduce trip times for commuters even though they may be travelling slightly further between suburban jobs. The shift probably conceals a widening time difference between car users (94.5 per cent) and public transit riders (5.5 per cent) travelling to sub-centres, given the difficult of cross-city commuting by bus or train.

Furthermore, the increase in the proportion of casual and part-time jobs to one in four by the end of the 1990s will help spread the peak load on the suburban road network and lead to marginal improvements in commuting time to car users. Simultaneously, casual and part-time workers without the use of a car – like many mothers leaving children at day-care centres – will be immeasurably worse-off if the public transport system continues to deteriorate.

Transportation planning under these conditions throws up a multitude of access and equity issues. To date the response of the State transport authorities to mounting deficits has been to halt or reschedule unprofitable services; or in the case of outer areas of the metropolitan catchment, privatise the operators who only respond to peak demand. This downward spiral discourages remaining commuters who have alternative means of transport, and privatises the costs of what has been regarded as a merit good by the travelling public. Only Western Australia has been actively trying to improve and expand Perth's urban transit system.

The burden of declining public transport services is highly inequitable since it penalises captive patrons like pensioners and students, while car users remain oblivious to the economic and social costs. As the State public transport providers try to make further economies in the 1990s, the existing fixed track/route services will prove increasingly ill-suited in an era of job flexibility and diversity, and as employment becomes more widely scattered in suburban mixed-use zones. If equality of access to transport services is to be upheld as a goal in the outer suburbs, local government bodies will have to consider building up their own or 'owner-operated' mini-bus fleets to service their communities.

A Disappearing Gender Division of Urban Space?

I have argued that, despite the mediating effect of female earnings on household income, it is likely that the bifurcation of occupations underway at present in the Australian workforce (Gregory 1992) will sharpen rather than dull the existing polarity between classes in our cities during the 1990s. By contrast, a further strengthening of female labour participation rates should work to break down even more the gender division of Australian cities into spaces devoted to production and control on the one hand (the central core area), and reproduction on the other (dormitory suburbs). By 2006, when only a quarter of households will include children (NHS 1991a:65), the domestic sphere of reproduction will obviously be the locus for far fewer women.

As we have already seen for the ageing inner suburbs, the growth in childless households will redistribute existing patterns of access to child-linked services like day-care, clinics and schooling. For example, if numbers of children in the local catchment, or in the workplace, say, fall below a critical threshold for day-care, will State support be withdrawn from those areas? What inequalities of access will arise in the process? Will households with children that can afford to, gravitate towards the private providers (or drop them off along the route to work) in the same way as they have to be near to private schools in the inner eastern suburbs of Melbourne?

Conclusion

Structural adjustment is the product of the Commonwealth's efforts to reorientate the Australian economy in light of rapid changes on the international front. In its determination to force the pace of change by deregulating the markets for finance and labour, the federal Labour government intensified the processes of 'de-industrialisation' and concentration in the banking and financial services sector. As a consequence, job losses and retrenchment have been unnecessarily high in the most vulnerable sectors of the economy, and some urban communities and parts of our cities are carrying a disproportionate share of the burden of economic restructuring. This is despite Hawke's reassurance that:

> if the community believes that change is necessary in the interests of the community as a whole, then that belief carries with it a necessary corollary –

that the whole community must not leave those individuals who are adversely affected to bear the whole burden of change. It must itself be prepared to share the burden of change as well as reaping the benefits of change. (Department of PM&C 1991:1.7)

To aggravate matters, the Commonwealth has used the Loans Council to limit the borrowing by the States and LGAs that might have provided some assistance for readjustment at the local level. Funds provided under the Local Capital Works Program 1992–1994 have been soaked up without any perceptible impact on regional unemployment. The Commonwealth's own social justice strategy (DHHCS 1992c) is impotent, while the major part of the BBC funds has been devoted to urban infrastructure. Without the fiscal capacity to even begin to match the needs of communities concentrating retrenched workers and their families, the States are hamstrung in implementing policies that offer some hope to resource-poor suburbs.

The indications are, then, that as structural adjustment proceeds in the deregulated markets for labour, housing and services in the 1990s, some Australians, and parts of our cities, will be more rather than less unequal in the future. For example, the British experience suggests that if the States begin to sell their stocks of public housing on any scale, then the receding tide of recession will inevitably leave the 'hard-core', long-term unemployed geographically concentrated in a residual welfare housing sector. Besides, there does not appear to be the political will in Australia to change a housing system that works to further accentuate these differences in income (Yates 1991) and wealth (Dilnot 1990); nor the commitment to a level of social expenditure that begins to address the backlog of needs in Australian cities.

In this sense, the 1980s mark the beginnings of a reversal of the post-war achievements including reasonably full employment, some levelling of incomes, and a commitment, in principle at least, to equal access to services regardless of where people lived in the city (Parkin 1982). Because of the highly selective nature of structural adjustment, the Federal government did anticipate that there would be an ongoing need to 'share the burden of change' (PM&C 1991:1.7). However the reality is that the Commonwealth has failed to act upon its own implicit undertaking, even as the process of labour shedding in the early 1990s extends well beyond official forecasts.

Of course there is also the related difficulty, as David Donnison (1973) explained two decades ago: the key to more equitable living arrangements in our cities does not really rest with a refocused metropolitan strategy, or planning subventions, or revised residential development codes. Ultimately the indirect effects of broader federal and State policies play a much more decisive role in redistributing income and wealth within Australian cities. On the one hand, the experience of the late 1980s proved that unregulated capital markets are capable of more than matching the misallocation that is always ascribed to public enterprise by its detractors: colossal over-investment in downtown property markets denied capital to the States for public housing and suburban infrastructure (Low & Moser 1991). On the other hand, employment programs, tax breaks for strategic investment, and industry policy (if only by default), impact quite unevenly on sectors and locations within cities. The huge public subsidies that help underwrite private infrastructure, the production of serviced allotments, and owner-occupied and rental investment housing are also frequently prejudicial to equitable outcomes in urban development.

Not only do these subsidies often distort the States' ordering of priorities, but part of the proceeds are indirectly capitalised into the value of private property to the benefit of most owners of housing. Since the principal place of residence is exempt from the tax on capital gains, there are strong grounds for taxing the inheritance when the housing wealth incorporated within an estate is transferred between genera-tions.[4] Besides, there is evidence to suggest that capital gains are exceedingly erratic in the residential property market and tend not to systematically favour any class of owner (Badcock 1994).

Lastly, there is a sense in which the unstoppable suburban growth around major Australian cities (Jay 1993) is a product of the Common-wealth's sponsorship of home ownership ahead of other tenures in Australia since 1945. Even when allowance is made for the different cultural traditions, it is fairly obvious that those societies with much larger social housing sectors (Britain, the Netherlands, Denmark, and Sweden), or more private rental stock (the former West Germany), have been more successful in containing the spread of their cities. This has been possible even though many European cities have been compre-hensively rebuilt since World War II; and still holds true, notwith-standing the amount of suburban growth that has occurred in the Randstad, Holland since the 1970s.

4 However, the sale of the parental home by dependants may be subject to the capital gains tax.

PART THREE

Avenues for Development

CHAPTER 10

Financing Urban Services

Max Neutze

Questions about the funding of urban infrastructure have become more topical in recent years as governments providing infrastructure have sought to limit their financial commitments. The evidence of the cutback in public investment is clear. Real gross fixed capital expenditure by the public sector was the same in 1991–1992 as in 1984–1985 and fell from 6.6 per cent to 5.5 per cent of Gross Domestic Product (GDP). For public enterprises, which are very largely concerned with provision of infrastructure, there was a fall of 6 per cent in real gross fixed capital expenditure over the same period.

One reason is a change in the prevailing economic orthodoxy in the government, and another is the recession.[1] As a result of the former, revenue from taxes, fines and fees fell from 30.7 per cent of GDP in 1984–1985 to 30.2 per cent in 1991–1992. As a result of the latter there was an increase in government expenditure on personal benefits from 9.9 per cent of GDP in 1984–1985 to 11 per cent in 1991–1992, and real GDP, which had risen by 20.5 per cent between 1984–1985 to 1989–1990, was lower in the following two years.

One of the planks of the increasingly neoclassical policies followed by government since 1980 is a reduction in the size of the government sector, because of a belief that lower taxes will stimulate private investment. Eligibility for, and levels of, social security benefits have been increasingly constrained and expenditure on infrastructure has been limited. In effect, governments have not been willing to tax heavily enough to pay for unemployment benefits and other current

---

1 A very useful analysis of the reason for these changes has been provided in a recent unpublished paper by Ian Manning (1993).

expenditure. One way to stop the resulting deficits from getting out of hand has been to reduce (or defer) both maintenance and capital expenditure on infrastructure. It is now commonly agreed, however, that there is too little investment resulting from too little saving. One way to increase investment is for investors such as infrastructure authorities to increase their savings by raising charges in order to finance their own investment from surpluses.

This was not the first occasion on which governments have been unable to keep up with the demand for urban infrastructure. Rapid population growth after World War II, following the war years when all civilian investment had been severely constrained (Neutze 1977:210–12) resulted in a backlog of services. The costs of providing services were high because much of the post-war housing was scattered across subdivisions. It was during this period that developers first offered, and later were required, to contribute to the cost of roads, drains, water and sewerage.

Most social infrastructure, including the large items such as education and health, can be funded only from tax revenue. But many items of physical infrastructure can be funded also from user charges, charges on, and requirements of, developers or from access charges. This chapter aims to provide a framework for considering alternative means of funding urban services provided through physical infrastructure, and makes proposals about appropriate funding sources.[2]

Generally, this chapter argues that user charges should play a greater role, and access charges and charges levied on developers should play a smaller role. Overall, there should be less reliance on revenue from taxation. It is assumed throughout that general tax revenue should continue to provide substantial funds for most kinds of social infrastructure, and that some should be completely funded from tax revenue. Much of the chapter deals solely with physical infrastructure.

Because of the shortage of public funds for investment in infrastructure, the location of new urban development is being driven too much by the availability and costs of infrastructure. One objective of the proposals in this chapter is to reduce this influence by introducing funding methods that achieve the major economic and social objectives. Then it should be possible to make decisions about urban development on the basis of the collective preferences of people who live and work in cities.

The first section of the chapter lists the main objectives to be pursued in funding urban infrastructure, and the second section discusses the

2 Other discussions of some of the issues in this paper are found in Mushkin (1972), Downing (1974), Turvey (1971), OECD (1987), Kirwan (1991) and Snyder & Stegman (1986).

advantages and disadvantages of the alternative sources of funds in terms of those objectives. Classifying urban services according to why they are provided by governments (or government-regulated private firms) in the third section helps to determine which of the objectives should be most important for each service. To evaluate the case for user charges, it is necessary to examine the main determinants of cost (fourth section) to see to what extent costs vary with use and, if they do, how much of the costs can be covered by charges set equal to marginal cost. The chapter then lists appropriate funding sources for urban infrastructure (fifth section), considers some institutional impacts on sources of funds (sixth section), and concludes with a general assessment of the proposals against the objectives.

Financing Objectives

The objectives to be pursued in choosing a method of financing urban services fall into four broad groups.

Economic Efficiency

For some services it is desirable to set charges at a level which requires users to pay the marginal cost of production. Faced with such charges, consumers will use the service only up to the level at which the value placed on the marginal use equals the cost of producing it. Charges that vary with location according to the cost of providing the service in different locations will encourage users to locate where services can be provided cheaply. Only charges that vary with costs in different locations can achieve this, and the main candidates are developer charges and user charges.

To achieve economic efficiency, users have to know the cost of using a service, which requires that charging systems be relatively simple and the levels of charges widely known. Most of all though, the charges need to vary with measures of use which are major determinants of cost.

Environmental Quality

The use of many urban services affects the quality of air and water and amenity in and around cities. It is desirable that funding mechanisms discourage uses of services which damage the environment and encourage uses which enhance it. To achieve economic efficiency, charges should take account of the external as well as the internal costs of providing a service.

Revenue which Covers Costs and is Cheap to Collect

Revenue from charges needs to cover total costs less any amount which it is decided should be covered from general taxation. The costs of collection should be a low proportion of revenue, and preferably should provide a stable and predictable source of revenue.

Equity between Users

For some services user-equity can be achieved by setting charges equal to marginal cost, and for others a charge according to the benefit received. For many services, however, it is desirable to charge for at least a part of their costs according to ability to pay. Since the political process might be expected to levy taxes according to ability to pay, one relatively simple way to do this is to finance part or all of their costs from general tax revenue.

Financing Options

Three broad kinds of charges are used to finance infrastructure services: charges according to use, access charges, and charges levied on developers either in cash or by requiring them to install services. In addition, funds can be obtained from taxes related to use of a service such as fuel taxes, or from property taxes or general taxes.

User charges vary with the volume of use. Common examples are water volume charges, public transport fares and charges for the use of electricity, gas and telephones. The level of charge may vary with the rate of use, with the time of day or year, and with the location of use. The advantage of user charges is that, when they reflect the marginal cost of providing the service, they encourage efficient use (Turvey 1971). They are more valuable in this respect: first, if the volume of use has a large effect on the cost of production and second, if the level of charge has a large effect on the volume of use.

A set of user charges which varies with all of the determinants of the cost of providing a service would often be very complex, and not understood by users. Charges should be set to reflect the most important determinants of cost (Paterson 1992) and often need to be accompanied by persuasion and regulation. Although cost-related user charges are equitable according to one definition of equity, they do not relate to ability to pay. By themselves, efficient user charges cannot be expected to produce efficient cities because of pervasive externalities. There is a need for collective choices and there are opportunities for different cities to develop different identities. User charges can, however, assist in efficient use of resources for providing infrastructure.

An advantage of user charges and of clearly defined developer requirements, compared with less well-defined developer charges and tax revenue, is that they provide fewer opportunities for corruption. User charges that have to be approved by a body such as the NSW Government Pricing Tribunal may be less subject to political interference than either property rates or access charges. Compared with access charges and property taxes, user charges are often more equitable; at least they give low-income users the opportunity to reduce their costs by reducing their use of the service.

Access charges are fixed charges which permit a user to use the service, for example a fixed charge for water or sewerage, vehicle registration charges, telephone rental and connection charges, and higher charges for the initial units of gas and electricity. These charges are primarily revenue-raising measures. They are regressive with respect to income. They can be justified when the revenue from user charges that equal marginal cost would not cover total costs, which occurs when there are significant economies of scale in providing the service. In this situation they are part of a two-part tariff. Where consumers have a real choice about whether or not to use a service (e.g. gas, telephones), an access charge that reflects the cost of providing access can promote efficiency, but where access is essential or compulsory they do nothing to encourage efficient use.

Developer charges are levies on new developments for permission to connect to services (mainly water, sewerage, drainage, roads and open space) (Snyder & Stegman 1986). It is generally believed that these charges are passed on to home buyers in the form of higher prices.[3] They comprise two distinct components:

- developer requirements – that the reticulation of water, sewerage, drainage and roads, and open space within a subdivision, and the cost of connecting the subdivision to existing networks, be provided by the developer at the developer's cost; and
- developer charges which are a contribution to the cost of headworks and networks of these services, and sometimes the cost of other

3 There are three reasons for this occurring. First, when the charges were introduced they permitted early and full servicing which increased the value of allotments. Second, while the supply of land for urban uses is relatively elastic, demand is inelastic in growing cities so that land owners had only to defer development to recoup the costs of the charges (Neutze 1987). Third, the charges were introduced throughout metropolitan areas at the same time so that developers could not move to locations where development would be cheaper.

services outside the subdivision, but which need to be amplified as a result of the increasing demands coming from the new housing. Most of these charges are levied at a fixed level per unit area or per dwelling rather than being an estimate of the cost of meeting the demands resulting from a particular subdivision.

The cost to developers of requirements that they reticulate services within a subdivision reflects the resource cost of providing access to those services. As a result they provide incentives for developers to choose sites and forms of development (density, layout) for which services can be provided cheaply. Thus they help to encourage an efficient form of urban development. Developer charges do not have this advantage because they are levied at a flat rate per dwelling or per hectare. Both the developer requirements and the developer charges have the financial advantage of providing capital resources and thus reducing the need for local councils (roads and drainage) and water and sewerage authorities to borrow and amortise loans from property rates, access charges or user charges.

Neither form of impost on developers encourages efficient use of services by the residents, and the freedom of developers to provide more efficient facilities is limited by the detailed requirements of the infrastructure authorities.

When introduced, developer charges caused serious inequities (Kirwan 1991b). The change from financing these capital costs through loans amortised from rates on property to developer requirements and charges, resulted in increased prices for all housing and therefore shifted the financial burden from all ratepayers to renters and first-time home buyers. This involved a transfer from younger to older households, from renters to owners, and from those without housing assets to owners of such assets.

In summary, the economic efficiency advantages derive almost solely from requirements that developers reticulate services on the site. Charges on developers for off-site costs of services, on the other hand, are a purely financial measure. Both have serious equity disadvantages.

Taxes need to be classified into several types. The first is those which vary with the use of a service and have some of the features of user charges, for example, the petrol tax. Their disadvantage as user charges is that they seldom relate closely to the costs of the use of the service, in this case roads. In particular, they do not vary sufficiently between peak-hour use of high-cost roads in congested urban areas and use of low-cost roads in suburban and rural areas.

The second is property taxes, which have been used extensively in Australia as a source of funding for local roads, water, sewerage, drainage, garbage, open space and the cultural and recreational facilities provided by local government. Among their advantages is that, since the value of property is increased by the availability of urban services, property taxes are, to some extent, a tax on those who benefit from provision of the service. To some degree also, the value of property owned reflects wealth and hence ability to pay, though this is weakened because no account is taken of mortgage debt. Property taxes tend to be regressive with respect to income.

Property taxes levied on the unimproved value of property have little if any effect on the allocation of resources. This is an advantage if the objective is a non-distorting tax to provide funds. It is a disadvantage if the objective is to use charges to encourage efficient use of resources. Taxes on improved value are more closely related to ability to pay. Most taxes on property are levied by local councils and metropolitan authorities. Property taxes have a role as a source of funds for local services, but they are of almost no value in stimulating efficiency or environmental quality and of very little value in achieving equity.

General tax revenue comes from (usually) progressive income taxes and a range of indirect taxes. Their main advantage as a source of funds for urban services is that they are levied to some degree according to ability to pay. Also, since these taxes are collected by the Commonwealth government and State governments, they spread the cost of services over the whole State, which is especially appropriate for funding services which are regarded as a right of citizens, or which are public goods that provide benefits over a very wide area.

Although a number of general taxes have the objective of discouraging particular activities, for example smoking, the only one which affects the use of urban services is the tax on motor fuels. It is both a source of general government revenue and a source of funds for roads.

Borrowing is a method by which the costs of capital works can be spread over a number of years – preferably the useful life of the asset – as the loan is amortised. It does not, however, create the necessary flow of resources to pay for the services. Whether capital works are funded by borrowing, from current revenue, or from charges on developers has important effects on the distribution of those costs, including distribution across generations. Borrowing is more appropriate when there are adequate savings flows available for investment, which is not the case in the first half of the 1990s.

Privatisation is not a method of funding. The private providers of a service have to raise revenue to cover costs, but they have fewer options than public providers. In particular they cannot levy taxes. Their borrowing costs are generally higher, but they might be able to provide services more efficiently if it is possible to establish competition between private suppliers. This might be possible in the generation of electricity and is possible in long-distance and mobile telecommunications. There are many areas, however, in which it is not possible.

Classification of Urban Public Services

Much can be learned about the appropriate sources of funds for these services by considering why they are provided by government (or by regulated private companies) rather than competitively by the private sector (Shoup 1969:chs 4 and 5). The reasons reveal which of the objectives of funding are the most important for each service, and that in turn helps in the choice of funding source. One reason is dominant for most services, although some services are publicly provided for more than one reason. The reasons fall under four main headings:
- natural monopolies
- public goods and externalities
- equity and the rights of citizens
- merit goods.

To give some idea of the order of magnitude of the costs involved, table 10.1 shows the current and capital outlays by all levels of government for the purposes that include the main forms of urban public services. The table includes, of course, outlays in rural as well as urban locations.

Natural Monopolies

Where the economies of scale in some major part of the operations of the enterprise supplying the service are sufficiently great, competition between suppliers is inefficient. It would probably also be unstable since the most efficient supplier would take over its competitors. The relevant economies of scale are usually in the networks of pipes, wires, roads, rails or routes through which the services are provided. Thus, it is cheaper for all users in a street to be served from one water main than to have a choice between the mains provided by competing suppliers. Competition between suppliers providing substitutable services – gas and electricity, buses and trains – can help to achieve efficiency. It is also more efficient to provide a public transport system in which services that feed passengers from one to another can be coordinated, and a road system in which users can move freely between all roads.

This is the main, though not the only, reason why most physical infrastructure services – water, sewerage, drainage, roads, public transport, electricity, gas, telephones and garbage collection – are provided by governments, or by regulated private monopolies. For other services, including ports and airports, the economies of scale occur in the terminal facilities themselves. A feature of these services is their capital intensity, as reflected in the relative importance of capital expenditures in table 10.1. The users of services which are provided by governments because they are natural monopolies might be expected to cover their full costs: the natural monopoly argument for government supply does not justify government subsidy. Even without competition, user charges provide information to suppliers about the value users place on their services.

Public Goods and Externalities

Some services have to be provided for the community as a whole because it is impossible or too costly to exclude from some or all of the benefits those who do not pay. The classic example is defence. Among urban services police, fire services, the courts and public open space are, to a considerable extent, public goods. The public health effects of water, sewerage and garbage services provide public goods also, though public health requirements could be satisfied with systems that are less costly than those we have currently, so the marginal cost of providing these services is not incurred to expand public goods. Nevertheless, the whole

Table 10.1 *Outlays on urban-type services by all levels of government, 1991–1992 ($m)*

	Current	Capital	Total
Public order and safety	4 974	668	5 642
Primary and secondary education	10 564	1 963	12 527
University education	4 119	305	4 424
Technical and further education	1 819	294	2 113
Hospitals and other institutional services	11 644	822	12 466
Clinics and other non-institutional services	6 223	51	6 274
Welfare services	3 522	267	3 789
Housing and community development	922	863	1 785
Water supply	135	833	968
Sanitation and protection of the environment	541	1 038	1 579
Recreational facilities and services	1 375	468	1 843
Cultural facilities and services	792	172	964
Fuel and energy	759	2 600	3 359
Road transport	3 335	2 821	6 165
Water transport	335	85	420
Rail and multi-mode transport	1 143	1 105	2 248
Air transport	417	1 811	2 228
Communication	33	2 216	2 249

Source: ABS 1990–1991 and 1991–1992 Government Finance Statistics (cat. no. 5512.0)

community benefits from a cleaner environment in a city with good sewerage and garbage services. Local roads are public goods because it is inefficient to charge for their use, but the use of freeways and arterial roads can be priced using currently available technology. Education also produces external economies since the whole country benefits from a well-educated workforce and well-informed citizens.

Since we cannot charge for public goods, the alternatives are to finance them from general tax revenue or from taxes or charges on those who benefit from their provision. For example, since police and fire services protect property as well as people, some part of the cost might come from a property tax. Since the provision of access roads and parks increases the value of properties, it is appropriate that either owners cover their cost through a property tax, or subdividers provide the roads or parks and pass on the cost to home buyers.

Equity and the Rights of Citizens

Some services are provided, at least at a basic level, to all citizens as a matter of right, irrespective of their ability to pay the cost of provision. One objective, then, is redistribution in kind between the rich and the poor. Provision of these services is seldom a public monopoly; that is not necessary, and charges for some of them cover part of the cost. The balance is generally paid from general tax revenue; charges that covered the total cost would exclude those who could not afford to pay and therefore defeat the purpose of public provision.

The most important services in this category are education, health and welfare services. Equity can be defined as equality of opportunity (education) or of outcome (health). Consistent with the redistributive objective, access to some of these public services, for example public housing, is means tested. The importance of the equity objective or of citizens rights varies among these services. For example, it is very important in infant health, mental health, primary and secondary education, but less important for tertiary education and elective surgery.

Although equity considerations are rarely important in determining the means of funding physical infrastructure services, they are taken into account, especially where the services are required to meet 'community service obligations'. These are obligations to provide services at less than full cost to particular users for equity reasons. Examples are a range of services provided to small towns and remote locations, public transport services outside peak hours for the benefit of people without access to cars, and lower charges to pensioners for a range of services. Often the costs of these obligations are met by cross-subsidisation from other revenue received by the supplying authority. The conventional view is that these obligations should be financed from tax revenue so that their costs are distributed according to ability to pay rather than being met by other users of particular services.

Merit Goods

Governments believe their citizens should use more of some services than they would if they had to pay the full cost. The paternalism implied in such judgements make this a controversial category, and it is often claimed that these goods provide benefits to others in the community (externalities, perhaps making them public goods) or that they should be available to all citizens for equity reasons. The main examples are cultural services, libraries, recreation facilities and a part of higher education, and they are funded partly by user charges and partly from tax revenue. Merit good as well as public good arguments are used to justify public provision of some health services such as vaccination and other aspects of public health.

Determinants of Cost

For those (mainly physical infrastructure) services where charges are to be used to encourage efficiency in the use of resources, it is necessary to know the determinants of cost in order to decide on a set of charges which will reflect the marginal cost of production and hence help to achieve efficiency.[4]

Volume of Use and Economies of Scale

The main determinant of the cost of almost all services is the volume of use. Large fixed costs and relatively low variable costs result in large economies of scale in the short term in the provision of physical infrastructure. These economies can occur at different levels of use and in different parts of the operations of authorities providing the services.[5]

The most pervasive economies of scale occur in the networks through which most of these services are provided. It is these scale economies which prevent effective competition between suppliers. Some of them are straightforward. The capacity of pipes used to deliver gas and water

4 It is also desirable to have information on the elasticity of demand with respect to alternative means of charging, but very little information is available on this matter. It is best discovered by trial and error.
5 In this chapter I ignore the fact that most authorities produce more than one product and there can be economies of scope (from producing multiple products) as well as scale (Bailey & Friedlander 1982).

and to collect sewage and stormwater increases as more than the square of the diameter, but their cost increases roughly in proportion to the diameter. A similar relationship occurs in the wires used to distribute electricity. The fixed costs of railway rights of way, tracks, stations and terminals are high relative to variable costs of urban railway services even in the long term. Higher demand on bus routes permits more frequent services and shorter waiting periods. Economies arise in telecommunications from greater use of the fixed capacity of local networks as volume of traffic increases. There are great economies in sharing the use of access roads with all other users, though most of these economies are exhausted by the capacity of urban freeways.

While these economies prevent competition for customers, they do not always operate at the level of the urban area as a whole. As a result, it is not particularly inefficient to have different electricity, gas or water suppliers serving different parts of a large city. Private bus companies can operate quite efficiently when franchised with coordinated service standards, fares and schedules. Such arrangements are efficient unless there are economies of scale at the level of a city as a whole. Such economies would have to result either from economies of connection between different parts of the network, or from scale economies in headworks at the level of the whole city, and it is doubtful whether they occur.

There are economies of scale in water supply dams, sewage treatment and electricity generation but increases in the cost of transmission are often incurred in order to reap them. The dam sites that can supply water to a city at lowest cost are exploited first as a city grows, and expansion of demand requires the use of less efficient harvesting and storage sites. The same applies to electricity to a lesser extent, though other reasons for economies of scale are outlined below.

Technological change, especially the use of membrane separation, is reducing the economies of scale in sewage treatment. Costs of piping sewage remain high so that small-scale treatment plants are becoming relatively more efficient. Costs of disposal would be expected to rise with the size of a city because of the limited capacity of the environment in and around the city to absorb pollutants. Even cities, such as Sydney, which use the vast capacity of the ocean are experiencing increasing cost. As a result, either standards and costs of treatment must rise or the effluent must be pumped at increasing cost to a more distant outfall if the environment is not to deteriorate.

The volume of stormwater drainage used by individual property owners can best be measured by the volume generated: the increase in the volume over natural run-off which would occur during a defined rainfall event, for example, the highest 24-hour fall during the previous decade. The costs of the drainage system in a particular urban catchment could be distributed according to this measure. In many cases, the cost of coping with the run-off will also vary with the location of the property in its catchment. For example, the direct cost of coping with run-off from a property draining directly into Sydney Harbour may be zero. In general, the costs of stormwater drainage increase as the proportion of the catchment covered with an impermeable surface increases, as it does when the extent and intensity of development increases.

As cities become larger through a combination of greater density and covering a larger area, the overall length of roads, railways, pipes and wires within them increases, but does that result in increased cost per unit of use, or are the economies of scale in the elements of these networks sufficient to produce declining costs? As long as water all comes from outside an urban area it seems likely that the cost per kilolitre delivered will increase with city growth. The same applies to sewerage for similar reasons. (There are, however, opportunities for reducing the cost of both of these services if increased use can be made of locally harvested stormwater and of treated effluent from small-scale local sewage-treatment plants.)

If the average cost of providing a service is either constant or increases with increasing use of the service as cities grow, user costs equal to the marginal cost of providing an extra unit of the service will cover the total cost or make a profit. In that case, there would be no need for access charges or taxes to cover the overheads.

The usual measure of use of roads and public transport is a vehicle kilometre or passenger kilometre. As a city grows, the average length of journeys does not grow proportionately to their radius because jobs and services become more decentralised. Also as cities grow, the value of land, and hence the cost of increasing road capacity and therefore the level of congestion near city centres, increases. Journeys in those congested areas are more expensive per kilometre. Recent technological developments allow charges for the use of roads to vary with the level of congestion. Such charges can encourage efficient use of roads and, as a result, efficient location decisions. Calculations by Small, Winston & Evans (1989) suggest that a high proportion of the cost of urban arterials and freeways would be covered by user charges set equal to the marginal cost of road use.

Public transport commonly requires large subsidies from general tax revenue. One reason is that fares for some journeys, especially long commuter journeys, are often well below marginal cost. Another is that some part of the cost is incurred to provide mobility for people without access to other forms of transport. A third is that public transport is subsidised to reduce the volume of traffic on congested roads. The first reason suggests an increase in some fares, the second an explicit subsidy from general revenue to cover the losses, and the third would lose its validity if congestion charges were levied. If all of these changes were made, it still seems likely that fares equal to marginal cost would leave large deficits because fixed costs are high relative to variable costs even in the long term, and demand is highly peaked.

Economies of scale occur in electricity generation, but only up to a level of production which is far exceeded by demand in large cities. There are, however, economies up to a larger scale in scheduling to make the best use of a number of sources of electricity which have different production characteristics. For example, older thermal stations have higher costs than newer ones and should be used only in peak hours; hydro stations can effectively store energy as water in dams and are therefore efficient producers of peak-period power; gas-fired stations can be brought to production more quickly than coal-fired stations and therefore can also meet peak demands efficiently. The limits to these economies is the cost of transmitting electricity over longer distances to reach a larger market, and these costs will depend also on the location of coal, natural gas and hydro sites. There are also scale economies in piping gas from remote sources.

Fluctuations in Demand

For all services in which capacity costs are a high proportion of total costs, it is more expensive to cater for demand that is highly peaked. The effect on costs is greater where it is not possible to store the service (transport, telecommunications) or very costly to do so (electricity, drainage, sewerage, gas, and water supply in roughly decreasing order of cost). The amount of capacity needed is determined by peak demand and much of the capacity is unused during off-peak periods. Peaked demand also increases some labour costs because of the higher cost of employing people for very short periods, for example to operate public transport.

For all of these services it costs more to supply the service during peak periods, and those additional costs should be reflected in higher user charges during those periods. As a generalisation, the entire marginal cost of capacity should be charged to peak-period users.

Security of Supply

Although it is possible to project demand for infrastructure services reasonably accurately, fluctuations in temperature and rainfall make it difficult to predict accurately maximum demand for energy, water supply, sewerage and drainage during any given period. To meet the maximum possible demand requires greater capacity and therefore a higher cost per unit supplied. The additional costs of ensuring adequate water supply during a drought are even greater where the source is direct harvesting of surface run-off, because supply ténds to vary inversely with demand. Costs are lower for cities that are willing to accept periodic restrictions in use or even cuts in supply.

Restrictions and cuts mean different things for the different services: reductions in electricity voltage and gas pressure can be dangerous and cuts can cause damage to equipment or to stored food. Flooding and overflow from sewage treatment cause environmental and property damage and sometimes danger to people. Restrictions on water supply, such as those on garden irrigation, or loss of water pressure are less damaging. A decision on security of supply is necessarily a collective decision.

Location

Location affects costs in several ways, some of which have been mentioned above. First, the cost of providing services may vary with the particular characteristics of the location including its elevation, topography and geology, which affect the cost of installing services. Second, the location of the site relative to established networks affects the cost of providing connections to them. Third, the location of the site relative to headworks or to sinks where wastes can be deposited can affect transmission costs or treatment costs. For example, it is cheaper to supply water to the south of Sydney which is closer to the supply dams and to dispose of sewerage generated in the east because effluent discharged into the ocean need not be treated as fully, but the fact that most electricity comes from the north and gas from the west has little effect on costs in different parts of the city. Fourth, in the case of roads and public transport, it is the location at which a service is used rather than the location of new development that affects costs.

Form of Development

There is much discussion in the literature of the impact of density of residential development on the cost of infrastructure services (Real Estate Research Corporation 1974; Industry Commission 1993). Higher planned density when an area is being developed from a greenfield site results in lower costs, largely because of economies of scale in the networks of roads and pipes outlined above. If developers are required to provide the roads, water and sewerage reticulation and drainage within subdivisions they will have an appropriate incentive to build at higher density. Faced with costs of sites that vary with net residential density, home buyers will be able to make appropriate choices (Industry Commission 1993).

Other aspects of the form of development also affect costs, especially drainage costs. Run-off increases with the proportion of a subdivision that is covered with hard surface, just as it does for an individual property. In particular, developers have opportunities to decide how much of the subdivision will be covered by impermeable road paving and hard standing surface. They can do more than the subsequent owners of individual properties to provide for pondage or absorption of run-off into the ground water, and the method of charging for storm-water drainage should encourage them to do so.

Environmental Costs

Environmental costs which result from the production and use of physical infrastructure services tend to increase with the size of a city and to vary between locations within cities. Nevertheless, the main determinant of these costs is the volume of use of the service. Even when they vary with location, they also vary with the volume of use at each location. It is instructive to examine each of the major physical infrastructure services.

Supplying water necessitates the flooding of river valleys and, when it is used for irrigation of lawns and gardens, results in nutrients being washed into streams and ground water. All of these effects depend on the volume of water used. The flooding, pollution of water courses and erosion caused by stormwater depend on the volume of run-off. The discharge of pollutants from sewerage systems following treatment depends on the volume of water from which they have to be separated as well as the volume of nutrients, heavy metals and other intractable wastes discharged into sewers.

The noise, collisions, greenhouse and ozone-depleting gases and other air pollutants from road use result mainly from the volume of use of roads. Electrified suburban railways create noise in the cities they serve, and are responsible for air pollution at the sites of thermal generating stations. The amount of pollution is again proportional to use. The same air pollutants are produced to cater for other demands for electricity. The use of gas generates its own air pollutants in proportion to use. Even more directly, the environmental effects of garbage depend on the volume produced.

It is difficult, if not impossible, to measure the costs of the environmental damage which results from the use of each of these services and thus to incorporate the marginal cost of damage along with the marginal cost of provision into the level of charges. But if there is a choice of funding source, a consideration of environmental effects suggests that it would be appropriate to set user charges above measurable marginal costs rather than to use some other funding source. Such charges, along with education, land-use planning, regulations and some subsidies, could form an effective urban environmental policy.

Funding Proposals

This chapter has little new to say about funding of social infrastructure. Because the objectives of the government in providing such infrastructure are mainly distributional, the part of its cost which is not collected from users should be funded from general taxation. There is a case for funding local open space from charges on developers because most of the benefits accrue to people who live nearby, but it is not a strong case because such a charge does nothing for either efficiency or equity.

The following propositions are advanced with respect to physical infrastructure:

- user charges should be set at least equal to the marginal cost of providing the service. Where such charges do not cover the total cost of providing the service (because of economies of scale), or where environmental costs result from the use of the service, user charges should be higher than marginal cost of provision
- user charges should vary with location where off-site costs of operation of the service vary to a major degree (e.g. sewerage in inland areas of Sydney, water supply in elevated suburbs, and roads in areas of high land cost)
- developers should be required to provide roads, water, sewerage and drainage reticulation within subdivisions
- developers should also be required to pay the additional off-site capital cost of out-of-sequence development and the additional off-site capital cost of developments that would be particularly costly to service (e.g. pumping equipment and service reservoirs for developments at high elevations)
- access charges should be levied only to cover costs which are not covered by the above charges
- taxes would be used to pay for community service obligations of service authorities, such as provision of public transport out of hours for people without access to cars, and to charge some overheads to the beneficiaries.

The overall effect of the proposals is that user charges would increase significantly, charges to developers for off-site capital costs would be much lower, and access charges and taxes would become much less important as sources of funds.

There is little disagreement that the marginal costs of headworks should be covered from user charges as they are for gas and electricity. Charges for water use to cover at least these costs are being introduced in most cities. It is also agreed that it is desirable that the cost of using the road network should be covered by revenue from user charges. Whether or not that occurs at present depends on the proportion of fuel taxes which are defined as user charges rather than general revenue, and on the opportunity cost of land (its value in an alternative use) occupied by roads.

There is less agreement about how to charge for transmission networks where there are large economies of scale. The two traditional approaches are user charges for telecommunications and access charges for water and sewerage. In my view, the environmental costs of use of water and sewerage services are sufficiently great to make it preferable to cover these overhead costs from user charges.

Individual Services

The implications of these proposals for individual services, especially the nature of the user costs, are described briefly below.

Stormwater Drainage As well as providing drainage facilities within sub-divisions, developers would be required to make a capital contribution to the cost of dealing with the run-off from the subdivision based on the estimated increase in run-off due to development during a defined rain-fall event. Such a charge would give developers an incentive to provide for on-site absorption, short-term storage and possible re-use on the site.

The annual user charge would be calculated on the basis of the total hard area on a property (mainly roofs, driveways and parking) with a discount for on-site storage or provision for absorption. In addition, there would be a surcharge on the cost of water to cover the environmental cost of run-off from urban irrigation. The level of the annual charge would vary between catchments, and in some cases between parts of catchments.

Sewerage Most of the cost of sewerage would be covered from a surcharge on the use of water indoors which goes into the sewers. Given the cost of measurement of discharge to the sewers, domestic indoor water use would be estimated from the level of use during the time of year when water use is lowest: winter in southern Australia. As described above for Sydney, in some cases the level of charge will vary between parts of a city.

Large commercial and industrial users should continue to be metered both for the volume and the composition of discharge. Composition should also be measured for small non-domestic establishments which produce discharges that are costly to separate in treatment facilities.

Water Supply Aside from the (smaller than at present) charges on developers, probably the whole cost of supplying water should be recovered from a flat charge per unit of water used.

It is possible that the optimal level of charges for these three services would exceed the cost of provision. In effect, then, the use of water would become a base for taxes as use of motor fuel is today. That might seem to be inequitable if it were applied only in large urban areas where environmental costs are high, though it would be only one of the many ways in which there are differences in government charges and expenditures between parts of States: one difference which favours large cities is the subsidies to public transport from State budgets.

A relatively high price for new water will encourage economy in use, saving of rainwater and the use of collected stormwater and treated sewage for irrigation, especially in public open space areas.

Roads Urban arterial roads and freeway roads should be funded from congestion charges which vary with the level of congestion between parts of the city and between times of the day and week. The simplest method is meters in cars which are activated by loops in the road. An alternative is electronic number plates read by sensors beside or in the road. In both cases the charge depends on the level of congestion. The cost of levying such charges is much lower than manual collection of tolls and looks relatively attractive as tolls are charged for more urban roads.

They have the great advantage over fuel taxes in that they permit higher charges where and when the cost of road use is high. Since the economies of scale in provision of roads are small (Small *et al.* 1989), optimal user charges which include an allowance for environmental cost would almost certainly cover the total cost of major urban roads. Such charges would provide an appropriate disincentive to live or locate a business in areas which required travel on congested roads.

Public Transport Fares for bus public transport would increase when buses are required to pay their share of road user charges, though it is unlikely that this would bring fares even close to covering total costs. Since the losses in public transport that arise from the obligation to provide out-of-hours services are incurred to achieve a redistributive objective, their cost should be covered from general tax revenue. A large part of the losses, however, arise from economies of scale in railways and from the high cost of providing peak-hour services. The high costs of travel in the peak are seldom fully reflected in the cost of peak-period fares. Similarly, fares seldom rise with the length of journeys in proportion to the increase in cost. The environmental cost of public transport, including greenhouse and ozone-depleting gas emissions in electricity generation, and from burning motor fuels, also seem to justify higher fares.

The public transport services that mainly serve the city centre – railways and buses in large cities (and trams in Melbourne) and buses in smaller cities – would be likely to continue to make losses even if they were compensated for their community service role and charged appropriate fares. Currently the taxpayers of the State as a whole cover the losses. It would seem to be equitable and to promote more efficient location if the main beneficiaries were required to cover the cost. They primarily serve city centres and a tax on property in the city centre, as occurs for example in Paris, would be an appropriate way to cover their remaining losses.

Electricity The cost of reticulation of electricity, except where the lines are underground, is a much smaller proportion of total costs than in the case of hydraulic services, so it is easier for electricity authorities to include most of their network costs in charges for use. The small access charges, which usually take the form of declining block tariffs, should probably be replaced by higher flat user charges to reflect environmental costs. Greater use of off-peak pricing would also be appropriate. Additional costs of underground mains in both commercial and residential areas are, and should be, generally covered by developers. In residential areas this permits home buyers to choose whether they want to pay the additional price for the additional amenity which results.

Gas The current situation and the proposed changes are much the same as for electricity, though the case for off-peak pricing is not as strong because gas can be more readily stored. Where the demand for mains gas is more seasonal, as when a major use is for space heating, there may be a case for off-peak season prices.

Telecommunications As reflected in table 10.1, this is the service where capacity costs probably are the highest proportion of total costs, and there are substantial economies in providing higher capacity in sections of the network. I cannot judge whether the current fixed charge of, for example, $195 per year for a Canberra residential service, returns too high or too low a proportion of total revenue. It is also the service for which environmental costs are lowest, so that there is not a strong case for increasing user charges to cover them.

Garbage Collection and Disposal Rather than recovering the cost of these services through a fixed charge or a tax on property values as is common at present, it would be preferable to charge for the volume of garbage collected. This is the practice, for example, in Seattle and occurs in varying degrees in Australian cities. It encourages recycling and can reflect the costs of collection and disposal. Most garbage is put into landfill sites beyond the urban fringe and the cost of disposal will vary a little with the distance of a local council from the landfill site.

Institutional Effects on Charging

The reasons for the current system of charging are partly historical and partly due to institutional constraints which have prevented the adoption of more appropriate funding sources. Those institutional impacts on charging can be grouped under four headings.

Geographic Area Served

Physical infrastructure services are provided by local governments, State authorities serving a State-wide market, and public authorities established under State legislation which serve metropolitan markets. The same services are provided by authorities with State-wide responsibilities in some States and by metropolitan authorities in others, and these differences affect the charging system used. Cross-subsidisation is generally more prevalent within the area served by a single authority than between areas served by different authorities. For example, the Western Australian Water Authority provides water services to Kalgoorlie at a fraction of their cost without any explicit subsidy. In New South Wales also, water and sewerage and electricity services to small centres are subsidised, but the subsidies are expressly authorised by State parliament.

Main roads in all States are provided by authorities with State-wide roles. There is no attempt to charge in an efficient manner for urban (relative to rural) roads partly because of the difficulties of doing so through fuel taxes. Similarly the State Electricity Commission of Victoria retails electricity throughout the State and has a policy of charging all consumers at the same rate despite very large differences in the cost of supply.

Local councils in rapidly growing suburbs are responsible for local roads and drainage, two of the services whose capital costs of reticulation were transferred to developers in the 1960s. Prior to this change the cost of providing these services fell heavily on ratepayers in rapidly growing suburbs. After the change they fell on those paying mortgages in the same suburbs; the redistribution of the burden was often large even though it was confined within a municipality.

The other two services whose funding changed in the same way at the same time were water and sewerage reticulation. This caused much more widespread changes in the distribution of the cost burden. In this case, the cost of providing new services at the fringe had been spread across those paying water and sewerage rates throughout the metropolitan areas, or across the State in Southern and Western Australia. Following the change, all house prices rose and the capital cost to developers was added to the mortgages of all first-time home buyers.

There is a long tradition of regarding metropolitan areas as single areas from the point of view of planning and the provision of major infrastructure. In some cases, the metropolitan area is serviced by authorities with State-wide responsibilities, but even then it is usually dealt with separately for planning purposes. In the period since World War II, however, Australian metropolitan areas have become less integrated spatially. Most people live, work, shop, go to school and find their entertainment and recreation mainly within a section of the metropolitan area.

Similarly, many of the efforts to deal with environmental problems have occurred within sections of these large cities. There is a good deal of discussion on water management within urban areas at the scale of local catchments. For stormwater this is an obvious unit of management, though it corresponds to neither local government nor metropolitan boundaries. Local storage and re-use of stormwater has both economic and financial advantages. As mentioned above, new techniques permit efficient treatment of sewage in small-scale plants, and this in turn facilitates the re-use of effluent since the costs of pumping it back from large peripheral and low-lying treatment plants is avoided. The large hierarchical authorities which provide hydraulic services in the large cities or across whole States, while they have incentives to economise on the volume of trunk sewerage, are not well-suited to exploiting these local opportunities.

Similarly, much of the road travel occurs within sections of cities. Road planning that paid more attention to these local trips would limit the extent to which local residents needed to feed into the main arterial routes, and would facilitate the growth of regional centres within large urban areas.

With more local responsibility for stormwater, it would be possible to extend the earlier proposals for charging for it by regionalisation within the larger units. An urban catchment authority which received payments from developers and property owners depending on the volume discharged could in turn be charged by a metropolitan authority according to the volume it discharged into a larger river.

Constraints on Funding Options

Some of the impetus to charge developers for a range of services resulted from constraints on other sources of funding. For reasons outlined at the beginning of this chapter, State governments have recently had few funds to invest in infrastructure. Indeed, they have raided some of the reserves of their infrastructure authorities. Furthermore, some States have limited the ability of both local councils and water and sewerage authorities to increase their property rates, largely because of the political unpopularity of higher rates.

Borrowing has been constrained also. In the 1980s this was largely a result of the constraints placed on State borrowing by the Loan Council. Following deregulation the States themselves have been restricting borrowing because of its possible effect on their credit rating and the negative political impact of a high level of State indebtedness.

Being constrained in both their borrowing and the level of property rates they have been permitted to strike has caused authorities to place increasing reliance on charging developers for the total estimated cost of extending infrastructure to service new residential areas, including increased capacity in headworks and transmission networks. One possible way to avoid this problem would be for State governments to cease to guarantee the debts of these authorities and to allow them to be secured by the assets of the authorities themselves and their future income-earning potential. Such a change would follow naturally from corporatisation, though it could, I believe, occur without it.

Funding of Roads

Partly because of the costs and difficulty of charging for public roads prior to the development of electronic charging for road use, and partly because roads were regarded as part of public open space, they have been regarded as a quasi-public good to be funded from tax revenue. Since no revenue is directly received for the use of roads, they have been funded from current revenue rather than regarded as an investment which was expected to earn a return. Yet road building often has been justified as yielding a good commercial rate of return. Because they yield no revenue directly, roads have been provided by a government department and regarded in the national accounts as part of general government while most other physical infrastructure services have been provided by public trading enterprises and expected to make a return on their investment. By any criteria roads are a long-lived capital asset investment in them has been included in national capital accounts, and should be expected to yield a return.

Few estimates have been made of whether revenue from roads cover their full economic costs and road authorities have been slower than other utilities in facing the need to earn a return on replacement costs including land. A recent 'Review of Road Cost Recovery' (Luck & Martin 1988) takes it as given that roads should be funded from current revenue, and ignores the opportunity cost of the land occupied by roads. It follows from this approach that there have been few, if any, estimates of the value of road assets in Australia, even though public trading enterprises have been required to have their assets valued at replacement costs and to pay a dividend based on that value to their owner-governments in recent years.

If roads were to be treated in the same way, road authorities would be required to earn an appropriate rent on the land they occupy, and would have to give serious attention to a charging system of the kind advocated in this chapter (and much earlier: Neutze 1964) which brings in more revenue from roads in locations where land value is high.

Preference for Stable and Low-Cost Funds

The slowness of water and sewerage authorities to move from property rates to user charges reflects the attraction of a source of revenue which is completely predictable, quite stable, and very cheap to collect, especially when the valuation of rateable properties is carried out by another authority. Rate capping, and the difficulty of authorities in funding the headworks required to meet increasing demand, has encouraged them to adopt a charging system that will discourage excessive demand.

The reluctance of road authorities to adopt congestion charging has several origins. Like water authorities, they found attractions in revenue from petrol taxes, especially when they did not have to collect it. They have been dissatisfied, however, with the limited fraction of that revenue which they have received. They believe that roads are seriously under-funded and are considering adoption of congestion charges, as well as making greater use of private funding of urban freeways. The two main constraints on the introduction of congestion charging are the costs of setting up the system and, probably even more importantly, the likely opposition from groups concerned that privacy would be threatened by the ability it could give the administering authority to monitor the movement of individual vehicles. The privacy problem could be overcome by having meters in cars which could be kept in credit (or limited debit) using the same technology as is used for public telephone cards.

Conclusions

A considerable increase in reliance on user charges as sources of funds for urban physical infrastructure would have a number of desirable effects. First, it would improve efficiency in the use of resources by discouraging the use of services beyond the level at which the value to the user falls to the marginal cost of supply. Second, by including an allowance for external environmental costs in charges to users, it encourages consumption patterns which have less damaging effects on the environment. Third, by varying user charges between parts of an urban area where the costs are markedly different, it discourages use of a service in localities where it is costly to provide the service.

This desirable-location incentive, for example from higher charges for road use in areas where land value and congestion are high, is supplemented by requiring developers to provide on-site reticulation of services whose costs vary with the location of development.

Some service costs vary with the particular form of development and those variations should be taken into account by continuing the requirement for developers to provide on-site reticulation. Some features of the development also affect costs off-site, such as the cost of dealing with stormwater. The proposal that there be a charge on developers which varies with volume of stormwater which would flow from a subdivision, provides an incentive to design it to be environmentally benign.

The proposals would result in less stable and predictable income for a number of authorities providing physical infrastructure services, especially water, sewerage and drainage. Those authorities would need to keep financial reserves for wet years when they have water nobody wants and dry years when users want more water than is available. The cost of collection of congestion charges would be greater than that of fuel taxes, and there would be additional cost of metering water in some cities and of more frequent reading in others.

The proposals do not give a great deal of weight to equity issues, though the reduction in developer charges will reduce the cost of becoming a home owner or being a renter, and therefore redistribute income from home owners to non-owners. The other proposals are equitable in the sense that users pay for the cost of the services they use, and are not obviously less equitable than current charging policies.

For the funding proposals to have their desirable effects, people will need to change where they live and work and to invest in equipment and outdoor planting that use less water and energy. Low-income people, especially heavy users who will be adversely affected by the proposed charges, will be less able to make these investments. This suggests two policy measures. First, the changes should be introduced gradually to give time for people to make adjustments. Second, there is a case for financially assisting those who, during the phasing-in period, want to move or to invest in equipment that will economise on the use of services.

It is possible that greater reliance on user charges that differ with location would result in greater residential segregation, as only the rich could afford to live in areas where the charges were high. That would be the case, however, only where it is more expensive to provide services to areas of high amenity, as for example water supply to elevated suburbs. It would not turn low-lying areas where drainage is costly into high-income areas. The users of congested roads at peak hours are mainly those who work in the central areas and live in the suburbs. Only the rich could afford to continue to do so: others would have to seek work closer to home or live closer to work.

On balance, the proposals provide major gains in terms of efficiency and environmental quality, some additional costs of collection, greater fluctuations of income and very little change in equity.

CHAPTER 11

Alternative Urban Policies:
The Case for Regional Development

Peter Self

Analysis of urban problems and policies cannot be confined to the big Australian cities, but needs to consider their relationship to the rest of this continent. Regional development presents itself as one possible route for ameliorating the problems of big-city growth and for promoting a more balanced and satisfactory settlement pattern for Australia as a whole. This chapter explores this possibility.

Initially certain objections must be confronted. First, it is often said that regional development and urban dispersal policies have been tried and have failed. Secondly, and more particularly, it will be claimed that there are neither the necessary resources nor the political will to push policies of this kind in the likely economic climate of the 1990s. Regional development as a prescription for urban problems is unfashionable in political circles, except among the enthusiasts for the development of particular towns or regions. The prevailing doctrine of market-led growth appears to rule out any striking public initiatives.

The Federal government views regional issues primarily in terms of encouraging economic restructuring and public service economy, and has confined its positive interventions to the advocacy of urban consolidation in the big cities through its 'better cities' projects and in other ways. State governments are less active in promoting regional development than was once the case, although with some exceptions. Western Australia, for example, is concerned about the still increasing dominance of Perth which now contains almost three-quarters of this vast State's population, and has followed up its promotion of Bunbury as an alternative growth point with other regional initiatives (Self 1991).

Despite these unpromising circumstances, the prospects for regional development will repay a closer look. In the first place, past experience is not adequate grounds for rejecting regional development initiatives, although it does contain lessons about the form which these should take. Secondly, regional development can be claimed now to be more not less relevant to the urban future of Australia than was the case in the past. This is so partly because the mounting disadvantages of further growth of the big cities cannot be resolved by the fashionable recipe of urban consolidation, and partly because Australia has reached the take-off point which will bring it closer to the more normal patterns of urban growth in other 'developed' countries. Finally, while the time is unpropitious for new Whitlam-like urban initiatives, government policies can and do influence urban patterns in a variety of ways, while the application of rational pricing policies would in some ways favour regional development.

Lessons of Earlier Regional Policies

Australia has a unique pattern of urbanisation. The uniqueness lies not so much in the high degree of urbanisation per se, as in its concentration in the five 'millionaire' cities of Sydney, Melbourne, Brisbane, Perth and Adelaide. There are no cities of between half a million and one million population and only eight between 100 000 and 500 000. Among this group Canberra stands out as the only major inland city, and Canberra, Hobart (a State capital) and Townsville are the only towns not close to a conurbation. There are fifteen towns between 50 000 and 100 000 and a very large number of small country towns, the products of early agricultural development, many in decline because of agricultural mechanisation, lack of social facilities and sometimes harsh living conditions. Conversely there has been some growth of the larger rural centres, due to the concentration of commercial and social facilities, and on the coast tourist and retirement developments.

The original causes of this demographic and economic concentration in a few big cities are well known. They included a transportation system based on the coastal cities, the concentration of migrants in those cities, economies of scale for manufacturing and distribution, the political and administrative pull of the State capitals, and the cumulative ratchet effect of urban concentration – backed up on the negative side by the great size and poor communications of the continental interior.

For most of this century the degree of concentration in the big cities grew steadily and substantially. Reasons for this were the parallel movements into the cities of both overseas migrants and surplus rural workers, and the growth of manufacturing in the cities behind protective tariffs. Between 1921 and 1976 Sydney increased its share of State population from 42.8 to 63.4 per cent, Melbourne from 50.1 to 71.5,

Brisbane from 27.8 to 47.8, Adelaide from 51.6 to 72.5, Perth from 46.6 to 70.7 per cent. Since 1976 the position has stabilised and there has been little change in the combined proportion of population living in capital cities (EPAC 1991:18).

Against this background it was natural that efforts should be made to promote regional development in the aftermath of World War II. The political environment and the existence of a Labor government were favourable for bold schemes of post-war reconstruction. The rural lobby was keen to reverse the decline of country towns. The Premiers' Conference of October 1944, called by Federal Prime Minister John Curtin, initiated a phase of intensive regional planning activity. However, within a few years the Federal government had changed its political colour and retired from the scene, leaving regional decentralisation to be pursued by the individual States.

This they all did in much the same way. The NSW government set up regional development committees to review regional resources and prepare development schemes, a move later followed by Victoria. By the early 1950s Queensland and Tasmania had introduced legislation to provide financial assistance for regional development, and New South Wales, Victoria and South Australia introduced similar schemes in the 1960s. The main instrument used was the offer of loans or the development of industrial sites to encourage firms to move to decentralised locations, supported by freight subsidies and sometimes by payroll tax rebates (EPAC 1991:3–4).

These State schemes achieved very little, although they did something to prevent urban concentration from increasing still further. The main reason was 'scattergun decentralisation' – the diffusion of a small quantum of assistance unselectively over very wide areas. In New South Wales, for example, decentralisation assistance was made available over virtually the whole State, even including less prosperous parts of the Sydney metropolitan area. This unselective assistance was the product of political pressures to offer something to everybody, despite the realisation of a few farsighted public servants that this strategy could not work (Harris & Dixon 1978).

The Whitlam victory in 1972 brought in the Federal government as a keen initiator of regional policies and the new Department of Urban and Regional Development (DURD) was keen to avoid the errors of 'scatteration' and to promote substantial new growth centres which could cumulatively change the urban framework of Australia. The eventual results were not impressive, but the main reasons for this outcome were the few projects which actually got off the ground and adverse political pressures, coming initially from some States over the choice of sites and then from the reversal of DURD policies which followed the election of the Fraser coalition government.

Briefly reviewing the projects which were started, Campbelltown new town basically represented a regionalisation of the outward growth of Sydney through the creation of a new centre and the provision of local industrial employment, low-income housing and recreational facilities. As such it can be counted a useful project but it did not constitute regional development in the broader sense (much the same could be said of the less realised Gosford–Wyong project which may eventually produce another example of regionalisation within Greater Sydney). The Bathurst–Orange project, also in New South Wales, was the choice of the State government and was badly flawed in its initial design and frustrated by non-cooperation of State agencies. The one reasonably successful growth centre was Albury–Wodonga where the political complexities, involving two States as well as the Federal government, may actually have assisted its realisation despite the necessity for a complex administrative structure. This development lies at a natural if distant growth point along the Sydney–Melbourne corridor, and the development corporation has been fairly successful in attracting firms and helping to create what will become a major city with some natural attractions.

Among the projects which did not get off the ground should be mentioned the case of Monarto, warmly supported at first by the South Australian government but later scrapped (after the land had been acquired and preparatory work done) because of a downward revision of the population forecasts for Adelaide and doubt about the project's economic prospects. However, as Adelaide continues to spread along its narrow coastal plain, South Australia may eventually regret the loss of this opportunity.

Some specific lessons can be drawn from the problems of the DURD growth centres:

- in a natural revulsion from earlier State policies, the projects were too ambitious. Not even Albury–Wodonga reached its population targets, and the development corporations set up for each town were allowed or encouraged to acquire too much land at inflated prices, which then contributed a lot to their subsequent financial problems. Of course, this difficulty would have been reduced if the Whitlam government had continued in office to nurse its projects.

- there was too little effective cooperation with local government. Partly, this failure stemmed from the political priority which DURD had to give to working with the State governments, but it also showed up in the planning of the growth centres. Thus, the Bathurst–Orange growth centre was located midway between the two towns, an unrealistic concept, and the growth of Albury–Wodonga was not related effectively to the existing centre of Albury, which could have become the focal point of the whole new town.

• it is essential to secure the cooperation of State agencies for a growth centre project to be successful. This point was clearly demonstrated in the history of Bathurst–Orange (Sproats 1983). In South Australia, with its stronger tradition of urban planning, the necessary cooperation would have been forthcoming for the development of Monarto, but unfortunately this demonstration could not proceed.

In conclusion then, the difficult political climate in which the growth centre projects were launched and later reversed has to be fully understood before judging these initiatives a failure (Lloyd & Troy 1981). Politics need not necessarily be so erratic in relation to future policies even if they are unlikely to take the same form as the DURD initiatives. Moreover the State decentralisation attempts and the DURD initiatives do offer useful lessons for future policy-making.

Growth Dilemmas of the Big Cities

Currently Australia's big coastal cities are continuing to swell outwards at a still rapid rate. It is 80 kilometres (50 miles) from the centre of Sydney to the end of the new south-west development area. It is much the same distance from the top to the bottom of the much smaller city of Adelaide. In Melbourne, only 42 per cent of the population lives within 15 kilometres (9 miles) of the city centre. Perth, like Adelaide, is growing to an enormous size along its coastal plain. Brisbane has expanded well beyond its city borders into adjacent shires and municipalities and threatens to join up with the rapid growth occurring on the Gold and Sunshine Coasts. A further complication here is the enormous area zoned by local governments as 'rural residential'.

These urban developments have rightly set the alarm bells ringing. Most of the fringe suburbs are poorly served for social facilities and public transport, which seriously disadvantages the many low-income families who live there. Environmental problems include the growth of traffic congestion, pollution of watercourses and beaches, smog, noise hazards, problems of sewage and waste disposal, and rapid consumption of environmental resources. Financial problems include the high cost of developing and servicing new neighbourhoods and the very large expenditures necessary to renew basic infrastructure, to improve roads and public transport, to mitigate pollution and to find suitable sites for the disposal of waste.

The current orthodoxy appears to be that the special problems of big cities are due not so much to the total size of the population as to the structure of the city and its means of communication and transport. There is no doubt that structure and communication systems are important factors for determining how well or badly a big city functions. However, it would be wrong to suppose that size of population has little relevance to urban problems, since a larger population (whether more concentrated or more dispersed) puts more demands on environmental resources and public services, produces more waste products and adds to the complexity of urban management and policing. In any event, the structure of a city can change only very slowly and no conceivable measures of restructuring can do more than modify the further outward expansion of the cities.

The current political recipe for solving urban problems is 'urban consolidation', coupled hopefully with a major switch from cars to public transport. In popular terms, this policy suggests an intensification of residential development within the inner areas of cities which would enable more people to live closer to public transport, work and social facilities. In particular, this change would be socially beneficial for many lower income households, single-parent families or pensioners who would otherwise be living in distant suburbs. Unfortunately the actual prospects of achieving these results have been much overstated. The physical capacity of inner areas to take more dwellings under tolerable conditions of space and daylighting is much less than is usually supposed, given that housing occupies only a third of urban land and such development is also limited by the high prices of land in inner areas and the opposition of existing residents (usually supported by their local governments) to any erosion of their amenities and lifestyle. Hence any hope of enabling more low-income households to live close in rather than far out depends in practice on strong political determination and a generous use of public subsidies – difficult conditions to be satisfied at the present time.

Hence, urban consolidation comes to mean in practice increasing housing densities wherever possible, and as much in new release areas on the fringe (where it is perhaps easier to achieve) as in existing urban areas. Its most promising prospect will be the development of medium-density housing near major sub-centres and transport stops, but it would be illusory to suppose that some intensification of development will produce a big shift in modes of travel. That shift depends on the adoption of policies for road pricing and improved public transport – which could assist urban consolidation but which are needed in any case if cities are to be made more 'habitable'. It seems certain that there will still be a strong market demand for single-storey detached dwellings, whose residents will experience a loss of garden space and privacy from developments that seem likely to add to the 'Australian ugliness' deplored by Robin Boyd (1960).

Urban consolidation policies will achieve the best results if they are pursued selectively and sensitively and coupled with special assistance for low-income groups so as to counter the growing geography of inequality described by other writers in this book; but in any event, they will make a rather minor difference to the outward growth of the big cities for a long time to come. Suppose, for example, average net residential density increased from 30 to 35 persons per hectare in a city of one million people – a process which would take many years – the city's radius would only fall from 14.6 to 14.1 kilometres, assuming expansion in all directions (McLoughlin 1991:153). All the metropolitan planning strategies (Melbourne 1987, Sydney 1988, Perth 1990, Adelaide 1991) embrace the principle of urban consolidation enthusiastically, but even the most ambitious program (such as Melbourne's) still has to allocate two-thirds of new growth to the periphery, and the Sydney strategy concluded that even a fully successful containment program would defer the need for additional release areas by only three years over a twenty-year period (Self 1988). An authoritative view is that nine-tenths of new development will continue to be near or on the urban fringe (HRSC–LTS 1992:87).

An important development is regionalisation within big cities. The proportion of employment concentrated in the central area has declined drastically – in Melbourne, for example, from 55 per cent in 1961 to 30 per cent in 1986, and the majority of workplaces are now in the suburbs. These trends will continue and contradict the concept of the concentrated city. Unfortunately, places of employment are widely dispersed (though increasingly located within favoured sectors of the city) and all State planning strategies hope to concentrate a much larger quantum of employment in major sub-centres that are accessible to public transport and offer a wide range of facilities.

This intended 'regionalisation' of the structure of the city offers considerable social and environmental advantages and accords with Lionel Orchard's concept (chapter 3) of the decentralised, socially oriented city; but it will not come about without substantial public initiative and investment. To avoid continued 'scatteration' of social facilities and workplaces, it is necessary to create new centres which offer a genuine alternative to the main city centre for social, cultural and entertainment facilities as well as shopping. Imaginative planning and steering of new developments are necessary to realise this vision, but the political will to pursue it is not yet evident.

Policies to make the big cities more 'habitable', equitable and efficient are urgently needed, but they have also to cope with the additional problems of further growth; for example, the enormous planned expansion of western Sydney is occuring in a bowl liable to severe air pollution and served by already polluted rivers. It is not surprising that some local councils are campaigning to shift development elsewhere – but where? If residents are faced with increasing smog and traffic congestion, and possibly restrictions on their choice of housing, they may themselves want to move. Regional development, in its wider sense, may offer at least one way of making growth problems of cities more solvable while offering alternative lifestyles which many would welcome.

Regional Development Prospects

It has been pointed out that the urban system of Australia is unlike that of other developed countries. In particular, there is a lack of the medium-sized cities which occur so abundantly in Europe and North America (even Canada, the closest geographical parallel to Australia, has an appreciably greater number of such cities). Cities have everywhere swollen through the accretion of suburbs, and the largest cities have developed into 'urban regions' comprising a ring (or even successive rings) of satellite or partly dependent towns. Another development is the growth of 'urban corridors' between major cities. A growing volume of economic activity has also become relatively 'footloose' and less tied to the traditional advantages of economic concentration possessed by major cities. The 'world cities' such as New York and London increasingly specialise in finance, management services and cultural facilities, while manufacturing industry and routine service employment move to the outer parts of the urban region and beyond – or disappear with 'deindustrialisation'.

This brief summary of international trends clearly has parallels in Australia, notably in the suburban growth of the big cities. However, there are also differences. Urban regions are coming into existence as a continuous urban spread rather than as a system of satellite towns at a variable distance (such factors as poor communications, mountain barriers and the climatic pull of living near the sea contribute to this result). Hence 'regionalisation' within cities is at present more relevant than the development of satellites, although Australia contains some country towns (for example, Ballarat and Bendigo in Victoria) which are well placed to grow as centres within a broader urban region (in these examples, one based upon Melbourne).

A second difference is that manufacturing and routine service employment remain closely tied to the major cities, especially Sydney and

Melbourne. This situation stems from the rather weak basis of Australian manufacturing and the fact that tariff reductions are hurting employment in country towns more than in the cities. In 1993 unemployment was high everywhere, but in every State (and especially New South Wales) it was higher in non-metropolitan than metropolitan areas. The fact that there is surplus labour in country towns has little relevance for employers when there is also a surplus in the city as well as a broader labour force. Economic recession leads to timidity over locational moves and an obsession among policy-makers for protecting such economic concentrations as already exist.

Potential 'urban corridors' certainly exist in Australia. The most obvious one follows the road and rail routes between Sydney, Canberra, Albury and Melbourne, which was the intended route of the Very Fast Train. Another emerging corridor, already being fostered by tourist and retirement developments, is the coastal route from Sydney to Brisbane. In the long run it seems certain that there will be a growth of urbanisation all along the coast from Cairns to Adelaide with probably a mini-corridor along the West Australian coast from Geraldton to Albany or Esperance. However, because of poor communications, the accumulated effects of existing urban concentrations and the adverse economic climate (especially for investment in major infrastructure), these potentialities have only just begun to be realised.

Demographers point out that there is already some movement of the aggregate population from metropolitan to non-metropolitan areas; but this switch is as yet a very minor one and can anyhow be explained by moves just across statistical boundaries. More to the point is the substantial migration out of Sydney and Melbourne, offset – at least until recently – by a much larger immigration into these cities from overseas. Much of this out-migration has been to coastal districts in New South Wales and Queensland. Brisbane has become the fastest growing major city, followed by Perth.

Any programs of regional development would need to build on the potential opportunities indicated above. It would be pointless to return to the unselective efforts of a previous era and impracticable (at least for the present) to revert to the idea of large Federal-initiated growth points. But within these limitations there would be scope for the gradual development of a considerable number of medium-sized towns. Some of these towns would be within the orbit of influence of a major city – sufficiently near to permit easy contact but sufficiently distant to establish an independent existence. (This is, in fact, the European and American pattern.) Other expanding towns would lie along the incipient growth corridors which have already been described. There are also other towns outside the main lines of development which possess particular opportunities for growth. The impact of such a program would affect only a relatively small part of the total area of Australia. The future of the more remote places and regions involves different considerations and a separate analysis. However, any extension of the poles of growth would have some knock-on effect on surrounding areas. For example, if some of the larger rural centres were to achieve an accession of economic activity, some of the benefit would flow back to rural areas in their vicinity.

The question which arises is not whether these kinds of regional development will occur or not. Eventually they seem certain to occur unless population and economic growth become indefinitely static. The question rather is whether regional development in this sense could and should be accelerated or alternatively, as some writers suggest, whether it should be held back in the interest of concentrating public investment and subsidies on the functioning of the largest cities, primarily Sydney and Melbourne (O'Connor 1992). That question will now be reviewed in terms of social desirability and economic feasibility.

The virtues of the free-standing medium-sized city – with a population of anything from 30 000 to 300 000 – are very considerable. As demonstrated in the pioneering work of Colin Clark, and confirmed by the findings of the Commonwealth Grants Commission, the service costs of such a city are distinctly lower than for either big cities or sparse rural areas. Such a city can cope comfortably (in a physical sense) with almost any type of housing demand, while keeping its facilities accessible to all citizens. Particularly in the upper levels (over 100 000 people), it can afford a good range of social facilities and can evoke a lively community and civic life. While the opera may be lacking, there is ample compensation to be had in lifestyle and recreation.

Social surveys in France, Britain and the USA have shown that a majority of people now living in a big city would sooner live in a smaller town (Self 1982:110–11). The most favoured option appears actually to be a relatively small town, but one with good access to a major centre. This preference could be satisfied by new developments within reasonable travel range of an existing big city centre, but it could also be met through Ebenezer Howard's concept of the 'social city' – a ring of smallish towns all with access to a new centre, the whole complex totalling about 250 000 people. Interestingly, present-day Canberra represents a rough if not perfect approximation to Howard's ideal (its main problem is Canberra's over-reliance upon the motor car facilitated by its good road system, a system which will become more costly and destructive as the city grows further).

At a minimum, the development of more medium-sized cities would increase the range of lifestyle opportunities for Australians by adding to the alternatives between life in the suburbs of a giant city or in a small country town. Indeed, there is already evidence of many Australians moving from a big city (especially Sydney) to some smaller place for social and environmental reasons, even at the cost of long-distance commuting or difficulties over finding a job. Employment is the main factor constraining the distribution of the population. However, is it realistic and economically efficient to envisage a gradual switch of employment to regional centres? While the current economic climate is certainly adverse, there are some reasons for answering this question in the affirmative:

- the reduction of industrial protection will give some differential advantage to regions specialising in agriculture and mining. Significant opportunities should arise for new employment in the processing of raw materials. The States that primarily benefit are expected to be Queensland and Western Australia, but some regional centres in all States could gain from this development (Industry Commission 1991).
- on the American model one can expect quite small towns to specialise in particular functions such as retail mail orders or health services and supplies. 'Major advances in telecommunications and transportation are creating a footloose economy that enables entrepreneurs to locate where they want to be rather than having to be in close physical proximity to their market' (EPAC 1991:48).
- the possibilities of telecommuting for enabling employees to work from home are becoming evident in the USA but have still to be realised in Australia. 'Telecommuting offers considerable potential for altering the regional pattern of employment and improving the efficiency with which our cities operate' (EPAC 1991:51).
- because of high rents and traffic congestion in the big cities, there are gains from decentralising routine office tasks to other locations which can be quite distant. This opportunity is as relevant for government as for business. For example, in Britain the government has decentralised civil service jobs from London to the point where London's employment in public administration is scarcely different from that of an average British city or region. One would hardly find the same result in respect of public employment in Australian States!

The decline of manufacturing and the growth of an information and service economy appear to favour a more decentralised pattern of employment. They increase the importance of the quality of life which a given location can offer (Hall 1992). Simultaneously, the old connection between size of city and average income (based on the increasing returns to joint economies of scale) no longer seems to apply, at least not beyond a certain city size, while the increasing costs of urban living seem to outweigh any income advantage which remains (Brotchie 1992). To function as an international financial, managerial and cultural centre, a city such as Sydney needs high quality facilities and an attractive image; but it does not require a still larger population or to spread itself over more than 80 kilometres – developments which will detract from rather than improve its functional efficiency. These considerations underpin the opportunities for regional development if it is intelligently pursued.

Influence of Federal Policies

Many Federal policies have some effects on patterns of urbanisation and regional development, but they are usually based on quite different criteria and are not directed at or concerned with those particular effects. As one consequence, different policies can and do have contrary effects. Since 1992 the Federal government has tried to take a more positive and coherent approach to urbanisation issues. Brian Howe, Minister for Housing, Local Government and Community Services, has initiated a wide-ranging study termed the Australian Urban and Regional Development Review (AURDR) (1994), to be spread over three years and involving six Federal departments; but there is also an Office of Regional Development, located in the Department of Industry, Technology and Regional Development, whose particular concern is the contribution of regions to national economic growth. These reviews, as well as the work of the Industry Commission, are all affected by the federal concern with micro-economic reform, economic efficiency and rational pricing. It may be doubted whether they will take a broad enough view of regional development or avoid some contradictory prescriptions. However, my concern here is not to second-guess federal reviews, but to consider briefly some of the Federal policies which have a major effect on patterns of urban growth.

Immigration

Federal immigration policies are crucial for the growth of the Australian population and economy. As in most other 'developed' countries, the Australian-born population is no longer reproducing itself, although due to the earlier baby boom and the higher birth rates of some recent immigrant groups, it will be many years before this effect of zero or negative growth occurs. Eventually (barring further changes in repro-duction habits) population growth will depend entirely on immigration, and even for the next thirty or so years this dependence will be considerable (Day 1992). For example, with a low immigration rate of 60 000 a year, the Australian population is expected to increase by 5 million to 22 million in 2030 and then level off; but with a high immigration rate of 160 000 it would increase by 11 million to 28 million in the same year and then go on growing (HRSC–LTS 1992:14).

Immigrants concentrate strongly in Sydney, Melbourne and Perth. In Sydney, their main destination, they accounted for 70 per cent of all household formation between 1981 and 1986 and in Melbourne for 50 per cent (NHS 1991a). A decline in the immigration rate, which began in the 1990s, should have the beneficial effect of alleviating the growth problems of the big cities. In the case of Sydney this effect has so far been offset by a reduction in the numbers leaving Sydney for other destinations and the ambitious development plans for the city still stand. In the longer run, a low immigration rate would slow up considerably population growth in the major cities, although much less so in the Brisbane region and possibly Perth. The fact that Queensland's population is growing twice as fast as that of New South Wales, although it receives only 10 per cent of immigrants, shows that substantial shifts in the settlement pattern could still occur.

In principle, Australia would seem to need population growth for economic and strategic reasons and has the resources to support a substantially larger population. Immigration will probably continue at a relatively low and possibly declining level until Federal economic policies tackle mass unemployment more effectively and allow sufficient investment in infrastructure to foster better communications and faster growth. As economic prospects improve, so will the scope for regional development. If (as the Fitzgerald Report (1988) recommended) more priority is given to highly skilled immigrants, many of them may also be attracted to new developments since workers in science and technology constitute the most mobile section of the population. Immigration policy is closely linked with macro-economic policy and both policies need to take account of their urban effects and potentialities.

Transportation Policies

The Federal government is deeply involved in the provision of a satisfactory national system of road and rail communications. Priority within this system needs to be given to the improvement of routes between the main cities and along the potential corridors of urban growth. A number of trunk roads, such as the Pacific Highway between Sydney and Brisbane, are in urgent need of improvement.

Particular attention needs to be given to the upgrading of rail services for passengers as well as freight. State rail authorities, following a narrow commercial principle which overlooks the environmental and social case for assisting rail services as well as the opportunity costs of existing rail investment, and which also reflect the political tendency to overlook the national value of good interstate services, have been further curtailing their already very limited rail services. During 1993 the strange situation occurred of there being no daytime rail service at all between Sydney and Melbourne, two cities of over three million people.

The situation is completely different in Europe. There an excellent system of fast and frequent rail services has been built up between the main European cities, which has also benefited intermediate towns along the main routes. Japan has an excellent and frequent rail system. In the USA much public opinion now deplores the disappearance of rail services due to lack of government involvement and support. Australia should learn from European experience and the advantages for regional development associated with it.

The Very Fast Train (VFT) proposal, if it ever comes to fruition, will produce a sharp stimulus to regional development along the routes between Sydney, Canberra and Melbourne and/or Sydney and Brisbane. It has emerged that the project's commercial viability probably depends upon either tax concessions or else on allowing the promoters to reap profits from the appreciation of land values around intermediate stations. However, if government undertook the project it could cover its costs through acquiring land at key locations in the same manner, an arrangement which would also much assist the planning of new urban growth. Short of settling for the VFT technology, against which some environmental objections can be raised in the Australian context, it is necessary to upgrade the existing rail tracks so as to reduce travel times substantially and much increase the frequency of services.

The VFT project put much weight on the need for rail travel times to be competitive with air travel between the main cities. This goal may have been somewhat unrealistic and overstated in terms of the general advantages from improved rail services. These services should be able to offer appreciably lower fares than air services, given the case for some subsidy on environmental and social grounds. Competition over fares is probably more significant than competition over time – although comparison with the time taken by coach or car is important. Also much of the benefit of good rail services will flow to inhabitants of intermediate towns, whose accessibility to both main cities and to other towns along the route will be much improved. The stimulus to regional development would be considerable.

Rational Pricing Policies

The Federal government's attempts to promote more economically rational ways of pricing public services and framing regulations could be very helpful to regional development. Application of the 'user pays' principle to the costs of urban infrastructure, as suggested by Max Neutze in chapter 10, would bring home the real costs of big-city life. The introduction of road pricing would substantially increase the price of travel by car to a much greater extent than in smaller towns, and public transport in the cities is also subsidised from general State and Commonwealth taxation. (However, the desirability of subsidising public transport on social and environmental grounds suggests that 'user pay' ought not to be applied here, although the subsidy to the cities should be recognised.) Many public utilities cost extra in the cities, because of high land prices, high costs of pollution control and waste disposal and more complex management. By contrast, many middle-sized towns would reap the advantage of lower service costs.

The Industry Commission's reports point in the same direction. Interestingly, the commission finds no clear evidence that development on the urban fringe is being subsidised compared with inner areas; and it delivers an agnostic verdict on whether urban consolidation can, in fact, deliver public service economies. However the commission's findings do suggest considerable undercharging for basic infrastructure and transportation in the cities. The commission has also suggested that environmental regulations that are suitable for big cities may be unduly burdensome for smaller towns, and that wage rates in smaller towns could reasonably be somewhat lower than in the cities since costs of living are also lower. The latter proposal might stimulate employment in some regional locations, but as presented it is associated with an undesirable erosion of basic wage rates (Industry Commission 1993a, 1993b).

The equalisation principle of the Commonwealth Grants Commission – which requires that every State should be enabled to provide (if it so chooses) the same level of public services for the same tax effort – has been attacked by New South Wales and Victoria for subsidising inefficient locations. Their main criticism is directed against the heavy subsidisation of public services in remote areas, which is especially helpful for Western Australia and Queensland. If support were withdrawn from remote areas they could become uninhabitable – which might be seen as desirable on ecological and financial grounds, and as assisting Aboriginal land claims, but strategically and socially as very questionable. In any event the commission is also giving differential support for public service costs in big cities, and it is uncertain how far the higher revenue per head derived from these cities is due to the efficiency of their economy as opposed to their capital status and dominance. If the commission's equalisation principle were modified by 'efficiency' arguments (which is not necessarily desirable), it seems likely that, once again, the results would favour medium-sized towns.

Federal Assistance for Local Government

The Federal government's financial assistance grant to local government is distributed according to a similar equalisation principle, although its details are still more complex because of the variety and number of local governments. The Federal government would like to introduce some 'efficiency' considerations into this grant and also to stimulate desirable forms of regional development.

The main beneficiaries of local government assistance are rural areas, which is equitable but wholly unselective in terms of development opportunities. However, the grant could fairly be used to encourage joint provision of services and the formation of regional councils which in some areas would assist regional development. Beyond this point an effective policy of regional development requires a much more selective form of grant. Fortunately it is fiscally possible to achieve this result without changing the equity basis and untied character of the present grant system. As urged by the National Inquiry into Local Government Finance (1985), the present federal grants for local roads could be merged with the federal equalisation grant and allocated on the same basis, since both grants deal with the finance of local roads and there seems no reason why local governments should not be free to establish their own priorities between local roads and other services. If this were done, the total equalisation funds would be substantially increased and, assuming (as is likely) that no further federal finance would be forthcoming, some money could be deducted from the total funds and allocated for a separate regional development grant. This grant would be available only to local governments who are willing and able to undertake development in an effective manner and according to some general criteria for regional development.

Regional Development Initiatives and Policies

Changes to existing federal policies could help regional development but would not amount to a satisfactory program. Two lessons need to be learned from past experience and the understanding of current trends and opportunities:

- regional development should be selective, well planned and responsive to social and environment requirements;
- regional development requires a working partnership between all three levels of government.

The first point can be demonstrated by the failures of previous unselective schemes and of over-ambitious single projects. It is also strongly indicated by the likely patterns of unconstrained market growth. Much of this growth may take place outside existing metropolitan areas. Many of the new high technology areas in the world, such as Silicon Valley, the North Carolina research and development triangle, Cambridge and the M4 corridor in England, are located outside metropolitan areas, although usually with good access to a major centre. Lifestyle considerations are becoming more important for many professional groups and skilled workers, and modern telecommunications is facilitating the dispersal of homes and often workplaces as well. Australia still has an abundance of attractive coastal and some inland sites which can meet these preferences. However, these overseas examples also show the dangers of market-led growth without effective public planning. Silicon Valley, for example, is not just a technological showcase but in some respects a depressed area, marred by environmental pollution and by inadequate and distant housing for the many relatively low-paid workers. Cambridge and the M4 corridor in England are suffering from the abolition of regional planning and the lack of affordable housing. New growth areas in Japan suffer severely from environmental pollution and weak housing policies. Left to itself, market-led growth has strong tendencies to scattered and lopsided development patterns which increase the cost of public services, produce undesirable environmental impacts and fail to consider the needs of lower-income households living in these new areas. Planning of balanced development at a limited, well-chosen number of sites is an equitable and economical answer to these very real dangers.

Secondly, the circumstances of Australia, as well as past experience, point to the need for effective partnership. State governments' role is plainly central because of their direct responsibilities for the planning of development, for local government and for the provision of most public services, but the Federal government's participation is also essential because of the impact of its existing policies and its dominant economic and financial role. Moreover it should be able to take a more national view of development possibilities than individual States can manage.

Local government has been the neglected partner in regional development, but numerous local governments are keen to undertake development and many are doing so actively (Wagga Wagga Conference 1992). Many local governments are not well placed to see their dreams come true – at least, not in the 1990s – although State and Federal policies ought to give some weight to their enthusiasm and capacities. A selective regional program could count on the support and participation of local governments, who should be given an active role in advising on and implementing development policies. Local government can sometimes be strengthened through the creation of regional councils of local government, which is also a long-standing aim of federal policy.

Admittedly the immediate prospects for regional development do not look bright. Large-scale unemployment, sluggish economic growth, reduced levels of immigration and especially strong curbs on public expenditure have inhibiting effects. Yet, whether the process occurs slowly or rapidly, randomly or deliberately, substantial shifts are likely in the distribution of the Australian population as it continues to grow. These shifts will occur both between States, with Queensland one obvious winner, and within States to favoured regional developments.

It is surely up to governments, and especially the Federal government, to take a long-term approach to national development. Public investment creates no larger burden of foreign debt than does equivalent private investment and if well-directed should bring more benefit to the nation than money invested in overseas assets. A basic input of public investment is often the essential basis for triggering off a much higher volume of private investment, as can be observed in many urban developments around the world. It can also be argued that a strong public initiative in the process of urban development would have a very beneficial effect on employment and economic growth and (after allowing for substantial savings in unemployment benefit and additional tax revenue) would be both economically and socially worthwhile in terms of its costs.

The starting point is a more effective system of regional planning. Here the Federal government should work closely with the State planning systems and do its utmost to strengthen their present weak impact, instead of launching into piecemeal experiments of its own. As Patrick Troy argues in chapter 12, political competition between governments needs to give way to effective cooperation upon a broad basis. One purpose of this enhanced regional planning would be to identify suitable regional growth points and draw up outline plans for their development. Local government would be involved in this planning process, but on the understanding that only a very limited number of projects are possible at one time.

Development, like planning, would proceed through a partnership process. In many cases, local governments themselves would be able and willing to provide much of the infrastructure and other requirements, but it would be desirable and often necessary to help them with financial support and high quality technical assistance. The most suitable instrumentality for this purpose would probably be a regional development corporation, not restricted to a particular area but with flexible powers to provide assistance to participating local governments or to undertake works itself on an agreed basis. It would also have the important task of marketing regional projects to prospective employers and residents. The corporation would presumably be State-appointed, but the Federal government should share financial responsibility for agreed development projects and should preferably have representation on the board of the corporation. The Federal government could initiate a planning and development process through offering appropriate incentives to participating States.

This sketch of possible political cooperation for regional development may seem premature to some and utopian to others. However, the ill-effects of unplanned urbanisation are already apparent along Australia's long and beautiful coastline and will intensify. Unguided market forces will also produce scattered and segregated development patterns. By contrast, an effective regional development policy would concentrate new growth in a more balanced way in a series of expanded towns located mainly along natural growth corridors served by improved communications. Australia has plenty of attractive locations for new development, and the time would seem ripe to ensure that these potentialities are not squandered but safeguarded for the long-term benefit of a growing society.

CHAPTER 12

Cooperation Between Governments

Patrick Troy

We have seen from the preceding chapters that the mainland capital cities in Australia have grown rapidly in the post-war period. Although only Sydney and Melbourne are large by international standards all of them are now of a size and complexity exceeding the imagination or expectations of the political leaders who at the end of the nineteenth century arranged the distribution of powers between the States and Commonwealth.

In defining the Constitutional responsibilities of the different levels of government at the end of the nineteenth century, urban issues appear not to have been raised (Deakin 1963). In the discussions which took place it was implicitly assumed that the States would continue with the responsibilities each had as colonies for urban affairs. As sovereign States they would each continue to oversee the distribution of functions between the towns and cities which formed their urban systems and they would each exercise whatever powers they chose over the form and structure of the towns and cities within their territories.

Local Government

The question of local government and its powers never arose. Local government was unevenly developed in the colonies. In some Australian colonies, communities had local government imposed on them, whereas in others colonists strenuously opposed it. Finn (1986:57) reports that 'By the turn of the century less than one per cent of the total area of New South Wales was incorporated.' It was implicitly assumed that local government would be the creature of each State government as it had been of each colonial government.

State Independence

Much of the independence each colony enjoyed was to be continued in the new States. The distinctiveness in the development of each colony would continue in each State. During the nineteenth century each colony developed its own laws and regulations governing the development of local government, housing, the provision, financing and pricing of a variety of urban services in ways which grew out of their own political experience, aspirations and economic development and with little reference to one another. Colonial governments, since their foundation, had been centrally involved in the provision of public works and facilities. The location of various government services, schools, roads, the construction of bridges and harbours, the development of building standards and health and local government regulations, the development of rail systems and of tramways, the provision of water supplies and of sewerage were all areas in which colonial governments were centrally involved. It could be argued that concern over these issues was the essence of political life in each of the colonies. The saliency of public investment in infrastructure was reflected in the importance attached to the Ministry of Public Works whose Minister ranked only slightly behind the Premier/Treasurer in importance and as a source of patronage in each colony. This investment was of crucial importance in the development or 'progress' of each colony but was also essential in the establishment and maintenance of their comparative advantages. By the end of the century Australia was one of the most urbanised nations in the world.

These different trajectories in the evolution of concern by colonial governments over urban issues continued in the early twentieth century as the colonies became States. For example, they developed their regulations covering housing, health and local government in different ways at different times. By and large, there was little government planning and regulation of the form and structure of urban growth in any State.

There were few urban services which required cooperation between towns and cities within one colony and fewer which required intercolonial cooperation for the services to be provided. In some cases, adjoining urban local authorities in a single urban area were required by the colonial governments to jointly sponsor or finance water supply and sewerage schemes.

Although there were local examples of noisome water pollution resulting from the discharge of sewage or the waste from the operation of tanneries and wool scouring establishments, reforms in these areas were resisted, especially by influential country interests in the colonial governments. When reforms were undertaken they were seen as public health issues, not as concern over the environment or general quality of life issues. By their nature they did not require inter-city cooperation or collaboration for their resolution. That is, externality issues or problems which in large measure result from concentration of population, which we now regard as environmental problems, could be resolved without cooperation with other cities or other governments. Issues of efficiency or the realisation of economies by means of collaboration and coordination were simply not considered.

Urban development in the nineteeenth century was relatively self-contained. Apart from the influence of each town or city on others, resulting from trade and exchange or competition between them, the operation of each city was independent of others. The primacy of each colonial capital within its colony in part grew out of a determination by the governments of each colony to focus development on it to prevent loss of markets and influence to other colonies (Butlin 1964). That is, colonial governments, especially in New South Wales and Victoria, sought to establish and retain the dominance or comparative advantage of their respective capitals over those of the other colonies. The way they focused development of their railway systems on their respective capitals and the fact that the systems were built to different specifications which limited interchange demonstrate this most eloquently. To some degree their investment in collective consumption or 'civic' services such as public libraries and universities can be seen as a way of maintaining their advantage by demonstrating their relative progress, superiority or modernity.

Form and Structure

The most important influences on the growth of cities which affected their form and structure during the nineteenth century were the working out of market pressures by the private investment in fixed assets. Householders continued to demand their own house on an individual block of land as they had throughout the nineteenth century (Fry 1972). The generally high standard of living meant that the aspirations of average income earners to own their own house on its own piece of land could be met. As Mullins has pointed out, domestic production was a major influence on the form of the Australian city during this period (Mullins 1981a, 1981b). Land developers and promoters supplied the land to meet the demand. Government authorities met the demand for water supply, railways and tramways by extending their services which in turn generated new demand. Apart from ensuring that health and building safety standards were met, governments were little exercised by the growth other than to encourage it and to ensure that it continued to be focused on the central area of the city which was where most employment was found and commerce conducted. The government's capacity to provide services was stretched and much of the growth occurred without appropriate services – roads were not sealed and they frequently had little provision for drainage, schools were often provided late which meant they were frequently inconveniently located. The only saving grace for the governments of the day was that community expectations of urban services were low.

The major cities in each State continued to grow in the early twentieth century and Sydney and Melbourne reached a size where problems of scale began to appear. State governments continued policies designed to reinforce the primacy of their own capital within the State and to protect it from competition from other States. The administration within the States did not change to reflect the changing complexity of urban issues. The distribution of power and the manner in which decisions were made at the State level continued much as they had under the early colonial administrations. Ministers for Works, Lands, Railways and Education continued to be the important members of governments. Individual government departments and authorities continued to pursue their own programs, each intent on optimising or expanding their operations with little consultation or regard for the consequences for others or the overall impact of their activities. There were attempts by advocacy groups, including town planning reformers early in the twentieth century, to get State governments to adopt more rational approaches to the problems of urban development. These were mainly focused on the growth problems of the State capitals; there was almost no attempt to take a State, let alone a national, approach to the issues and even at the State capital level they were unsuccessful (Sandercock 1975). The major reshaping of Sydney's port facilities at the turn of the century and its Daceyville housing project in 1912 were two major initiatives which required inter-departmental cooperation and consideration of what, in modern times, we would call city-wide issues but in both cases the interactions were minimal. In the former case, the reforms were accomplished because the agency involved had strong political/administrative backing even though it lacked cooperation from the Sydney City Council whereas the failure of the second reflected the relative weakness of the proponents of the initiative.

Commonwealth Powers

In the new Commonwealth the Federal government's responsibilities were set out under section 51 of the Constitution (Sawer 1975) with the States having the remainder. The Commonwealth had no direct powers over urban development other than the responsibility under section 125 for a seat of government and for which it did not need State co-operation; powers over urban development resided with the States. The Commonwealth was, however, given powers under section 96 to make grants of financial assistance to the States under conditions established by the Federal parliament.

The Federal government was slowly drawn into urban issues as urban growth continued, new technologies were taken up, demand for higher quality services rose and the cities became more complex. By the early 1920s the pressure for increased investment in and a more rational approach to the development of the national road system led to the Commonwealth making grants to the States under section 96 for the construction and maintenance of main roads (Lloyd & Troy 1978). Although the grants were initially and essentially for the development of the non-urban elements of the national road system they required an increasing degree of communication between the States and Common-wealth and between the States themselves for the program to be effective. The increasing communication was followed by increasing cooperation between governments, which was reflected in the departure from a system of allocation to each State according to a formula related to factors such as area and numbers of vehicles to one where the funds made available to the States were allocated according to assessment of needs and national priorities.

At the time of Federation the States had substantially different capacities to finance the provision of services (particularly urban services). The new Commonwealth Constitution made interim arrange-ments to provide for a degree of financial equalisation between the States through the allocation of special grants to those which were at a disadvantage. Early Federal governments continued to make such equalising grants after the interim period expired in 1910, but they were the subject of much dispute. By 1933 these arrangements were accepted as inadequate and the Commonwealth Grants Commission was created to develop and apply principles for assessing grants to the States (AGPS 1983). The purpose of the grants was to enable States to provide services to relatively equal standards. Although States made submission to the commission about their needs there was no formal requirement for cooperation between them or with the Commonwealth. The Whitlam government's reforms of the Grants Commission were designed to allow local government to make submissions to and receive grants from it. These measures required a degree of cooperation between State governments and their local authorities.

Meanwhile the major cities continued to grow over the post-Federation period (see table (i)). The growth in size was accompanied by an increase in the expectations of their residents in the standard and range of urban services they enjoyed. For example, whereas early in the twentieth century few expected roads in the suburbs to be paved or their houses to be sewered when they took up residence, by mid-century local authorities were refusing to allow developments unless they had paved roads and by the 1960s they were permitting only developments which were sewered. There are many other examples of services whose standards of provision rose over the period and there were services, such as telecommunications, which were not a commonplace at the beginning of the century but which were ubiquitous by its end.

Increasing Expectations

Some part of the demand for higher standard services arose out of the higher expectations of what was a reasonable standard for a modern advanced society and the correct way to order urban expansion (resulting from the adoption of modernist ideas), some as a way of preventing sprawl and some out of the realisation that provision of the service after settlement of an area was often much more expensive. Although State and local governments were attaching conditions to urban development to enable them to cope with problems of financing the urban growth, much of which occurred or was exacerbated by the Commonwealth's policies (especially its immigration program), there was virtually no recognition by the Commonwealth of the seriousness of the issues let alone any contemplation of cooperation between it and the States to resolve them.

Housing

In the post-war period the Commonwealth established a public housing program which was funded under the Commonwealth State Housing Agreement. The States were presented with an offer of financial support for housing programs from the Commonwealth providing they met certain conditions set down by the Commonwealth. Although the Commonwealth had limited responsibility for housing it had explored the housing situation in Australia through the Commonwealth Housing Commission but had not involved the States in any joint review of housing (Lloyd & Troy 1981). Its offer of assistance was similarly asymmetrical – the offer was on a take-it-or-leave-it basis. The States protested and one refused the offer for some time although they were all ultimately forced by their limited resources into agreement. In spite of the uniformity in the terms of the financial assistance made available to the States their performance varied widely. South Australia, for example, vigorously pursued opportunities available to it under the Agreement. This led to South Australia having a substantial proportion of all houses built in that State built by the Housing Trust or on land acquired by the Trust. It also led to that State having the highest proportion of all dwellings in public ownership. Queensland, however, had the lowest level of activity and the lowest level of dwellings in public ownership.

The history of the housing program is not one of cooperation although the States themselves initiated a regular meeting of their Ministers and officials to share knowledge and experience. The Commonwealth sought permission to attend and was invited initially with observer status. The Commonwealth gradually assumed the leading role although it has not functioned as a forum for the cooperative exploration or resolution of housing issues. The Commonwealth has traditionally approached the meetings with the States as though it was laying down policy and has succeeded in large measure by taking advantage of traditional rivalries between the States and because the financial independence of the States has been progressively reduced over the period. We should also note that there have frequently been tensions between the Commonwealth and States over the support for housing with the States claiming that they had better knowledge of housing requirements in their respective States. These tensions have been exacerbated because the Commonwealth has never had senior policy advisers or program administrators who were experienced in the area. That is, there has been a lack of symmetry in education and training and experience between those engaged in the consideration of housing issues at the State and Commonwealth levels.

The States have had officers experienced at managing housing programs and the Commonwealth has had officers who have been more skilled at examining housing at the macro-economic policy level – the Commonwealth officers have also had the strength which comes from the knowledge that they control the purse strings. At the State level, until recently, public servants tended to remain with one department or agency and were recruited by their department or agency because they had relevant qualifications or experience. There were clear disadvantages to this policy but the major advantage was that there was a substantial accumulation of experience and deep corporate knowledge of housing development and management at that level. At the Commonwealth level public servants are regarded as interchangeable from one area to another, with the result that there is no necessary connection between those in policy analytical roles or senior managerial levels and qualifications or experience in the area. State public servants in housing are more likely to have relevant training and experience than their Commonwealth counterparts.

This asymmetry in knowledge and experience has not always resulted in mutual respect or harmonious relations between officers of the two levels or between their respective ministers. This in turn has reduced opportunities for cooperation between governments on housing issues. The differences between Commonwealth and States do not seem to have been a function of differences in ideology between Commonwealth and State governments but rather continuing tensions between the Commonwealth on the one hand and the State-level governments on the other over their relative authority. The tensions originate in the fact that while the States have the constitutional authority the resources increasingly lie at the Commonwealth level. They may also be explained by the different perspectives of the politicians at the two levels, with Commonwealth-level politicians having wider horizons and less immediate contact with those in need of publicly provided housing services.

The States, having the continuing responsibility for delivering housing services and having some commitment to notions of equitable support for the lower income members of society, must seek to maximise their programs and to seek commitment to those programs running over an extended period. State governments are, of course, much more vulnerable to pressure for reform of the whole range of areas of housing policy – whether in the field of landlord–tenant relations, housing standards or supply – than the Commonwealth. The Commonwealth, on the other hand, seeks maximum flexibility in its management of economic policy and, in particular, to demands on the Commonwealth budget leading it to resist commitment of resources for more than one year.

In more recent periods as the 'first generation' of housing officers have retired and/or administrations have been restructured, State governments have themselves appointed to senior positions officers with no special training or experience in housing. This pursuit of managerialist philosophy has resulted in loss of skill and corporate knowledge or institutional memory at the State level. Pursuit of the same philosophy at the Commonwealth level led to the distribution of responsibility for housing policy and program administration between a number of departments following the 1987 restructuring of administrative arrangements (AAO 1987). This led to the devaluation of such corporate knowledge as existed in the middle levels of Commonwealth housing administration. The immediate consequence of these two processes occurring simultaneously at the two levels of government was that opportunities for development of a shared understanding of housing issues were reduced. It also meant that opportunities for cooperation between the different levels of government were limited if only because of the number of departments at the Commonwealth level with an interest in housing issues, thus creating confusion in the States.

National Approaches

Few initiatives are national approaches arising from a shared understanding of the nature of urban problems or determination to resolve them in a way which produces a more equitable system more efficiently. This may be a consequence of the nature of political discourse in Australia, the inevitable outcome of the institutional arrangements or the fact that urban issues are, and are perceived, differently in different regions.

The different institutional structures and political timetables in each State and the Commonwealth will result in differing priorities and therefore perceptions. That is, the differences in the structure of State parliamentary systems (whether uni- or bicameral), the distribution of power between city and country interests, the different periods between elections, and the different electoral systems all combine to create different contexts and timetables in which urban issues are considered.

The different functions discharged by urban areas in each State, the differences between States in terms of their urban systems and scale of problems, form and structure of the major cities inevitably mean that State politicians and administrators bring differing understandings into play when discussing urban problems. The scale and complexity of urban problems in Sydney, for example, are compounded by the topography and geology of its site as well as its inherited infrastructure, making Sydney's problems different from those experienced in Melbourne; the saliency of water supply and sewerage issues differ between Adelaide and Perth; the need for and type of public transport in Brisbane differs from that in Hobart.

The Commonwealth must treat each State equally; it cannot provide services to one State and not provide the same services to others. It can provide support for a location-specific or area service such as education out of a concern for social justice and the rights of citizenship and according to some uniform conditions even when no interstate issues are involved. The Commonwealth is on stronger ground when it attempts to improve the functioning of network services such as roads or transport and communications services, in which there are interdependencies across State boundaries. There are, however, urban network services such as water supply, sewerage and drainage which, although of central importance to the operation of a city, have no impact on other cities in other States. Although the provision of hydraulic services is essential they are usually seen as the responsibility of the cities they serve. This set of services provides few opportunities for cooperation between governments other than the sharing of information and experience about operations, technology, financing and pricing and the joint sponsorship of research. The Australian Water Resources Commission (AWRC) is a felicitous example of such cooperation. Given that many of the issues identified as urban have features which make them unique to a city, it might be too much to expect the development of a shared understanding let alone the articulation of a consensus of how the problems might be resolved.

Nonetheless, the political realities are that Commonwealth governments are pressed to, or perceive opportunities to, take initiatives to resolve urban problems. The initiatives are usually 'top down' and are frequently 'product' oriented: they originate at the Commonwealth level and are offered to the States, they are rarely a response by the Commonwealth to State pressures or analyses. They are often designed to deliver a 'product' rather than change the decision-making process at the urban level – sometimes the offer of a product is rationalised on the grounds that the demonstration effects of the delivery of the product will lead to the States changing their decision processes or administrative arrangements (the current Better Cities Program is an example of this type of program). A charitable view would be that this is the result of a superior analysis of the situation (although it would be hard to sustain such an explanation in many cases) coupled with a recognition of the inherent difficulty of trying to reach agreement with a set of States locked in competition, and each with a political agenda whose imperatives are only coincidentally congruent with those of the Commonwealth.

In many situations a Commonwealth initiative can be too easily characterised as intervention in the States' affairs. The States may respond to 'product' programs by dusting off plans for pet projects and using them to extract finance from the Commonwealth with little intention of changing the way they order their affairs. States can take advantage of Commonwealth offers under this kind of program because, having made the offer and publicised it, the Commonwealth needs the States' cooperation to get political kudos from the initiative. This makes the identification of issues problematic and the chances that the States will respond favourably to initiatives to modify or reform processes remote.

The limited and reducing discretionary resources available to State governments mean that they can always be forced to appear to play the game with the Commonwealth but, to excuse their own failure to address problems, they can always also blame the Commonwealth for its parsimony.

The difficulties faced by the Commonwealth in trying to achieve a cooperative approach with the States may also arise because of the way the Commonwealth takes initiatives where it is itself unsure of what its position should be. The lack of specificity and the way the Commonwealth engaged with the States over the recent proposal to develop a 'Multi Function Polis', whatever its merits or demerits, ensured that the idea would not receive the cooperative response the Commonwealth desired. That may have been because nobody involved at the Commonwealth level associated with the initiative had substantial knowledge of the context from which the Japanese proposal emerged, nor of the Australian urban system, the way cities within it operated or of the history of utopian proposals. The lack of knowledge and professional competence at the Commonwealth level together with the lack of a detailed proposal meant that States had great difficulty in working out how to cooperate with the Commonwealth, and in any event they were put into competition with one another so the probability of a positive outcome emerging from it was low.

Another recent illustration of the limited capacity of the Commonwealth to cooperate with the States is its response to the Very Fast Train (VFT) proposal. Here a private consortium proposed to build a new high-speed passenger train system to operate between Sydney, Canberra and Melbourne with possible long-term extension of the system to Brisbane and Adelaide. In a situation where there was general agreement that the national rail system needed to be reformed and upgraded the Commonwealth was presented with an opportunity to focus attention on the issue without necessarily accepting the high technology proposal. While generally determined to withdraw from public investment in infrastructure and to encourage private investment, its reaction was to reject the proposal after what seemed an inadequate consideration of the issues. Later consideration confirmed the initial decision but by then there was some suspicion that the Commonwealth was doing so to show consistency rather than as a result of more mature rigorous exploration of the proposal. The failure by the Commonwealth to use the proposal as a way of developing cooperation with the States to address a major national transport infrastructure issue could not have been encouraging. It may also have been due to the lack of experience and knowledge of transport issues at the senior levels of the Commonwealth's Department of Transport and Communications.

The States' response to the Commonwealth's proposal to reform the national rail freight system which followed soon after the VFT proposal thus did not result in the degree of cooperation which the Commonwealth sought. The Commonwealth's determination to give as little as possible to the States revived their fears that the Commonwealth was simply trespassing in their area of responsibility and seeking the credit which would flow from the improved efficiency of the national transport system while effectively forcing the States to shoulder the burden of the reform. The Commonwealth strategy of requiring all States to agree before proceeding with this much needed reform simply meant that the opportunity of improving cooperation between those States most affected, at least in the early stages of the new system, was lost. The most recalcitrant States effectively had a veto which limited cooperation with the States most prepared to proceed with the reform. The result was that microeconomic reform of those industries whose export and import performance is most affected by transport services and a significant Commonwealth employment creation program were delayed.

Within States, the fact that local government is the creature of each State government breeds resentment and limits cooperation. Local authorities attempt to assert their independence but, as we have seen in the debate over consolidation, State governments have typically over-ruled them. The propensity of State governments to remove local control over areas in which the State's government has an interest weakens local government and contributes to public scepticism of the effectiveness of local authorities. The independence of many of the urban service authorities, including those which receive Commonwealth funds, led to them pursuing their own agendas and a marked reluctance to cooperate with one another.

There was probably more cooperation between State roads authorities which had a high degree of independence because of their Common-wealth funds than there was between each road authority and its respective State planning agency. The creation of the Australian Road Research Board is an example of the cooperation between the States and Commonwealth in sharing information and experience as well as joint sponsorship of research into road transport issues. Soon after they were created in the early post-war period planning authorities sought co-operation with other State agencies out of a notion that there was a scientific or systematic relationship between where urban activities were pursued and the development of an equitable, efficient city. More recent notions of city development and the corporatising of service agencies have emphasised the 'accidental' or unpredictable nature of the outcome of urban development initiatives. Although it may be argued that this has the benefit of increasing the local focus or involvement of local communities in local economic development, it has actually reduced the opportunities for cooperation, especially as the agencies have dispensed with or reduced their capacity for forward planning. State governments have simultaneously reduced the significance of local involvement as they have removed powers of discretion from them; for example, the State governments have imposed development rules and consolidation policies on local authorities.

Environmental Issues

Concern over environmental issues has risen throughout Australia. Some of the issues involve localised pollution such as the environmental stress at sewer outfalls in the ocean. While these issues have no immediate interdependence because the cities which generate the pollution are separated by large distances, there is an increasing concern for the ecosystem which leads communities across the nation to agree that they must all act to ameliorate the condition. The general climate of opinion is that solving local pollution problems is the correct thing to do.

Other water pollution problems, such as algal blooms, may affect entire river systems and the industries and communities which depend on them. The initial response to the algal bloom problem in the Darling/Murrumbidgee river system was for agencies, industries and communities to each deny that their activities caused the problem and to search for some culprit to take the burden of responsibility and blame. Cooler consideration led to the realisation that the problem had multiple causes and was the result of practices they had all followed and that it could be successfully tackled only if there was cooperation between State and local governments and the industries in the river catchment. The danger of further algal blooms continues but the remedial programs now being developed reduce the risk and provide further evidence of the need for inter-governmental cooperation to solve system-wide environmental problems.

Air pollution problems have emerged in a number of the cities. Air pollution of Sydney is not exacerbated by that in Melbourne, nor will reducing the pollution of the one beneficially affect the other. There is, however, general agreement that it is inherently a 'bad thing' and that it should be reduced, not only to improve the lives of the residents of each city but to display some moral leadership by reducing Australia's contribution to the global greenhouse effect and to ozone depletion. The States have responded differently to air pollution problems in regulating emissions and there are limits to the extent to which they are prepared to go. The limits are set, in part, by States' responses to threats, implicit and explicit, from industry that if the regulations are too severe it will either shift to or only invest in States with the lower standards although, paradoxically, market-based solutions would probably benefit from the existence of national standards.

The States, all of which desperately pursue growth, are caught in a dilemma. The States with weaker economic bases do not wish to further

reduce their competitiveness by introducing standards which discourage
investment, so they will not take initiatives aimed at reducing pollution.
They also fear that if they adopt common standards the stronger States
will retain their relative advantage. The stronger States fear that if they
adopt higher standards they will lose out to the weaker States. Cooperation between them, probably brokered by the Commonwealth, is
the only feasible route to reducing air or water pollution in any given
city. The major problem with this approach is that there are no sanctions
available to encourage States to rigorously apply regulations, even their
own, or mechanisms to reward them for adopting regulations and
policies encouraging urban development which minimises environmental stress.

The dilemma created by fear that one State will succeed in attracting
investment at the expense of another affects the way States compete to
provide cheap power to industry – even though in doing so they create
significant pollution problems and pressure on the natural environment
and on their budgets. In their contemporary responses the States behave
in much the same way as their colonial predecessors.

A Cooperative Approach

It may be expecting too much of State politicians and administrators to
initiate policies aimed at developing a consensus on how urban policies
should be applied, especially if they feel their constituencies will not be
prepared to accept short-run disadvantages which could flow from their
adoption. They would be in a stronger position to espouse the same policies if they felt their constituents could be convinced that the policies
had emerged from an informed exploration of the issues and that they
were to be adopted across the nation. State politicians may be constrained because their understanding of national needs is in advance of
that of their constituents but they may be willing to 'deliver' their State's
support for a national approach if they can appeal to national interest.

Appeals to conceptions of the rights of citizenship are potent
arguments if they imply commitment to equality in the minimum
standards which citizens should be accorded in access to shelter,
schooling, health, cultural and social facilities and services. These are all
facilities and services for which the Commonwealth has either constitutional responsibility or an implicitly conferred responsibility born
out of pragmatic acknowledgment over the post-war period that the
Commonwealth is the only level of government with the resources to
accept such responsibility and that there is strong political support for
initiatives in those areas. This leaves open the risk that opportunistic
politicians, especially at the State level, will take populist stances to

oppose such national initiatives if they feel the need to attack the Commonwealth to bolster their local position – but this is a risk which has to be taken.

The evolving perception of the Constitution means that the Commonwealth is increasingly seen as having the power in its own right to take initiatives in the delivery of urban services. Occasionally the perception has been reinforced by legal interpretation but both levels of government are on firmer ground if they can cooperate in the development of programs in these areas. This will test the political discourse in Australia which has not been noted for exploration, in any systematic way, of the range of urban issues with which the cities are faced.

Urban growth and management issues confirm the truism that 'everything is connected to everything else'. Banal and all as the statement is, it nonetheless provides the opening for a greater degree of cooperation between governments for the resolution of urban and environmental problems (most of which are urban in origin) than we have hitherto seen. The institutions of the cities and their State governments have been unable to meet the challenges the national urban system faces, both in terms of the equity outcomes of its operations and its efficiency of operation. A significant part of this lies in what must now be seen as an archaic distribution of responsibility between Commonwealth, State and local governments – given the way the society has developed and the kinds of social and environmental externalities which have accompanied that development. It may also be seen as a result of the unequal access to revenue.

One approach would be to take advantage of the fact that we are now approaching the centenary of Federation. This provides an opportunity to mark the occasion by reviewing progress over the period, including a reconsideration of the way we order our affairs. If we assume that constitutional readjustment will not be accomplished in the short run but there is an urgent need for resolution of urban problems, cooperation between governments seems the only practicable option. This might be seen as a counsel of perfection with little chance of popular support. Nonetheless there seems to be growing recognition that, although we have been prepared recently to acquiesce with the departure from previously strongly held commitments to egalitarian notions, we must resolve urban environmental issues on some common basis.

Most interest in environment issues has been directed to the non-urban questions, such as the fight to save old growth forests, the 'Daintree', the 'Franklin' or the Gouldian Finch. All of these are important but the concentration on them has been at the cost of 'the urban'. That is, there has not been the development of an urban lobby. Although most Australians live in cities and, in a fundamental sense, form an urban constituency, they have not articulated a defence of or mounted campaigns for the improvement of the urban system and they have only rarely responded to political leadership which emphasised urban issues. It is easy to understand why proponents of particular development proposals who stand to gain from favourable decisions are energised. It is much harder to identify ways in which members of the public who defend a public interest can be encouraged to act or form an urban lobby other than by appealing to their sense of citizen obligation.

There is, however, some encouraging evidence of community acceptance that we need to establish standards for vehicle emissions and, despite current controversy, for lower lead levels in the atmosphere. These are two illustrations of willingness to cooperate. Another is the agreement between Commonwealth and States to reduce the use of CFCs as propellants and refrigerants. There is similar evidence in the cooperative setting of water quality standards and the acceptance of the need for national standards for waste water quality.

Although there are few firms which operate nationally, the States and Commonwealth have been able to cooperate and reach agreement on uniform building regulations. We have similarly seen cooperative development of traffic control and safety regulations.

While environmental issues highlight concern for intergenerational equity, the quest for equality of access to housing, education and health services arises from a consideration of the rights of citizens and the recognition of the need for policies to redistribute wealth between rich and poor to enable the latter to have access to those services. States are forced, to some degree, to cooperate with one another and with the Commonwealth over these issues because the presence of a national media and a highly mobile population means that understanding of the situation in the various States is soon communicated to the others. This in turn produces pressures for convergence which States cannot resist except at high political risk.

Finally, States and Commonwealth must cooperate because to do otherwise leads them into a phoney competitiveness in pursuit of growth which is inefficient and wasteful. It is a competition which creates a 'prisoner's dilemma' leaving the States vulnerable to the pressures and manipulations of private investors – particularly foreign investors. The States each refuse to act in concert out of a fear that another State will undercut them: it is harder for them to recognise the benefits of cooperation. This provides an opportunity for the Commonwealth to play a constructive role.

We might accept that cooperation between governments is the only rational approach to the resolution of urban growth problems but the question is: how can this be achieved? Although it might seem utopian, answers will not be forthcoming until political leaders and administrators from different levels of government recognise their differences but accept their essential equality in the contributions they can each make and the understandings they can bring to the resolution of urban problems. The Commonwealth will probably have to take the initiative as convenor of the debate but will need to display a greater degree of modesty and humility than it has hitherto revealed, and it will need to be prepared to respond openly to the States' perception of the issues. The present institutions of the city and the forums for developing and monitoring Commonwealth/State relations may themselves need to be reformed before much progress can be made on a cooperative resolution of urban growth issues.

Summary

This account suggests that cooperation between governments in tackling urban issues has been limited by:
- interstate rivalry;
- differences in power between the Commonwealth and the States;
- differences between the Commonwealth and States in their access to economic resources;
- differences in technical competence and understanding between the public servants of the States and Commonwealth;
- the adoption of managerialist philosophy and consequent loss of institutional memory and corporate knowledge at both Commonwealth and State levels;
- imperfect communication between States and between the Commonwealth and States;
- the lack of a shared understanding of the nature of urban problems.

It has been argued that cooperation is needed to ensure:
- that citizens' rights are respected and obligations enforced;
- that issues of equity both between generations and between social classes are taken into account;
- that States eliminate the power of corporations to create 'prisoners' dilemmas';
- that Australia meets its obligations to reduce the impact of urban growth on the ecosystem;
- more efficient urban growth and development;
- the development of a community better informed about the nature of urban problems and felicitous ways they can be solved.

This chapter proposes that cooperation can be achieved by a reconsideration of the distribution of powers between the States and

Commonwealth and by a redesign of the institutions of the city. It suggests that progress will not be made unless a more charitable view is developed between Commonwealth and State politicians and administrators in their approach to urban problems. It implies that this will not develop unless the public is educated to the nature of urban issues and the benefits cooperation can bring. The optimism of the chapter is sustained by the recognition that the States and Commonwealth have successfully cooperated in the creation and operation of the ARRB and the AWRC and in the adoption of several environmental initiatives. The Commonwealth must take the initiative in framing the institutional arrangements with the States if we are to resolve the problems our cities are faced with. In doing so it must accept that the States have a significant role to play.

References

AAO 1987. Administrative Arrangements Order.

Agenda 1991a. 74, Feb.

Agenda 1991b. 75, Mar.

Agenda 1991c. 76, Apr.

Alexander, I. 1986. Land use and transport planning in Australian cities: capital takes all?, in *Urban Planning in Australia: Critical Readings*, eds J.B. & M. Huxley, Melbourne, Longman Cheshire, 11–130.

Alexander, I. 1994. DURD revisited? Federal policy initiatives for urban and regional planning 1991–94, *Urban Policy and Research*, 12(1):6–26.

Allbrook, M. & Cattalini, H. 1988. Community relations in a multicultural society, in *The Challenge of Diversity: Policy Options for a Multicultural Australia*, ed. James Jupp, Office of Multicultural Affairs, Canberra, Australian Government Publishing Service.

Allport, C. 1980. The unrealised promise: plans for Sydney housing in the forties, in *Twentieth Century Sydney: Studies in Urban and Social History*, ed. Jill Roe, Sydney, Hale and Iremonger.

Allport, C. 1983. Women and suburban housing: post-war planning in Sydney, 1943–61, in *Social Process and the City*, ed. P. Williams, Sydney, Allen and Unwin, 64–87.

Arnold, L. 1993a. *Meeting the Challenge*, an economic statement to the parliament of South Australia, 22 Apr., Adelaide, Government Printer of South Australia.

Arnold, L. 1993b. *Meeting the Social Challenge*, a statement to the parliament of South Australia, 21 Oct., Adelaide, Government Printer of South Australia.

Ashton, P. 1993. *The Accidental City: Planning Sydney since 1788*, Sydney, Hale and Iremonger.

Auster, M. 1984. Spot zoning: an American perspective on a New South Wales phenomenon, 1 Environment and Planning, *Law Journal*, 1:347–53.

Australian Bureau of Statistics 1993. *1991 Census of Population and Dwellings*, CD-rom database.

Australian Government Publishing Service 1983. *Equality in Diversity: Fifty Years of the Commonwealth Grants Commission*, Canberra, Australian Government Publishing Service.

283

Australian Institute of Family Studies 1993. *The Australian Living Standards Study: Berwick Report. Part 1: The Household Survey*, Melbourne, Australian Institute of Family Studies.

Australian Local Government Association (ALGA) 1992. Making the Connections, Towards Integrated Local Area Planning, Sydney.

Australian Local Government Association (ALGA) 1993. *Local Government Urban Strategy*, Canberra, ALGA.

Australian Urban and Regional Development Review (AURD) 1994. *Information paper no.1*, Australian Government Publishing Service.

Badcock, B. 1984. *Unfairly Structured Cities*, London, Basil Blackwell.

Badcock, B. 1986. Land and housing provision, in *The State as Developer: Public Enterprise in South Australia*, ed. Kyoko Sheridan, Adelaide, Wakefield Press.

Badcock, B. 1989. *Metropolitan Planning in South Australia*, Urban Research Unit working paper no.10, Canberra, Urban Research Unit, Australian National University.

Badcock, B. 1991. With hindsight who needs 2020 vision? The planning review in context, *Australian Planner*, 29:48–53.

Badcock, B. 1992. Adelaide's heart transplant, 1970–88: 1. creation, transfer, and capture of 'value' within the built environment, *Environment and Planning*, A 24:215–41.

Badcock, B. 1993. The urban programme as an instrument of crisis management in Australia, *Urban Policy and Research*, 11:72–80.

Badcock, B. 1994. Snakes or ladders?: the housing market and wealth distribution in Australia, *International Journal of Urban and Regional Research*, 18:3.

Badcock, B. forthcoming, The 'family home' and transfers of wealth in Australia in *Housing and Family Wealth in Comparative Perspective*, eds R. Forrest & R. Murie, London, Routledge.

Badcock, B. & Browett, M. 1992. Adelaide's heart transplant, 1970–88: 3. The deployment of capital in the renovation and redevelopment submarkets, *Environment and Planning*, A 24:1167–90.

Bagguley, P., Mark-Lawson, J., Shapiro, D., Urry, J., Warlby, S. & Warde, A. 1990. *Restructuring: Place, Class and Gender*, London, Sage.

Bailey, E.E. & Friedlander, A.F. 1982. Market Structures and Multiproduct Industries, *Journal of Economic Literature*, 20:1024–48.

Balmain Association 1991. *New Sheet*, 26(1). Feb.

Balmain Association v *Planning Administrator for Leichhardt Council* 1991a. 25 New South Wales Law Reports.

Balmain Association v *Planning Administrator for Leichhardt Council* 1991b. unreported, Land and Environment Court, 40292/90, 24 Jan.

Balmain Residents Case 1975. *Impact of Cargo Trucking on Balmain*, Sydney.

Batten, D., Fincher, R. & Gleeson, B. 1993. Review of a place to live, urban development 1992–2031: shaping Victoria's future, *Urban Policy and Research*, 11:57–9.

Bauman, Z. 1988. Sociology and postmodernism, *Sociological Review*, 36:790–813.

Beauregard, R.A. 1993. Descendants of ascendant cities and other urban dualities, *Journal of Urban Affairs*, 15(3):217–29.

Beilharz, P., Considine, M. & Watts, R. 1992. *Arguing about the Welfare State: The Australian Experience*, Sydney, Allen and Unwin.

Bell, C. & Newby, H. 1972. *Community Studies*, London, George Allen and Unwin.

Bell, P. 1992. *Multicultural Australia in the Media*, Office of Multicultural Affairs, Canberra, Australian Government Publishing Service.

Berry, M. 1988. To buy or rent? the demise of a dual tenure policy in Australia 1945–60, in *New Houses for Old. Fifty Years of Public Housing in Victoria 1938–1988*, ed. R. Howe, Melbourne, Ministry of Housing and Construction.

Berry, M. 1992. Rediscovering the cities: prospects for a national urban policy in the 1990s, *Urban Policy and Research*, 10:37–44.

Bethune, G. 1978. Urban Home Ownership in Australia: some aspects of housing demand and policy, Ph.D. thesis, Australian National University.

Bianchini, F. & Parkinson, M. eds 1993. *Cultural Policy and Urban Regeneration*, Manchester, Manchester University Press.

Blecher, E.M. 1971. *Advocacy Planning for Urban Development*, New York, Praeger.

Bocock, R. 1993. *Consumption*, London, Routledge.

Boddy, M. & Fudge, C. 1984. *Local Socialism? Labour Councils and New Left Alternatives*, London, Macmillan.

Boehm, E.A. 1979. *Twentieth Century Economic Development in Australia*, 2nd edn, Melbourne, Longman Cheshire.

Bonyhady, T. 1993. *Places Worth Keeping: Conservationists, Politics and Law*, Sydney, Allen and Unwin.

Bottles, S.L. 1987. *Los Angeles and the Automobile: The Making of the Modern City*, Berkeley and Los Angeles, University of California Press.

Bounds, M. 1993a. Planning for post modernity, unpublished paper delivered to the Postmodern Cities Conference, University of Sydney, Apr.

Bounds, M. 1993b. Property values and popular politics: resistance to urban consolidation in inner Sydney, *Australian Planner*, Mar.:14–18.

Bourdieu, P. 1984. *Distinction*, Cambridge, MA, Harvard University Press.

Boyd, R. 1968. *The Australian Ugliness*, Sydney, Penguin.

Brannen, J. & Moss, P. eds 1987. *Give and Take in Families*, London, Allen and Unwin.

Brigden, J.B. *et al.* 1929. *The Australian Tariff. An Economic Enquiry*, Parkville, Melbourne University Press.

Brisbane City Council 1992. Urban renewal – inner North Eastern suburbs, Brisbane, *Urban Futures*, 2(1):9–17.

Brotchie, G. 1992. The changing structure of cities, *Urban Futures*, special issue 5:13–26.

Brown, A.J. & Sherrard, H.M. 1951. *Town and Country Planning*, Parkville, Melbourne University Press.

Brown, A.J. & Sherrard, H.M. 1969. *Town and Country Planning*, 2nd edn, Parkville, Melbourne University Press.

Bryson, L. & Thompson, F. 1972. *An Australian Newtown*, Ringwood, Penguin.

Bunker, R. 1978. Cooperative planning, in *Federal Power in Australia's Cities*, ed. P. Troy, Sydney, Hale & Iremonger, 39–51.

Bunker, R. 1989a. A decade of urban consolidation, in *Metropolitan Planning Australia: Urban Consolidation*, working paper no.11, Canberra, Urban Research Unit, Australian National University.

Bunker, R. 1989b. Property, propriety and purpose: planning in Adelaide since the Second World War, *Environmental and Planning Law Journal*, 6:169–87.

Bunker, R. & Minnery, J. 1992. *Recent Commonwealth Initiatives in Urban Affairs*, Urban Studies National Monograph Series no.1, Adelaide, Australian Institute of Urban Studies.

Burbidge, A. & Gondor, G. 1992. Housing costs and unemployed families, *Family Matters*, 31:35.

Burgess, R. & Skeltys, N. 1992. *The Findings of the Housing and Locational Choice Survey: an Overview*, National Housing Strategy, background paper no.11, Canberra, Commonwealth of Australia.

Burke, T. & Hayward, D. 1990. Housing Melburnians for the next twenty years, *Urban Policy and Research*, 8(3):122–51.

Burrell, S. 1989. Keating to 'rescue' cities from developers, *Australian Financial Review*, 28 Aug.:1.

Burrell, S. 1993. Why jobs will stay scarce, *Australian Financial Review*, 17 Feb.:17.

Butlin, N.G. 1962. *Australian Domestic Product, Investment and Borrowing, 1861–1938/39*, Cambridge, Cambridge University Press.

Butlin, N.G. 1964. *Investment in Australian Economic Development 1861–1900*, Cambridge, Cambridge University Press.

Calhoun, C. 1991. Indirect relationships and imagined communities, in *Social Theory for a Changing Society*, eds P. Bourdieu & J. Coleman, Boulder, Westview.

Campbell, I. 1991. Private sector investment in housing and urban development, *Urban Futures*, special issue 2:1–6.

Cardew, R.V. & Rich, D. 1982. Manufacturing and industrial property development in Sydney, in *Why Cities Change: Urban Development and Economic Change in Sydney*, eds Richard V. Cardew, John V. Landale & David C. Rich, Geographical Society of New South Wales/Sydney, George Allen and Unwin, 124.

Cass, B. 1989. Defending and reforming the Australian welfare state: some ideas for the next decade, in *Markets, Morals and Public Policy*, eds Lionel Orchard & Robert Dare, Sydney, Federation Press.

Cass, B. 1991. *The Housing Needs of Women and Children*, National Housing Strategy discussion paper, Canberra, Australian Government Publishing Service.

Castells, M. 1983. *The City and the Grassroots*, London, Edward Arnold.

Castells, M. 1989. *The Informational City. Information Technology, Economic Restructuring, and the Urban-Regional Process*, Oxford, Basil Blackwell.

Castles, F. 1988. *Australian Public Policy and Economic Vulnerability*, Sydney, Allen and Unwin.

Castles, I. 1992. Living standards in Sydney and Japanese cities: a comparison, in *The Australian Economy in the Japanese Mirror*, ed. K. Sheridan, Brisbane, University of Queensland Press.

Castles, I. 1994. *How Australians Use their Time*, (revised publication), Canberra, Australian Bureau of Statistics (cat. no.4153.0).

Caulfield, J. 1992. Planning policy options for Brisbane's growth, *Power and Policy in Brisbane*, Centre for Australian Public Sector Management, Griffith University.

Caulfield, J. & Davies, R. 1992. Growth politics and group activities in Brisbane, paper delivered at conference *Policy and Power in Brisbane*, 30–31 Oct., Centre for Australian Public Sector Management, Griffith University.

Charles, C. 1990. Urban consolidation, an answer?, *Shelter – National Housing Journal*, 6:17–24.

Cheal, D. 1990. Social construction of consumption, *International Sociology*, 5(3):299–317.

Cohen, A. & Fukui, K. eds 1993. *Humanising the City?*, Edinburgh, Edinburgh University Press.

Coker, A. 1991. What happened in Balmain, *New Planner*, 5:8–9.

Colman, J. 1991. Fouling the nest, *Urban Futures*, 1(2):30–2.

Commissioner of Inquiry for Environment and Planning 1989. *Operation and Practices Associated with Contributions under Section 94 of the Environmental Planning and Assessment Act 1979*, Sydney.

Commissioners of Inquiry for Environment and Planning 1991. Draft local environmental plans nos. 76, 77, 78 and 81, Balmain Peninsula, Sydney.

Commonwealth Census 1911–1947.

Commonwealth Housing Commission 1944. *Final Report*.

Cook, M. 1993. Go-ahead for $20m Richmond Mill, *Age*, 9 Sept.

Cooke, P. 1989. Locality, economic restructuring and world development, in *Localities: The Changing Face of Urban Britain*, ed. Philip Cooke, London, Unwin Hyman.

Cooke, P. 1990. *Back to the Future*, London, Unwin Hyman.

Coupe, B. & Jakubowicz, A. 1992. *Nextdoor Neighbours: Ethnic Group Discussion of the Australian Media*, Office of Multicultural Affairs, Canberra, Australian Government Publishing Service.

Crofts, D. 1992. *Integrated Planning for Housing, Employment and Services: The Role of Local Government in Building Better Cities*, Canberra, Office of Local Government.

Cutts, L. 1992. *Immigration and Local Government Budgets*, Bureau of Immigration Research, Canberra, Australian Government Publishing Service.

Davidoff, P. 1965. Advocacy and pluralism in planning, *Journal of the American Institute of Planners*, 31:331–8.

Davies, W. & Herbert, D. 1993. *Communities within Cities*, London, Belhaven.

Davis, M. 1990. *City of Quartz: Excavating the Future in Los Angeles*, London, Verso.

Davison, G. 1978. *The Rise and Fall of Marvellous Melbourne*, Parkville, Melbourne University Press.

Davison, G. 1993. *The Past and Future of the Australian Suburb*, Urban Research Program working paper no.33, Canberra, Urban Research Program, Australian National University.

Day, G. & Murdoch, J. 1993. Locality and community: coming to terms with place, *Sociological Review*, 41(1):82–111.

Day, L.H. 1992. *The Future of Low-Birthrate Populations*, London and New York, Routledge.

Deakin, A. 1963. *The Federal Story: the Inner History of the Federal Cause 1880–1900*, edited and with an introduction by J.A. La Nauze, Parkville, Melbourne University Press.

Dear, M. 1989. Privatization and the rhetoric of planning practice, *Environment and Planning*, D7:449–62.

Dear, M. 1990. Understanding and overcoming the NIMBY syndrome, *Journal of the American Planning Association*, 58(3).

Department of Environment and Planning, New South Wales 1988. *Sydney Into Its Third Century*.

Department of Environment and Planning, South Australia. 1991. *Ideas for Metropolitan Adelaide: Planning Review*.

Department of Health, Housing and Community Services (DHHCS) 1991. Local Area Research Studies: Elizabeth/Munno Para, South Australia, Canberra, Australian Government Publishing Service.

Department of Health, Housing and Community Services (DHHCS) 1992a. *Better Cities: National Developments 1991–92*, Canberra, Australian Government Publishing Service.

Department of Health, Housing and Community Services (DHHCS) 1992b. Building better cities: South Australia pamphlet, in *Better Cities Information*, Canberra, Australian Government Publishing Service.

Department of Health, Housing and Community Services (DHHCS) 1992c. Social Justice for the Community. Portfolio of Health, Housing and Community Services. Social Justice Plan (incorporating the Second Access and Equity Plan), Canberra, Australian Government Publishing Service.

Department of Health, Housing and Community Services (DHHCS) 1992d. Towards a Fairer Australia. Social Justice Strategy 1990–1991. Local Area Research Studies: project report, Canberra, Australian Government Publishing Service.

Department of Health, Housing, Local Government and Community Services (DHHLGCS) 1993. Budget 1993–1994, Canberra.

Department of Planning and Urban Development, Western Australia, 1990. *Metroplan: A Planning Strategy for the Perth Metropolitan Region*, Perth, Department of Planning and Urban Development.

Department of Planning, New South Wales 1991. *Modernising the Planning System in New South Wales*, a discussion paper, Sydney, Department of Planning.

Department of the Premier and Cabinet, South Australia 1993. Draft Public Consultation Report on the Planning Review.

Department of the Prime Minister and Cabinet 1991. *Building a Competitive Australia*, statements by Prime Minister, Treasurer, and Industry Minister, 12 Mar. Canberra, Australian Government Publishing Service.

Department of Urban and Regional Development 1975. *Third Annual Report 1974–75*, Canberra, Australian Government Publishing Service.

Dilnot, A. 1990. The distribution and composition of personal sector wealth in Australia, *Australian Economic Review*, 1st quarter:33–40.

Dingle, A.E. 1984. *The Victorians*, vol. 2 *Settlings*, Sydney, Syme, Fairfax, Weldon.

Dingle, A.E. & Merrett, D.T. 1972. Home owners and tenants in Melbourne 1891–1911, *Australian Economic History Review*, 12:21–35.

Dingle, A. & Rasmussen, C. 1991. *Vital Connections: Melbourne and its Board of Works 1891–1991*, Melbourne, McPhee Gribble.

Donnison, D. with Soto, P. 1980. *The Good City: A Study of Urban Development and Policy in Britain*, London, Heinemann.

Donnison, D. 1973. What is the 'good city'? *New Society*, 13 Dec.:647–9.

Downing, P.B. ed. 1974. *Local Service Pricing Policies and their Effect on Urban Spatial Structure*, Vancouver, University of British Columbia Press.

Doyle, J. 1993. From joint venture to privatised planning: two inner urban housing developments in Melbourne, *Urban Policy and Research*, 11:50–3.

Duncan, S. & Goodwin, M. 1987. *The Local State and Uneven Development: Behind the Local Government Crisis*, New York, St Martin's Press.

Eccles, D. 1991. Dual occupancy households and their neighbours in Melbourne, *Urban Policy and Research*, 9:34–46.

Economic Development Board, South Australia 1993. *Building Prosperity*, discussion paper, Adelaide, Economic Development Board.

Economic Planning Advisory Council (EPAC) 1990. *Regional Policies, Future Directions*, Canberra, Australian Government Publishing Service.

Economic Planning Advisory Council (EPAC) 1991. *Background Papers on Urban and Regional Issues*, Canberra, Australian Government Publishing Service.

Economic Planning Advisory Council (EPAC) 1993. *Medium-Term Review: Opportunities for Growth*, Canberra, Australian Government Publishing Service.

Edgar, D. 1992. Families in unemployment, *Family Matters*, 32:3.

Elizabeth–Munno Para Project 1992. *Community Consultation Report*, Adelaide, Elizabeth–Munno Para Project.

Ellis, D. 1993. Metropolitan Strategic Planning, paper presented to the Winter Planning Seminar, Adelaide, 28 Jul.

England, K. 1991. Gender relations and the spatial structure of the city, *Geoforum*, 22:135–47.

Environmental Planning and Assessment Act (EPAA) 1979a. New South Wales.

Environmental Planning and Assessment Act (EPAA) 1979b. New South Wales, s.70(1)(a)(ii), discussed in *Shellharbour Municipal Council v Minister for Environment* 1985, 58 Local Government Reports of Australia, 18.

Environmental Services 1993. Memorandum from Head to Town Clerk, 12 Feb.

Esping-Anderson, G. 1990. *The Three Worlds of Welfare Capitalism*, Cambridge, Polity Press.

Esping-Andersen, G. ed. 1993. *Changing Classes*, London, Sage.

Ethnic Affairs Commission of NSW 1990. *Planning for Religious Development in NSW*.

Fainstein, S.S., Gordon, I. & Harloe, M. eds 1992. *Divided Cities. New York and London in the Contemporary World*, Oxford, Basil Blackwell.

Featherstone, M. 1991. *Consumer Culture and Postmodernism*, London, Sage.

Fincher, R. 1990. Women in the city: feminist analyses of urban geography, *Australian Geographical Studies*, 28:29–37.

Fincher, R. 1991a. *Immigration, Urban Infrastructure and the Environment*. Bureau of Immigration Research, Canberra, Australian Government Publishing Service.

Fincher, R. 1991b. Locational disadvantage: an appropriate policy response to urban inequity?, *Australian Geographer*, 22:132–5.

Finn, P. 1986. *Law and Government in Colonial Australia*, Melbourne, Oxford University Press.

Fishman, R. 1987. *Bourgeois Utopias: the Rise and Fall of Suburbia*, New York, Basic Books.

Fitzgerald, Shirley 1987. *Rising Damp: Sydney 1870–90*, Melbourne, Oxford University Press.

Fitzgerald, Shirley 1992. *Sydney 1842–1992;* Sydney, Hale and Iremonger.

Fitzgerald, Stephen 1988. Immigration: A Commitment to Australia, Report of the Committee to Advise on Australia's Immigration Policy, Canberra, Australian Government Publishing Service.

Fletcher, B. 1989. Sydney: a southern emporium, in *The Origins of Australia's Capital Cities*, ed. Pamela Statham, Melbourne, Cambridge University Press.

Flood, J. 1993. Housing subsidies 1990–1991, paper presented to the Institute of Australian Geographers Annual Conference, Monash University, Sept. 1993.

Forester, J. 1989. *Planning in the Face of Power*, Berkeley and Los Angeles, University of California Press.

Forrest, J. 1985. Urban conflict patterns, in *Living in Cities: Urbanism and Society in Metropolitan Australia*, eds Ian Burnley & James Forrest, Sydney, Allen and Unwin/Geographical Society of New South Wales, 183.

Forrest, J. & Burnley, I. 1985. Themes and issues, in *Living in Cities: Urbanism and Society in Metropolitan Australia*, eds Ian Burnley & James Forrest, Sydney, Allen and Unwin/Geographical Society of New South Wales, 5–6.

Forrest, R. & Murie, A. 1988. *Selling the Welfare State: The Privatization of Public Housing*, London, Routledge.

Forster, C. 1964. *Industrial Development in Australia 1920–1930*, Canberra, Australian National University Press.

Forster, C. 1984. Metropolitan Adelaide: who are the planners and what should we expect of them? *Urban Policy and Research*, 2:40–4.

Forster, C. 1986. Economic restructuring, urban policy and patterns of urban deprivation in Adelaide, *Australian Planner*, 24:6–10.

Franklin, N. 1992. Initiative and referendum: participatory democracy or rolling back the State? in *Citizen Participation in Government*, ed. Margaret Munro-Clark, Sydney, Hale and Iremonger.

Fraser, N. 1989. *Unruly Practices: Power, Discourse and Gender in Contemporary Social Theory*, Cambridge, Polity Press.

Freeland, J.M. 1972. *Architecture in Australia: a History*, Melbourne, Penguin.

Friend, J. & Hickling, A. 1987. *Planning Under Pressure: the Strategic Choice Approach*, Oxford, Pergamon Press, Urban and Regional Planning Series, vol. 37.

Friend, J. & Jessop, N. 1969. *Local Government and Strategic Choice*, London, Tavistock Publications.

Frost, L. 1990. *Australian Cities in Comparative View*, Melbourne, McPhee Gribble.

Frost, L. 1991a. Nineteenth-century Adelaide in a global context, *Australian Economic History Review*, 31:28–44.

Frost, L. 1991b. *The New Urban Frontier: Urbanisation and City-Building in Australasia and the American West*, Kensington, New South Wales University Press.

Frost, L. 1992. Government and economic development: the case of irrigation in Victoria, *Australian Economic History Review*, 32:47–65.

Fry, E.C. 1972. Growth of an Australian metropolis, in *The Politics of Urban Growth*, eds R.S. Parker & P.N. Troy, Canberra, Australian National University Press.

Gapps, B. 1990. Consolidation for people: the impact of urban consolidation on the planning and provision of human services, *Proceedings: Western Sydney Regional Organisation of Councils*.

Garlick, F.J. 1983. Melbourne Suburban Expansion in the 1920s, MA thesis, University of Melbourne.

Garreau, J. 1991. *Edge City: Life on the New Frontier*, New York, Doubleday.

Gettler, L. 1993. Reform expected for two years in 'over-governed' city, *Age*, 29 Sept.

Gibbons, R. 1983. The 'fall of the giant': trams versus trains and buses in Sydney, 1900–61, in *Sydney's Transport: Studies in Urban History*, ed. Garry Wotherspoon, Sydney, Hale and Iremonger.

Glass, R. 1964. *London: Aspects of Change*, London, Centre for Urban Studies.

Glover, J. & Woollacott, T. 1992. *A Social Health Atlas of Australia*, Adelaide, South Australian Health Commission.

Goldsmith, M. 1993. The Europeanisation of Local Government, *Urban Studies*, 30 (4/5).

Gondor, G. & Burbidge, A. 1992. Capital gains and locational disadvantage, *Family Matters*, 32:20–1.

Gooding, A. 1990. *Consolidating for People: The Impact of Urban Consolidation on the Planning and Provision of Human Services*, Sydney, Western Regional Organisation of Councils.

Government Gazette of the State of New South Wales 1990. 30 Aug., 108:7841.

Government of South Australia 1993. *Development Act 1993*, Adelaide, South Australian Government Printer.

Government of Victoria 1987. *Shaping Melbourne's Future*.

Government of Victoria Department of Planning and Housing 1992. *A Place to Live, Urban Development 1992–2031: Shaping Victoria's Future*, Victorian Government Printer.

Grattan, M. 1989. Howe wants urban revival back on Labor agenda, *Age*, 11 Sept.:13.

Gregory, R. 1992. Aspects of Australian labour force living standards: the disappointing decades 1970–1990, Copland Oration, 21st Conference of Economists, University of Melbourne, Jul.

Hall, P. 1992. Cities in the informational economy, *Urban Futures*, special issue 5:1–12.

Hamley, B. 1992. The housing costs study – an overview, *Urban Futures*, 2(2):15–24.

Hamnett, C. 1991. The blind men and the elephant: the explanation of gentrification, *Transactions of the Institute of British Geographers*, 16:173–89.

Hamnett, S. & Parham, S. 1992. 2020 vision: a planning strategy for metropolitan Adelaide, *Urban Futures*, 2(2):78–85.

Harman, E. 1988. Capitalism, patriarchy and the city, in *Women, Social Welfare and the State*, 2nd edn, eds C. Baldock & B. Cass, Sydney, Allen and Unwin, 108–33.

Harris, C.P. & Dixon, K.E. 1978. *Regional Planning in New South Wales and Victoria since 1944*, Centre for Research on Federal Financial Relations, Canberra, Australian National University.

Harris, J. 1991. Hands off Hunter's Hill: a Case Study of the Rezoning of the Mobil Oil Terminal Site at Pulpit Point in Hunter's Hill, Diploma in Urban and Regional Planning, University of New England.

Harrison, P. 1970. Measuring urban sprawl, in *Analysis of Urban Development: Proceedings of the Tewksbury Symposium*, ed. N. Clark, Department of Civil Engineering, University of Melbourne, 3.3–3.6.

Harvey, D. 1989. *The Condition of Postmodernity: An Enquiry into the Origins of Cultural Change*, Oxford, Basil Blackwell.

Harvey, D. 1992. Social justice, postmodernism and the city, *International Journal of Urban and Regional Research*, 16:588–601.

Hay, D. 1990. Letter to Issy Wyner, 15 Jun.

Hayes, B. 1993. Strategic planning and development controls, *Australian Environmental Law News*, Mar./Apr.:42–50.

Hayward, D. 1993. Dual politics in a three-tiered state, *Urban Policy and Research*, 11(3):166–81.

Head, B. 1986. *The Politics of Development in Australia*, Sydney, Allen and Unwin.

Hedgecock, D., Hillier, J. & Wood, D. 1991. Planning, postmodernism and community power, *Urban Policy and Research*, 9:220–6.

Hill, M.R. 1959. *Housing Finance in Australia 1945–1956*, Parkville, Melbourne University Press.

Hirst, J.B. 1973. *Adelaide and the Country: Their Social and Political Relationship*, Parkville, Melbourne University Press.

House of Representatives Standing Committee for Long Term Strategies (HRSC–LTS) 1992. *Patterns of Urban Settlement: Consolidating the Future?*, Canberra, Australian Government Publishing Service.

Howard, A. ed. 1979. *The Crossman Diaries*, condensed version, London, Magnum Books.

Howe, B. 1990. Building a secure and sustainable base for the future, *Australian Journal of Public Administration*, 49:211–15.

Howe, R. & Norman, B. 1992. Vision and Reality; Metropolitan Strategic Planning in Australia, Urban Research Program seminar, Research School of Social Sciences, Australian National University.

Industry Commission 1991. *Industry assistance trends and regional implications*, in EPAC 1991, background papers on Urban and Regional Trends and Issues, Canberra, Australian Government Publishing Service, 105–48.

Industry Commission 1993a. *Impediments to Regional Industry Adjustment*, Canberra, Industry Commission, Australian Government Publishing Service.

Industry Commission 1993b. *Taxation and Financial Policy Impacts on Urban Settlement*, vol.1, Canberra, Industry Commission, Australian Government Publishing Service.

Institute of Public Affairs 1993. *Reforming Local Government in Victoria*, Melbourne.

Ironmonger, D. ed. 1990. *Households Work*, Sydney, Allen and Unwin.

Jackson, J. & O'Connor, K. 1993. Beyond the fringe: social and physical planning problems in shires adjacent to Melbourne's metropolitan statistical division, *Urban Policy and Research*, 11:81–95.

Jackson, K.T. 1985. *Crabgrass Frontier. The Suburbanization of the United States*, New York, Oxford University Press.

Jakubowicz, A. 1972. A new politics of suburbia, *Current Affairs Bulletin*, 48:338–51.

Jamrozik, A. 1983. Universality and selectivity: social welfare in a market economy, in *Retreat from the Welfare State: Australian Social Policy in the 1980s*, ed. Adam Graycar, Sydney, Allen and Unwin.

Jay, C. 1993. Urban consolidation: push for new policies, *Australian Financial Review*, 2 Apr.:41–2.

Johnston, R. 1979. Participation in local government: Leichhardt 1971–74, in *The Pieces of Politics*, 2nd edn, ed. Richard Lucy, Melbourne, Macmillan, 230–57.

Jonathon Falk Planning Consultants 1987. Study into the processing of development applications, rezoning requests and other matters: summary of report, Sydney.

Jones, F.L. 1975. The changing shape of Australian income distribution, 1914–15 and 1968–69, *Australian Economic History Review*, 15:21–34.

Judd, B. 1993. *Designed for Urban Living: Recent Medium-Density Group Housing in Australia*, Canberra, Royal Australian Institute of Architects and Department of Health Housing and Community Services.

Kass, T. 1987. Cheaper than rent: aspects of the growth of owner-occupation in Sydney 1911–1966, in *Sydney: City of Suburbs*, ed. Max Kelly, Sydney, New South Wales University Press.

Keating, P. 1993. Only option is to become master of our own destiny, *Weekend Australian*, 13–14 Mar.:34.

Kee, P. 1992. *Home Ownership and Housing Conditions of Immigrants and Australian Born*, Office of Multicultural Affairs, Canberra, Australian Government Publishing Service.

Keller, S. 1988. The American dream of community: an unfinished agenda, *Sociological Forum*, 3(2):167–83.

Kelly, M. 1980. Pleasure and profit: the eastern suburbs come of age 1919–1929, in *Twentieth Century Sydney. Studies in Urban and Social History*, ed. Jill Roe, Sydney, Hale and Iremonger.

Kemeny, J. 1986. The ideology of home ownership, in *Urban Planning in Australia: Critical Readings*, eds J. Brian McLoughlin & Margo Huxley, Melbourne, Longman Cheshire.

Kilgour, A. 1994. Planning by Numbers, *Planning News*, Melbourne, RAPI, Victorian Division.

Kirwan, R. 1991a. *Financing Urban Infrastructure: Equity and Efficiency Considerations*, NHS background paper no.4, Canberra, Australian Government Publishing Service.

Kirwan, R. 1991b. Financing urban infrastructure: equity and efficiency considerations, *Urban Futures*, 1(2):1–5.

Kirwan, R. 1991c. Planning for affordable housing: a challenge for the 1990s, *Urban Futures*, special issue 2:17–22.

Kirwan, R. 1992a. Urban development, in *The Impact of Federalism on Metropolitan Strategies in Australia*, eds C. Fletcher & C. Walsh, Canberra, Federalism Research Centre, Australian National University.

Kirwan, R. 1992b. Urban form, energy and transport: a note on the Newman–Kenworthy thesis, *Urban Policy and Research*, 10(1):6–23.

Kirwan, R., Neutze, M., Stretton, H. & Walsh, C. 1992. *The Role of State Government in the Provision of Urban Infrastructure*, South Australian Planning Papers, working paper no.2, Adelaide, Planning Education Foundation of South Australia and University of South Australia.

Kymlicka, W. 1989. *Liberalism, Community and Culture*, Oxford, Clarendon.

Lack, J. 1991. *A History of Footscray*, Melbourne, Hargreen.

Lang, J. 1990. The provision of social infrastructure in new urban development in three Australian states, *Urban Policy and Research*, 8(3).

Lang, J. 1991. *Local Government's Role in Urban Infrastructure*, Canberra, Office of Local Government.

Laws, G. 1989. Privatization and dependency on the local welfare state, in *The Power of Geography: How Territory Shapes Social Life*, eds Jennifer Wolch & Michael Dear, Boston, Unwin Hyman.

Lee, M. 1993. *Consumer Culture Reborn*, London, Routledge.

Leichhardt Assistant Treasurer 1991. Memorandum to Town Clerk, 12 Nov.

Leichhardt Metropolitan Town Planner 1990. Memorandum to Town Clerk, 21 Jun.

Leichhardt Council 1990a. Report on the proposed rezoning of the Ampol, Unilever, Balmain Power Station, Monsanto and Caltex Sites, Aug.:66, 107, 120, 145, 149, 150, 157, 163.

Leichhardt Council 1990b. Report, Dec.

Leichhardt Council 1992a. *Balmain Peninsula: Five Major Sites*, Mayoral minute, 28 Sept.

Leichhardt Council 1992b. Letter from Local Government Association to Chief Clerk, 28 Apr.

Leichhardt Council v *Minister for Planning* 1992. 77 Local Government Reports of Australia.

Leichhardt Council 1993. *Issue Paper: Open Space Strategy.*

Leichhardt Council v *Minister for Planning* 1993. 78 Local Government and Environmental Reports of Australia.

Leichhardt Town Planner 1990. Memorandum to Town Clerk, 1 May.

Leichhardt Public Inquiry 1990/91. Report to the Hon. G.B. Peacocke (MP), Minister for Local Government.

Lennon, M. 1993. Report to Conference of Central City Mayors.

Little, A.D. 1992. *New Directions for South Australia's Economy,* final report of the Economic Development Strategy Study prepared for the Government of South Australia, Adelaide.

Llewellyn-Smith, J. & Watson, S. 1992. Issues in cross-cultural planning, *Australian Planner,* 30(2).

Lloyd, C.J. & Troy, P.N. 1978. A history of federal intervention in federal power, in *Australia's Cities, Essays in Honour of Peter Till,* ed. P.N. Troy, Sydney, Hale and Iremonger.

Lloyd, C.J. & Troy, P.N. 1981a. *Innovation and Reaction: The Life and Death of the Federal Department of Urban and Regional Development,* Sydney, Allen and Unwin.

Lloyd, C.J. & Troy, P.N. 1981b. *The Commonwealth Housing Commission and a National Housing Policy,* paper delivered at an Urban Research Unit seminar, Research School of Social Sciences, ANU, 21 Sept.

Local Government Bulletin 1987. May.

Logan, T. 1984. Local planning, in *Conflict and Development,* ed. Peter Williams, Sydney, Allen and Unwin.

Low, N. & Moser, S.T. 1991. The cause and consequences of Melbourne's central city property boom, *Urban Policy and Research,* 9:5–27.

Luck, D.P. & Martin, I.J. 1988. *Review of Road Cost Recovery,* Bureau of Transport and Communication Economics, occasional paper no.90, Canberra, Australian Government Publishing Service.

Lunt, P.K. & Livingstone, S.M. 1992. *Mass Consumption and Personal Identity,* Buckingham, Open University.

MacDermott, K. 1993. Rapid change the planners' challenge, *Australian Financial Review,* 26 Mar.:42.

Mackay, H. 1993. The house must fit its family, *Australian Financial Review,* 20 Apr.:15.

Maher, C. 1982. *Australian Cities in Transition,* South Yarra, Shillington House.

Maher, C. 1993. Recent trends in Australian urban development: locational change and policy quandary, *Urban Studies,* 30(4/5):797–826.

Maher, C. *et al.* 1992. *Mobility and Locational Disadvantage within Australian Cities: Social Justice Implications of Household Relocation,* Canberra, Australian Government Publishing Service.

Manning, I. 1993. Cities and economic growth (unpublished).

Marsh C. & Arber, S. eds 1992. *Families and Households,* London, Macmillan.

Mathews, R. 1992. *Immigration and Local State Budgets,* Bureau of Immigration Research, Canberra, Australian Government Publishing Service.

McAllister, I. 1993. Immigration, bipartisanship and public opinion, in *The Politics of Australian Immigration,* eds James Jupp & Maril Kabala, Bureau of Immigration Research, Canberra, Australian Government Publishing Service.

McClelland, J.R. 1992. Participation and the law, in *Citizen Participation in Government*, ed. Margaret Munro-Clark, Sydney, Hale and Iremonger.

McLoughlin, B. 1991. Urban consolidation and urban sprawl: A question of density, *Urban Policy and Research*, 9(3):148–56.

McLoughlin, B. 1992. *Shaping Melbourne's Future? Town Planning, the State and Civil Society*, Melbourne, Cambridge University Press.

Meade, K. 1994. Mayoral race unleashes naked ambition, *Weekend Australian*, 15–16 Jan.

Merrett, D.T. 1978. Australian capital cities in the twentieth century, in *Australian Capital Cities. Historical Essays*, eds J.W. McCarty & C.B. Schedvin, Sydney, Sydney University Press.

Milburn, C. 1993. Grim future for casual workers, says report, *Age*, 15 Jul.:1.

Minister for Planning NSW 1990. Press release, 30 Aug., Sydney.

Minister for Planning, Victoria 1993. *Planning a Better Future for Victorians*, Melbourne, Department of Planning and Development.

Minnery, J.R. 1992. *Urban Form and Development Strategies: Equity, Environment and Economic Implications*, NHS background paper no.7, Canberra, Australian Government Publishing Service.

Morrissey, M., Mitchell, C. & Rutherford, A. 1991. *The Family in the Settlement Process*, Bureau of Immigration Research, Canberra, Australian Government Publishing Service.

Mullins, P. 1981a. Theoretical perspectives on Australian urbanisation. I: material components in the reproduction of Australian labour power, *Australian and New Zealand Journal of Sociology*, 17(1):65–76.

Mullins, P. 1981b. Theoretical perspectives on Australian urbanisation. II: social components in the reproduction of Australian labour power, *Australian and New Zealand Journal of Sociology*, 17(3):35–43.

Mullins, P. 1987. Community and urban movements, *Sociological Review*, 35(2):347–69.

Mullins, P. 1988. Is Australian urbanisation different?, in *A Sociology of Australian Society*, 2nd edn, eds J. Najman & J. Western, Melbourne, Macmillan.

Mullins, P. 1991. Tourism urbanisation, *International Journal of Urban and Regional Research*, 15(3):326–42.

Mullins, P. 1993. Decline of the old, rise of the new: late twentieth century Australian urbanisation, in *A Sociology of Australian Society*, 2nd edn, eds J. Najman & J. Western, Melbourne, Macmillan.

Munro, A. 1993. *A Strategic Approach to the Role of Local Government in Economic Development*, Melbourne, Municipal Association of Victoria.

Munro-Clark, M. ed. 1992. *Citizen Participation in Government*, Sydney, Hale and Iremonger.

Murphy, P. & Watson, S. 1990. Restructuring of Sydney's central industrial area: processes and local impacts, *Australian Geographical Studies*, 28:187–203.

Murray, R. & White, K. 1992. *A Bank for the People: A History of the State Bank of Victoria*, Melbourne, Hargreen.

Mushkin, S. 1972. *Public Prices for Public Products*, Washington DC, Urban Institute.

National Housing Strategy (NHS) 1991a. *Australian Housing: The Demographic, Economic and Social Environment*, issues paper no.1, Canberra, Australian Government Publishing Service.

National Housing Strategy (NHS) 1991b. *The Efficient Supply of Affordable Land and Housing: The Urban Challenge*, issues paper no.4, Canberra, Australian Government Publishing Service.

National Housing Strategy (NHS) 1992a. *Housing Location and Access to Services*, issues paper no.5, Canberra, Australian Government Publishing Service.

National Housing Strategy (NHS) 1992b. *National Housing Strategy: Agenda for Action*, issues paper no.7, Canberra, Australian Government Publishing Service.

National Housing Strategy (NHS) 1992c. *The Findings of the Housing and Locational Choice Survey, An Overview*, background paper no.11, Canberra, Australian Government Publishing Service.

National Inquiry into Local Government Finance 1985. Report, Canberra, Australian Government Publishing Service.

Neilson, L. & Spiller, M. 1992. *Managing the Cities for National Economic Development: the Role of the Building Better Cities Program*, paper presented to the Biennial Congress of RAPI, Canberra, the Local Government Planners Association, and the Australian Association of Consulting Planners, 26–30 Apr.

Neutze, M. 1964. Pricing road use, *Economic Record*, 40:175–86.

Neutze, M. 1977. *Urban Development in Australia*, Sydney, Allen and Unwin.

Neutze, M. 1987. The supply of land for a particular use, *Urban Studies*, 24:379–88.

Neutze, M. & Kendig, H. 1991. Achievement of home ownership among post-war Australian cohorts, *Housing Studies*, 6(1):3–14.

Newman, P. 1992. The compact city: an Australian perspective, *Built Environment*, 18(4):285–300.

Newman, P. & Kenworthy, J. 1992a. Transit-oriented urban villages: design solution for the 90s, *Urban Futures*, 2(1):50–8.

Newman, P. & Kenworthy, J. 1992b. *Winning Back the Cities*, Sydney, Australian Consumers' Association & Pluto Press.

Newman, P., Kenworthy, J. & Vintila, P., 1993. Can we build better cities? Physical planning in an age of urban cynicism, *Urban Futures*, 3(2):17–24.

New Planner 1991. 6 Dec.:10.

New South Wales Census, 1901–1947.

New South Wales Department of Planning 1991. *Modernising the Planning System in New South Wales*, Sydney.

New South Wales Parliamentary Debates (NSWPD) 1990. Feb., Mar., Sept.

New South Wales Parliamentary Debates (NSWPD) 1991. Feb.

New South Wales Parliamentary Debates (NSWPD) 1992. May.

Nittim, Z. 1980. The coalition of resident action groups, in *Twentieth Century Sydney*, ed. Jill Roe, Sydney, Hale and Iremonger, 232.

North Shore Gas Company v *North Sydney Municipal Company* 1991. Unreported, Land and Environment Court, 10452/90, 27 Jun.

O'Connor, K. 1992. Economic Activity in Australian Cities: National and Local Trends and Policy, *Urban Futures*, special issue 5:86–95.

O'Donovan, T. & Ferretti, D. 1993. Elizabeth–Munno Para Social Justice Project, *Australian Planner*, 31:70–4.

Office of Planning and Urban Development, South Australia 1993. *Choices for the Future, Area Planning in Northern Adelaide*, Adelaide, SA Office of Planning and Urban Development.

Ohlin, J. 1992. *A Change of Culture – Local Government and Planning for Quality of Life*, Municipal Association of Tasmania, Hobart.

Olsen, D.J. 1986. *The City as a Work of Art: London, Paris, Vienna*. New Haven, Yale University Press.

Orchard, L. 1992. *A Blinkered Vision? The Emerging National Agenda for Australian Cities and Housing or Where's the Social Democratic Middle?*, South Australian planning papers no.1, Adelaide, Planning Education Foundation of South Australia.

Orchard, L. 1993. *Then and now: twenty-five years of national urban policy in Australia*, paper presented to the Conference of the Australian Institute of Urban Studies, Adelaide.

Organization for Economic Co-operation and Development (OECD) 1987. *Pricing Water Services*, Paris, OECD.

Organization for Economic Co-operation and Development (OECD) 1988. *Ageing Populations*, Paris, OECD.

Organization for Economic Co-operation and Development (OECD) 1993. *Employment Outlook*, Paris, OECD.

Origlass, N. 1991. Webster Goes Hay Wire, 21 Oct., roneoed manuscript.

Pahl, R. 1984. *Divisions of Labour*, Oxford, Blackwell.

Pahl, R. 1988. Some remarks on informal work, social polarization and the social structure, *International Journal of Urban and Regional Research*, 12:247–67.

Painter, M. 1992. Participation and power, in *Citizen Participation in Government*, ed. Margaret Munro-Clark, Sydney, Hale and Iremonger.

Parham, S. 1992. 2020 Vision: Strategic Planning for Metropolitan Adelaide, *Urban Policy and Research*, 10:33–45.

Paris, C. 1992. Social rental housing: are there British lessons for Australia?, *Urban Policy and Research*, 10:49–55.

Parkin, A. 1982. *Governing the Cities: the Australian Experience in Perspective*, Melbourne, Macmillan.

Paterson, J. 1992. Water Utilities and Water Resources, in Economic Planning and Advisory Council, *Issues in the Pricing and Management of Natural Resources*, background paper no.16, Canberra, Australian Government Publishing Service.

Peel, M. 1993a. A place made poor: the past and the future in Elizabeth, *Arena*, 7, Oct.-Nov.

Peel, Mark 1993b. Consultation and renovation: producing a new Elizabeth, *South Australian Planner*, Dec.:6–13.

Peel, Mark 1993c. Who speaks, who gets heard: women and planning in poor suburbs, *Urban Futures*, 3(2):27–30.

Perlgut, D. ed. 1983. Community Participation in the Development of Western Sydney, proceedings, Planning Research Centre.

Pickles, I. 1983. Section 94 in established areas, *Plan*, 2(1):14.

Pikusa, S. 1986. *The Adelaide House 1836 to 1901: the Evolution of Principal Dwelling Types*, Netley, Wakefield Press.

Pinch, S. 1993. Social polarization: a comparison of evidence from Britain and the United States, *Environment and Planning*, A 25:779–95.

Planning Review 1992a. *Development Bill, Regulations, Explanation of Clauses*, Planning Review, Adelaide.

Planning Review 1992b. *Final Report: A Planning System*, Planning Review, Adelaide.

Planning Review 1992c. *Planning Strategy for Metropolitan Adelaide*, Planning Review, Adelaide.

Planning Workshop 1990. Letter to Leichhardt Council, 20 Apr.

Podder, N. 1971. Patterns of household consumption expenditure in Australia, *Economic Record*, 47.

Population Issues Committee 1992. *Population Issues and Australia's Future: Environment, Economy and Society*, Canberra, Australian Government Publishing Service.

Powell, D. 1993. *Out West: Perceptions of Sydney's Western Suburbs*, St Leonards, NSW, Allen and Unwin.

Power, J. 1969. The new politics in the old suburbs, *Quadrant*, 13:60–5.

Preteceille, E. & Terrail, J-P. 1985. *Capitalism, Consumption, and Needs*, Oxford, Basil Blackwell.

Pusey, M. 1991. *Economic Rationalism in Canberra: A Nation Building State Changes its Mind*, Cambridge, Cambridge University Press.

Rance, C. 1992. Huge Potential for Resource Sharing, *Age*, 5 May.

Randolph, B. 1993. *A Review of Community Housing in Australia*, working paper no.40, Canberra, Urban Research Program, Australian National University.

Raskall, P. 1993. Widening income disparities in Australia, in *Beyond the Market: Alternatives to Economic Rationalism*, eds Stuart Rees, Gordon Rodley & Frank Stilwell, Sydney, Pluto Press.

Real Estate Research Corporation 1974. *The Costs of Sprawl: Environmental and Economic Costs of Alternative Development Patterns at the Urban Fringe*, Washington DC, US Government Printing Office.

Redclift, N. & Mingione, E. eds 1985. *Beyond Employment: Household, Gender, and Subsistence*, Oxford, Basil Blackwell.

Rehak, P. 1988. Stoking up Dreams: Some Aspects of Postwar Housing in the Suburbs of Melbourne, MA thesis, Monash University.

Reich, R. 1991. *The Work of Nations. Preparing ourselves for 21st-century Capitalism*, New York, Alfred Knopf.

Revay & Scott v *Leichhardt Municipal Council* 1981. Land and Environment Notes, 625.

Revcourt Pty Ltd v *Wingecarribee SC* 1993. Unreported, Land and Environment Court, 10034/1993, 10035/1993, 24 May.

Review Group to the State Planning Commission of Western Australia 1987. *Planning for the Future of the Perth Metropolitan Region*, Perth, State Planning Commission.

Richard Smyth Planning Consultants Pty Ltd 1991. Report to Council: Local Environment Plans, 76, 77, 78 & 81, 9 Dec.

Richards, L. 1990. *Nobody's Home: Dreams and Realities in a New Suburb*, Melbourne, Oxford University Press.

Roberts, M. 1992. *Outdoor Recreation and Open Space: Planning Guidelines for Local Government*, Sydney, Department of Planning.

Rojek, C. 1993. *Ways of Escape*, London, Routledge.

Royal Australian Planning Institute (RAPI), ACT branch, 1993. Consultation and Planning Workshop.

Ryan, P. 1987. *Urban Development: Law and Policy*, Law Books, Sydney, 199.

Saegert, S. 1980. Masculine cities and feminine suburbs: polarized ideas, contradictory realities, *Signs*, 5.

Sandercock, L. 1975. *Cities for Sale. Property, Politics and Urban Planning in Australia*, Parkville, Melbourne University Press.

Sandercock, L. 1983. Urban development on the cheap, *Plan*, Dec. 1982–Jan. 1983:16.

Sandercock, L. 1986. Economy versus community, *Australian Society*, 5(7):12–15.

Sandercock, L. & Berry, M. 1983. *Urban Political Economy: the Australian Case*, Sydney, George Allen and Unwin.

Sant, M. & Jackson, S. 1991. Strategic planning and urban restructuring: the case of Pyrmont-Ultimo, *Australian Geographer*, 22:136–46.

Sassen, S. 1991. *The Global City. New York, London, Tokyo*, Princeton NJ, Princeton University Press.

Saunders, P. 1984a. Re-Thinking Local Politics, in *Local Socialism? Labour Councils and New Left Alternatives*, eds Martin Boddy & Colin Fudge, London, Macmillan.

Saunders, P. 1984b. The crisis of local government in Melbourne: the sacking of the city council, in *Australian Urban Politics*, eds John Halligan & Chris Paris, Melbourne, Longman Cheshire.

Saunders, P. 1990. *A Nation of Homeowners*, London, Unwin Hyman.

Saunders, P. 1994. *Welfare and Inequality: National and International Perspectives on the Australian Welfare State*, Melbourne, Cambridge University Press.

Savage, M. & Warde, A. 1993. *Urban Sociology, Capitalism and Modernity*, Basingstoke, Macmillan.

Savage, M., Barlow, J., Dicken, A. & Fielding, T. 1992. *Property, Bureaucracy and Culture*, London, Routledge.

Sawer, G. 1975. *The Australian Constitution*, Canberra, Australian Government Pubishing Service.

Sayer, A. & Walker, R. 1992. *The New Social Economy*, Cambridge, MA, Basil Blackwell.

Schedvin, C.B. 1970. *Australia and the Great Depression*, Sydney, Sydney University Press.

Self, P. 1982. *Planning the Urban Region*, Tuscaloosa Alabama, Alabama University Press.

Self, P. 1988. The resurgence of metropolitan planning in Australia, *The Planner*, London, Dec.:16–19.

Self, P. 1991. Comments on State Planning Strategy, discussion paper 4b, Department of Planning and Urban Development, Western Australia.

Shields, R. 1989. Social spatialisation and the built environment: the case of the West Edmonton Mall, *Society and Space*, 7(2):147–64.

Shiels, G. 1989. More quality, less quantity in open space planning, *Australian Parks and Recreation*, Autumn 25(1):12.

Shoup, C.S. 1969. *Public Finance*, Chicago, Aldine.

Siebert, K. 1993. Cross-sectoral co-odination in planning processes, *Strategic Planning in the 90s*, Canberra, RAPI, ACT branch, Sept.

Sinclair, W.A. 1970. Capital formation, in *Australian Economic Development in the Twentieth Century*, ed. Colin Forster, Sydney, Allen and Unwin.

Sklair, L. 1991. *Sociology of the Global System*, New York, Harvester Wheatsheaf.

Small, K.A., Winston, C. & Evans, C. 1989. *Road Work: A New Highway Pricing and Investment Policy*, Washington DC, Brooking Institution.

Smith, J. & Wallerstein, I. eds 1992. *Creating and Transforming Households*, Cambridge, Cambridge University Press.

Smith, J., Wallerstein, I. & Evers, H-D. eds 1984. *Households and the World Economy*, Beverly Hills, Sage.

Smith, M. 1988. *City, State and Market. The Political Economy of Urban Society*, Oxford, Basil Blackwell.

Smith, N. 1987. Of housing and yuppies, *Society and Space*, 5:151–72.

Smith, N. & Williams, P. (eds) 1986. *Gentrification of the City*, Boston, Allen and Unwin.

Smyth, R. 1992. Urban consolidation cowboys: some notes and lessons from Balmain, *Inner Voice*, Winter.

Snooks, G.D. 1994. *Portrait of the Family within the Total Economy: A Study in Longrun Dynamics, Australia 1788–1990*, Cambridge, Cambridge University Press.

Snyder, T.P. & Stegman, M.A. 1986. *Paying for Growth: Using Development Fees to Finance Infrastructure*, Washington DC, Urban Land Institute.

Social Justice Consultative Council 1991. *Report to the Premier: Improving Services for People*, Melbourne, Department of the Premier and Cabinet.

Social Justice Consultative Council 1992. *Social Justice, Economic Restructuring and Job Loss*, Melbourne, Department of the Premier and Cabinet.

Soja, E. 1989. *Postmodern Geographies*, London, Verso.

South Australian Housing Trust 1993. Rosewood Village sales pamphlet.

South Australian Planning Review 1992. *2020 Vision: Planning Strategy for Metropolitan Adelaide*, Adelaide, Department of Environment and Planning.

South East Queensland 2001 (SEQ 2001) Project 1993. Creating Our Future; Towards a Framework for Growth Management in South East Queensland, draft document for public comment, Brisbane.

South East Queensland Regional Organisation of Councils (SEQROCs) 1992. Regional Growth Co-Ordination Study, vol.1, Morton Consulting Services Pty Ltd & Brannock Humphreys Town Planning.

Spearritt, P. 1978. *Sydney Since the Twenties*, Sydney, Hale and Iremonger.

Spenceley, G. 1990. *A Bad Smash. Australia in the Depression of the 1930s*, Melbourne, McPhee Gribble.

Spiller, M. 1992. Federal Initiatives on Better Cities, paper presented to Winter Planning Seminar of the Planning Education Foundation of South Australia.

Sproats, K.W. 1983. A Tale of Two Towns, unpublished thesis, Armidale, University of New England.

Statham, P. 1989. Patterns and perspectives, in *The Origins of Australia's Capital Cities*, ed. Pamela Statham, Cambridge, Cambridge University Press.

Stevens, C., Baum, S. & Hassan, R. 1992. The housing and location preference of Adelaide residents, *Urban Policy and Research*, 10(3):6–22.

Stilgoe, J.R. 1988. *Borderland: Origins of the American Suburb, 1820–1939*, New Haven, Yale University Press.

Stilwell, F. 1989. Structural change and spatial equity in Sydney, *Urban Policy and Research*, 7:3–14.

Stilwell, F. 1993a. Economic rationalism: sound foundations for policy?, in *Beyond the Market: Alternatives to Economic Rationalism*, eds Stuart Rees, Gordon Rodley and Frank Stilwell, Sydney, Pluto Press.

Stilwell, F. 1993b. From 'Fightback' and 'One Nation' to an alternative economic strategy, in *Beyond the Market: Alternatives to Economic Rationalism*, eds Stuart Rees, Gordon Rodley and Frank Stilwell, Sydney, Pluto Press.

Stilwell, F. & Hardwick, J.M. 1973. Social inequality in Australian cities, *Australian Quarterly*, 45:18–36.

Stimson, R. 1991. *Brisbane – Magnet City*, a report to the Brisbane City Council, Brisbane, Brisbane City Council.

Stokes, R. & Hill, R. 1992. The evolution of metropolitan planning in Western Australia, in *Urban and Regional Planning in Western Australia*, eds David Hedgecock & Oren Yiftachel, Perth, Curtin University of Technology, Paradigm Press.

Stretton, H. 1987. *Political Essays*, Melbourne, Georgian House.

Stretton, H. 1989a. *Ideas for Australian Cities*, 3rd edn, Sydney, Transit Australia.

Stretton, H. 1989b. Women and the future of work, in *Markets, Morals and Public Policy*, eds L. Orchard & R. Dare, Sydney, Federation Press, 245–64.

Stretton, H. 1993. Transport and the Structure of Australian Cities, paper presented to Monash Transport Forum, 1993: Transport policies for the new millennium.

Styles, H. 1991. Speech at Balmain Development Trust dinner, Parliament House NSW, 14 Feb.

Sulzberger, M. 1990. The surburban road to social justice, *Australian Society*, 12:11–12.

Susskind, A. 1992. Government to Override Councils, *Sydney Morning Herald*, 22 May.

Taskforce on Regional Development 1993. *Developing Australia: A Regional Perspective*, vols 1 and 2.

Tatz, C.M. 1972. Four kinds of domination, inaugural public lecture, Armidale, NSW, University of New England.

Taylor, M. 1992a. *Labour market change and the regional pattern of unemployment in Australia*, Canberra, Office of Local Government, DILGEA.

Taylor, M. 1992b. *The Regional Impact of Changing Levels of Protection in Australian Industries*, Canberra, Office of Local Government, DILGEA.

Toon, J. 1987. The role of the town planner in urban design, *Australian Planner*, 25(1).

Troy, P. ed. 1978. *Federal Power in Australia's Cities*, Sydney, Hale and Iremonger.

Troy, P. 1987. Planners and social justice, *Australian Planner*, 25(1).

Troy, P. 1992a. Let's look at that again, *Urban Policy and Research*, 10(1):41–9.

Troy, P. 1992b. The new feudalism, *Urban Futures*, 2(2):36–44.

Turvey, R. 1971. *Economic Analysis and Public Enterprise*, London, George Allen and Unwin.

Urban Futures 1992. Planning strategies, 2(2):49–85.

Urwin, N. & Searle, G. 1991. Ecologically sustainable development and urban development, *Urban Futures*, special issue 4:4–12.

Vamplew, R. 1987. *Australians: Historical Statistics*, Broadway, Fairfax, Syme and Weldon.

Victorian Census, 1911–1947.

Victorian Department of Planning and Development 1993. *Urban Villages in Melbourne*, Melbourne, Department of Planning and Development.

Victorian Department of Planning and Housing 1990. *Urban Development Options for Victoria: A Discussion Paper*, Melbourne, Department of Planning and Housing.

Victorian Ministry of Planning and Environment 1987. *Shaping Melbourne's Future*, Melbourne, Victorian Government.

Viviani, N., Coughlan, J. & Rowland, T. 1993. *Indochinese in Australia: The Issues of Unemployment and Residential Concentration*, Bureau of Immigration Research, Canberra, Australian Government Publishing Service.

Wagga Wagga Conference 1992. *Regional Development in the 1990s: Fact or Fiction?*, City of Wagga Wagga, New South Wales.

Walker, R. 1981. A theory of suburbanisation, in *Urbanisation and Urban Planning in Capitalist Society*, eds M. Dear & A.J. Scott, London, Methuen.

Wallerstein, I. & Smith, J. 1992. Households as an institution of the world economy, in *Households and the World Economy*, eds J. Smith & I. Wallerstein, Beverly Hills, Sage.

Wallman, S. 1993. Reframing context: pointers to the post-industrial city, in *Humanising the City?*, eds A. Cohen & K. Fukui, Edinburgh, Edinburgh University Press.

Wanna, J. & Davies, R. 1992. Resource Allocation, Policy Provision and Budgetary Management in the Brisbane City Council, *Power and Policy in Brisbane*, Centre for Australian Public Sector Management, Griffith University.

Ward, A.J. 1983. The Development of Melbourne in the Interwar Years, Ph.D. thesis, Monash University.

Watson, S. 1988. *Accommodating Inequality: Gender and Housing*, Sydney, Allen and Unwin.

Watson, S. 1993. Work and Leisure in Tomorrow's Cities, in *Beyond the Market: Alternatives to Economic Rationalism*, eds Stuart Rees, Gordon Rodley & Frank Stilwell, Sydney, Pluto Press.

Watts, R. 1993. The cost to Victorians of economic rationalism: private investment in public infastructure, *Urban Policy and Research*, 11:48–50.

Wellman, B. & Wortley, S. 1990. Different strokes for different folks: community ties and social support, *American Journal of Sociology*, 96:558–88.

Wensing, E. 1993. Recent and Foreshadowed Changes to State and Northern Territory Local Government Acts, Canberra, Office of Local Government.

Western Sydney Regional Organisation of Councils (WESROC) 1994. *Western Sydney's Future – Developing a New Metropolitan Planning Strategy*, Sydney, WESROC.

Wheelwright, T. 1983. New South Wales: the dominant right, in *Machine Politics in the Australian Labor Party*, eds Andrew Parkin & John Warhurst, Sydney, George Allen and Unwin, 48–50.

Whitwell, G. 1989. *Making the Market. The Rise of Consumer Society*, Melbourne, McPhee Gribble.

Williams, P. 1984. The politics of property: home ownership in Australia, in *Australian Urban Politics: Critical Perspectives*, eds J. Halligan & C. Paris, Melbourne, Longman Cheshire.

Wilmoth, D. (convenor) 1990. Urban Futures: Towards an Agenda for Australian Cities, conference papers, 5–6 Apr. 1990, Melbourne, Australian Government Publishing Service.

Wilmoth, D. 1987. Metropolitan Planning for Sydney, in *Urban Australia: Planning Issues and Policies*, eds S. Hamnet & R. Bunker, London, Mansell.

Wilmoth, D. 1990. Urban infrastructure finance issues in Australia: a review in the context of international experience, *Urban Policy and Research*, 8:159–68.

Wilson, W. 1987. *The Truly Disadvantaged: The Inner City, the Underclass, and Public Policy*, Chicago, University of Chicago Press.

Wulff, M. 1993. An overview of Australian housing and locational preference studies, *Urban Policy and Research*, 11(4):230–7.

Yates, J. 1991. *Australia's owner-occupied housing wealth and its impact on income distribution*, Social Policy Research Centre, reports and proceedings no.92, Social Policy Research Centre, University of NSW.

Yates, J. & Vipond, J. 1991. Housing and urban inequalities, in *Inequality in Australia*, eds J. O'Leary & R. Sharp, Melbourne, Heinemann, 234–57.

Yiftachel, O. & Kenworthy, J. 1992. The planning of metropolitan Perth: some critical observations, in *Urban and Regional Planning in Western Australia*, eds David Hedgecock & Oren Yiftachel, Perth, Curtin University of Technology, Paradigm Press.

Young, I.M. 1990. *Justice and the Politics of Difference*, Princeton, Princeton University Press.

Zukin, Sharon 1991. *Landscapes of Power: From Detroit to Disney World*, Berkeley, University of California Press.

Index

urban consolidation (*continued*)
75; and role of government, 75–6, 86;
criticism of, 43–7, 72–5
urban density, and residential density, 28,
38, 58, 73, 76; and non-residential urban
space, 73; *see also* urban development;
urban form
urban development, 27, 33, 36, 40, 46, 50,
180; and standard of living, 270;
projections, 70; *see also* planning; urban
planning; urban policy
urban form, 34, 38, 40, 42, 45–6, 90, 267;
and housing, 171–4; and democracy,
193
urban growth, 180, 250–3, 258; *see also*
urban development
urban institutions, 24, 152–9, 271–7;
inadequacies of, 9–10, 271, 272, 279; *see
also* inter-government relations;
planning
urban planning, 25, 142–3, 163, 195; *see
also* area planning; planning; strategic
planning
urban policy, 62, 69, 71, 197, 246, 262, 274;
future prospects, 80–2, 85; phases of, 65,
67–8
Urban Research Program, 180
urban reform, 40, 66; *see also* inequality;
inter-government relations; urban policy
urban services, *see* infrastructure; public
investment; public services
urban structure, 2, 5, 10, 251, 252
urban system, 77, 80
urban theory, 62–3

urban village, 57–62; *see also* planning;
inequality
urbanisation, 33, 37, 247; *see also*
suburbanisation; urban development
Uren, Tom, 68

Very Fast Train, 8, 254, 259, 275
Victoria, 24, 25, 81, 82; and planning
reform, 160–1; and urban growth, 199;
Victorian AAT Planning Division, 191
Vietnamese, 166, 168, 172
'Visions of Adelaide', 147

War Service Homes Act, 30
War Service Homes scheme, 30, 35
Water Board (NSW), 140
Webster, Robert, 135, 136, 137, 138, 140
Western Australia, 161–2, 182, 246, 256;
Water Authority, 240
western Sydney, 166–7, 171, 174
Western Sydney Regional Organisation of
Councils (WESROC), 184
Whitlam, Gough, Prime Minister, 8, 65, 67,
68, 184, 199, 269
Williamson, David, 130
Wollongong (NSW), 100
Woods, Peter, 129, 131, 138, 139
Woodward, John, 133, 134
Woollahra (NSW), 29
workforce *see* industrial restructuring,
labour force
World War I, 27, 28
World War II, 2, 26, 125, 179, 248
Wran government, 139